CENTURY 21
Computer Keyboarding
SEVENTH EDITION

Jack P. Hoggatt, Ed.D.
Professor of Business Communication and Administrative Management
University of Wisconsin
Eau Claire (WI)

Jon A. Shank, Ed.D.
Professor of Education
Robert Morris College
Moon Township (PA)

Jerry W. Robinson, Ed.D.
Former Keyboarding Instructor
Moeller High School
Cincinnati (OH)

This publication is dedicated to the memory of two Keyboarding pioneers, Dr. T. James Crawford and Dr. Jerry W. Robinson. Dr. Crawford, who passed away on August 15, 2000, was Professor Emeritus at Indiana University, Bloomington, Indiana, and a 50-year author on *Century 21 Keyboarding*. Dr. Robinson, a noted business educator, publisher, and *Century 21* author, passed away in 1997. Both men were visionaries in the field of business education. Their research contributed to the development of learning principles that have guided more than 75 million students and will continue to have an impact on learners for decades to come.

Australia • Canada • Mexico • Singapore • Spain • United Kingdom • United States

SOUTH-WESTERN
THOMSON LEARNING™

Century 21 Computer Keyboarding
by Hoggatt, Shank, & Robinson

Executive Editor:
Karen Schmohe

Project Manager/ Production Manager:
Jane Congdon

Editor:
Kim Kusnerak

Fee Writer:
Elaine Langlois

Technology Project Manager:
Gayle Statman

Technology Editor:
Mike Jackson

Consulting Editor:
Penworthy Learning Systems

Production Services:
Thomas N. Lewis, Diane Bowdler, Gary Morris

Channel Coordinator:
Nancy Long

Marketing Coordinator:
Cira Brown

Manufacturing Manager:
Carol Chase

Art and Design Coordinator:
Michelle Kunkler

Cover/Internal Design:
Ann Small, a small design studio

Cover/Internal Illustration:
Matsu, Jeffrey Pelo

Photo Stylist:
Fred M. Middendorf

Compositor:
D&G, Limited, LLC

Printer:
Quebecor World Versailles

ISBN: 0-538-69919-1/0-538-69920-5

Printed in the United States of America
7 8 9 10 11 12 13 14
09 08 07 06 05 04

For more information, contact
South-Western Educational Publishing
5191 Natorp Blvd.
Mason, OH 45040
Or you can visit our internet site at
www.swep.com

For permission to use material from this text or product, contact us by
Phone: 1-800-730-2214
Fax: 1-800-730-2215
www.thomsonrights.com

Photo Credits:
pp. xv, R5, R34: © Courtesy of PhotoDisc, Inc.
pp. 2, R2: © Photo by Erik Snobeck/Digital Imaging Group
pp. 3, R3, R7, R8, R9, R10, R12, R14, R16, R17, R18, R20, R21, R22, R24, R26, R28, R29, R30, R33: © Greg Grosse

Reviewers:
Karen Bean, Harker Heights High School, Harker Heights, TX
Eileen Dittmar, Kent Career/Technical Center, Grand Rapids, MI
Lisa J. Karr, High School Academy, Irving Independent School District, Irving, TX
Janet Knox, Public Schools of North Carolina, Raleigh, NC
Mary Ann Mann, Palestine High School, Palestine, TX
Sue Miller, Shiloh High School, Hume, IL
Carol Mitzner, Reseda High School, Reseda, CA
Barbara Small, Fairfax County Public Schools, Falls Church, VA
James R. Smith, Jr., Public Schools of North Carolina, Raleigh, NC

CENTURY 21

Computer Keyboarding 7E

KEYBOARDING
going forward

Use the following materials to customize your course and increase your students' skills and knowledge.

KEYBOARDING SOFTWARE

- *MicroType Multimedia* Lessons cover alphabetic, numeric, skill building, and keypad instruction. Graphics, games, audio, video, and word processor with timer. Available for Windows and Macintosh.
- *Quick Check* Assessment software that checks documents and timed writings from ***Century 21*** keyed in a built-in word processor. Available for Windows and Macintosh.
- *CheckPro* New to this edition, this checking software works with commercial word processing software. Available for Windows.
- *MicroPace Pro* Diagnoses errors and focuses students on areas that need improvement. Paced and timed writings, drills, and practices. Available for Windows and Macintosh.
- *KeyChamp* Develops speed by analyzing students' two-stroke key combinations (digraphs) and recommending speed-building drills. Available for Windows and Macintosh.
- *Skillbusters* An interactive mystery game that builds speed and accuracy. Clues surface only after students achieve keyboarding goals. Available for Windows and Macintosh.

WORD PROCESSING SIMULATIONS

- *The Candidate: Beginning Simulation* Develop word processing skills while formatting letters, memos, tables, press releases, and reports. Softcover text and CD available together or separately.
- *Line Rollering* Students complete keyboarding, alphabetizing, computation, and proofreading tasks as an assistant for an in-line skating club. Simulation is available with optional data disk.

SPEECH RECOGNITION

Learn the fundamentals of continuous speech recognition and achieve speech-writing proficiency of 110-150 words per minute with 95-99% accuracy.

- *L&H® VoiceXpress™ for the Office Professional* (download available at www.swep.com/ebooks)
- *IBM® ViaVoice™ for the Office Professional*
- *Dragon® NaturallySpeaking™ for the Office Professional*

SPANISH KEYBOARDING

Designed for the user who wants to learn keyboarding, but is more comfortable reading Spanish. All instructions are written in Spanish, allowing the user to focus on keyboarding rather than language translation. The lessons, skill checks, and assessment exercises themselves are still in English.

- *Digitacion para el dominio de la computadora (Keyboarding for Computer Success)*

MOUS CERTIFICATION

Master all of the key functions of Microsoft Word on both the Core and Expert levels.

- *MOUS Certification Review, Microsoft Word 2000* Text/CD Package

CHOICE + COVERAGE = FLEXIBILITY

PART 1

Lessons 1-40

- Review Letter Keys
- Build Keyboarding Skill
- Review Figure Keys
- Build Keyboarding Skill
- Learn/Review Symbol Keys
- Build Keyboarding Skill
- Learn to Format Memos and E-mail
- Learn to Format Unbound Reports
- Learn to Format Personal-Business Letters
- Learn to Format Tables
- Prepare for Document Formatting Assessment
- Assessing Document Formatting Skills
- Communication Skills 1-5
- Word Processing 1-4
- Skill Builder 1-2
- Learn Numeric Keypad Operation
- Your Perspective

PART 2

Lessons 41-75

- Building Basic Skill
- Improving E-mail and Memo Formatting Skills
- Improve Report Formatting Skills
- Building Basic Skill
- Improving Letter Formatting Skills
- Improving Table Formatting Skills
- *HPJ Communication Specialists: A Workplace Simulation*
- Preparing for Assessment
- Assessing Document Formatting Skills
- Communication Skills 6-8
- Word Processing 5-8
- Skill Builder 3
- Your Perspective

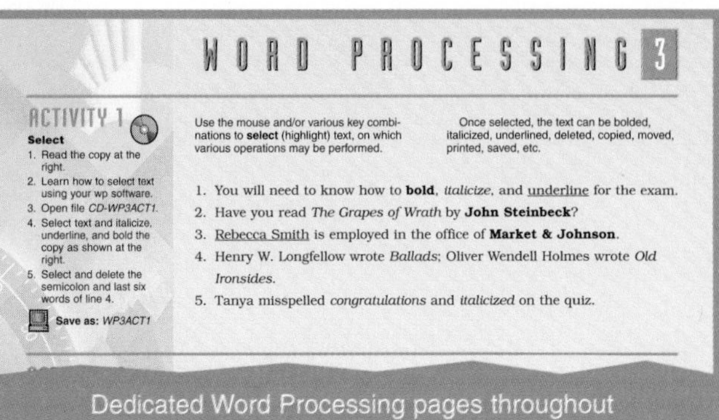

WORD PROCESSING 3
ACTIVITY 1
Select
1. You will need to know how to bold, italicize, and underline for the exam.
2. Have you read The Grapes of Wrath by John Steinbeck?
3. Rebecca Smith is employed in the office of Market & Johnson.
4. Henry W. Longfellow wrote Ballads; Oliver Wendell Holmes wrote Old Ironsides.
5. Tanya misspelled congratulations and italicized on the quiz.
Save as: WP3ACT1
Dedicated Word Processing pages throughout

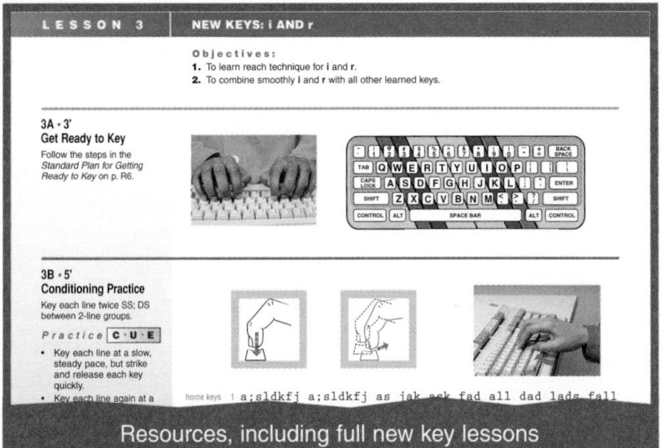

LESSON 3
NEW KEYS: i AND r
Objectives:
1. To learn reach technique for i and r.
2. To combine smoothly i and r with all other learned keys.
3A • 3'
Get Ready to Key
3B • 5'
Conditioning Practice
Resources, including full new key lessons

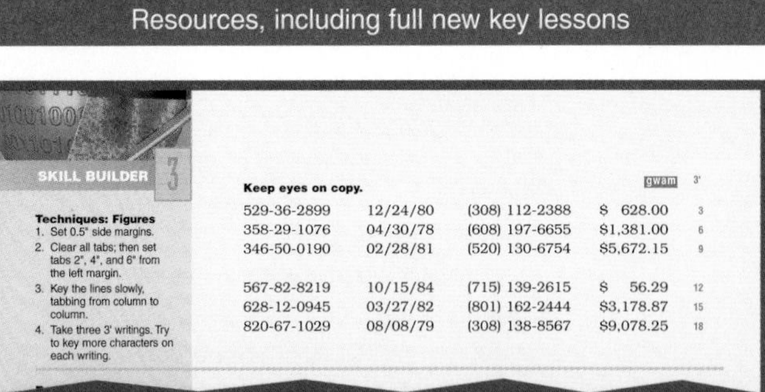

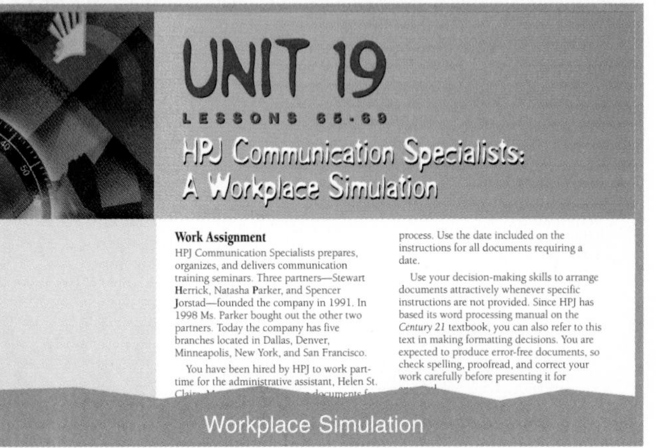

UNIT 19
LESSONS 65-69
HPJ Communication Specialists: A Workplace Simulation
Work Assignment
Workplace Simulation

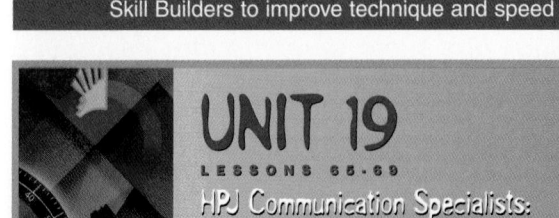

FOUNDATIONS OF INSTRUCTION

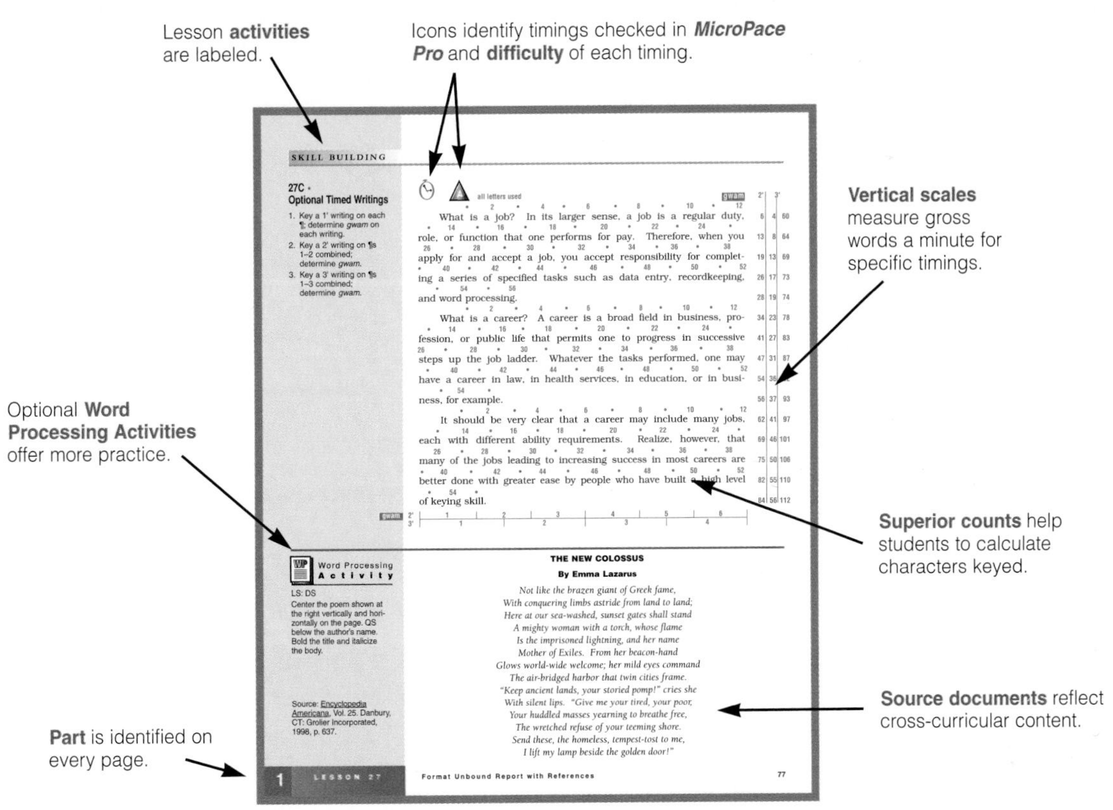

Lesson **activities** are labeled.
Icons identify timings checked in ***MicroPace Pro*** and **difficulty** of each timing.
Vertical scales measure gross words a minute for specific timings.
Optional **Word Processing Activities** offer more practice.
Superior counts help students to calculate characters keyed.
Source documents reflect cross-curricular content.
Part is identified on every page.

SKILL BUILDING

27C • Optional Timed Writings

1. Key a 1' writing on each ¶; determine *gwam* on each writing.
2. Key a 2' writing on ¶s 1–2 combined; determine *gwam*.
3. Key a 3' writing on ¶s 1–3 combined; determine *gwam*.

all letters used

What is a job? In its larger sense, a job is a regular duty, role, or function that one performs for pay. Therefore, when you apply for and accept a job, you accept responsibility for completing a series of specified tasks such as data entry, recordkeeping, and word processing.

What is a career? A career is a broad field in business, profession, or public life that permits one to progress in successive steps up the job ladder. Whatever the tasks performed, one may have a career in law, in health services, in education, or in business, for example.

It should be very clear that a career may include many jobs, each with different ability requirements. Realize, however, that many of the jobs leading to increasing success in most careers are better done with greater ease by people who have built a high level of keying skill.

Word Processing Activity

LS: DS

Center the poem shown at the right vertically and horizontally on the page. QS below the author's name. Bold the title and italicize the body.

THE NEW COLOSSUS

By Emma Lazarus

Not like the brazen giant of Greek fame,
With conquering limbs astride from land to land;
Here at our sea-washed, sunset gates shall stand
A mighty woman with a torch, whose flame
Is the imprisoned lightning, and her name
Mother of Exiles. From her beacon-hand
Glows world-wide welcome; her mild eyes command
The air-bridged harbor that twin cities frame.
"Keep ancient lands, your storied pomp!" cries she
With silent lips. "Give me your tired, your poor,
Your huddled masses yearning to breathe free,
The wretched refuse of your teeming shore.
Send these, the homeless, tempest-tost to me,
I lift my lamp beside the golden door!"

Source: Encyclopedia Americana, Vol. 25. Danbury, CT: Grolier Incorporated, 1998, p. 637.

1 LESSON 27 Format Unbound Report with References 77

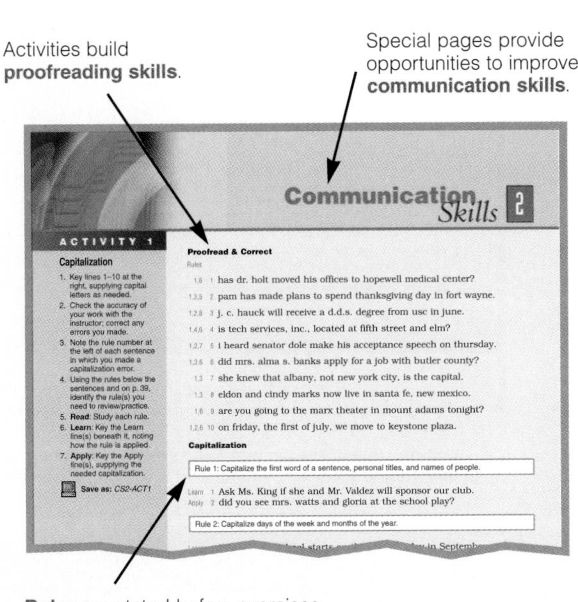

Activities build **proofreading skills**.
Special pages provide opportunities to improve **communication skills**.
Rules are stated before exercises.

Communication Skills 2

ACTIVITY 1

Capitalization

1. Key lines 1–10 at the right, supplying capital letters as needed.
2. Check the accuracy of your work with the instructor; correct any errors you made.
3. Note the rule number at the left of each sentence in which you made a capitalization error.
4. Using the rules below the sentences and on p. 39, identify the rule(s) you need to review/practice.
5. **Read:** Study each rule.
6. **Learn:** Key the Learn line(s) beneath it, noting how the rule is applied.
7. **Apply:** Key the Apply line(s), supplying the needed capitalization.

Save as: *CS2-ACT1*

Proofread & Correct

1. has dr. holt moved his offices to hopewell medical center?
2. pam has made plans to spend thanksgiving day in fort wayne.
3. j. c. hauck will receive a d.d.s. degree from usc in june.
4. is tech services, inc., located at fifth street and elm?
5. i heard senator dole make his acceptance speech on thursday.
6. did mrs. alma s. banks apply for a job with butler county?
7. she knew that albany, not new york city, is the capital.
8. eldon and cindy marks now live in santa fe, new mexico.
9. are you going to the marx theater in mount adams tonight?
10. on friday, the first of july, we move to keystone plaza.

Capitalization

Rule 1: Capitalize the first word of a sentence, personal titles, and names of people.

Learn 1 Ask Ms. King if she and Mr. Valdez will sponsor our club.
Apply 2 did you see mrs. watts and gloria at the school play?

Rule 2: Capitalize days of the week and months of the year.

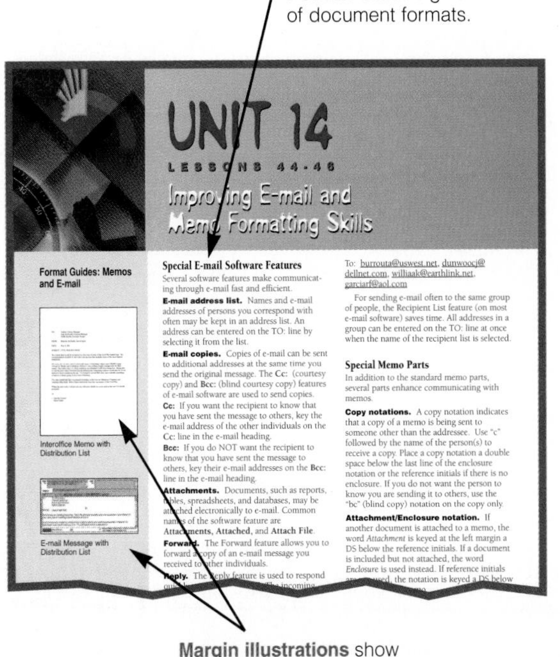

Format Guides give overviews of document formats.
Margin illustrations show correct **document formatting**.

UNIT 14

LESSONS 44-46

Improving E-mail and Memo Formatting Skills

Format Guides: Memos and E-mail

Interoffice Memo with Distribution List

E-mail Message with Distribution List

Special E-mail Software Features

Several software features make communicating through e-mail fast and efficient.

E-mail address list. Names and e-mail addresses of persons you correspond with often may be kept in an address list. An address can be entered on the TO: line by selecting it from the list.

E-mail copies. Copies of e-mail can be sent to additional addresses at the same time you send the original message. The **Cc:** (courtesy copy) and **Bcc:** (blind courtesy copy) features of e-mail software are used to send copies.

Cc: If you want the recipient to know that you have sent the message to others, key the e-mail address of the other individuals on the Cc: line in the e-mail heading.

Bcc: If you do NOT want the recipient to know that you have sent the message to others, key their e-mail addresses on the **Bcc:** line in the e-mail heading.

Attachments. Documents, such as reports, tables, spreadsheets, and databases, may be attached electronically to e-mail. Common names of the software feature are **Attachments, Attached,** and **Attach File**.

Forward. The Forward feature allows you to forward a copy of an e-mail message you received to other individuals.

Reply. The Reply feature is used to respond

To: burrouta@uswest.net, dunwoocj@dellnet.com, williaak@earthlink.net, garciarf@aol.com

For sending e-mail often to the same group of people, the Recipient List feature (on most e-mail software) saves time. All addresses in a group can be entered on the TO: line at once when the name of the recipient list is selected.

Special Memo Parts

In addition to the standard memo parts, several parts enhance communicating with memos.

Copy notations. A copy notation indicates that a copy of a memo is being sent to someone other than the addressee. Use "c" followed by the name of the person(s) to receive a copy. Place a copy notation a double space below the last line of the enclosure notation or the reference initials if there is no enclosure. If you do not want the person to know you are sending it to others, use the "bc" (blind copy) notation on the copy only.

Attachment/Enclosure notation. If another document is attached to a memo, the word *Attachment* is keyed at the left margin a DS below the reference initials. If a document is included but not attached, the word *Enclosure* is used instead. If reference initials are not used, the notation is keyed a DS below

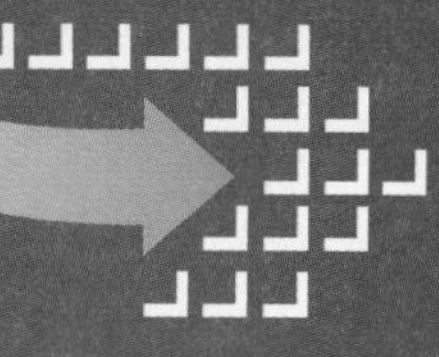

FOUNDATIONS OF LEARNING

Warm-up drills prepare students to key lesson material.

Lesson **objectives** are identified throughout.

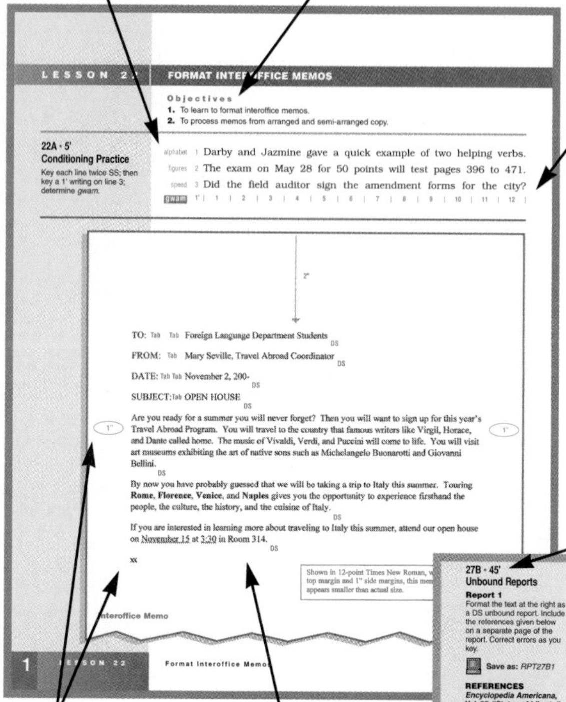

Scales identify ***gwam*** to measure keying productivity.

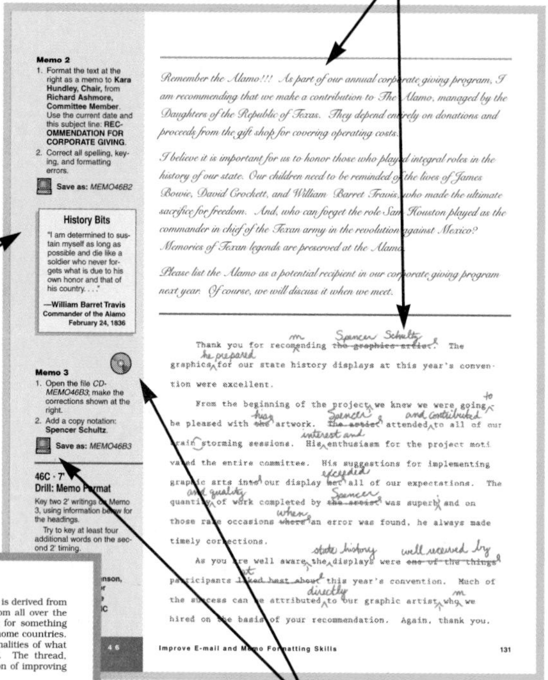

Script and rough-draft copy provide real-world keying experience.

Features enforce cross-curricular themes.

Times are given for lesson activities.

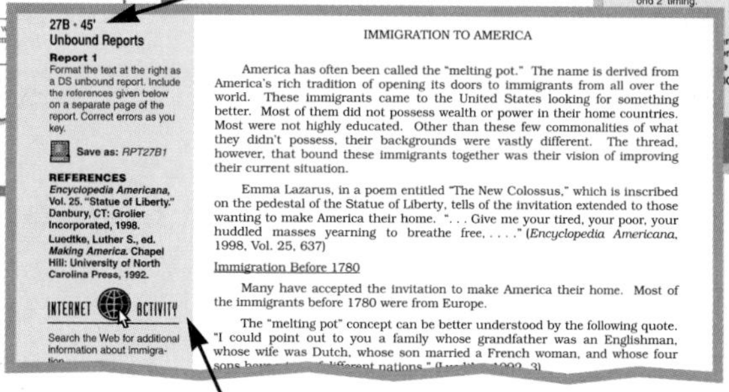

Model documents illustrate correct formatting.

Documents illustrate **cross-curricular** themes.

Icons identify **data file instructions.**

New-key review lessons provide an alternative for experienced students.

Internet Activities enhance lessons and follow cross-curricular themes.

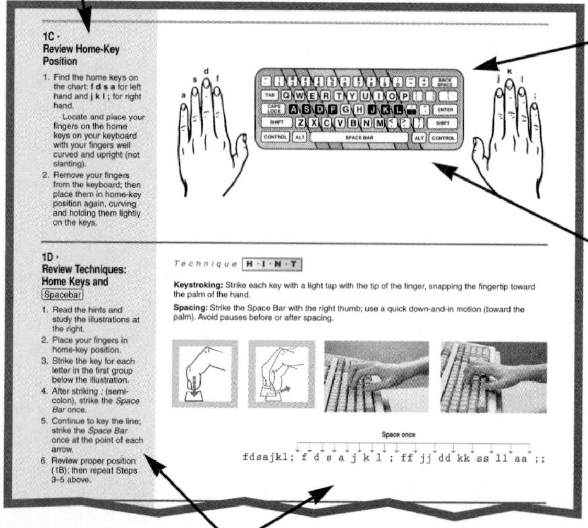

Keyboards help students with **correct hand and finger** positions.

Special pages invite individual and **group participation**.

Activities combine keying with **research** and **critical thinking**.

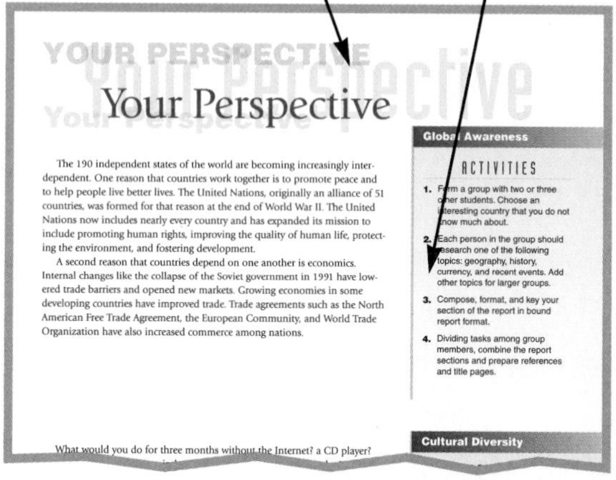

Keys being taught are shown in **black**; identifiers on previously taught keys are **gray**.

Correct **keying techniques** are emphasized **visually**.

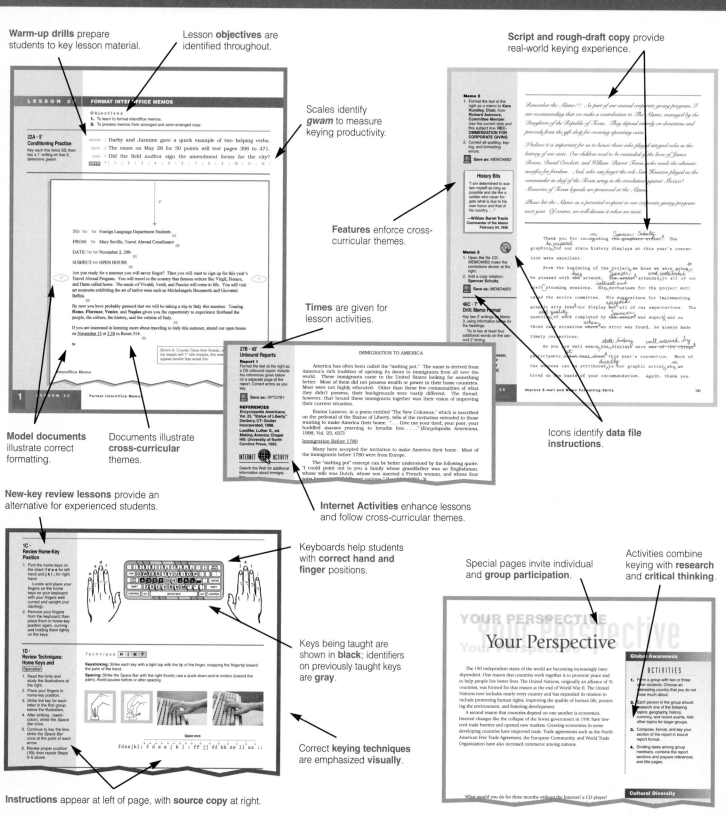

Instructions appear at left of page, with **source copy** at right.

TECHNOLOGY LEADER TAKES YOU FORWARD

MicroType Multimedia
Lessons cover alphabetic, numeric, skillbuilding, and keypad instruction. Graphics, games, audio, video, and word processor with timer. Available for Windows and Macintosh.

KeyChamp
Develops speed by analyzing students' two-stroke key combinations (digraphs) and recommending speed-building drills. Available for Windows and Macintosh.

Quick Check
Assessment software that checks documents and timed writings from *Century 21,* keyed in a built-in word processor. Available for Windows and Macintosh.

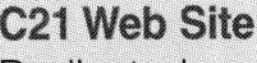

C21 Web Site
Dedicated Web site with materials for students and instructors. Instructor materials include Placement and Performance Tests, Solution Keys, PowerPoint presentations, Activity Pak, Exploring Cultural Diversity, E-Term Dictionary, Certificates, Workplace Enrichment correlations and data files, Formatting Templates, MicroPace Pro Timed Writing Templates, Lesson Plans, and Transparency Masters for Word and Corel.

Century 21 Computer Keyboarding, Seventh Edition

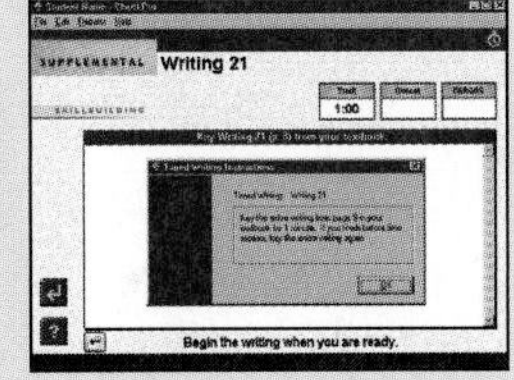

CheckPro
New to this edition, this checking software works with commercial word processing software. Available for Windows.

Skillbusters
An interactive mystery game that builds speed and accuracy. Clues surface only after students achieve keyboarding goals. Available for Windows and Macintosh.

Instructor Resource CD Materials include Placement and Performance Tests, Solution Keys, Exploring Cultural Diversity, Instructor's Manual, Certificates, Workplace Enrichment correlations and data files, Formatting Templates, MicroPace Pro Timed Writing Templates, Lesson Plans, and Transparency Masters for Word and Corel.

MicroPace Pro
Diagnoses errors and focuses students on areas that need improvement. Paced and timed writings, drills, and practices. Available for Windows and Macintosh.

Preface

Century 21 Computer Keyboarding provides a bridge from keyboarding to computer applications by teaching keying skills, word processing functions, and document formatting in a 75-lesson format.

Flexibility is key in the new *Century 21* family. *Century 21 Computer Keyboarding* provides options for instructors to determine where students will begin—with refresher lessons for those who have had prior touch keyboarding instruction, or with new-key lessons designed for true beginners.

Century 21 Computer Keyboarding can be used in a one-semester course or combined with a simulation, South-Western Educational Publishing 10-Hour Series course, or other module for a full-year solution.

In planning this product, South-Western/Thomson Learning surveyed business teachers, employed content reviewers, and met with focus groups to determine the needs of today's keyboarding students and instructors. The features of *Century 21 Computer Keyboarding* address those needs.

The *Century 21* family includes supplementary items for both students and instructors. You will find a full range of high-quality materials, including a Web site at http://www.c21key.swep.com. Thank you for choosing *Century 21 Computer Keyboarding*. We know that you will find this edition an exciting solution for your classes.

ABOUT THE AUTHORS

Dr. Jon A. Shank is a Professor of Education at Robert Morris College in Moon Township, Pennsylvania. For more than 20 years, he served as Dean of the School of Applied Sciences and Education at Robert Morris. Dr. Shank retired as Dean in 1998 to return to full-time teaching. He currently teaches methods courses to students who are studying to become business education teachers. Dr. Shank holds memberships in regional, state, and national business education organizations. He has received many honors during his career, including Outstanding Post-Secondary Business Educator in Pennsylvania.

Dr. Jack P. Hoggatt is Department Chair for the Department of Business Communications at the University of Wisconsin-Eau Claire. He has taught courses in Business Writing, Advanced Business Communications, and the communication component of the university's Masters in Business Administration (MBA) program. Dr. Hoggatt has held offices in several professional organizations, including the Wisconsin Business Education Association. He has served as an advisor to local and state business organizations. Dr. Hoggatt is involved with his community and the school activities of his four children.

Dr. Jon Shank (left) and Dr. Jack Hoggatt

Contents

PART 1 ARTS & LITERATURE

UNIT 1	**REVIEW LETTER KEYS**	**2**
1	Review Home Keys (fdsa jkl;)	2
2	Review Letter Keys (h, e, i, and r)	5
3	Review Letter Keys (o, t, n, and g)	7
4	Review Letter Keys (left shift, period, u, and c)	9
5	Review Letter Keys (w, right shift, b, and y)	11
6	Review Letter Keys (m, x, p, and v)	13
7	Review Letter Keys (q, comma, z, and colon)	15
8	Review Letter Keys (caps lock, ?, tab, ', -, and ")	17
UNIT 2	**BUILD KEYBOARDING SKILL**	**19**
9	Skill Building	19
10	Skill Building	21
11	Skill Building	23
12	Skill Building	25
	COMMUNICATION SKILLS 1	27
UNIT 3	**REVIEW FIGURE KEYS**	**29**
13	Review Figure Keys (8, 1, 9, 4, and 0)	29
14	Review Figure Keys (5, 7, 3, 6, and 2)	31
UNIT 4	**BUILD KEYBOARDING SKILL**	**34**
15	Skill Building	34
16	Skill Building	36
	COMMUNICATION SKILLS 2	38
UNIT 5	**LEARN/REVIEW SYMBOL KEYS**	**40**
17	Learn/Review Symbol Keys (/, $, !, %, <, and >)	40
18	Learn/Review Symbol Keys (#, &, +, @, and ( ))	42
19	Learn/Review Symbol Keys (=, _, *, \, and [ ])	43
UNIT 6	**BUILD KEYBOARDING SKILL**	**45**
20	Skill Building	45
21	Skill Building	47
	COMMUNICATION SKILLS 3	49
	LEARN NUMERIC KEYPAD OPERATION	51
	WORD PROCESSING 1	55
	Insert and Typeover, Underline, Italic, and Bold Alignment: Left, Center, Right Undo and Redo Hyphenation Speller View and Zoom Hard Page Break Tabs	
UNIT 7	**LEARN TO FORMAT MEMOS AND E-MAIL**	**59**
22	Format Interoffice Memos	60
23	Format E-mail Messages	62
24	Format Memos and E-mail	64
	SKILL BUILDER 1	66
	WORD PROCESSING 2	67
	Margins Line Spacing Widow/Orphan Indentation Page Numbers Review Tabs	
UNIT 8	**LEARN TO FORMAT UNBOUND REPORTS**	**70**
25	Format Unbound Reports	72
26	Format Unbound Report with Textual Citations	72
27	Format Unbound Report with References	75
	COMMUNICATION SKILLS 4	78
	WORD PROCESSING 3	80
	Select Cut, Copy, and Paste Center Page Envelopes	
UNIT 9	**LEARN TO FORMAT PERSONAL-BUSINESS LETTERS**	**82**
28	Format Personal-Business Letters	84
29	Format Personal-Business Letters	85
30	Format Personal-Business Letters	87
	SKILL BUILDER 2	89
	WORD PROCESSING 4	90
	Insert Table Insert and Delete Rows and Columns Join Cells and Change Column Width Change Table Format Center Tables Horizontally and Vertically Sort Tables Change Row Height and Vertical Alignment	
UNIT 10	**LEARN TO FORMAT TABLES**	**94**
31	Format Two-Column Tables with Column Headings	96
32	Format Two-Column Tables with Main, Secondary, and Column Headings	97
33	Format Three-Column Tables	99
34	Format Four-Column Tables	100
	COMMUNICATION SKILLS 5	102
UNIT 11	**PREPARE FOR DOCUMENT FORMATTING ASSESSMENT**	**104**
35	Prepare for Assessment: E-mail, Memos, Letters	104
36	Prepare for Assessment: Reports	106
37	Prepare for Assessment: Tables	108
UNIT 12	**ASSESSING DOCUMENT FORMATTING SKILLS**	**110**
38	Assess E-mail, Memo, and Letter Formatting Skills	110
39	Assess Report Formatting Skills	112
40	Assess Table Formatting Skills	114
	YOUR PERSPECTIVE 1	116
	Ethics, Global Awareness, Cultural Diversity	

PART 2 SOCIAL STUDIES

UNIT 13	**BUILDING BASIC SKILL**	**119**
41	Improve Keying Technique	119
42	Improve Keying Technique	121
43	Improve Keying Technique	122

WORD PROCESSING 5 124
Review WP Features · Copy Text to Another File · Reinforce Copying Files

UNIT 14 IMPROVING E-MAIL AND MEMO FORMATTING SKILLS 126
44 Improve E-mail Formatting Skills 127
45 Improve Memo Formatting Skills 129
46 Improve E-mail and Memo Formatting Skills 130
COMMUNICATION SKILLS 6 132
WORD PROCESSING 6 134
Review WP Features: Margins, Spacing, and Left (Paragraph) Indent · Review WP Features: Margins, Alignment, and Hanging Indent · Review WP Feature: Copy Text from File to File · Footnotes and Endnotes · Superscript · Bullets and Numbering · Insert File · Dot Leader Tab

UNIT 15 IMPROVE REPORT FORMATTING SKILLS 137
47 Improve Report Formatting Skills 139
48 Format Bound Report with Footnotes 141
49 Improve Report Formatting 144
50 Format Bound Reports with Endnotes 146
51 Improve Report Formatting Skills 148
52 Extend Report Formatting Skills 150

UNIT 16 BUILDING BASIC SKILL 152
53 Improve Keying Technique 152
54 Improve Keying Technique 154
COMMUNICATION SKILLS 7 156
WORD PROCESSING 7 158
Insert Date, AutoComplete · Navigate a Document · Macro · Reinforce Use of Macro

UNIT 17 IMPROVING LETTER FORMATTING SKILLS 160
55 Review Personal-Business Letter Format 161
56 Format Business Letters 162
57 Format Business Letters 163
58 Format Letters with Special Parts 165
59 Improve Business Letter Formatting 167
WORD PROCESSING 8 169
Review Table Formatting Features · Split Cells/Join Cells · Shading · Borders · Gridlines

UNIT 18 IMPROVING TABLE FORMATTING SKILLS 172
60 Improve Table Formatting Skills 173
61 Apply Shading to Tables 175
62 Present Information in Tables 176
63 Apply Borders to Tables 179
64 Improve Table Formatting Skills 181
COMMUNICATION SKILLS 8 183
SKILL BUILDER 3 185

UNIT 19 HPJ COMMUNICATION SPECIALISTS: A WORKPLACE SIMULATION 186
65–69 HPJ Communication Specialists 187

UNIT 20 PREPARING FOR ASSESSMENT 195
70 Prepare for Assessment: E-mails, Memos, Letters 195
71 Prepare for Assessment: Reports 197
72 Prepare for Assessment: Tables 199

UNIT 21 ASSESSING DOCUMENT FORMATTING SKILLS 201
73 Assess Correspondence Formatting 201
74 Assess Report Formatting 203
75 Assess Table Formatting 205
YOUR PERSPECTIVE 2 207
Ethics, Global Awareness, Cultural Diversity

RESOURCES

NEW-KEY LEARNING R2
1 Home Keys (fdsa jkl;) R2
2 New Keys: h and e R6
3 New Keys: i and r R8
4 New Keys: o and t R10
5 New Keys: n and g R12
6 New Keys: left shift and period (.) R14
7 New Keys: u and c R16
8 New Keys: w and right shift R18
9 New Keys: b and y R20
10 New Keys: m and x R22
11 New Keys: p and v R24
12 New Keys: q and comma (,) R26
13 New Keys: z and colon (:) R28
14 New Keys: caps lock and question mark (?) R30
15 New Keys: tab key, apostrophe ('), hyphen (-), and quotation mark (") R32

REPETITIVE STRESS INJURY R34

WINDOWS TUTORIAL R37

INTERNET GUIDE WITH APPLICATIONS R40

FORMAT GUIDES R44

SOFTWARE FEATURES INDEX R46

INDEX I-1

Computer Concepts

A **computer** is a machine that processes data and performs tasks according to a set of instructions. To do anything, computers must be given specific directions to follow. They get these directions from software. **Software**, such as that used for word processing, is a set of step-by-step instructions for the computer, written by computer programmers in a programming language like BASIC, Pascal, or C.

Computers also get instructions from you, the user. When you use the mouse (more in a moment about this tool) or the keyboard, you are giving instructions, or *input*, to your computer. That is why the mouse and keyboard are sometimes referred to as **input devices**.

Hardware is computer equipment. It carries out the software instructions. Hardware includes the central processing unit (CPU) as well as the monitor, keyboard, mouse, printer, and other *peripherals*. **Peripheral** is the name used for a piece of hardware that works with the CPU.

USING YOUR COMPUTER SAFELY

Follow these guidelines to use your computer safely:

1. Keep air vents unobstructed to prevent the computer from overheating.
2. Keep food and liquids away from your computer. If something does spill, unplug the computer and notify your instructor immediately.
3. Do not expose disks to excessive heat, cold, or moisture or to magnets, x-ray devices, or direct sunlight.
4. Use a felt-tip marker, not a ballpoint pen or a pencil, to write on disk labels.
5. Do not remove a disk from the drive when the in-use light is on.

STARTING YOUR COMPUTER

Follow these steps to start your computer:

1. Remove any 3.5" disk from that disk drive.
2. Turn on the power. You may need to flip a switch or press a button on the CPU or press a button or key on the keyboard. You may also have to turn on the monitor separately.

Your computer may take a few moments to power up. The computer will execute a series of automatic steps that will load the **operating system**. The operating system—Windows® 98, for example—is the program that manages other programs on the computer.[1] It will prepare the computer to receive your instructions and run software.

GETTING AROUND THE DESKTOP

The screen on your monitor is your **desktop.** Like the desk where you are sitting, your computer desktop is your main work area. It likely contains **icons** (picture symbols) for programs and documents, some resembling file folders that contain programs and documents. You probably have a taskbar or menu bar at the top or bottom of the screen (more about these in a moment). From here, you can start programs, find files, get information about your computer, and shut down the computer when you are finished.

A **mouse** is a tool for getting around the desktop. The same mouse actions are used in any software, though the results may vary depending on the software and version. Here are the basic ways to use a mouse:

- **Point**. Move the mouse (roll it on the work surface) so that the **pointer** (the arrow that represents the mouse's position on the screen) points to an item.
- **Click**. Press the left mouse button once and let go.
- **Double-click**. Press the left mouse button twice quickly and let go.
- **Drag**. Press and hold down the left mouse button and move the pointer to another location.

WHAT IS APPLICATION SOFTWARE?

You have probably heard the terms *application*, *application software*, and *application program*. They all mean the same thing. **Application software** is a computer program designed to perform a specific task directly for the user or for another application. Some common types of application software are word processing, spreadsheet, database, presentation, and Internet software.

---

[1] Windows® is a registered trademark of Microsoft Corporation in the United States and/or other countries.

STARTING SOFTWARE

Your computer gives you several different ways of starting programs, depending on the operating system and version. Here are two ways:

- If you have the Microsoft® Windows® operating system, click the ***Start*** button on the taskbar, point to ***Programs***, and click the name of the program you want to open. Your program may be inside a folder. If so, open the folder (by pointing to it) to get to the program.
- With Microsoft® Windows® operating system and Macintosh® computers, double-click the program icon on the desktop. Your program may be inside a folder. If so, open the folder (by double-clicking it) to get to the program.

Application software is displayed in a **window** on the monitor. The features of all windows are the same. At the top is the **title bar.** The title bar displays the name of the file you are working on and, for some programs, the name of the software (such as *Microsoft® Word*). If you haven't yet saved the document with a filename, the title bar will say something like *Document* or *unmodified*, along with the name of the software. Under the title bar, you may see a menu bar and one or more toolbars or button bars. These bars allow you to choose commands in your software. We'll talk more about them in the next section.

The title bar contains boxes that allow you to resize and close the window. At the bottom and right sides of the window are **scroll bars.** You can click or drag these bars with the mouse to navigate (move around in) your document. To learn more about resizing and navigating a window, go to the Windows® Tutorial on pages R37–R39.

CHOOSING COMMANDS

Most software gives you several different ways to choose commands. As you work with a program, you will find the ways that are easiest for you.

Menus. A **menu bar** may appear at the top of your application window, just under the title bar. Like a menu in a restaurant, a menu bar offers you choices. From the menu bar, you can open a document, spell-check it, and so on. To open a menu and see its options, click the menu name in the menu bar. For example, to open the File menu, click *File.* For some software, you have to hold the mouse button down to keep the menu displayed. To choose a command, click it (Windows®) or drag down to it (Macintosh®). In some software, you can also open menus by pressing ALT plus the underlined letter in the menu name. For example, ALT + F opens the File menu. Menu names vary a little but are much the same across application software.

File Edit View Insert Format Tools Window Help

Corel® WordPerfect® 8 Program Menu Bar[2]

Toolbars. **Toolbars** let you choose commands quickly and easily. Most applications have toolbars. They have different names, such as *button bars*, in different software; but all toolbars are similar. They consist of icons or buttons that represent commands; some of the same commands found on menus. The standard toolbar contains icons for basic, often-used commands, such as saving and printing. Toolbars also exist for certain tasks, like formatting text or creating tables. In most software, pointing to a toolbar icon displays the name of the command. Clicking the icon executes the command.

Microsoft® Word 2000 Standard Toolbar[3]

Keyboard shortcuts. Each application has its own set of **keyboard shortcuts** for opening menus and executing commands. Keyboard shortcuts usually consist of pressing a function key (e.g., F1, F2, F3) or pressing the ALT, CTRL, or COMMAND key plus some other key. For example, to open a file in *Microsoft® Word 2000* for PCs, you would key CTRL + O. These shortcuts are often displayed on the menus and can also be found in the software's Help feature.

The following sections tell you how to use menus and toolbars to start, save, print, close, and open documents. The names for menus, commands, and icons in your software may differ slightly from those used here.

[2] Corel® and WordPerfect® are registered trademarks of Corel Corporation or Corel Corporation Limited in Canada, the United States, and/or other countries.

[3] Microsoft® is a registered trademark of Microsoft Corporation.

STARTING A NEW DOCUMENT 

For many applications, starting the program starts a new document automatically. You can simply begin working on the blank screen that is displayed when the program has been loaded. If your software doesn't display a blank screen on starting up, if you want to start a new document later in your working session, or if you want to start a new document with another document already on the screen, do *one* of the following:

- Select the *New* command on the File menu.
- Click the *New* icon, usually the first icon to the left on the standard toolbar.
- Use the keyboard shortcut for the *New* command.

A new document window will display. In some software, you may first see a **dialog box** that gives you setup options for your document. To learn more about dialog boxes, go to the Windows® Tutorial on pages R37–R39. Pressing ENTER or RETURN or clicking *New* or *OK* will take you from the dialog box to a blank document window.

KEYING TEXT

Keying text in a new word processing document is easy. Simply begin keying. Text is entered to the left of the **insertion point** (the flashing line). You will use many features of your word processing software in the special Word Processing pages of this book.

USING HELP

If you need assistance in the form of "how-to" information while working with software, you can get it through the program's Help menu or the Help icon on the toolbar. Help options vary but generally include a table of contents and a searchable index. If you enter the topic or a keyword, the software can search for information about it.

SAVING A DOCUMENT 

Saving a document places a copy of it on a disk in one of the computer's disk drives. This may be the hard (internal) disk of the computer or some kind of removable **medium,** such as a 3.5" disk or Zip disk. This copy will not be erased when your computer is shut down. It is permanent until you delete or modify it.

Save any documents that you think you will need later. You can save a document anytime the document is on the screen—just after starting it, while you are working on it, or when you are done. Save often as you work on a document so that you will not lose your changes in case of a power failure or other problem. Follow these steps to save a document:

1. Select the *Save* command from the File menu, click the *Save* icon on the standard toolbar, or use the keyboard shortcut for the *Save* command.
2. If you did not save the document before, the software will display the Save As dialog box. In this dialog box, look at the *Save in,* ___ *Folder* box, or something similar. If the drive and/or folder where you want to save the file does not show, click the down arrow and double-click drives and folders until the box shows the correct location. The computer's hard drive is most often (C:); the drive that takes 3.5" disks, (A:).
3. If you are saving the file to any kind of removable medium, insert that disk into the disk drive.
4. Key a name for the document in the box that says *File name, Name,* or something similar. Click *Save* or *OK* or press ENTER or RETURN.

If you modify a document after saving it, resave the document by selecting the Save command (Step 1). The Save As dialog box will not appear this time because you already named the file.

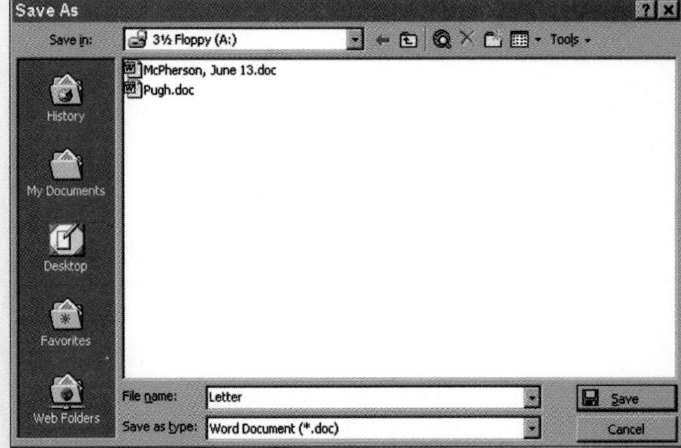

The Microsoft® Word 2000 Save As Dialog Box[4]

PRINTING A DOCUMENT 

Follow these steps to print a document:

1. Turn on the printer. Make sure it is loaded with paper.
2. Display the document on the screen.

[4] Microsoft® is a registered trademark of Microsoft Corporation.

3. Select the *Print* command from the File menu, click the *Print* icon on the standard toolbar, or use the keyboard shortcut for the *Print* command.
4. In the Print dialog box, select the print settings you want or use the settings that are already there (the **default settings**). In most software, the default settings print one copy of the document. When you are ready to print, click *OK* or *Print* or press ENTER or RETURN.

CLOSING A DOCUMENT

Closing a document removes it from the window. If you have not yet saved the document, or if you have made changes to it that you haven't saved, you will be asked when you choose the **Close** command whether you first want to save the document. Choosing *No* will erase a document that has not yet been saved. For a document that has been saved, choosing No will erase any changes you have made to the document since last saving it. You can close a document in any of these ways:

- Select the *Close* command from the File menu.
- Click the *Close* icon on the standard toolbar.
- Click the *Close* box or *Close* button. In Macintosh® applications, the Close box is at the top left of the window. The Close button in applications based on the Microsoft® Windows® operating system is the button containing an *x* at the far right of the title or menu bar. Each document window has a Close button, as does the software window. Be sure to choose the Close button for the document, not the software, if you want to continue working in the program.
- Use the keyboard shortcut for the Close command.

OPENING A DOCUMENT 

Opening a document means retrieving it from wherever it is stored and displaying it on the screen. Follow these steps to open a document:

1. Select *Open* from the File menu, click the *Open* icon on the standard toolbar, or use the keyboard shortcut for the Open command.
2. Choose or key the filename of the document. If you don't see the filename displayed in the Open dialog box, navigate with the mouse to where the file is stored by choosing the appropriate disk drive (and folder, if any), just as you do when saving a document. If you are retrieving a file from a 3.5" disk, CD-ROM, or Zip disk, you will need to insert that disk into the disk drive to get the file.

CLOSING THE SOFTWARE

Choose one of these options for closing the application software:

- Select the *Exit* or *Quit* command from the File menu.
- Click the *Close* button or *Close* box.

If you still have a file open and have not saved it, or if you have made changes to the file since your last save, you will be *prompted* to save the file. The computer is programmed to remind you of certain steps. These reminders are called **prompts**.

TURNING OFF THE COMPUTER

Follow these steps to turn off your computer:

1. Close all application software.
2. Remove any media from the disk drives.
3. Select *Shut Down* from the Start menu (Microsoft® Windows® operating system), Apple menu (Macintosh® computers), or Special menu (Macintosh® computers). On some Macintosh® computers, you can press the ON/OFF key instead.
4. If you get a prompt asking whether you really want to shut down, click *Yes* or *Shut Down*. On some Macs, you may be prompted to press the ON/OFF key.
5. After the computer has shut down, turn off the power switch on the CPU or keyboard (and monitor, if necessary).

Know Your Computer

The numbered parts are found on most computers. The location of some parts will vary.

1. **CPU (Central Processing Unit):** Internal operating unit or "brain" of computer.
2. **Disk drive:** Reads data from and writes data to a disk.
3. **Monitor:** Displays text and graphics on a screen.
4. **Mouse:** Used to input commands.
5. **Keyboard:** An arrangement of letter, figure, symbol, control, function, and editing keys and a numeric keypad.

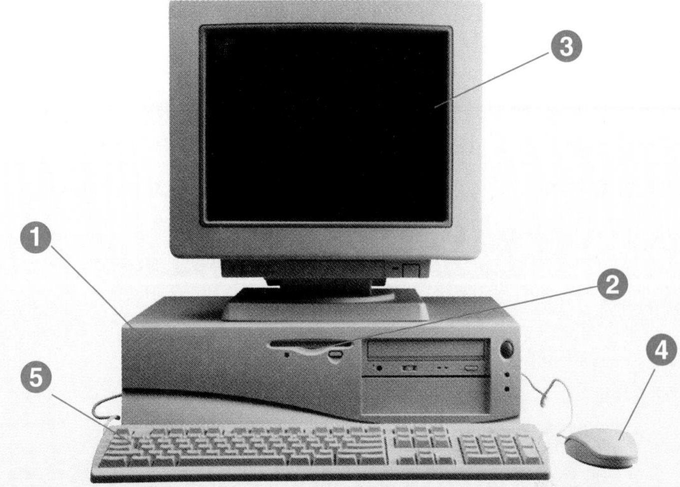

KEYBOARD ARRANGEMENT

1. **Alphanumeric keys:** Letters, numbers, and symbols.
2. **Numeric keypad:** Keys at the right side of the keyboard used to enter numeric copy and perform calculations.
3. **Function (F) keys:** Used to execute commands, sometimes with other keys. Commands vary with software.
4. **Arrow keys:** Move insertion point up, down, left, or right.
5. ESC **(Escape):** Closes a software menu or dialog box.
6. TAB**:** Moves the insertion point to a preset position.
7. CAPS LOCK**:** Used to make all capital letters.
8. SHIFT**:** Makes capital letters and symbols shown at tops of number keys.
9. CTRL **(Control):** With other key(s), executes commands. Commands may vary with software.
10. ALT **(Alternate):** With other key(s), executes commands. Commands may vary with software.
11. **Space Bar:** Inserts a space in text.
12. ENTER **(**RETURN**):** Moves insertion point to margin and down to next line. Also used to execute commands.
13. DELETE**:** Removes text to the right of insertion point.
14. NUM LOCK**:** Activates/deactivates numeric keypad.
15. INSERT**:** Activates insert or typeover.
16. BACKSPACE**:** Deletes text to the left of insertion point.

COMMAND **(Mac® keyboards only):** With another key, executes commands that vary with software.

Welcome to MicroType Multimedia

MicroType Multimedia is the multimedia-enhanced version of *MicroType Pro*. With this full-featured software, you can use the power of your computer to learn alphabetic and numeric keyboarding and keypad operation. The Alphabetic Keyboarding and the Numeric Keyboarding modules of *MicroType* correspond to the new-key lessons in the *Century 21 Computer Keyboarding* textbook. After you complete Lesson 15 (ending on p. R33), you can use Keyboarding Skill Builder to boost your speed and accuracy.

MAIN MENU

Alphabetic Keyboarding

These 20 lessons teach the alphabetic keys, operational keys, and basic punctuation keys. Material on this disk may be used with review Lessons 1–8 (pp. 2–18), also.

Numeric Keyboarding

These 16 lessons teach/review the top-row figure keys and the more commonly used symbols. They are related to Lessons 13 and 14 (pp. 29–33) in the textbook. Activities focus on building skill as well as learning the top-row and symbol keys.

Keyboarding Skill Builder

After you learn the alphabetic keys, use these 20 lessons to boost your keyboarding speed and control. Each lesson can focus on either speed or accuracy, so you really have 40 lessons.

Numeric Keypad

You will learn numeric keypad operation by completing this module. It is related to lessons on pp. 51–54 in the textbook.

Open Screen

The Open Screen is a full-featured word processor that includes a spell checker and a built-in timer. You can practice your keyboarding skills, key letters and reports, or take a timed writing. These features can be accessed from the Menu bar, and many of them are available on the toolbar. When you take a timed writing in the Open Screen, click the Timer button and save each timing with its own name; for example, *16b-t1* would be Lesson Part 16b, timing 1.

OTHER FEATURES

Games

Each keyboarding module incorporates a game into every lesson. The games offer exciting graphics and action to help you build skill while having fun. Top-ten lists provide a way for students to compare scores.

Reports

The Lesson Report shows which lesson parts were completed as well as your speed scores and keying lines for *Build Skill* and the game. You can access performance graphs by clicking the Graph button on the Lesson Report.

In addition to the Lesson Reports, *MicroType* software provides a Summary Report, Keypad Data Sets, Top-Ten Lists, Certificate of Completion, and Performance Graphs. All of these reports, except the Lesson Report, are accessed from the Reports menu.

Diagnostic Writings

This feature checks speed and accuracy and provides simple error diagnostics. The writings are keyed from hard copy printed from the File menu in the Diagnostic Writings screen.

Quick Review

This feature of the Skill Builder module presents drill lines for practicing alphabetic and numeric reaches and operational keys. The Quick Review Report displays the average *gwam* (gross words a minute) for each section attempted.

3D Animations

This feature demonstrates proper posture and hand positioning from all angles.

Movies

This feature shows proper keystroking in action. Video clips emphasize how keyboarding is used in every profession.

PART 1

UNITS 1-12

Computer Keyboarding: Reinforce & Apply

Computers are not just for business anymore—they are for *every*one, *every*where! In our world of fast-paced communication, almost everything we see on TV and the Internet, hear at rap concerts and Broadway musicals, or read in books and newspapers began as keystrokes entered into a computer by a keyboard operator.

To get the most value from high-speed computers, users must be competent at the input end—the keyboard. A computer processes data and text at the same speed for everyone. But a person who keys 50 words a minute produces twice as much work as a person who keys 25 words a minute for the same amount of time.

Lessons in Part 1 *reinforce* your keying skills. E-mail, reports, letters, and tables are some of the ways you then *apply* those skills, using the features of your word processing software. The Internet activities in these lessons represent an increasingly important use of keyboarding. A series of Communication Skills activities can help you do error-free work.

Here you have an opportunity to develop skills for traveling the Information Superhighway. Take it—straightaway!

Your Perspective

The 190 independent states of the world are becoming increasingly interdependent. One reason that countries work together is to promote peace and to help people live better lives. The United Nations, originally an alliance of 51 countries, was formed for that reason at the end of World War II. The United Nations now includes nearly every country and has expanded its mission to include promoting human rights, improving the quality of human life, protecting the environment, and fostering development.

A second reason that countries depend on one another is economics. Internal changes like the collapse of the Soviet government in 1991 have lowered trade barriers and opened new markets. Growing economies in some developing countries have improved trade. Trade agreements such as the North American Free Trade Agreement, the European Community, and World Trade Organization have also increased commerce among nations.

Global Awareness

ACTIVITIES

1. Form a group with two or three other students. Choose an interesting country that you do not know much about.
2. Each person in the group should research one of the following topics: geography, history, currency, and recent events. Add other topics for larger groups.
3. Compose, format, and key your section of the report in bound report format.
4. Dividing tasks among group members, combine the report sections and prepare references and title pages.

What would you do for three months without the Internet? a CD player? How about electricity or an indoor toilet? A television station in the United Kingdom took a suburban London row house—and a modern British family—back in time 100 years to answer questions like these.

The house was stripped of modern conveniences and restored to what it would have been like at the end of the nineteenth century. The Bowler family lived, for three months, exactly like a London family in 1900, and their experiences were the subject of a TV series.

Each person in the family—two parents and four children—had three outfits and three sets of underwear, all that a middle-class Victorian family could have afforded. Washing clothes took 12 hours, with the two younger girls staying home from school to help. No pizza or fast-food burgers were allowed. The family ate food that would have been served in Victorian England and brushed their teeth with hog-bristle brushes dipped in bicarbonate of soda. They had no telephones, but the mail arrived three times a day.

The Bowlers could ride bikes and swim. The children played cards, took old-time photographs, wrote and acted a play, and read. The pace of life slowed down. When the series was over, the Bowlers returned to modern life with a new appreciation of some of their things—and the knowledge that they could do fine without some things.

Cultural Diversity

ACTIVITIES

1. Read the material at the left.
2. Key a list of items invented in the last 100 years that you use daily.
3. Compare lists as a class activity. Make a list that represents the best thinking of the group.
4. Try to spend one day without some of the items on your list. What was most difficult to live without? What was the easiest? Key a paragraph about your experiences. Be prepared to share them with the class.

UNIT 1

LESSONS 1-8

Review Letter Keys

LESSON 1 REVIEW HOME KEYS (fdsa jkl;)

Objectives:

1. To review control of home keys (**fdsa jkl;**).
2. To review control of **Space Bar** and **Enter** key.

1A • Review Work Area Arrangement

Arrange work area as shown at the right.

- alphanumeric (main) keyboard directly in front of chair; front edge of keyboard even with edge of table or desk
- monitor placed for easy viewing
- disk drives placed for easy access and disks within easy reach (unless using a network)
- book behind or at side of keyboard; top raised for easy reading

Properly arranged work area

1B • Review Keying Position

The features of proper position are shown at right and listed below:

- fingers curved and upright over home keys
- wrists low, but not touching keyboard
- forearms parallel to slant of keyboard
- body erect, sitting back in chair
- feet on floor for balance

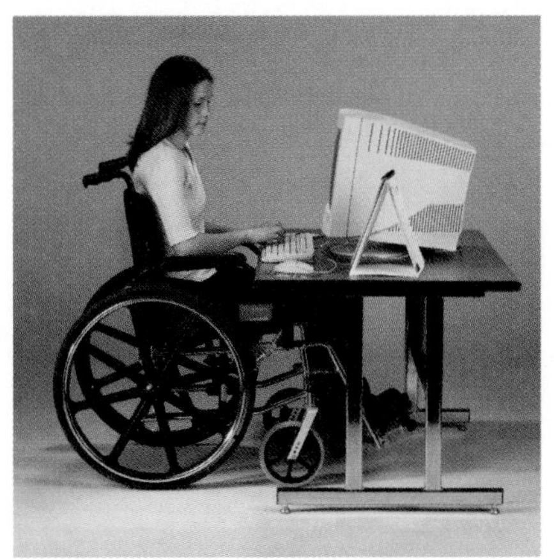

Proper position at computer

Your Perspective

Ethical issues confront us every day. They occur in our community, nation, and world. They also arise in our personal and professional lives.

- A stadium promises money and jobs, but some taxpayers would rather see the public funds to be expended on it spent on schools instead.
- A hydroelectric dam would provide a reservoir as well as electricity, but it would also destroy a wildlife habitat.
- In a grocery store, you see a student you know putting items under her coat.

Deciding what to do in situations like this isn't easy. What is a good way to think them through? What is a good way to make an ethical decision?

1. **Get the facts.** You can read about the new stadium and listen to what people on both sides of the issue have to say about it. You can learn more about reservoirs and how they affect the environment. You can try to find out more about the student from other people at school.
2. **Don't let assumptions get in the way of the facts.** As the actor and comedian Will Rogers said, "It isn't what we don't know that gives us trouble[;] it's what we know that ain't so." You don't like it when people make assumptions about you. Make sure your judgment isn't colored by preconceptions or stereotypes.
3. **Consider the consequences for everyone.** Try to see the situation from the point of view of each party involved. What is each person or group likely to lose or gain as a result of your decision?
4. **Consider your personal values.** Apply your own beliefs and standards to the problem.
5. **Make your decision.**

Ethics: The Right Thing to Do

ACTIVITIES

1. Read the material at the left.
2. Key a paragraph telling how you would use the five-step process to make a decision about the student in the grocery store.
3. Form a group with some other students. Discuss an ethical issue in your community. Make sure everyone contributes. Did everyone in the group agree?
4. Compose, format, and key a one-page personal-business letter to the editor of your local or school newspaper. Briefly explain the issue chosen in Step 3 and state your point of view. Include your reasons. Always present your viewpoint in a professional and respectful manner.

1C • Review Home-Key Position

1. Find the home keys on the chart: **f d s a** for left hand and **j k l ;** for right hand.

   Locate and place your fingers on the home keys on your keyboard with your fingers well curved and upright (not slanting).
2. Remove your fingers from the keyboard; then place them in home-key position again, curving and holding them lightly on the keys.

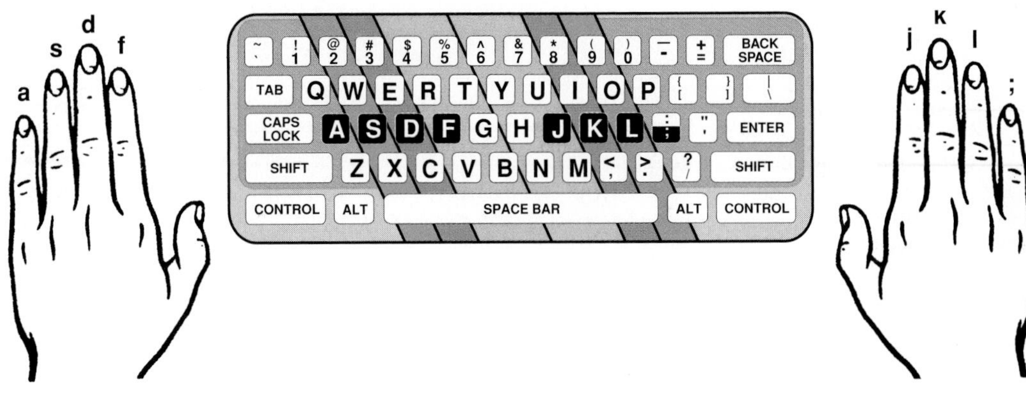

1D • Review Techniques: Home Keys and Spacebar

1. Read the hints and study the illustrations at the right.
2. Place your fingers in home-key position.
3. Strike the key for each letter in the first group below the illustration.
4. After striking *;* (semi-colon), strike the *Space Bar* once.
5. Continue to key the line; strike the *Space Bar* once at the point of each arrow.
6. Review proper position (1B); then repeat Steps 3–5 above.

Technique **H·I·N·T**

Keystroking: Strike each key with a light tap with the tip of the finger, snapping the fingertip toward the palm of the hand.

Spacing: Strike the Space Bar with the right thumb; use a quick down-and-in motion (toward the palm). Avoid pauses before or after spacing.

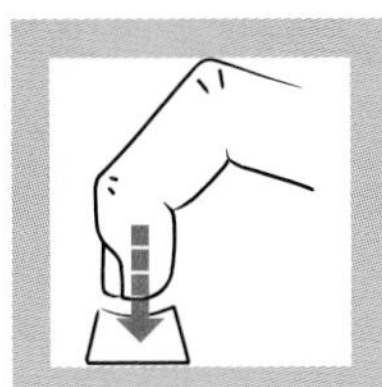

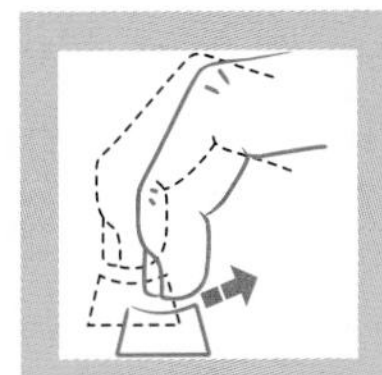

Space once

```
fdsajkl; f d s a j k l ; ff jj dd kk ss ll aa ;;
```

1E • Review Technique: Hard Return at Line Endings

Read the information and study the illustration at the right.

Practice the ENTER key reach several times.

Hard Return
To return the insertion point to the left margin and move it down to the next line, strike ENTER.

This is called a **hard return**. Use a hard return at the end of all drill lines in this unit. Use two hard returns when directed to double-space.

Hard Return Technique
Reach the little finger of the right hand to the ENTER key, tap the key, and return the finger quickly to home-key position.

Table 2

Format the table at the right. Adjust column widths: Columns A and B, 1"; Columns C and D, 0.75"; Columns E and F, 1.25". Adjust row height: 0.25" (all rows). In cells, use *bottom* vertical alignment and the horizontal alignment shown. Apply bold and shading (gray-5%, gray-10%, red, and light blue) and a triple-line border around every cell (as shown). Center the table horizontally and vertically.

 **Save as:** *TBL75B2*

UNITED STATES WOMEN GOVERNORS

Name		**Party Affiliation**		**State**	**Years Served**
Last	**First**	**Dem.**	**Rep.**		
Collins	Martha	X		Kentucky	1984-1987
Ferguson	Miriam	X		Texas	1925-1927
Finney	Joan	X		Kansas	1991-1995
Grasso	Ella	X		Connecticut	1975-1980
Hollister	Nancy		X	Ohio	1998-1999
Hull	Jane		X	Arizona	1997-present
Kunin	Madeleine	X		Vermont	1985-1991
Mofford	Rose	X		Arizona	1988-1991
Orr	Kay		X	Nebraska	1987-1991
Ray	Dixy	X		Washington	1977-1981
Richards	Ann	X		Texas	1991-1995
Roberts	Barbara	X		Oregon	1991-1995
Ross	Nellie	X		Wyoming	1925-1927
Shaheen	Jeanne	X		New Hampshire	1997-present
Wallace	Lurleen	X		Alabama	1967-1968
Whitman	Christine		X	New Jersey	1994-present

Source: "GenderGap in Government." http://www.gendergap.com/government/governor.htm (21 March 2000).

Table 3

Format the table at the right. Use a 2" top margin. Adjust column width: Column A, 1.5"; Columns B-E, 0.5". Adjust row height: 0.3" (all rows). In cells, use *bottom* vertical alignment and the horizontal alignment shown. Apply bold and shading (gray-5%) as shown. Remove the outside table border. Center the table horizontally.

 **Save as:** *TBL75B3*

SALARY COMPARISON

Employee	**Proposed Salary**		**Current Salary**	
	Salary	**Rank**	**Salary**	**Rank**
Douglas, Jason	$39,790	8	$39,000	7
Hazelkorn, Rebecca	41,230	7	38,500	8
Jackson, Charla	37,952	9	37,000	9
Loomis, Scott	25,796	10	23,000	10
Market, Michael	47,682	5	45,500	4
Nelson, Tim	62,265	1	59,725	1
Reed, Maja	52,980	3	51,900	2
Sutherland, Tara	54,769	2	51,695	3
Tekulve, Jaycee	49,780	4	44,500	6
Welsch, Gary	47,290	6	45,000	5

SKILL BUILDING

1F • Home-Key and Spacebar Review

Key the lines once; single-spaced (SS) with a double space (DS) between 2-line groups. Do not key line numbers.

Spacing **C • U • E**

Strike the ENTER key twice to insert a DS between 2-line groups.

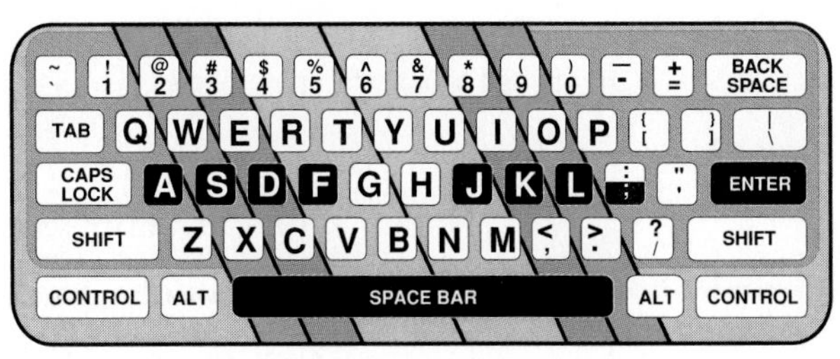

1 j jj f ff k kk d dd l ll s ss ; ;; a aa jkl; fdsa
2 j jj f ff k kk d dd l ll s ss ; ;; a aa jkl; fdsa

Strike the ENTER key twice to double-space (DS).

3 a aa ; ;; s ss l ll d dd k kk f ff j jj fdsa jkl;
4 a aa ; ;; s ss l ll d dd k kk f ff j jj fdsa jkl;

DS

5 jf jf kd kd ls ls ;a ;a fj fj dk dk sl sl a; a; f
6 jf jf kd kd ls ls ;a ;a fj fj dk dk sl sl a; a; f

DS

7 a;fj a;sldkfj a;sldkfj a;sldkfj a;sldkfj a;sldkfj
8 a;fj a;sldkfj a;sldkfj a;sldkfj a;sldkfj a;sldkfj

Strike the ENTER key 4 times to quadruple-space (QS).

1G • Review Technique: Enter

Key each line twice SS; DS between 2-line groups.

Reach with little finger; tap the ENTER key quickly; return finger to home key.

1 a;sldkfj a;sldkfj
2 ff jj dd kk ss ll aa ;;
3 fj fj dk dk sl sl a; a; asdf ;lkj
4 fj dk sl a; jf kd ls ;a fdsa jkl; a;sldkfj

1H • Keyboard Reinforcement

Key each line twice SS; DS between 2-line groups.

1 a lad; a jak; a lass; all ads; add all; ask a lass
2 as a lad; a fall fad; ask all dads; as a fall fad;
3 as a fall fad; add a jak salad; as a sad lad falls
4 ask a lad; ask a lad; all jaks fall; all jaks fall
5 as a fad; as a dad; ask a lad; as a lass; all lads
6 add a jak; a fall ad; all fall ads; ask a sad lass
7 a sad lad; ask a dad; all jaks; ask a jak; sad dad
8 a sad fall; all fall ads; as a lass asks a sad lad

ASSESS TABLE FORMATTING

Objective:
To assess table formatting skills.

75A • 5' Conditioning Practice

Key each line twice SS; then take a 1' writing on line 3; determine *gwam* and errors.

alphabet 1 Hazel Jackson reported quite extensive damage to the big freeway.

fig/sym 2 Model #80-93 sells for $425 plus 6% sales tax and 17% excise tax.

speed 3 He may pay us to work for the men when they dismantle the chapel.

gwam 1' | 1 | 2 | 3 | 4 | 5 | 6 | 7 | 8 | 9 | 10 | 11 | 12 | 13 |

75B • 45' Assess Table Formatting Skills

Table 1

Format the table at the right. Adjust column widths: Columns A and B, 2"; Column C, 1.75". Adjust row height: 0.3" (all rows). Use the horizontal and vertical alignment in cells as shown. Apply bold and shading (gray–5%) and a double-line border around every cell (as shown). Center the table horizontally and vertically.

Save as: *TBL75B1*

Fan Balloting

MAJOR LEAGUE ALL-CENTURY TEAM

Position	Player	No. of Votes
Catcher	Johnny Bench	1,010,403
	Yogi Berra	704,208
Pitcher	Nolan Ryan	992,040
	Sandy Koufax	970,434
First Baseman	Lou Gehrig	1,207,992
	Mark McGwire	517,181
Second Baseman	Jackie Robinson	788,116
	Rogers Hornsby	630,761
Shortstop	Cal Ripken Jr.	669,033
	Ernie Banks	598,168
Third Baseman	Mike Schmidt	855,654
	Brooks Robinson	761,700
Outfield	Babe Ruth	1,158,044
	Hank Aaron	1,156,782
	Ted Williams	1,125,583
	Willie Mays	1,115,896
	Joe DiMaggio	1,054,423
	Mickey Mantle	988,168

Source: USA Today. http://www.usatoday.com/sports/baseballmlbfs28.htm (25 October 1999).

LESSON 2 — REVIEW LETTER KEYS (h, e, i, AND r)

Objectives:

1. To review reach technique for **h** and **e**.
2. To review reach technique for **i** and **r**.

2A • 8'* Review [H] and [E]

Key each line twice single-spaced (SS); double-space (DS) between 2-line groups.

*Suggested number of minutes.

Review h

1 j j hj hj ah ah ha ha had had has has ash ash hash

2 hj hj ha ha ah ah hah hah had had ash ash has hash

3 ah ha; had ash; has had; a hall; has a hall; ah ha

Review e

4 d d ed ed el el led led eel eel eke eke ed fed fed

5 ed ed el el lee lee fed fed eke eke led led ale ed

6 a lake; a leek; a jade; a desk; a jade eel; a deed

SKILL BUILDING

2B • 14' Keyboard Reinforcement

Key each line twice SS; DS between 2-line groups.

home row

1 ask ask | has has | lad lad | all all | jak jak | fall falls

2 a jak; a lad; a sash; had all; has a jak; all fall

h/e

3 he he | she she | led led | held held | jell jell | she shed

4 he led; she had; she fell; a jade ad; a desk shelf

all keys learned

5 elf elf | all all | ask ask | led led | jak jak | hall halls

6 ask dad; he has jell; she has jade; he sells leeks

all keys learned

7 he led; she has; a jak ad; a jade eel; a sled fell

8 she asked a lad; he led all fall; she has a jak ad

all keys learned

9 had a jade; she fell; a lake; see dad; he fed dad;

10 she fell | has dad | he had a keel | she has a jade sash

Document 2 (References Page)
Format a references page from the information below.

Clinton, Susan. The Story of Susan B. Anthony. Chicago: Children's Press, 1986.

"An Overview of Abraham Lincoln's Life." http://www.home.att.net/~rjnorton/Lincoln77.html (27 April 2000).

Powell, Jim. "The Education of Thomas Edison." http://www.self-gov.org/freeman/9502powe.htm (25 April 2000).

 **Save as:** *RPT74B2*

Document 3 (Title Page)
Format a title page for the report.

 **Save as:** *RPT74B3*

Anthony continued to fight for women's rights, however, for the next 33 years of her life. Even though hse died in 1906 and the amendment granting women the right to vote (nineteenth amendment) was not passed until 1920, that amendment is often called the Susan B. Anthony Amendment in honor of Anthony's eforts to advance women's rights.

Thomas Alva Edison

Imagine life without the incandescent light bulb, phonograph, kinetoscope (a small box for viewing moving films), or any of the other 1,090 inventions pattented by Edison. Life certainly would be different without these inventions or later inventions that came as a result of Edison's ~~his~~ work.

Interestingly enough, most of Edison's learning took place at home under the guidance of his mother. "Nancy Edison's secret: she was more dedicated than any teacher was likely to be, and she had the flexibility to experiment with various ways of nurturing her son's live for learning.[2]

Benjamin Franklin

Benjamin Franklin was a man of many talents. He was an inventor, printer, diplomat, philosopher, author, postmaster, and leader. A few of his more noteworthy accomplishments included serving on the committee that created the Declaration of Independence; publishing Poor Richard's Almanac; and inventing the lightning rod, ~~the~~ Franklin stove, ~~the~~ odometer and bifocal glasses.

Abraham Lincoln

For many Americans the impact of Abraham Lincoln is as great today as it was during his life time.

> Abraham Lincoln is remembered for his vital role as the leader in preserving the Union and beginning the process that led to the end of slavery in the United States. He is also remembered for his character, his speeches and letters, and as a man of humble origins whose determination and perseverance led him to the nation's highest office.[3]

DS Lincoln is a great example of one who dealt positively with adversity in his personal and professional life. His contributions towards the shaping of America will be long remembered.

2C • 8'
Review [I] and [R]

Key each line twice SS; DS between 2-line groups.

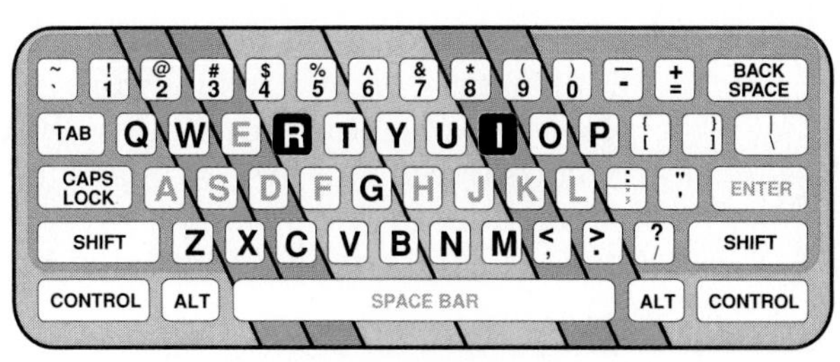

Review i

1 k k ik ik if if is is ill ill did did kid kid sail
2 ik ik is is did did his his lie lie side side hail
3 if he; she did; his side; a kid is a; if he is ill

Review r

4 f f rf rf are are jar jar red red ark ark far read
5 rf rf herd herd read read free free rare rare real
6 a jar; a rake; a lark; red jar; hear her; are dark

SKILL BUILDING

2D • 11'
Keyboard Reinforcement

1. Key the lines once SS with a DS between 2-line groups.
2. Key the lines again at a faster pace.

Technique Goals:
- fingers deeply curved
- wrists low, but not resting
- hands/arms steady
- eyes on copy as you key

reach review
1 hj ed ik rf hj de ik fr hj ed ik rf jh de ki fr hj
2 he he|if if|all all|fir fir|jar jar|rid rid|as ask

h/e
3 she she|elf elf|her her|hah hah|eel eel|shed shelf
4 he has; had jak; her jar; had a shed; she has fled

i/r
5 fir fir|rid rid|sir sir|kid kid|ire ire|fire fired
6 a fir; is rid; is red; his ire; her kid; has a fir

all keys learned
7 if if|is is|he he|did did|fir fir|jak jak|all fall
8 a jak; he did; ask her; red jar; she fell; he fled

2E • 9'
Technique: [Enter]

Key each line twice SS; DS between 2-line groups.

Practice 

Keep up your pace to the end of the line, return quickly, and begin the new line without a pause or stop.

1 if he is;
2 as if she is;
3 he had a fir desk;
4 she has a red jell jar;
5 he has had a lead all fall;
6 she asked if he reads fall ads;
7 she said she reads all ads she sees;
8 his dad has had a sales lead as he said;

Document 3 (E-mail)

Send the text at the right as e-mail to your instructor. (If you do not have e-mail software, prepare the text as a memo to **Sachiko Yang**. DATE: **April 24, 200-**). Use **RESPONSE TO YOUR QUESTION** for the subject.

 **Save as:** *MAIL73C3*

Your question is a good one. Yes, Nellie Tayloe Ross of Wyoming and Miriam (Ma) Ferguson of Texas were elected on the same day, November 4, 1924. However, Ms. Ross took office 16 days before Ms. Ferguson; therefore, Ms. Ross is considered the first woman governor in the United States, and Ms. Ferguson is considered the second. It should also be noted that Ms. Ross completed her husband's term as governor of Wyoming prior to being elected in 1924.

If you have other questions before the exam on Friday, please let me know. I hope you do well on it.

LESSON 74 ASSESS REPORT FORMATTING

Objective:

To assess report formatting skills.

74A • 5' Conditioning Practice

Key each line twice SS; then take a 1' writing on line 3; determine *gwam* and errors.

alphabet 1 Jeff Pizarro saw very quickly how Jason had won the boxing match.

figures 2 Our team average went from .458 on April 17 to .296 on August 30.

speed 3 Nancy may go to the big social at the giant chapel on the island.

gwam 1' | 1 | 2 | 3 | 4 | 5 | 6 | 7 | 8 | 9 | 10 | 11 | 12 | 13 |

74B • 45' Assess Report Formatting Skills

Document 1

Format the text at the right as a *bound* report with footnotes. Use **FOUR OUTSTANDING AMERICANS** for the title.

Footnotes

[1]Susan Clinton, The Story of Susan B. Anthony (Chicago: Children's Press, 1986), p. 5.

[2]Jim Powell, "The Education of Thomas Edison" (April 25, 2000).

[3]"An Overview of Abraham Lincoln's Life" (April 27, 2000).

 **Save as:** *RPT74B1*

Many outstanding Americans have influenced the past, and many more will impact the future. Choosing the "Four Greatest American" does injustice to the hundreds of others who left there mark on our country and diminishes their contributions. This report simply recognizes four great Americans who made America what it is today.

Without these four individuals America perhaps would be quite different than what it is today. The four individuals included in this report are: Susan B. Anthony, Thomas A. Edison, Benjamin Franklin, and Abraham Lincoln.

Susan B. Anthony

Susan B. Anthony is noted for her advancement of womens rights. She and Elizabeth Cady Stanton organized the national woman suffrage association. The following quote shows her commitment to the cause.

> At 7 a.m. on November 5, 1872, Susan B. Anthony broke the law by doing something she had never done before. After twenty years of working to win the vote for women, she marched to the polls in Rochester, New York, and voted. Her vote—for Ulysses S. Grant for president—was illegal. In New York state, only men were allowed to vote.[1]

LESSON 3

REVIEW LETTER KEYS (o, t, n, AND g)

Objectives:

1. To review reach technique for **o** and **t**.
2. To review reach technique for **n** and **g.**

3A • 5' Conditioning Practice

Key each line twice SS; DS between 2-line groups.

home row 1 a sad fall; had a hall; a jak falls; as a fall ad;

3d row 2 if her aid; all he sees; he irks her; a jade fish;

all keys learned 3 as he fell; he sells fir desks; she had half a jar

3B • 7' Review O and T

Key each line twice SS (slowly, then faster); DS between 2-line groups.

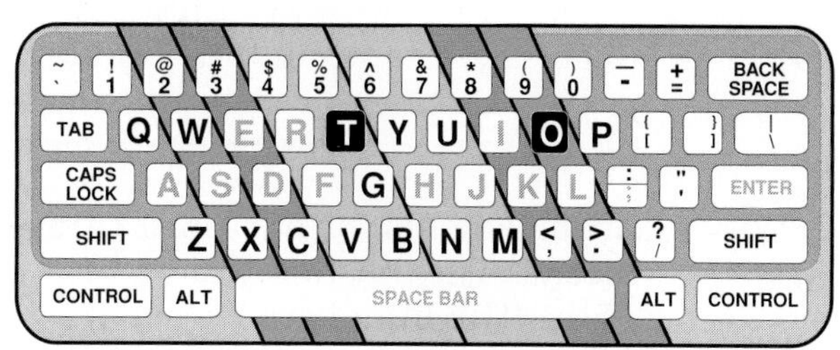

Review o

1 l l ol ol do do of of so so lo lo old old for fore

2 ol ol of of or or for for oak oak off off sol sole

3 do so; a doe; of old; of oak; old foe; of old oak;

Review t

4 f f tf tf it it at at tie tie the the fit fit lift

5 tf tf ft ft it it sit sit fit fit hit hit kit kite

6 if it; a fit; it fit; tie it; the fit; at the site

SKILL BUILDING

3C • 13' Keyboard Reinforcement

1. Key the lines once SS; DS between 2-line groups.
2. Key the lines again at a faster pace.

Technique Goals:

- curved, upright fingers
- wrists low, but not resting
- down-and-in spacing
- eyes on copy as you key

reach review

1 hj ed ik rf ol tf jh de ki fr lo ft hj ed ol rf tf

2 is led fro hit old fit let kit rod kid dot taj sit

h/e

3 he he|she she|led led|had had|see see|has has|seek

4 he led|ask her|she held|has fled|had jade|he leads

i/t

5 it it|fit fit|tie tie|sit sit|kit kit|its its|fits

6 a kit|a fit|a tie|lit it|it fits|it sits|it is fit

o/r

7 or or|for for|ore ore|fro fro|oar oar|roe roe|rode

8 a rod|a door|a rose|or for|her or|he rode|or a rod

space bar

9 of he or it is to if do el odd off too for she the

10 it is|if it|do so|if he|to do|or the|she is|of all

73C • 35'
Assess E-mail, Memo, and Letter Formatting Skills

Document 1 (Memo)

Format the text at the right as a memo to **Kathleen Maloney** from **Miguel Gonzalez**. Date: **May 5, 200-**. Subject: **BUDGET REQUEST**.

 **Save as:** *MEMO73C1*

As I searched the Internet for teaching resources, I came across some audiocassettes that would be an excellent addition to my World History course. The audiocassette collection, *The World's 100 Greatest People*, currently sells for $295, plus sales tax and shipping and handling charges of $9.95.

According to the advertisement (http://www.4iq.com/iquest16.html), "The 50 tapes included in this collection represent an audio treasury of 100 biographies detailing the life, time, achievement, and impact of some of history's greatest personalities, including philosophers, explorers, inventors, scientists, writers, artists, composers, religious, political, and military leaders." These tapes could be used in many classes outside the Social Studies Department. Perhaps some of the other departments would be willing to share the cost of the tapes.

When you have a few minutes, I would like to discuss how we should proceed to get these tapes in time for next year.

Document 2 (Letter)

Format the text at the right as a two-page letter to:

Mr. Michael Kent, President
Quote of the Month Club
97 Liberty Sq.
Boston, MA 02109-3625

Use **March 3, 200-** for the date; the letter is from **Patricia Fermanich**, who is the **Program Chair**. Use **Dear Michael** for the salutation and **Sincerely** for the complimentary closing.

Insert these quotations in the letter where indicated:

- **Wendell Lewis Willkie—"Our way of living together in America is a strong but delicate fabric. It is made up of many threads. It has been woven over many centuries by the patience and sacrifice of countless liberty-loving men and women."**
- **Althea Gibson—"No matter what accomplishments you make, somebody helps you."**

 **Save as:** *LTR73C2*

Arrangements for our April **Quote of the Month Club** meeting are progressing nicely. The meeting will be held at Pilgrims' Inn in Plymouth on Saturday, the 15th. The Inn offers excellent accommodations and food. I worked out special pricing with the manager. The cost will be $199.50 per member. This includes a single room, lunch and dinner on Saturday, and a continental breakfast on Sunday. I've asked the Inn to reserve 25 rooms for our members and guests. They will hold them until April 10. I've enclosed the Inn's brochure and list of food options. We can discuss them at the officers' meeting in Boston next week.

Members didn't like the format of our last meeting, so I'm proposing this plan: Each person attending will be assigned to a team, and each team will be given four quotes. The team will select one quote and prepare a five-minute presentation, explaining the meaning of the quote (their opinion). Each team will select a member to present to the entire group. Teams will evaluate each presenter in writing, rather than with oral comments. Some presenters at the last meeting felt uncomfortable being critiqued in front of the entire group.

I selected these four quotations:

- **Walter Elias Disney**—"Our greatest natural resource is the mind of our children."
- **Ayn Rand**—"Throughout the centuries there were men who took first steps down new roads armed with nothing but their own vision."

Insert two bulleted quotations shown at the left.

These topics should provide for excellent discussions leading up to the presentations. When you send the meeting notice, please send the quotes so the members will have time to think about them prior to the meeting.

I'm looking forward to our officers' meeting next week. I may be a few minutes late since I have a 4 p.m. meeting that I must attend.

3D • 7'
Review (N) and (G)

Key each line twice SS; DS between 2-line groups.

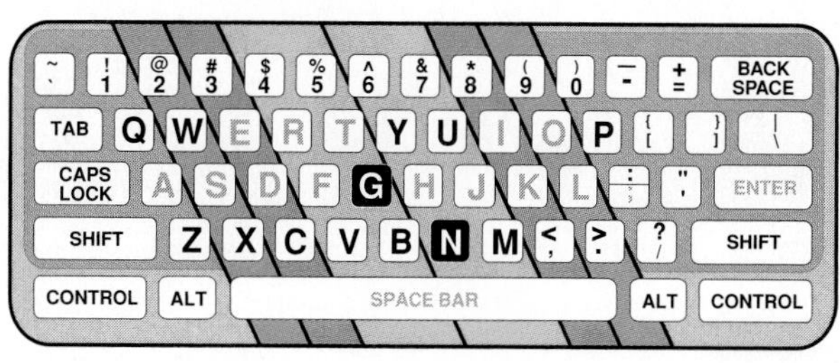

Review n

1 j j nj nj an an and and end end ant ant land lands
2 nj nj an an en en in in on on end end and and hand
3 an en; an end; an ant; no end; on land; a fine end

Review g

4 f f gf gf go go fog fog got got fig figs jogs jogs
5 gf gf go go got got dig dig jog jog logs logs golf
6 to go; he got; to jog; to jig; the fog; is to golf

SKILL BUILDING

3E • 13'
Keyboard Reinforcement

1. Key the lines once SS with a DS between 2-line groups.
2. Key the lines again at a faster pace.

Technique Goals:

- fingers deeply curved
- wrists low, but not resting
- hands/arms steady
- eyes on copy as you key

reach review

1 a;sldkfj ed ol rf jh tf nj gf lo de jh ft nj fr a;
2 he jogs; an old ski; do a log for; she left a jar;

n/g

3 an an|go go|in in|dig dig|and and|got got|end ends
4 go to; is an; log on; sign it; and golf; fine figs

space bar

5 if if|an an|go go|of of|or or|he he|it it|is is|do
6 if it is|is to go|he or she|to do this|of the sign

all keys learned

7 she had an old oak desk; a jell jar is at the side
8 he has left for the lake; she goes there at eight;

all keys learned

9 she said he did it for her; he is to take the oars
10 sign the list on the desk; go right to the old jet

3F • 5'
Technique: (Enter)

Key each line twice SS; DS between 2-line groups.

Practice **C • U • E**

Keep up your pace to the end of the line, return quickly, and begin the new line without a pause or stop.

1 she is gone;
2 she got the dogs;
3 she jogs on the roads;
4 he goes to the lake at one;
5 he has to go get their old dogs;
6 he is a hand on the rig in the north;

UNIT 21

LESSONS 73-75

Assessing Document Formatting Skills

LESSON 73 ASSESS CORRESPONDENCE FORMATTING

Objectives:

1. To assess e-mail, memo, and letter formatting skills.
2. To assess straight-copy skill.

73A • 5' Conditioning Practice

Key each line twice SS; then take a 1' writing on line 3; determine *gwam* and errors.

alphabet 1 Bugs quickly explained why five of the zoo projects cost so much.

figures 2 Jo's office phone number is 632-0781; her home phone is 832-4859.

speed 3 Pamela may go with us to the city to do the work for the auditor.

gwam 1' | 1 | 2 | 3 | 4 | 5 | 6 | 7 | 8 | 9 | 10 | 11 | 12 | 13 |

73B • 10' Check Keying Skill

Key two 3' writings on ¶s 1–3 combined; determine *gwam* and errors.

  all letters used

gwam 1' | 3'

Attitude is the way people communicate their feelings or 11 4
moods to others. A person is said to have a positive attitude 24 8
when he or she anticipates successful experiences. A person such 37 12
as this is said to be an optimist. The best possible outcomes 50 17
are expected. The world is viewed as a great place. Good is 62 21
found in even the worst situation. 69 23

Individuals are said to have negative attitudes when they 12 27
expect failure. A pessimist is the name given to an individual 24 31
with a bad view of life. Pessimists emphasize the adverse 36 35
aspects of life and expect the worst possible outcome. They 48 39
expect to fail even before they start the day. You can plan on 61 43
them to find gloom even in the best situation. 70 46

Only you can ascertain when you are going to have a good or 12 50
bad attitude. Keep in mind that people are attracted to a 24 54
person with a good attitude and tend to shy away from one with a 37 59
bad attitude. Your attitude quietly determines just how success- 50 63
ful you are in all your personal relationships as well as in 62 67
your professional relationships. 68 69

gwam 1' | 1 | 2 | 3 | 4 | 5 | 6 | 7 | 8 | 9 | 10 | 11 | 12 | 13 |
3' | 1 | 2 | 3 | 4 |

LESSON 4 REVIEW LETTER KEYS (left shift, period, u, AND c)

Objectives:

1. To review reach technique for **left shift** and **.** (period).
2. To review reach technique for **u** and **c**.

4A • 5' Conditioning Practice

Key each line twice SS (slowly, then faster); DS between 2-line groups.

```
reach review            1 ed ik rf ol gf hj tf nj de ki fr lo fg jh ft jn a;
space bar               2 or is to if an of el so it go id he do as in at on
all keys learned        3 he is; if an; or do; to go; a jak; an oak; of all;
```

4B • 7' Review Left Shift and .

Key each line twice SS (slowly, then faster); DS between 2-line groups.

Spacing **C • U • E**

Space once after . following abbreviations and initials. Do not space after . within abbreviations. Space twice after . at end of a sentence* except at line endings. There, return without spacing.

*Although desktop publishing calls for just one space after terminal punctuation, the standard two spaces are specified in this textbook.

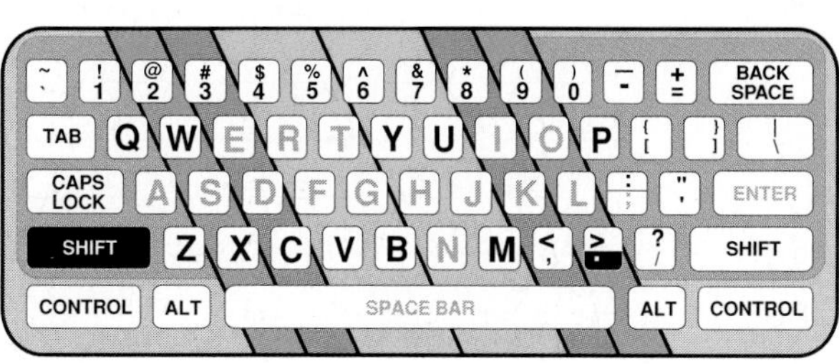

Shifting **C • U • E**

Shift, strike key, and release both in a quick 1-2-3 count.

Review left shift key

```
1 a a Ja Ja Ka Ka La La Hal Hal Kal Kal Jae Jae Lana
2 Kal rode; Kae did it; Hans has jade; Jan ate a fig
3 I see that Jake is to aid Kae at the Oak Lake sale
```

Review . (period)

```
4 l l .l .l fl. fl. ed. ed. ft. ft. rd. rd. hr. hrs.
5 .l .l fl. fl. hr. hr. e.g. e.g. i.e. i.e. in. ins.
6 fl. ft. hr. ed. rd. rt. off. fed. ord. alt. asstd.
```

SKILL BUILDING

4C • 13' Keyboard Reinforcement

1. Key the lines once SS; DS between 2-line groups.
2. Key the lines again at a faster pace.

Technique Goals:

- curved, upright fingers
- wrists low, but not resting
- quick-snap keystrokes
- eyes on copy as you key

```
h/e          1 hj ed jhj ded ha el he she led had eke her ale die
             2 Heidi had a good lead at the end of the first set.

i/r          3 ik rf kik frf is or sir ire ore his risk fire ride
             4 Kier is taking a high risk if he rides that horse.

o/t          5 ol tf lol ftf so it of too oft hot toe lot the old
             6 Ola has lost the list she took to that food store.

n/g          7 nj gf jnj fgf go an got and nag gin hang gone sign
             8 Lang and she are going to sing nine songs at noon.

left shift/. 9 Oak Lake; N. J. Karis; Lt. L. J. Oates; Lara Nador
            10 J. K. Larkin is going to Idaho to see Linda Jakes.
```

Tables 2 & 3

Format the tables at the right. Use the table formatting features you have learned to arrange the information attractively on the page. Apply a border of your choice.

Save as: *TBL72B2* and *TBL72B3*

Determine the current value of this portfolio, using an Internet site such as http://quote.yahoo.com/ to determine the value per share of each stock.

Stock Portfolio **EASTWICK INVESTMENT CLUB** **As of April 20, 200-**				
Stock		**Shares Owned**	**Price per Share**	**Value of Stock**
Company Name	**Symbol**			
Best Buy	BBY	200	78.875	$ 15,775.00
Ford	F	250	55.125	13,781.25
Intel	INTC	150	115.305	17,295.75
Kohls	KSS	200	102.375	20,475.00
McDonald's	MCD	200	35.625	7,125.00
Michael Foods	MIKL	150	20.125	3,018.75
Microsoft	MSFT	100	78.125	7,812.50
Pepsico	PEP	100	37.000	3,700.00
U.S. Airway	U	100	28.125	2,812.50
U.S. Bancorp	USB	200	21.305	4,261.00
Cash				23,495.77
Total Portfolio Value				$119,552.52

MAJOR UNITED STATES RIVERS		
River	**Length**	
	Miles	**Kilometers**
Arkansas	1,459	2,348
Colorado	1,450	2,333
Columbia	1,243	2,000
Mississippi	2,340	3,766
Missouri	2,315	3,726
Red	1,290	2,080
Rio Grande	1,900	3,060
Snake	1,038	1,670
Yukon	1,979	3,185

Source: The 1996 Information Please Almanac. Boston: Houghton-Mifflin.

72C • 9'
Skill Check

1. Key a 1' writing on each ¶ of 71C, p. 198; determine *gwam* and errors.
2. Take a 3' writing on ¶s 1–3 of 71C, p. 198; determine *gwam* and errors.

4D • 7' Review (U) and (C)

Key each line twice SS; DS between 2-line groups.

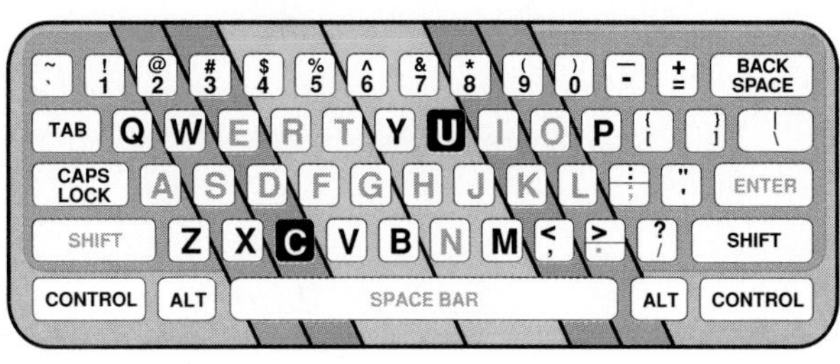

Review u

1 j j uj uj us us us jug jug jut jut due due fur fur

2 uj uj jug jug sue sue lug lug use use lug lug dues

3 a jug; due us; the fur; use it; a fur rug; is just

Review c

4 d d cd cd cod cod cog cog tic tic cot cot can cans

5 cd cd cod cod ice ice can can code code dock docks

6 a cod; a cog; the ice; she can; the dock; the code

SKILL BUILDING

4E • 13' Keyboard Reinforcement

1. Key the lines once SS with a DS between 2-line groups.
2. Key the lines again at a faster pace.

Technique Goals:

- Reach up without moving hands away from your body.
- Reach down without moving hands toward your body.
- Use quick-snap keystrokes.
- Eyes on copy as you key.

3d/1st

1 in cut nut ran cue can cot fun hen car urn den cog

2 Nan is cute; he is curt; turn a cog; he can use it

left shift and .

3 Kae had taken a lead. Jack then cut ahead of her.

4 I said to use Kan. for Kansas and Ore. for Oregon.

key words

5 and cue for jut end kit led old fit just golf coed

6 an due cut such fuss rich lack turn dock turf curl

key phrases

7 an urn|is due|to cut|for us|to use|cut off|such as

8 just in|code it|turn on|cure it|as such|is in|luck

all keys learned

9 Nida is to get the ice; Jacki is to call for cola.

10 Ira is sure that he can go there in an hour or so.

4F • 5' Technique: (Enter)

Key each line twice SS; DS between 2-line groups.

Practice **C · U · E**

Keep up your pace to the end of the line, return quickly, and begin the new line without a pause or stop.

1 Jan has gone to ski;

2 she took a train at nine.

3 Hans lost the three old disks;

4 he needs to find another disk soon.

5 Jack said he left the disks at the lake;

6 Nanci and I can go get the disks at the lake.

Keep eyes on copy as you strike the ENTER key.

PREPARE FOR ASSESSMENT: TABLES

Objective:
To prepare for assessment of table formatting skills.

72A • 5'
Conditioning Practice

Key each line twice SS; then key a 1' writing on line 3; determine *gwam.*

alphabet 1 Zachary James always purchased five or six large antique baskets.

figures 2 Only 1,548 of the 1,967 expected guests had arrived by 12:30 p.m.

speed 3 The neighbor may fix the problem with the turn signal on the bus.

gwam 1' | 1 | 2 | 3 | 4 | 5 | 6 | 7 | 8 | 9 | 10 | 11 | 12 | 13 |

72B • 36'
Reinforce Table Formatting Skills

Table 1

Format the table at the right. Use the table formatting features you have learned to arrange the information attractively on the page. Use the following source note.

Source: Fodor's 2000, San Francisco and Fodor's 2000, USA.

Use a border similar to the one shown.

 **Save as:** *TBL72B1*

PLACES TO EXPLORE

San Francisco

Place to Explore	Description	Major Attractions
Union Square	Heart of San Francisco's downtown, major shopping district	• Westin St. Francis Hotel • Old San Francisco Mint
Chinatown	Home to one of the largest Chinese communities outside Asia	• Chinese Culture Center • Old Chinese Telephone Exchange
Nob Hill	Home of the city's elite and some of its finest hotels	• Pacific Union Club • Cable Car Museum • Grace Cathedral • Mark Hopkins Hotel
Civic Center	One of the country's great city, state, and federal building complexes	• City Hall • Civic Center Plaza • Performing Arts Center • War Memorial Opera House
The Embarcadero	Waterfront promenade great for walking and jogging	• Ferry Building • Embarcadero Center • Hyatt Regency Hotel • Justin Herman Plaza
Fisherman's Wharf	Hyde cable-car line, waterfront, Ghirardelli Square, Piers 39 and 41	• Lombard Street • National Maritime Museum • Museum of the City of San Francisco
Financial District	Cluster of steel-and-glass high-rises and older, more decorative architectural monuments to commerce	• Transamerica Pyramid • Bank of America • Pacific Stock Exchange • Stock Exchange Tower

LESSON 5 — REVIEW LETTER KEYS (w, right shift, b, AND y)

Objectives:

1. To review reach technique for **w** and **right shift**.
2. To review reach technique for **b** and **y**.

5A • 5' Conditioning Practice

Key each line twice SS (slowly, then faster); DS between 2-line groups.

reach review 1 rf gf de ju jn ki lo cd ik rf .l ed hj tf ol gf ft

u/c 2 us cod use cut sue cot jut cog nut cue con lug ice

all letters learned 3 Hugh has just taken a lead in a race for a record.

5B • 7' Review W and Right Shift

Key each line twice SS (slowly, then faster); DS between 2-line groups.

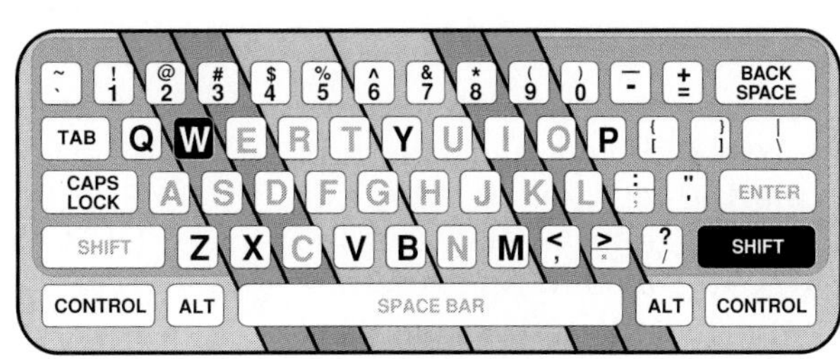

Review w

1 s s ws ws sow sow wow wow low low how how cow cows

2 sw sw ws ws ow ow now now row row own own tow tows

3 to sow; is how; so low; to own; too low; is to row

Review right shift key

4 A; A; Al Al; Cal Cal; Ali or Flo; Di and Sol left.

5 Ali lost to Ron; Cal lost to Elsa; Di lost to Del.

6 Tina has left for Tucson; Dori can find her there.

5C • 13' Keyboard Reinforcement

1. Key the lines once SS; DS between 2-line groups.
2. Key the lines again at a faster pace.

Practice **C · U · E**

Key at a steady pace; space quickly after each word; keep the insertion point moving steadily.

w and right shift

1 Dr. Rowe is in Tulsa now; Dr. Cowan will see Rolf.

2 Gwinn took the gown to Golda Swit on Downs Circle.

n/g

3 to go|go on|no go|an urn|dug in|and got|and a sign

4 He is to sign for the urn to go on the high chest.

key words

5 if ow us or go he an it of own did oak the cut jug

6 do all and for cog odd ant fig rug low cue row end

key phrases

7 we did|for a jar|she is due|cut the oak|he owns it

8 all of us|to own the|she is to go|when he has gone

all keys learned

9 Jan and Chris are gone; Di and Nick get here soon.

10 Doug will work for her at the new store in Newton.

ment of the Ohio, adventure in the Kentucky wilderness, conquest of the frontier lands of Illinois and the winning of the West for a new nation." Clark's explorations brought new options for people.

Delia Denning Akeley. Akeley explored Equatorial Africa, collecting specimens of Africa's wild animals for American natural history museums (1905–1929). Armed with little more than courage and an empathetic understanding of the Africans, she proved that a woman could travel in a dangerous country at a dangerous time.[5] Akeley's explorations brought new knowledge to the American people.

Everyone Explores

Not everyone will have the urge to explore as these noted explorers did, but everyone has a little bit of an exploring nature. It may not be the urge to explore for glory or discovery; it may simply be an urge to travel to an area that the individual has not yet visited. The urge may be in the form of exploring a book, museum, or Web site to expand one's knowledge. Or it may be exploring educational and career options. Regardless of the type of exploration done, all explorers are changed by their explorations. Their horizons become much broader.

Footnotes

[1]"A Profile of Greatness: The 10 Characteristics of the Achieving Personality" (April 25, 2000).

In Reference List only, add this Web address in front of date: http://www.4iq.com/great.html

[2]Milton Rugoff, The Great Travelers (New York: Simon and Schuster, 1960), p. xix.

[3]Samuel Eliot Morrison, "Christopher Columbus, Mariner." In Helen Wright and Samuel Rapport (eds.), The Great Explorers (New York: Harper & Row, 1957), pp. 80-81.

[4]Walter Havinghurst, "The Old Frontiersman—George Rogers Clark." In Helen Wright and Samuel Rapport (eds.), The Great Explorers (New York: Harper & Row, 1957), p. 21.

[5]Marion Tinling, Women into the Unknown (New York: Greenwood Press, 1989), p. 10.

71C • 9' Skill Check

1. Key a 1' writing on each ¶; determine *gwam* and count errors.
2. Take a 3' writing on ¶s 1–3 combined; determine *gwam* and count errors.

A all letters used

	gwam 3'	5'	
People in business are concerned about what is communicated	4	2	36
by the written word. As they write memos, letters, and reports,	8	5	38
they may plan for the content but may not plan for the image of	13	8	41
the message. Experts, however, realize that neglecting the way	17	10	43
a document looks can be costly.	19	11	45
Many times a written piece of correspondence is the only	23	14	47
basis on which a person can form an impression of the writer.	27	16	49
Judgments based on a first impression that may be formed by the	31	19	52
reader about the writer should always be considered before mail-	35	21	54
ing a document.	36	22	55
The way a document looks can communicate as much as what it	40	24	57
says. Margins, spacing, and placement are all important features	45	27	60
to consider when you key a document. A quality document is one	49	29	63
that will bring the interest of the reader to the message rather	53	32	65
than to the way it appears.	55	33	66

gwam 3' 1 2 3 4
5' 1 2 3

5D • 7' Review (B) and (Y)

Key each line twice SS; DS between 2-line groups.

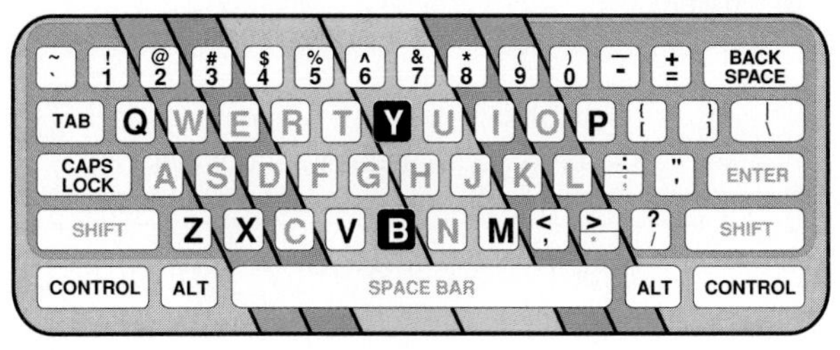

Review b

1 f f bf bf fib fib rob rob but but big big fib fibs

2 bf bf rob rob lob lob orb orb bid bid bud bud ribs

3 a rib; to fib; rub it; an orb; or rob; but she bid

Review y

4 j j yj yj jay jay lay lay hay hay day day say says

5 yj yj jay jay eye eye dye dye yes yes yet yet jays

6 a jay; to say; an eye; he says; dye it; has an eye

5E • 13' Keyboard Reinforcement

1. Key the lines once SS with a DS between 2-line groups.
2. Key the lines again at a faster pace.

Technique Goals:

- Reach up without moving hands away from your body.
- Reach down without moving hands toward your body.
- Use quick-snap keystrokes.
- Eyes on copy as you key.

reach review
1 fg sw ki gf bf ol ed yj ws ik rf hj cd nj tf .l uj
2 a kit low for jut led sow fob ask sun cud jet grow

3d/1st rows
3 no in bow any tub yen cut sub coy ran bin cow deck
4 Cody wants to buy this baby cub for the young boy.

key words
5 by and for the got all did but cut now say jut ask
6 work just such hand this goal boys held furl eight

key phrases
7 to do | can go | to bow | for all | did jet | ask her | to buy
8 if she | to work | and such | the goal | for this | held the

all letters learned
9 Becky has auburn hair and wide eyes of light jade.
10 Juan left Bobby at the dog show near our ice rink.

gwam 1' | 1 | 2 | 3 | 4 | 5 | 6 | 7 | 8 | 9 | 10 |

5F • 5' Technique: (Enter)

Key each line twice SS; DS between 2-line groups.

Practice **C • U • E**

Keep up your pace to the end of the line, return quickly, and begin the new line without a pause or stop.

Nancy has her coats.

Dan took her to the show.

Jay barely lost the last race.

Becky can go to the dance with Bob.

Jessica said he has brown eyes and hair.

Rebecca was not able to attend the late show.

gwam 1' | 1 | 2 | 3 | 4 | 5 | 6 | 7 | 8 | 9 |

LESSON 71 PREPARE FOR ASSESSMENT: REPORTS

Objective:
To prepare for assessment of reports.

71A • 5'
Conditioning Practice
Key each line twice SS; then key a 1' writing on line 3; determine *gwam.*

alphabet 1 An exclusive photo of a mosque by Dr. Kjelstad was quite amazing.
figures 2 They were born on May 22, 1964, July 13, 1975, and June 18, 1980.
speed 3 Gus paid the men for the work they did on the shanty by the lake.
gwam 1' | 1 | 2 | 3 | 4 | 5 | 6 | 7 | 8 | 9 | 10 | 11 | 12 | 13 |

71B • 36'
Reinforce Report Formatting Skills

Document 1
Format and key the copy below and on p. 198 as an unbound report with footnotes.

Save as: *RPT71B1*

Document 2
Prepare a reference list on a separate page. Insert the page number.

Save as: *RPT71B2*

Document 3
Prepare a title page for the EXPLORERS report.

Save as: *RPT71B3*

EXPLORERS

Explorers are men and women who have the courage to test existing boundaries. Explorers are men and women who aspire for something more out of life than what currently exists. Explorers are men and women who are willing to chart the unknown at a cost to their own comfort and security. It can be argued that explorers possess the ten characteristics of the "achieving" personality type:[1]

- Focus
- Preparedness
- Conviction
- Perseverance
- Creativity
- Curiosity
- Resilience
- Risk taking
- Independence
- A sense of higher purpose

<u>Motivation of Explorers</u>

What motivates explorers? The earliest explorers traveled for the purposes of discovery and adventure. Many of the early explorers mentioned conquest, acquisition of wealth, and territorial acquisition as their reasons for exploring.

<u>Backgrounds of Explorers</u>

Explorers come from all walks of life. Marco Polo was a merchant; Robert Louis Stevenson was a novelist; and Mary Kingsley was a well-born Englishwoman. Noted explorers included conquistadors, lawyers, naturalists, priests, and surgeons. No station in life is immune from the "fever."

> The itch, the fever, the urge—whatever one chooses to call it—is recurrent, if not constant. Once they have gone off, they go again and again. . . . Often the fever manifests itself in childhood . . . and sometimes it stops only with death, violent death.[2]

There are many examples of individuals who had the fever. Three such examples are Christopher Columbus, George Rogers Clark, and Delia Denning Akeley.

<u>Christopher Columbus</u>. Columbus is recognized as one of the earliest noteworthy explorers. On his first voyage Columbus landed on the Bahamas, then Cuba, and Haiti (1492-93). At the time of his explorations, "No other sailor had the persistence, the knowledge and the sheer guts to sail thousands of miles into the unknown ocean until he found land."[3] Columbus' explorations whittled away at the unknown.

<u>George Rogers Clark</u>. Clark was an American frontiersman explorer during the last half of the eighteenth century. Like many frontiersmen who are driven to explore by their need for wide open spaces, Clark explored vast areas of wilderness. According to Havinghurst[4], Clark's name is "synonymous with the settle-

LESSON 6 — REVIEW LETTER KEYS (m, x, p, AND v)

Objectives:

1. To review reach technique for **m** and **x**.
2. To review reach technique for **p** and **v**.

6A • 5' Conditioning Practice

Key each line twice SS (slowly, then faster); DS between 2-line groups.

reach review
```
1 bf ol rf yj ed nj ws ik tf hj cd uj gf by us if ow
```
b/y
```
2 by bye boy buy yes fib dye bit yet but try bet you
```
all letters learned
```
3 Robby can win the gold if he just keys a new high.
```

6B • 7' Review M and X

Key each line twice SS (slowly, then faster); DS between 2-line groups.

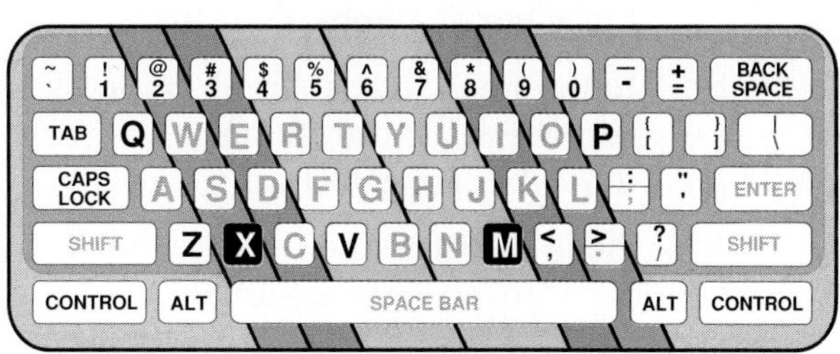

Review m
```
1 j j mj mj am am am me me ma ma jam jam ham ham yam
2 mj mj me me me may may yam yam dam dam men men jam
3 am to; if me; a man; a yam; a ham; he may; the hem
```

Review x
```
4 s s xs xs ox ox ax ax six six fix fix fox fox axis
5 xs xs sx sx ox ox six six nix nix fix fix lax flax
6 a fox; an ox; fix it; by six; is lax; to fix an ax
```

6C • 13' Keyboard Reinforcement

1. Key the lines once SS with a DS between 2-line groups.
2. Key the lines again at a faster pace.

Technique Goals:

- Reach up without moving hands away from your body.
- Reach down without moving hands toward your body.
- Use quick-snap keystrokes.
- Eyes on copy as you key.

3d/1st rows
```
1 by am end fix men box hem but six now cut gem ribs
2 me ox buy den cub ran own form went oxen fine club
```
space bar
```
3 an of me do am if us or is by go ma so ah ox it ow
4 by man buy fan jam can any tan may rob ham fun guy
```
key words
```
5 if us me do an sow the cut big jam rub oak lax boy
6 curl work form born name flex just done many right
```
key phrases
```
7 or jam|if she|for me|is big|an end|or buy|is to be
8 to fix|and cut|for work|and such|big firm|the call
```
all letters learned
```
9 Jacki is now at the gym; Lex is due there by four.
10 Joni saw that she could fix my old bike for Gilda.
```

Document 3 (Letter)

Format and key the text at the right as a business letter. Include a second-page heading. Place the following inserts in the body where indicated.

Insert 1

- **Depression**
- **Hard times**
- **Better**
- **Depressing/Sad**
- **Recovery**

Insert 2

- **Happy/Peaceful**
- **Rock 'n' Roll**
- **Great/Fun**
- **Getting better**
- **Prosperous**

Insert 3

- **Radio (96%)**
- **Automobile (91%)**
- **Computer (87%)**
- **Highway system (84%)**
- **Airline travel (77%)**

Proofread your copy; correct all keying and format errors.

 **Save as:** *LTR70B3*

Note:
The initials ASAP stand for the words *as soon as possible.*

March 11, 200- | Dr. Haley Morgan | 327 Redwood Dr. | Chattanooga, TN 37421-3619 | Dear Haley

I am excited about researching the "Generation Gap" with you. I have a vested interest in the problem since I have two teenagers who often ask which planet I came from.

The study I mentioned was a 1999 millennium survey entitled *Public Perspectives on the American Century: Technology Triumphs, Morality Falters.* The http: address is www.people-press.org/mill1que.htm. After studying the results, I'm convinced we are products of "Where we were when." For example, note the difference in the top five words used to describe each decade of the twentieth century. First, the 1930s:

Place Insert 1 here.

References to the Great Depression and economic hard times of the thirties were replaced by much happier terms two decades later. The top five terms to describe the 1950s:

Place Insert 2 here.

Who can forget Elvis and Rock 'n' Roll? I've finally achieved a semblance of success in getting my children to appreciate some of the great music of the fifties and sixties—of course, only when none of their friends are around.

Two other parts of that 1999 survey relate to our study: "A Century of Inventions" and "A Century of Social Change." The following list shows the top five inventions of the century and the percentage of respondents who thought the invention represented a change for the better.

Place Insert 3 here.

Television—interestingly—was not rated in the top five; it came in sixth. Seventy-three percent of the respondents said TV was a change for the better, while 27 percent responded "change for the worse," "made no difference," or "I don't know." Nuclear weapons were at the bottom of the list; only 19 percent of those surveyed said nuclear weapons were a change for the better.

Social changes of the century were not viewed as positively as the century's inventions. As shown below, only three categories were viewed as being a change for the better by 50 percent or more of the respondents.

- ✔ Civil rights movement (84%)
- ✔ Women in workplace (83%)
- ✔ Growth of suburbs (52%)
- ✔ Rock 'n' Roll (45%)
- ✔ Legalized abortion (34%)

I will continue to look for materials we can use in the review of related literature. I have cleared my calendar for April 2-3. Let me know ASAP the details for our meeting on those dates.

Cordially | Shawn Spielberg | Associate Professor | xx

6D • 7'
Review P and V

Key each line twice SS; DS between 2-line groups.

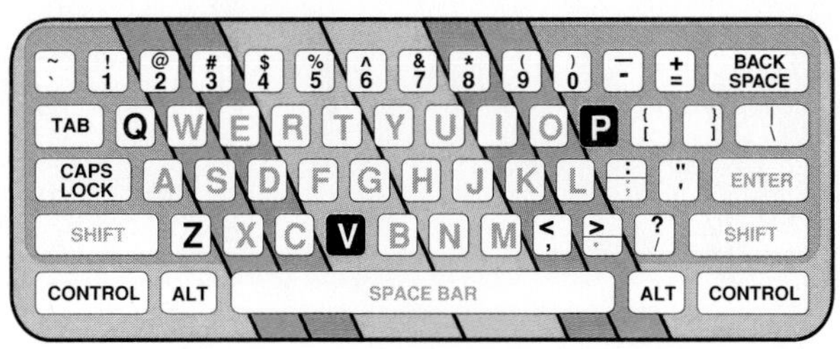

Review p

```
1 ; ; p; p; pa pa up up apt apt pen pen lap lap kept
2 p; p; pa pa pa pan pan nap nap paw paw gap gap rap
3 a pen; a cap; apt to pay; pick it up; plan to keep
```

Review v

```
4 f f vf vf via via vie vie have have five five live
5 vf vf vie vie vie van van view view dive dive jive
6 go via; vie for; has vim; a view; to live; or have
```

6E • 13'
Keyboard Reinforcement

1. Key the lines once SS; DS between 2-line groups.
2. Key the lines again at a faster pace.

Practice **C•U•E**

- Reach up without moving hands away from your body.
- Reach down without moving hands toward your body.
- Use quick-snap keystrokes.
- Eyes on copy as you key.

reach review

```
1 vf p; xs mj ed yj ws nj rf ik tf ol cd hj gf uj bf
2 if lap jag own may she for but van cub sod six oak
```

3d/1st rows

```
3 by vie pen vim cup six but now man nor ton may pan
4 by six but now may cut sent me fine gems five reps
```

key words

```
5 with kept turn corn duty curl just have worn plans
6 name burn form when jury glad vote exit came eight
```

key phrases

```
7 if they|he kept|with us|of land|burn it|to name it
8 to plan|so sure|is glad|an exit|so much|to view it
```

all letters learned

```
9 Kevin does a top job on your flax farm with Craig.
10 Dixon flew blue jets eight times over a city park.
```

6F • 5'
Technique: Spacing with Punctuation

Key each line twice SS; DS between 2-line groups.

Spacing **C•U•E**

Do not space after an internal period in an abbreviation, such as Ed.D.

```
1 Dr. Kennedy has a Ph.D., not an Ed.D., in physics.
2 Lynn may send a box c.o.d. to Ms. Fox in St. Paul.
3 J. R. and Tim will go by boat to St. Louis in May.
4 Lexi keyed ect. for etc. and lost the match to me.
5 Mr. and Mrs. D. J. Keaton set sail for the island.
6 Ms. Fenton may take her Ed.D. exam early in March.
```

UNIT 20

LESSONS 70-72

Preparing for Assessment

LESSON 70 PREPARE FOR ASSESSMENT: E-MAILS, MEMOS, LETTERS

Objective:
To prepare for assessment of e-mail, letter, and memo formatting skills.

70A • 5' Conditioning Practice

Key each line twice SS; then key a 1' writing on line 3; determine *gwam*.

alphabet 1 Extensive painting of the gazebo was quickly completed by Jerome.

figures 2 At least 456 of the 3,987 jobs were cut before November 18, 2001.

speed 3 Janel and I may go to the island to dismantle the bicycle shanty.

gwam 1' | 1 | 2 | 3 | 4 | 5 | 6 | 7 | 8 | 9 | 10 | 11 | 12 | 13 |

70B • 45' Reinforce Correspondence Formatting Skills

Document 1 (E-mail)
Format and key the text at the right as e-mail to your instructor. Attach the *CD-SALESRPT* file. Proofread your message; correct all errors.

 **Save as:** *MAIL70B1*

Note: Prepare this message as a memo to your instructor if you do not have e-mail software.

SUBJECT: SALES REPORT

The sales figures you requested are attached. This month's sales figures should be available on Friday. As soon as I receive them, I'll update the file to include those figures and e-mail them to you.

If there is any other information I can provide for the meeting next month, let me know. I'm looking forward to seeing you again in San Francisco.

Document 2 (Memo)
Format and key the text at the right as a memo to **Investment Club Members** from **Gordon Chandler**. Date the memo **April 20, 200-** and use **PORTFOLIO UPDATE** for the subject line.

 **Save as:** *MEMO70B2*

The attached table shows the current value of our portfolio. As you are well aware, market results have been mixed this year. The total value of the portfolio increased 12 percent since January 1. Most of this increase is due to additional contributions by members rather than increases in the value of stocks in the portfolio.

Our cash balance ($23,495.77) is quite large. We should decide at our next meeting what we want to do with this cash. As I recall, we are scheduled to meet on May 6 and will have potential investment opportunity reports from Catherine Cloninger and Mario Fernandez by then.

If you have questions about the report, please call me.

LESSON 7 — REVIEW LETTER KEYS (q, comma, z, AND colon)

Objectives:

1. To review reach technique for **q** and , (comma).
2. To review reach technique for **z** and : (colon).

7A • 5' Conditioning Practice

Key each line twice SS (slowly, then faster); DS between 2-line groups; if time permits, key the lines again.

all letters learned
1 an dog fix all via own buy for the jam cop ask boy

p/v
2 a pan; a vote; apt to; vie for; her pay; have five

all letters learned
3 Darby will pack sixty pints of guava jam for Beth.

7B • 7' Review Q and ,

Key each line twice SS (slowly, then faster); DS between 2-line groups.

Spacing **C • U • E**

Space once after , used as punctuation.

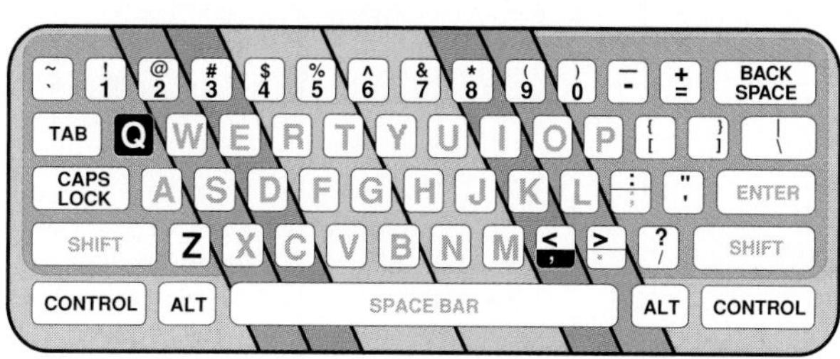

Learn q

1 a qa qa aq aq quo quo qt. qt. quad quad quit quits

2 qa quo quo qt. qt. quay quay aqua aqua quite quite

3 a qt.; pro quo; a quad; to quit; the quay; a squad

Learn , (comma)

4 k k ,k ,k kit, kit; Rick, Jan, or I will go, also.

5 a ski, a ski; a kit, a kit; a kite, a kite; a bike

6 Tom, I see, is here; Pam, I am told, will be late.

7C • 13' Keyboard Reinforcement

1. Key lines once SS; DS between 2-line groups.
2. Key the lines again at a faster pace.

Technique Goals:

- Reach up without moving hands away from your body.
- Reach down without moving hands toward your body.
- Use quick-snap keystrokes.

reach review
1 qa .l ws ,k ed nj rf mj tf p; xs ol cd ik vf hj bf

2 yj gf hj quo vie pay cut now buy got mix vow forms

3d/1st rows
3 six may sun coy cue mud jar win via pick turn bike

4 to go | to win | for me | a peck | a quay | by then | the vote

key words
5 pa rub sit man for own fix jam via cod oak the got

6 by quo sub lay apt mix irk pay when rope give just

key phrases
7 an ox | of all | is to go | if he is | it is due | to pay us

8 if we pay | is of age | up to you | so we own | she saw me

all letters learned
9 Jevon will fix my pool deck if the big rain quits.

10 Verna did fly quick jets to map the six big towns.

Job 14

HPJ From the Desk of
Helen St. Claire

Here is the company organization chart we have on file (CD-HPJJOB14). Some of the information is missing or outdated. Each branch's Web site contains the most up-to-date information. Print a copy of the file; then verify the information against that on the Web site. Mark the changes on the printed copy; finally, make the changes to the master file.
June 12
HSC

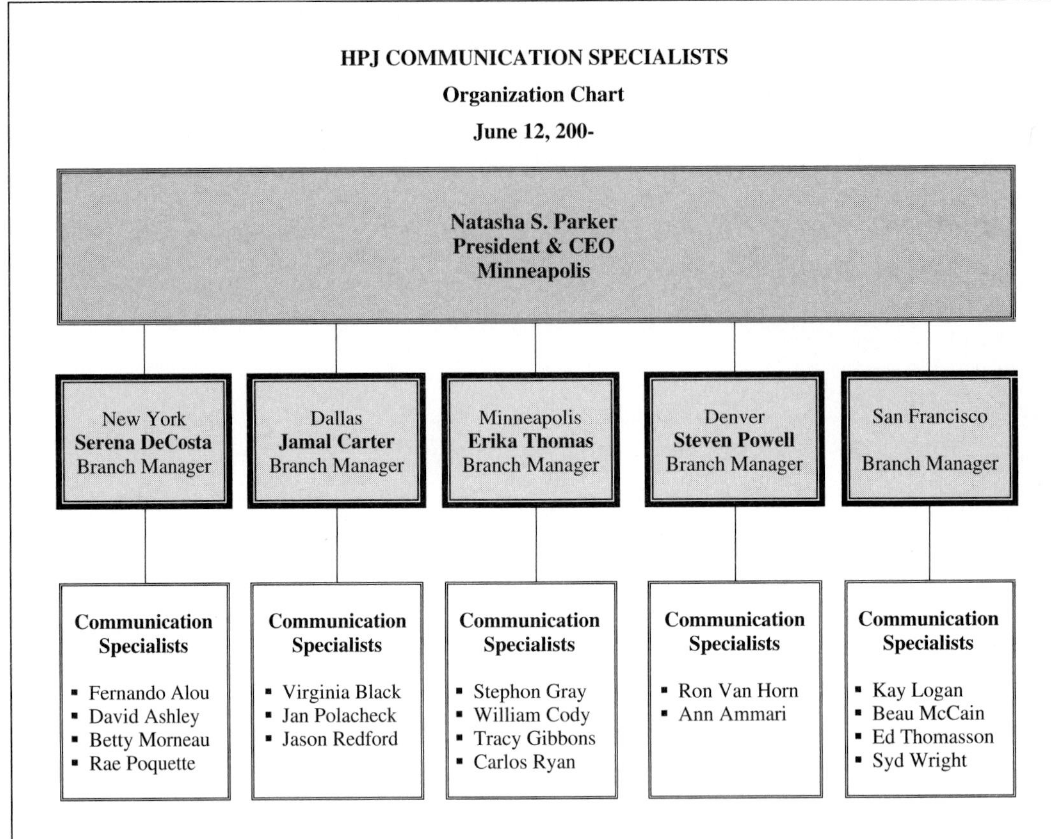

Job 15

HPJ From the Desk of
Helen St. Claire

Prepare (don't send) this message as e-mail to the communication specialists in the Minneapolis branch from Erika Thomas. You will need to get the e-mail addresses from their Web page. New Communication Specialist is the subject.
June 30
HSC

Stewart Peters will join our branch as Communication Specialist on Monday, July 15.

Stewart grew up in New york, where he completed an undergraduate degree in organizational communication at New york University. He recently completed his Master's degree at the University of Minnesota.

Stewart's thesis dealt with interpersonal conflict in the corporate environment. Since we intend to develop a seminar in this area, he will be able to make an immediate contribution.

Please welcome Stewart to HPJ and our branch when he arrives on the 15th.

7D • 7' Review Z and :

Key each line twice SS (slowly, then faster); DS between 2-line groups.

Language Skill **C • U • E**

- Space twice after : used as punctuation.
- Capitalize the first word of a complete sentence following a colon.
- Do not capitalize a sentence fragment following a colon.

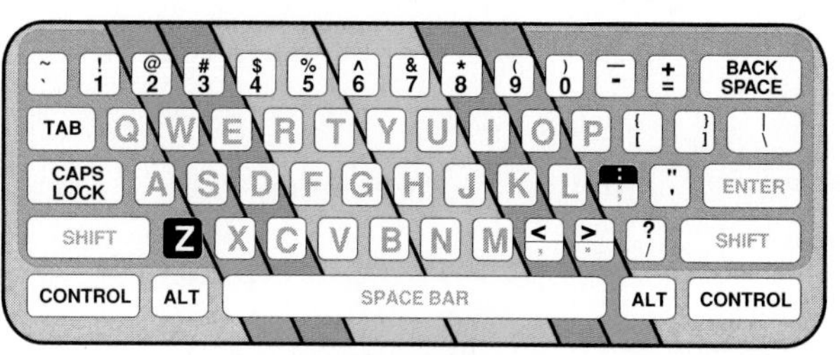

Review z

1 a a za za zap zap zap zoo zoo zip zip zag zag zany
2 za za zap zap zed zed oz. oz. zoo zoo zip zip maze
3 zap it, zip it, an adz, to zap, the zoo, eight oz.

Review : (colon)

4 ; ; :; :; Date: Time: Name: Room: From: File:
5 :; :; To: File: Reply to: Dear Al: Shift for :
6 Two spaces follow a colon, thus: Try these steps:

7E • 13' Keyboard Reinforcement

1. Key the lines once SS with a DS between 2-line groups.
2. Key the lines again at a faster pace.

Technique Goals:

- curved, upright fingers
- quiet hands and arms
- steady keystroking pace

q/z
1 zoo qt. zap quo zeal quay zone quit maze quad hazy
2 Zeno amazed us all on the quiz but quit the squad.

p/x
3 apt six rip fix pens flex open flax drop next harp
4 Lex is apt to fix apple pie for the next six days.

v/m
5 vim mam van dim have move vamp more dive time five
6 Riva drove them to the mall in my vivid lemon van.

easy
7 Glen is to aid me with the work at the dog kennel.
8 Dodi is to go with the men to audit the six firms.

alphabet
9 Nigel saw a quick red fox jump over the lazy cubs.
10 Jacky can now give six big tips from the old quiz.

7F • 5' Block Paragraphs

1. Read the note at the right below.
2. Key each paragraph (¶) once SS; DS between them; then key them again faster.
3. If your instructor directs, key a 1' writing on each ¶; determine your *gwam*.

Paragraph 1 — gwam 1'

The space bar is a vital tool, for every fifth or 10
sixth stroke is a space when you key. If you use 20
it with good form, it will aid you to build speed. 30

Paragraph 2

Just keep the thumb low over the space bar. Move 10
the thumb down and in quickly toward your palm to 20
get the prized stroke you need to build top skill. 30

gwam 1' | 1 | 2 | 3 | 4 | 5 | 6 | 7 | 8 | 9 | 10 |

Note: At the end of a full line, the copy and insertion point move to the next line automatically. This is called a **soft return**. Another name for it is **word wrap**. Use word wrap when you key a paragraph. At the end of a paragraph, though, use two hard returns to place a double space between it and the next paragraph.

Job 13, cont.

Internal barriers. Internal barriers are those that dal with the mental or psychological aspects of listening. The perception of the importance of the message, the emotional state, and the running in and out of the speaker by the listener are examples of internal barriers.

External Barriers. External barriers are barriers other than those that deal the mental and psychological makeup of the listner that tend tokeep the listener from devoting attention to what is being said. Telephone interruptions, visitors, noise, and the physical environment are examples of external barriers.

Ways to Improve Listening

Barrier to listening can be over come. However it does take a sincere efort on the part of the speaker. Neher and Waite suggest the following ways to improve listening skills.[3]

- Be aware of the barriers that are especially troublesome for you. Listening difficulties are individualistic. Developing awareness is an important step in overcoming
- Listen as though you will have to paraphrase what is being said. Listen for ideas rather than for facts.
- Expect to work t listening. work at overcoming distractions, such as the speaker's delivery or gestures.
- Concentrate on summarizing the presentation as you listen. If possible, think of additional supporting material that would fit with the point that the speaker is making. Avoid trying to refute the speaker. Try not to be turned off by remarks disagree with.

[1]H. Dan O'Hair, James S. O'Rourke IV, and Mary John O'Hair, Business Communication: A Framework for Success (Cincinnati: South-Western Publishing, 2001), p. 211.

[2]Judy C. Nixon and Judy F. West, "Listening--The New Competency," The Balance Sheet (January/February 1989), pp. 27-29.

[3]William W. Neher and David H. Waite, The Business and Professional Communicator (Needham Heights, MA: Allyn and Bacon, 1993), p. 28.

LESSON 8 REVIEW LETTER KEYS (caps lock, ?, tab, ', -, AND “)

Objectives:

1. To review reach technique for **Caps Lock**, **?** (question mark), **'** (apostrophe), **-** (hyphen), and **“** (quotation mark).
2. To review reach technique for the **Tab** key.

8A • 5' Conditioning Practice

Key each line twice SS; then key a 1' writing on line 3; determine *gwam* on the scale below line 3.

alphabet 1 Lovak won the squad prize cup for sixty big jumps.

z/: 2 To: Ms. Mazie Pelzer; from: Dr. Eliza J. Piazzo.

easy 3 He is to go with me to the dock to do work for us.

gwam 1' | 1 | 2 | 3 | 4 | 5 | 6 | 7 | 8 | 9 | 10 |

Note: Your **gwam** (gross words a minute) is the figure under the last letter keyed if you key only part of the line. If you key the line and start over, add 10 to that figure.

8B • 7' Review Caps Lock and ?

Key each line twice SS (slowly, then faster); DS between 2-line groups.

Note:
To key a series of capital letters, press CAPS LOCK, using the left little finger. To release CAPS LOCK, tap the CAPS LOCK key again.

Spacing **C•U•E**

Space twice after a ? at end of a sentence except at line or paragraph endings.

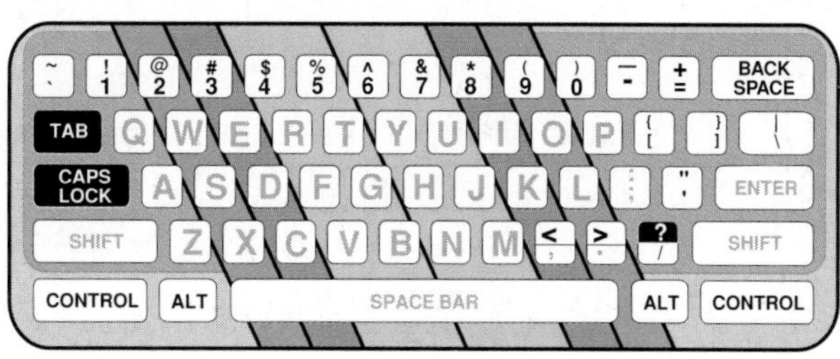

Review caps lock

1 Hal read PENTAGON and ADVISE AND CONSENT by Drury.

2 Oki joined FBLA when her sister joined PBL at OSU.

3 Zoe now belongs to AMS and DPE as well as to NBEA.

Review ? (question mark)

4 ; ; ?; ?; Who? What? When? Where? Why? Is it?

5 Who is it? Is it she? Did he go? Was she there?

6 Is it up to me? When is it? Did he key the line?

8C • 10' Review Tab

Indent and key each ¶ once SS, using word wrap (soft returns); DS between ¶s.

Note:
To indent the first line of a ¶, press TAB, using the left little finger. Usually tabs are set every 0.5" to the right of the left margin.

Tab → The tab key is used to indent blocks of copy such as these.

Tab → It should also be used for tables to arrange data quickly and neatly into columns.

Tab → Learn now to use the tab key by touch; doing so will add to your keying skill.

Tab → Strike the tab key firmly and release it very quickly. Begin the line without a pause.

Tab → If you hold the tab key down, the insertion point will move from tab to tab across the line.

Job 12, cont.

- Videoconferencing
- Teleconferencing
- Data conferencing
- GroupSystems
- Internet resources

Graphic Designer

A graphic artist has been hired to design all of the materials for the new seminar. He will design promotional items as well as content-related items. Currently he is working on the manual cover and divider pages. These items will be coordinated with the emblems used in the slide show portion of the presentation, along with name tags, promotional paraphernalia, and business cards. This should give our seminar a more professional appearance. If it works as well as I think it is going to, we will have the designer work on materials for our existing seminars to add the "professional" look.

Job 13

HPJ From the Desk of
Helen St. Claire

Format this text as an unbound report with footnotes (shown at bottom of attached copy). The report will be a handout for the "Listen Up!" seminar.

June 12
HSC

LISTEN UP!

According to Raymond McNulty, " Everyone who expects to succeed in life should realize that success only will come if you give careful consideration to other people."[1] To acomplish this you must be an excellent listener. One of The most critical skills that an individual acquires is the ability to listen. studies indicate that a person spends 70 percent to 80 percent of ~~their~~ his or her time communicating, of which 45% is spent listening. Nixon and West give the following breakdown for the average an individual of time spent communicating.[2]

- Writing 9%
- Reading 16%
- Speaking 30%
- Listening 45%

Since almost half ~~most~~ of the time spent communicating is spent listening, it is important to overcome any obstacles that obstruct our ability to listen and to learn new ways to improve our listening ability.

Barriers to Listening

Anything that interferes with our ability to listen is classified as a barrier to listening. These Barriers ~~that obstruct our ability to listen~~ can be divided into two basic categories—external and internal barriers.

(Report continued on next page)

8D • 10'
Review ', -, and "

Key each line twice SS (slowly, then faster); DS between 2-line groups.

Note:
On your screen, apostrophes and/or quotation marks may look different from those shown in these lines. Whatever their differences in appearance, the marks serve the same purpose.

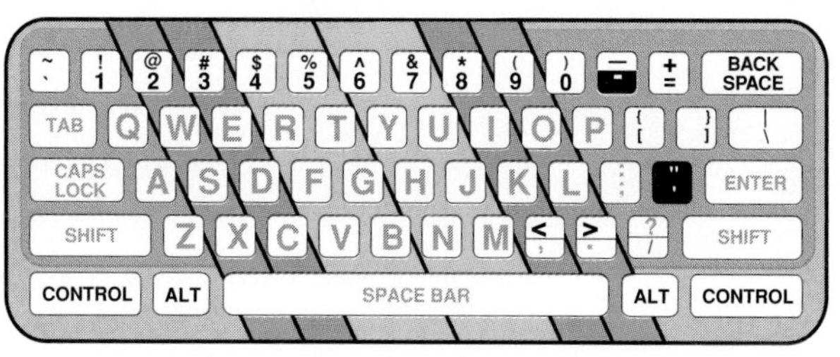

Review ' (apostrophe)

1 ;; ‘; ‘; ;’ ;’ I’ve told you it’s hers, haven’t I?
2 I’m sure it’s Jay’s. I’ll return it if he’s home.
3 I’ve been told it isn’t up to us; it’s up to them.

Review - (hyphen)

4 ; - -; -; ;- ;- -; -; -;- -;- We use a 2-ply tire.
5 We have 1-, 2-, and 3-bedroom condos for purchase.
6 He rated each as a 1-star, 2-star, or 3-star film.

Review “ (quotation mark)

7 ;; “; “; “;” “;” “I believe,” she said, “you won.”
8 “John Adams,” he said, “was the second President.”
9 “James Monroe,” I said, “was the fifth President.”

8E • 18'
Keyboard Reinforcement

1. Key lines once SS; DS between 2-line groups.
2. Key the lines again at a faster pace.
3. Key a 1' writing on lines 10–12.

Reach review (Keep on home keys the fingers not used for reaching.)

1 old led kit six jay oft zap cod big laws five ribs
2 pro quo | is just | my firm | was then | may grow | must try
3 Olga sews aqua and red silk to make six big kites.

Space Bar emphasis (Think, say, and key the words.)

4 en am an by ham fan buy jam pay may form span corn
5 I am | a man | an elm | by any | buy ham | can plan | try them
6 I am to form a plan to buy a firm in the old town.

Shift key emphasis (Reach up and reach down without moving the hands.)

7 Jan and I are to see Ms. Han. May Lana come, too?
8 Bob Epps lives in Rome; Vic Copa is in Rome, also.
9 Oates and Co. has a branch office in Boise, Idaho.

Easy sentence (Think, say, and key the words at a steady pace.)

10 Eight of the girls may go to the social with them.
11 Corla is to work with us to fix the big dock sign.
12 Keith is to pay the six men for the work they did.

gwam 1' | 1 | 2 | 3 | 4 | 5 | 6 | 7 | 8 | 9 | 10 |

Job 11

HPJ From the Desk of
Helen St. Claire
Prepare the seminar objectives list in final form for Erika Thomas.
June 9
HSC

Seminar Objectives for:
TECHNOLOGY IN THE WORKPLACE
Minneapolis Branch

1. Discuss the role of communication technology in today's business environment and how it has changed over the past ten years.
2. Inform participants of various technological communication tools presently available.
3. Highlight the advantages/disadvantages of these communication technologies.
4. Demonstrate:
   - Videoconferencing
   - Teleconferencing
   - Data conferencing
   - GroupSystems
   - Internet resources
5. Inform participants of various technological communication tools that are in development.
6. Discuss Internet resources available to participants.
7. Discuss how using high-speed communication in today's business environment can give a firm a competitive advantage in the global marketplace.

Job 12

HPJ From the Desk of
Helen St. Claire
Prepare a final draft of the attached memo to Natasha from Erika Thomas. The subject is Monthly Progress Report. Be sure to include the attachment.
June 9
HSC

Here is an update on recent progress of the Minneapolis Branch.

<u>Seminar Bookings</u>

We are fully booked through April and May. Additional communication specialists are desperately needed if we are going to expand into other states in our region. Most of our current bookings are in Minnesota, Iowa, and Wisconsin. We will be presenting in Illinois for the first time in May. I anticipate this will lead to additional bookings that we won't be able to accommodate. This is a problem that I enjoy having. Michigan, Indiana, and Ohio provide ample opportunities for expansion, when resources are made available.

<u>New Seminar</u>

A lot of progress has been made on the new seminar we are developing, "Technology in the Workplace" (see attachment for seminar objectives). Our branch will be ready to preview the seminar at our annual meeting. Not only will the seminar be a great addition to our seminar offerings, but also I believe HPJ can use it to communicate better internally. I will present my ideas when I preview the seminar. The seminar covers:

(Memo continued on next page)

UNIT 2

LESSONS 9-12

Build Keyboarding Skill

LESSON 9 SKILL BUILDING

Objectives:

1. To develop proper response patterns to gain speed.
2. To learn to key script copy.

9A • 5' Conditioning Practice

Key each line twice SS; then key a 1' writing on line 3; determine *gwam.*

```
alphabet 1 Levi Lentz packed my bag with six quarts of juice.
 spacing 2 it is|to me|may be|at my|to the|was it|is he|of us
    easy 3 A box with the forms is on the mantle by the bowl.
gwam  1' | 1 | 2 | 3 | 4 | 5 | 6 | 7 | 8 | 9 | 10 |
```

9B • 18' Technique: Response Patterns

1. Key each line twice SS (slowly, then faster); DS between 2-line groups.
2. Key 1' writings on lines 7–9; determine *gwam* (total words keyed) on each writing.

Technique **H·I·N·T**

Word response: Key easy (balanced-hand) words as a word—instead of letter by letter.

Letter response: Key the letters of one-hand words steadily and evenly.

Balanced-hand words (Think and key by word response.)

```
1 if it to me ox am so do he go is ha an us of to by
2 so men did jam fit pan dog lap fur ham cut own for
3 mend paid city land form they make work it's goals
```

One-hand words (Think and key by letter response.)

```
4 in we up as no at on be my ax oh at we no at my as
5 pin was pop tea ink fax imp tax him sad ill car no
6 lump save look were pill rest poll dear jump reads
```

Balanced-hand phrases (Think and key by word response.)

```
7 it is|to us|if it|to do|do so|to go|by us|if it is
8 did fit|for the|fix the|may make|paid for|may work
9 for the man|when did she|for the bid|may turn down
```

One-hand phrases (Think and key by letter response.)

```
10 as we|be my|in on|my ax|oh no|in my|be sad|was ill
11 car tax|you saw|pink ink|fast car|pin him|were you
12 save my water|saw my|oil taxes|water rates|a fever
gwam  1' | 1 | 2 | 3 | 4 | 5 | 6 | 7 | 8 | 9 | 10 |
```

Job 8

HPJ From the Desk of
Helen St. Claire
Format the attached agenda for the annual meeting in outline format.
June 9
HSC

AGENDA

I. Greetings
II. Overview of past year
III. Seminars
  A. Enhancement
  B. Expansion
  C. Client base
IV. Leadership
V. Company growth
  A. Regional expansion
  B. International expansion
VI. Employee incentives
  A. Branch managers
  B. Communication specialists
VII. Technology
VIII. Miscellaneous
IX. Adjournment

Job 9

HPJ From the Desk of
Helen St. Claire
Ms. Parker would like the attached letter sent to the branch managers. Enclose a copy of the agenda and the hotel confirmation (when it's available) with the letter.
June 9
HSC

Attached is the agenda for the annual meeting. I didn't hear from any of you about additions to the agenda; so if you have items to discuss, we can include them under Miscellaneous.

Your accommodations have been made for the McIntyre Inn. Your confirmation is enclosed. A limousine will pick you up at the Inn at 8:30 a.m. on Monday. Activities have been planned for Monday and Wednesday evenings. Tuesday and Thursday mornings have been left open. You can arrange something on your own, or we can make group arrangements. We'll decide on Monday before adjourning for the day.

I'm looking forward to seeing you on the 26th.

Job 10

HPJ From the Desk of
Helen St. Claire
Create tables for each of the branch managers similar to the attached one for Carter. The information for these tables is saved in the master interview schedule (CD-HPJJOB10). Copy and paste the information from the master to each individual table.
June 9
HSC

HPJ Communication Specialists

Interview Schedule for **Jamal Carter**

June 29, 200-, Room 101

Time	Name of Interviewee
1:00 - 1:15	Joan Langston
1:20 - 1:35	Tim Wohlers
1:40 - 1:55	Mark Enqvist
2:00 - 2:15	Stewart Peters
2:20 - 2:35	Felipe Valdez
2:40 - 2:55	Katarina Dent
3:00 - 3:15	Jennifer Kent
3:20 - 3:35	Sandra Baylor

9C • 10' Handwritten Copy (Script)

Key each line twice SS (slowly, then faster); DS between 2-line groups.

1 Now and then the copy you will key is from script.
2 Script is copy that is written with pen or pencil.
3 Copy that is written poorly is often hard to read.
4 Read script a few words "ahead of your fingers."
5 Doing so will help you produce an error-free copy.
6 Leave proper spacing after punctuation marks, too.
7 With practice, you will key script at a good rate.

SKILL BUILDING

9D • 12' Speed Building

1. Key a 1' writing on each ¶; determine *gwam* (the figure/dot above the last letter you keyed).
2. Key two 2' writings on ¶s 1–2 combined; determine *gwam*, using the *gwam* scale at the right (complete lines) and below (partial lines).

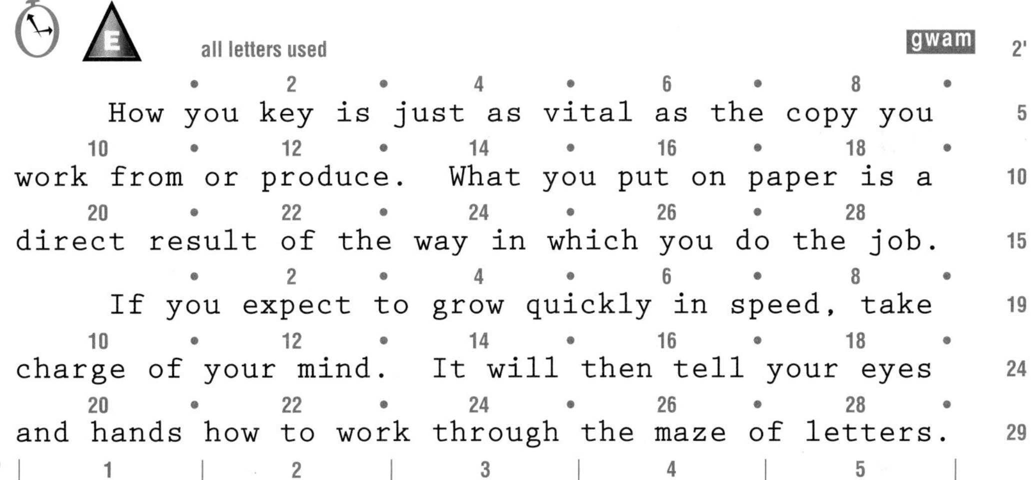

all letters used

	gwam 2'
How you key is just as vital as the copy you	5
work from or produce. What you put on paper is a	10
direct result of the way in which you do the job.	15
If you expect to grow quickly in speed, take	19
charge of your mind. It will then tell your eyes	24
and hands how to work through the maze of letters.	29

gwam 2' | 1 | 2 | 3 | 4 | 5 |

9E • 5' Technique: Spacebar and Enter

1. Key each line once SS; DS at end of line 6.
2. Key the drill again at a faster pace.

Technique **H•I•N•T**

- Quickly strike the Space Bar immediately after keying last letter in the word.
- Quickly strike ENTER after keying the period at the end of each line.

1 Sue ran to catch the bus.
2 Jan will be ready before noon.
3 Tim will bring his dog to the lake.
4 Mark did not fill the two cars with gas.
5 Don will take the next test when he is ready.
6 Karen is to bring two or three copies of the play.

Speed level of practice
When the purpose of practice is to reach a new speed, use the speed level. Take the brakes off your fingers and experiment with new stroking patterns and new speeds. Do this by:

- reading two or three letters ahead of your keying to foresee stroking patterns;
- getting the fingers ready for the combinations of letters to be keyed;
- keeping your eyes on the copy in the book.

Jobs 5 & 6

HPJ From the Desk of
Helen St. Claire
Prepare (don't send) the attached message as e-mail from Ms. Parker to the branch managers. Attach the job description that you created. Get e-mail addresses from the Web site. While you are doing that, please update the address list (Job 1) to include e-mail addresses and phone numbers.
June 7
HSC

SUBJECT: JOB DESCRIPTION FOR COMMUNICATION SPECIALISTS

I've attached a draft of the job description for the communication specialists that we will be hiring for each branch. I wanted to give each of you an opportunity to review it before we advertise for the positions in the newspaper.

If there are additional responsibilities that you would like to see included with the job description before we post it, please let me know by Friday. The advertisement will run in the Star on Sunday and appear on its Job Board Web site next week. I'm confident that we will have an even greater interest in the positions than we had when we hired a couple of communication specialists last January.

Job 7

HPJ From the Desk of
Helen St. Claire
Create the attached seminar description table. You will need to copy seminar descriptions from our Web site. Add color and other enhancements. Your document may be posted on the Web page if NSP approves.
June 8
HSC

NEW SEMINAR DESCRIPTIONS

Seminar Title	Seminar Description	Cost per Person
Business Etiquette: You Cannot Not Communicate!		$99
Gender Communication: "He Says, She Says"		$75
International Communication		$75
Listen Up!		$99
Technology in the Workplace		$125

LESSON 10 SKILL BUILDING

Objectives:

1. To build straight-copy speed and control.
2. To improve keying technique.

10A • 5' Conditioning Practice

Key each line twice SS; then key a 1' writing on line 3; determine *gwam*.

alphabet	1	Kevin can fix the unique jade owl as my big prize.
caps lock	2	JAY used the CAPS LOCK key to key CAPITAL letters.
easy	3	The small ornament on their door is an ivory duck.

gwam 1' | 1 | 2 | 3 | 4 | 5 | 6 | 7 | 8 | 9 | 10 |

Note: To determine *gwam*, see 8A directions if necessary.

10B • 15' Technique: Response Patterns

1. Key each line twice SS (slowly, then faster); DS between 2-line groups.
2. Key a 1' writing on lines 3, 6, 9, and 12.
3. If time permits, take additional timings on lines 3, 6, 9, and 12.

Technique **H • I • N • T**

Combination response: Most copy requires word response for some words and letter response for others. In such copy (lines 7–9), use top speed for easy words, lower speed for words that are harder to key.

letter response	1	In we up be my are pin tar lip car him sad joy set
	2	were you|at my|red kiln|as you see|you are|fat cat
	3	My cat darted up a tree as we sat in Jim's garage.
word response	4	it do am me so men did and lap fit ham pan got hen
	5	to us|by the|it is|to go|she may|for me|to fix the
	6	She may fix the dock if I do the work for the man.
combination response	7	he as is my to in is no am we by on it up do at or
	8	to be|is up|to my|or up|is at|go in|do we|if we go
	9	Steve and Dave may be by my dock; we may see them.
letter	10	Jon was up at noon; Rebecca gave him my red cards.
combination	11	Jay was the man you saw up at the lake in the bus.
word	12	I may go to the lake with the men to fix the door.

10C • 8' Speed Check: Sentences

1. Key a 30" writing on each line. Your rate in *gwam* is shown word-for-word above and below the lines.
2. Key another 30" writing on each line. Try to increase your keying speed.

| 2 | 4 | 6 | 8 | 10 | 12 | 14 | 16 | 18 | 20 | 22 |

1 He may go with us to the city.
2 Pamela may do half the work for us.
3 Ruth may go with us to the city to work.
4 Sign the forms for the firm to pay the girls.
5 Jan may make all the goal if she works with vigor.
6 He may sign the form if they make an audit of the firm.

gwam 30" | 2 | 4 | 6 | 8 | 10 | 12 | 14 | 16 | 18 | 20 | 22 |

Note: If you finish a line before time is called and start over, your *gwam* is the figure at the end of the line PLUS the figure above or below the point at which you stopped.

Job 3

> **HPJ** From the Desk of
> **Helen St. Claire**
> *I've started the attached letter from Ms. Parker to the branch managers. It is saved as CD-HPJJOB3. Please finish the letter.*
> *June 6*
> *HSC*

Technology. The changed marketplace is demanding that we explore new ways of delivering our seminars. How can we better use technology to deliver our product? This may include putting selected seminars online, inter- and intra-company communication, etc.

Company growth. What steps can we take to increase company growth? Last year revenues grew by 15 percent; our expenses grew by 8 percent.

Employee incentives. Last year we implemented a branch manager profit sharing plan. Some of you have indicated that we need to expand this profit sharing plan to include our communication specialists.

Regional expansion. Some of the regions have been very successful. How do we capitalize on that success? Is it time to divide the successful regions?

International expansion. **HPJ** has put on several seminars overseas—at a very high cost. Is it time to start thinking about creating a branch of **HPJ** at a strategic overseas location?

I am proud of what we have been able to accomplish this year. The foundation is in place and we are ready to grow. Each of you plays a critical role in the success of **HPJ**. Thank you for your dedication and commitment to making our company the "leader in providing corporate and individual communication training." Best wishes for continued success. I'm looking forward to discussing **HPJ**'s future at this year's annual meeting. If you have additional items that you would like included on the agenda, please get them to me before June 8.

Job 4

> **HPJ** From the Desk of
> **Helen St. Claire**
> *Format the attached job description. I've included some notes. (Directions for the Outline feature can be found in software Help.)*
> *June 6*
> *HSC*

(2" TM) HPJ COMMUNICATION SPECIALIST bf

(DS) Job Description (QS)

HPJ Communication Specialists (bf) work cooperatively with other branch members to develop and deliver communication seminars throughout the United States.

~~I.~~ II. Duties and Responsibilities

a. Research seminar topics
b. Develop seminars
c. Prepare PowerPoint® presentations for seminars
d. Prepare seminar manual
e. Present seminars

~~II.~~ I. Position Requirements

a. College degree
b. Excellent oral and written communication skills
c. Excellent interpersonal skills
d. Technology skills
e. Knowledge of business concepts

10D • 15' Speed Check: Paragraphs

1. Key a 1' writing on each paragraph (¶); determine *gwam* on each writing.
2. Using your better *gwam* as a base rate, select a goal rate and key two 1' guided writings on each ¶ as directed below.

Note:

Copy used to build or measure skill is triple-controlled for difficulty: E = easy; LA = low average; A = average

E — all letters used

```
                                                          gwam  2'
        •    2    •    4    •    6    •    8    •
     Are you one of the people who often look from          5
 10   •   12   •   14   •   16   •   18   •
the copy to the screen and down at your hands?  If         10
 20   •   22   •   24   •   26   •   28   •
you are, you can be sure that you will not build a         15
 30   •   32   •   34   •   36   •   38   •
speed to prize.  Make eyes on copy your next goal.         20
        •    2    •    4    •    6    •    8    •
     When you move the eyes from the copy to check         24
 10   •   12   •   14   •   16   •   18   •
the screen, you may lose your place and waste time         30
 20   •   22   •   24   •   26   •   28   •
trying to find it.  Lost time can lower your speed         35
 30   •   32   •   34   •   36   •   38   •
quickly and in a major way, so do not look away.           39
gwam 2' |    1    |    2    |    3    |    4    |    5    |
```

Quarter-Minute Checkpoints				
gwam	1/4'	1/2'	3/4'	Time
16	4	8	12	16
20	5	10	15	20
24	6	12	18	24
28	7	14	21	28
32	8	16	24	32
36	9	18	27	36
40	10	20	30	40

Guided (Paced) Writing Procedure

Select a practice goal

1. Key a 1' writing on ¶ 1 of a set of ¶s that contain word-count dots and figures above the lines, as in 10D above.
2. Using the *gwam* as a base, add 4 *gwam* to determine your goal rate.
3. Choose from Column 1 of the table at the left the speed nearest your goal rate. In the quarter-minute columns beside that speed, note the points in the copy you must reach to maintain your goal rate.
4. Determine the checkpoint for each quarter minute from the dots and figures in ¶ 1. (Example: Checkpoints for 24 *gwam* are 6, 12, 18, and 24.)

Practice procedure

1. Key two 1' writings on ¶ 1 at your goal rate, guided by the quarter-minute signals (1/4, 1/2, 3/4, time). Try to reach each of your checkpoints just as the guide is called.
2. Key two 1' writings on ¶ 2 of a set of ¶s in the same way.
3. If time permits, key a 2' writing on the set of ¶s combined, without the guides.

10E • 7' Keying Technique

Key each line twice.

Double letters

1 bill foot berry letter deep pool groom egg balloon

2 Matt will look at a free scanner tomorrow at noon.

Balanced hands

3 risk usual to maid the corn box did pan rifle dish

4 He may go with me to the city by the lake to work.

Shift keys

5 Los Angeles Dodgers | PowerPoint | The Book of Virtues

6 The New York Yankees will play the Boston Red Sox.

Space Bar

7 to do a be box and the or was it see me by ten ask

8 As near as I can tell, it is five or six days old.

LESSONS 65-69

HPJ COMMUNICATION SPECIALISTS

Objectives:

1. To use your decision-making skills to process documents.
2. To improve your ability to read and follow directions.

65A-69A • 5' (daily) Conditioning Practice

Key each line twice.

alphabet 1 Seven complete textbooks were required for the new zoology major.

fig/sym 2 Shipping charges ($35.18) were included on the invoice (#426097).

speed 3 A sick dog slept on the oak chair in the dismal hall of the dorm.

gwam 1' | 1 | 2 | 3 | 4 | 5 | 6 | 7 | 8 | 9 | 10 | 11 | 12 | 13 |

65B-69B • 45' (daily) Work Assignments

Job 1

HPJ From the Desk of
Helen St. Claire

I would like an updated name and address list for the CEO and branch managers. Please get this information from the Web site and create a table similar to the one attached. Addresses are shown at the top of each Web page. Keep a copy of the list. Suggestion: Create a macro for each branch manager's address to use for later jobs.

June 5
HSC

HPJ COMMUNICATION SPECIALISTS
CEO and Branch Manager Address List
June 5, 200-

Ms. Natasha S. Parker, President & CEO HPJ Communication Specialists Address City, State ZIP	Name of Branch Manager, Branch Manager HPJ Communication Specialists Address City, State ZIP
Name of Branch Manager, Branch Manager HPJ Communication Specialists Address City, State ZIP	Name of Branch Manager, Branch Manager HPJ Communication Specialists Address City, State ZIP
Name of Branch Manager, Branch Manager HPJ Communication Specialists Address City, State ZIP	Name of Branch Manager, Branch Manager HPJ Communication Specialists Address City, State ZIP

Job 2

HPJ From the Desk of
Helen St. Claire

Ms. Parker wants the attached letter sent to each of the branch managers. Find mailing addresses on your address list.

June 5
HSC

Dear

Each of you has indicated a need for additional personnel. I've heard your requests. With this quarter's increase in seminar revenues, I am now in a position to respond to them. Five new communication specialist positions, one for each branch, have been added.

Since training for the positions takes place here at the home office, it is more cost effective to hire communication specialists from this area. I will take care of recruitment and preliminary screening. However, since each of you will work closely with the individual hired, I think you should make the final selection.

When you are here for the annual meeting, I'll schedule time for you to interview eight individuals. If you are not satisfied with any of the eight, we will arrange additional interviews. I should have a job description created within the next week. When it is completed, I'll send it to you for your review.

LESSON 11 SKILL BUILDING

Objectives:

1. To build straight-copy speed and control.
2. To improve keying technique on script and rough-draft copy.

11A • 5' Conditioning Practice

Key each line twice SS; then key a 1' writing on line 3; determine *gwam*.

alphabet 1 Lock may join the squad if we have six big prizes.

? 2 Do I get a locker? Where is it? Do I need a key?

easy 3 Pam may name a tutor to work with the eight girls.

gwam 1' | 1 | 2 | 3 | 4 | 5 | 6 | 7 | 8 | 9 | 10 |

11B • 10' Speed Building

1. Key each line twice SS with a DS between 2-line groups.
2. If time permits, key the lines again to improve keying ease and speed.

Technique Goals:

- Reach up without moving hands away from you.
- Reach down without moving hands toward your body.
- Use quick-snap keystrokes.

za/az

1 zap lazy lizard pizza hazard bazaar frazzle dazzle

2 Zack and Hazel zapped the lazy lizard in the maze.

ol/lo

3 old load olive look fold lost bold loan allow told

4 Olympia told the lonely man to load the long logs.

ws/sw

5 swing cows sweet glows swept mows sword knows swap

6 He swung the sword over the sweaty cows and swine.

ju/ft

7 often jury draft judge left just hefty juice after

8 Jud, the fifth juror on my left, just wants juice.

ed/de

9 deal need debit edit deed edge deli used dent desk

10 Jed needed to edit the deed made by the defendant.

ik/ki

11 kick like kind bike kiln hike kids strike king ski

12 I like the kind of kids who like to hike and bike.

11C • 13' Speed Check: Straight Copy

LS: DS

1. Key one 1' unguided and two 1' guided writings on ¶ 1 and then on ¶ 2, as directed on p. 22.
2. Key two 2' unguided writings on ¶s 1–2 combined; determine *gwam* on each.

all letters used — gwam 2'

Time and motion are major items in building 4
our keying power. As we make each move through 9
space to a letter or a figure, we use time. So we 14
want to be sure that every move is quick and direct. 20
We cut time and aid speed in this way. 24

A good way to reduce motion and thus save time 28
is just to keep the hands in home position as you 33
make the reach to a letter or figure. Fix your 38
gaze on the copy; then, reach to each key with a 43
direct, low move at your very best speed. 47

gwam 2' | 1 | 2 | 3 | 4 | 5 |

UNIT 19

LESSONS 65-69

HPJ Communication Specialists: A Workplace Simulation

Work Assignment

HPJ Communication Specialists prepares, organizes, and delivers communication training seminars. Three partners—Stewart **H**errick, Natasha **P**arker, and Spencer **J**orstad—founded the company in 1991. In 1998 Ms. Parker bought out the other two partners. Today the company has five branches located in Dallas, Denver, Minneapolis, New York, and San Francisco.

You have been hired by HPJ to work part-time for the administrative assistant, Helen St. Claire. Ms. St. Claire processes documents for the President and CEO, Natasha S. Parker, as well as for Erika Thomas, the Minneapolis branch manager.

During your training program, you were instructed to use the unbound format for reports and block format for all company letters. Ms. Parker likes all her letters closed as follows:

```
Sincerely



Natasha S. Parker
President & CEO
```

When a document has more than one enclosure, format the enclosure notation as follows:

```
Enclosures: Agenda
            Hotel Confirmation
```

General processing instructions will be attached to each document you are given to process. Use the date included on the instructions for all documents requiring a date.

Use your decision-making skills to arrange documents attractively whenever specific instructions are not provided. Since HPJ has based its word processing manual on the *Century 21* textbook, you can also refer to this text in making formatting decisions. You are expected to produce error-free documents, so check spelling, proofread, and correct your work carefully before presenting it for approval.

If you need help with software features to complete your work, refer to Software Features Index in this text. Use the Help features in your software, too. Using Help, you can recall or review a feature that you have forgotten. Also use it to learn any new features you may need.

HPJ Files and Web Site

Some jobs will require you to use documents stored in HPJ company files. Some documents will require you to gather information from the company's Web site at http://www.hpj.swep.com. All files you create should be named with *HPJ*, followed by the job number (*HPJ1*, *HPJ2*, etc.).

Getting Started

Create macros for closing lines of letters and other text, such as *HPJ Communication Specialists*, that you will use often.

11D • 10' Rough Draft (Edited Copy)

1. Study the proofreaders' marks shown below and in the sentences.
2. Key each sentence DS, making all handwritten (editing) changes.
3. Key the lines again to improve your editing speed.

∧ = insert

= add space

∽ = transpose

ℓ = delete

⁀ = close up

≡ = capitalize

1 A first draft is a preleminary orr tentative one.

2 It is where the creator gets his thoughts on paper.

3 After the draft is created, it will be looked over.

4 Reviewing is the step where a persone refines copy.

5 Proof readers marks are used edit the original copy.

6 The edting changes will be then be made to the copy.

7 After the change have been made read the copy agian.

8 more changes still may need to be made to the copy.

9 Edting proof reading does take a lot time and effort.

10 error free copy is worth the trouble how ever.

11E • 12' Skill Transfer: Straight Copy to Script and Rough Draft

1. Key each ¶ once SS; DS between ¶s.
2. Key a 1' writing on each ¶; determine *gwam* on each writing; compare the three rates.

Your highest speed should be on ¶ 1 (straight copy); next highest on ¶ 2 (script); lowest on ¶ 3 (rough draft).

3. Key one or two more 1' writings on the two slowest ¶s to improve skill transfer.

Recall

1' *gwam* = total words keyed

A standard word = 5 strokes (characters and spaces).

Straight copy — gwam 1'

Documents free of errors make a good impression. 10
When a document has no errors, readers can focus on 20
the content. Errors distract readers and may cause 31
them to think less of the message. 38

Script

Therefore, it is important to proofread the final 10
copy of a document several times to make sure it 20
contains no errors before it leaves your desk. 29
Readers of error-free documents form a positive image 40
of the person who wrote the message. 47

Rough draft

When a negative image of the per son who wrote the the 10
messge is formed the message is less likely to succeed. 22
remembre you never get a another chance tomake a good 33
impression. 35

SKILL BUILDER 3

Techniques: Figures

1. Set 0.5" side margins.
2. Clear all tabs; then set tabs 2", 4", and 6" from the left margin.
3. Key the lines slowly, tabbing from column to column.
4. Take three 3' writings. Try to key more characters on each writing.

Keep eyes on copy.

				gwam 3'
529-36-2899	12/24/80	(308) 112-2388	$ 628.00	3
358-29-1076	04/30/78	(608) 197-6655	$1,381.00	6
346-50-0190	02/28/81	(520) 130-6754	$5,672.15	9
567-82-8219	10/15/84	(715) 139-2615	$ 56.29	12
628-12-0945	03/27/82	(801) 162-2444	$3,178.87	15
820-67-1029	08/08/79	(308) 138-8567	$9,078.25	18

Reading/Keying Response Patterns

Lines 1–3: each word 3 times (slowly, faster, top speed).

Lines 4–6: each phrase 3 times (slowly, faster, top speed).

Lines 7–9: each sentence 3 times (slowly, faster, top speed).

Goal:
Word-level keying.

Emphasize quick finger reaches, wrists low and relaxed.

balanced-hand words

1 us if he an by is jam fur hen row pay map man sit the and big may
2 dusk dock corn busy both keys firms land rock sign owns mend sick
3 docks bucks eight goals right they shame social towns vivid turns

Emphasize high-speed phrase response.

balanced-hand phrases

4 he owns it | make the signs | paid the man | go to work | if they fix the
5 go to the | they may make | to the problem | with the sign | and the maps
6 with the city | the eighth neighbor | social problem | the big ornament

Emphasize high-speed, word-level response; quick spacing.

balanced-hand sentences

7 Jaynel paid the man by the city dock for the six bushels of corn.
8 Keith may keep the food for the fish by the big antique fishbowl.
9 The haughty girls paid for their own gowns for the island social.

gwam 1' | 1 | 2 | 3 | 4 | 5 | 6 | 7 | 8 | 9 | 10 | 11 | 12 | 13 |

Number Expression Check

Key the sentences at the right; correct number expressions as needed.

1. When you buy 3 cups, they will give you 1 free.
2. 12 of the 26 charter members were at the reunion.
3. If you place your order before two p.m., it will be shipped the next day.
4. Ms. King placed an order for eight copies of The Secretary and 14 copies of Modern Office Technology.
5. Approximately 2/3 of the parents attended the special meeting.
6. The package needs to be delivered to 1 Lakeshore Drive.
7. About 60 students voted for class officers on April seven.
8. The next assignment was Chapter seven, not Chapter eight.
9. Roy is 6 ft. eleven in. tall and weighs 180 lbs.
10. The final flight on July six going to Reno leaves at 8 p.m.

LESSON 12 SKILL BUILDING

Objectives:

1. To build straight-copy speed and control.
2. To improve keying technique.

12A • 5' Conditioning Practice

Key each line twice SS; then key a 1' writing on line 3; determine *gwam.*

alphabet	1	J. Fox made five quick plays to win the big prize.
spacing	2	It will be fun for us to try to sing the old song.
easy	3	The sorority may do the work for the city auditor.
gwam	1'	1 | 2 | 3 | 4 | 5 | 6 | 7 | 8 | 9 | 10

12B • 12' Difficult-Reach Mastery

1. Key each line twice SS; DS between 2-line groups.
2. Note the lines that caused you difficulty; practice them again to increase rate.

Adjacent (side-by-side) keys (lines 1–4) can be the source of many errors unless the fingers are kept in an upright position and precise motions are used.

Long direct reaches (lines 5–8) reduce speed unless they are made without moving the hands forward and downward.

Reaches with the outside fingers (lines 9–12) are troublesome unless made without twisting the hands in and out at the wrist.

Adjacent keys

1 Jerry and Jason were not ready to buy a newspaper.
2 Polly dropped my green vase on her last trip here.
3 Marty opened the carton to retrieve the power saw.
4 Bert and I were there the week before deer season.

Long direct reaches

5 My niece may bring the bronze trophy back to them.
6 Manny broke his thumb when he spun on the bicycle.
7 Betty is under the gun to excel in the ninth race.
8 They must now face many of the facts I discovered.

Reaches with 3d and 4th fingers

9 A poet told us to zip across the road to get away.
10 Zack saw the sapodilla was almost totally sapless.
11 A poet at our palace said to ask for an allowance.
12 Was it washed when you wore it to our school play?

12C • 13' Script Copy

1. Key the ¶s twice DS (slowly, then faster).
2. Key a 1' writing on ¶ 1.
3. Key a second 1' writing on ¶ 1, trying to key two additional words.
4. Key a 1' writing on ¶ 2.
5. Key a second 1' writing on ¶ 2, trying to key two additional words.
6. To determine *gwam*, count the words in partial lines.

gwam 1'

Thomas Jefferson was a very persuasive writer. Perhaps his most 13
persuasive piece of writing was the Declaration of Independence, which he was 29
asked to prepare with John Adams and Benjamin Franklin to explain the need 44
for independence. 47

We all should recognize parts of that document. For example, "We 13
hold these truths to be self-evident, that all men are created equal, that they are 30
endowed by their Creator with certain unalienable Rights, that among these are 46
Life, Liberty and the pursuit of Happiness." 54

Internal Punctuation: Colon

Rule 4: Use a colon to introduce an enumeration or a listing.

Learn 13 These students are absent: Adam Bux, Todd Cody, and Sue Ott.
Apply 14 Add to the herb list parsley, rosemary, saffron, and thyme.
Apply 15 We must make these desserts a cake, two pies, and cookies.

Rule 5: Use a colon to introduce a question or a quotation.

Learn 16 Here's the real question: Who will pay for the "free" programs?
Learn 17 Who said: "Freedom is nothing else but a chance to be better"?
Apply 18 My question stands Who are we to pass judgment on them?
Apply 19 He quoted Browning "Good, to forgive; Best, to forget."

Rule 6: Use a colon between hours and minutes expressed in figures.

Learn 20 They give two performances: at 2:00 p.m. and at 8:00 p.m.
Apply 21 You have a choice of an 11 15 a.m. or a 2 30 p.m. appointment.
Apply 22 My workday begins at 8 15 a.m. and ends at 5 00 p.m.

ACTIVITY 2

Listening

Complete the listening activity as directed at the right.

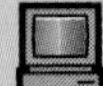
Save as: *CS8-ACT2*

You answered a telephone call from George Steward, your father's business associate. Mr. Steward asked you to take a message for your father.

1. Open the sound file (*CD-CS8LISTN*). As you listen to Mr. Steward's message, take notes as needed.
2. Close the sound file.
3. Key or handwrite the message—in complete sentences—for your father.
4. Check the accuracy of your work with the instructor.

ACTIVITY 3

Composing

1. Key the paragraph, correcting the word-choice errors it contains. (Every line contains at least one error; some lines contain two or more errors.)
2. Check the accuracy of your work with the instructor; correct any errors you made.
3. Compose a second paragraph to meet these two goals:
   - Express your viewpoint about special treatment of "stars."
   - State your view about whether *same offense/same penalty* should apply to everyone alike.

Save as: *CS8-ACT3*

Some people think that because their good at sum sport, music, or other activity, there entitled to respect and forgiveness for anything else they choose to do in the passed. Its not uncommon, than, when such people break the law or violate sum code of conduct, four them to expect such behavior to be overlooked buy those who's job it is to enforce the law or to uphold an established code of conduct. Sum parents, as well as others in hour society, think that a "star's" misbehavior ought too be treated less harshly because of that person's vary impressive "celebrity" status; but all people should be treated equally under and threw the law.

SKILL BUILDING

12D • 12'
Technique: Response Patterns

1. Key each line twice SS; DS between 2-line groups.
2. Key a 1' writing on lines 10–12 to increase speed; find *gwam* on each line.

Technique **H • I • N • T**

Letter response (lines 1–3): Key the letters of these words steadily and evenly.

Word response (lines 4–6): Key these easy words as words—instead of letter by letter.

Combination response (lines 7–9): Key easy words at top speed; key harder words at a lower speed.

letter response
```
1 milk faced pill cease jump bread join faster jolly
2 were you|up on|are in fact|my taxes are|star gazed
3 My cat was in fact up a tree at my estate in Ohio.
```

word response
```
4 oak box land sign make busy kept foal handle gowns
5 go to the|it may work|did he make|she is|he may go
6 Did he make a big profit for the six formal gowns?
```

combination response
```
7 is pin when only their dress forms puppy kept care
8 when fate|east of|right on|nylon wig|antique cards
9 Pam was born in a small hill town at the big lake.
```

```
letter      10 Edward gave him a minimum rate on state oil taxes.
combination 11 Their eager neighbor may sign up for a tax rebate.
word        12 He may work with the big firms to fix the problem.
```

gwam 1' | 1 | 2 | 3 | 4 | 5 | 6 | 7 | 8 | 9 | 10 |

12E • 8'
Skill Building

1. Key a 1' writing on each ¶; determine *gwam*.
2. Key two 2' writings on ¶s 1–2 combined; determine *gwam*.

Quarter-Minute Checkpoints				
gwam	1/4'	1/2'	3/4'	Time
16	4	8	12	16
20	5	10	15	20
24	6	12	18	24
28	7	14	21	28
32	8	16	24	32
36	9	18	27	36
40	10	20	30	40

E all letters used — gwam 2'

```
     Do you think someone is going to wait around          5
just for a chance to key your term paper?  Do you         10
believe when you get out into the world of work that      15
there will be someone to key your work for you?           20
Think again.  It does not work that way.                  24
     Even the head of a business now uses a keyboard      29
to send and retrieve data as well as other informa-       34
tion.  Be quick to realize that you will not go far       39
in the world of work if you do not learn how to key.      44
Excel at it and move to the top.                          47
```

gwam 2' | 1 | 2 | 3 | 4 | 5 |

ACTIVITY 1

Internal Punctuation: Comma and Colon

1. Key lines 1–14 at the right, supplying the needed commas and colons.
2. Check the accuracy of your work with the instructor; correct any errors you made.
3. Note the rule number at the left of each sentence in which you made a comma or colon error.
4. Using the rules below the sentences and on p. 184, identify the rule(s) you need to review/practice.
5. **Read**: Study each rule.
6. **Learn**: Key the Learn line(s) beneath it, noting how the rule is applied.
7. **Apply**: Key the Apply line(s), adding commas and colons as needed.

 **Save as:** *CS8-ACT1*

Proofread & Correct

Rules

1,3 1 The memorial was dedicated on November 13 1982—not 1,983.
1 2 We played in the Hoosier Dome in Indianapolis Indiana.
1 3 I cited an article in the May 8 1999, *Wall Street Journal.*
2 4 Carl sent Diana a dozen bright red long-stem roses.
2 5 He buys most of his clothes at a store for big tall men.
3 6 Our enrollment for 1999, 1,884; for 2000 2040.
3 7 Where is the request for books and supplies for Room 1,004?
1,3 8 Policy #HP294,873 took effect on September 20 1999.
3 9 Della and Eldon Simms paid $129000 for their new condo.
4 10 Dry cleaning list 1 suit; 2 jackets; 3 pants; 2 sweaters.
5 11 Golden Rule Do unto others as you would have them do unto you.
5 12 I quote Jean Racine "Innocence has nothing to dread."
6 13 Glynda asked me to meet her 2 15 p.m. flight at JFK Airport.
6 14 Ten o'clock in the morning is the same as 10 00 a.m.

Internal Punctuation: Comma

Rule 1: Use a comma to separate the day from the year and the city from the state.

Learn 1 Lincoln delivered the Gettysburg Address on November 19, 1863.
Learn 2 The convention will be held at Cobo Hall in Detroit, Michigan.
Apply 3 Did you find this table in the March 16 1999, *USA Today*?
Apply 4 Are you entered in the piano competition in Austin Texas?

Rule 2: Use a comma to separate two or more parallel adjectives (adjectives that could be separated by the word *and* instead of a comma).

Learn 5 The big, loud bully was ejected after he pushed the coach.
Learn 6 Cynthia played a black lacquered grand piano at her concert.
Apply 7 The big powerful car zoomed past the cheering crowd.
Apply 8 A small, red fox squeezed through the fence to avoid the hounds.

Rule 3: Use a comma to separate (a) unrelated groups of figures that occur together and (b) whole numbers into groups of three digits each. (Policy, year, page, room, telephone, invoice, and most serial numbers are keyed without commas.)

Learn 9 By the year 2000, 1,100 more local students will be enrolled.
Learn 10 The supplies listed on Invoice #274068 are for Room 1953.
Apply 11 During 1999 2050 new graduates entered our job market.
Apply 12 See page 1,069 of *Familiar Quotations*, Cat. Card No. 68-15,664.

(continued on next page)

Communication Skills 1

ACTIVITY 1

Simple Sentences

1. Study the guides and the simple sentences beneath them.
2. Key the Learn sentences as shown, noting the subjects and predicates.
3. For each sentence 1 through 8, key the sentence number, followed by the subject and predicate.
4. For each line 9 through 11, combine the two sentences into one simple sentence with two nouns as the subject and one verb as the predicate.
5. Revise Sentence 12 by combining the two sentences into one simple sentence with two nouns as the subject and two verbs as the predicate.

 **Save as:** *CS1-ACT1*

> A **simple** sentence consists of one independent clause that contains a subject (noun or pronoun) and a predicate (verb).

Learn 1 Pam is president of her class.

Learn 2 Kevin walks to and from school.

Learn 3 Reading mystery novels is my favorite pastime.

Learn 4 The captain of the team is out with a badly sprained ankle.

> A **simple** sentence may have as its subject more than one noun or pronoun (compound subject) and as its predicate more than one verb (compound predicate).

Learn 5 She bought a new bicycle. (single subject/single predicate)

Learn 6 Marv and I received new bicycles. (compound subject/single predicate)

Learn 7 Alice washed and waxed her car. (single subject/compound predicate)

Learn 8 He and I cleaned and cooked the fish. (compound subject/compound predicate)

Apply 9 Jorge read AURA by Fuentes. Rosa read it, also.

Apply 10 Hamad cooks his own meals. So does Janelle.

Apply 11 Sara talked with Mona at the concert. Lee talked with her, also.

Apply 12 Mel chooses and buys his own training shoes. Suzy also chooses and buys hers.

ACTIVITY 2

Compound Sentences

1. Study the guides and the sentences beneath them at the right and on the top of p. 28.
2. Key the Learn sentences, noting the words that make up the subjects and predicates of each sentence.
3. For each sentence 13 through 20, key the sentence number, followed by the subjects and predicates.

> A **compound** sentence contains two or more independent clauses connected by a coordinating conjunction **(and**, **but**, **for**, **or**, **nor**, **yet**, **so)**.

Learn 13 Jay Sparks likes to hike, and Roy Tubbs likes to swim.

Learn 14 The computer is operative, but the printer does not work.

Learn 15 You may eat in the hotel, or you may choose a café nearby.

Learn 16 The sky is clear, the moon is out, and the sea is very calm.

> Each clause of a compound sentence may have as its subject more than one noun/pronoun and as its predicate more than one verb.

Learn 17 Ben and I saw the game, and Bob and Maria went to a movie.

Learn 18 Nick dived and swam, but the others fished off the boat.

Learn 19 You may play solitaire, or you and Joe may play checkers.

(continued on next page)

Table 2

Information about 12 states is shown at the right. Create and format a table that shows all of the information in one table. Use **INFORMATION ABOUT SELECTED STATES** as a title. Data about each state should make up one row of the table. Include this source note: **James R. Giese, et al. The American Century, 1999, pp. 922-925.**

Place a border around each cell that has a **1** or a **50** to show the states that rank first and last. Shade or color these bordered cells to highlight them even more.

 **Save as:** *TBL64B2*

Alaska Rank Entering Union: 49 Rank Land Area: 1 Rank Population: 49	**Idaho** Rank Entering Union: 43 Rank Land Area: 13 Rank Population: 42	**Montana** Rank Entering Union: 41 Rank Land Area: 4 Rank Population: 44
California Rank Entering Union: 31 Rank Land Area: 3 Rank Population: 1	**Illinois** Rank Entering Union: 21 Rank Land Area: 24 Rank Population: 6	**Nebraska** Rank Entering Union: 37 Rank Land Area: 15 Rank Population: 36
Delaware Rank Entering Union: 1 Rank Land Area: 49 Rank Population: 46	**Kansas** Rank Entering Union: 34 Rank Land Area: 14 Rank Population: 32	**Rhode Island** Rank Entering Union: 13 Rank Land Area: 50 Rank Population: 43
Hawaii Rank Entering Union: 50 Rank Land Area: 47 Rank Population: 41	**Michigan** Rank Entering Union: 26 Rank Land Area: 23 Rank Population: 8	**Wyoming** Rank Entering Union: 44 Rank Land Area: 9 Rank Population: 50

Table 3

Format the table at the right. Use the table formatting features that you have learned to arrange the information attractively on the page. Use a border and shading color similar to the one shown.

 **Save as:** *TBL64B3*

NATIVE AMERICAN NAMES OF PLACES

State: New York

Name of Place	Tribe	Derivation
Adirondacks	Iroquoian	Name of town, park, and mountain range; derived from tribal name, meaning "bark eaters."
Allegheny	Delaware	Name of plateau and reservoir; probably from the name for Allegheny and Ohio rivers.
Manhattan	Algonkian	Name of island and borough; derived from tribal name, probably meaning "island-mountain."
Niagara	Iroquoian	Name of town, county, river, and falls, meaning "point of land cut in two."
Poughkeepsie	Algonkian	Name of town, meaning "little rock at water."
Seneca	Mohegan	Name of county, river, lake, and falls; derived from tribal name, probably meaning "people of the stone."
Susquehanna	Iroquoian	Name of river; derived from tribal name.

Source: The Native North American Almanac, 1994.

Table 4 - Optional Editing Activity

Open *TBL64B2* (64B, Table 2). Insert a column for showing the **Electoral Votes** for each state.

AK 3; CA 54; DE 3; HI 4; ID 4; IL 22; KS 6; MI 18; MT 3; NE 5; RI 4; WY 3

 **Save as:** *TBL64B4*

4. For lines 21 through 24, combine the two sentences into a compound sentence. Choose carefully from the coordinating conjunctions *and*, *but*, *for*, *or*, *not*, *yet*, and *so*.

 **Save as:** *CS1-ACT2*

Learn 20 Bobby huffed and puffed, but Erin scampered up the hill.

Apply 21 Karen listened to Ravel's BOLERO. Matt read FORREST GUMP.

Apply 22 You may watch STAR TREK. You and Edie may play dominoes.

Apply 23 Ken may play football or basketball. He may not play both.

Apply 24 Linda skated to CABARET music. Jon chose WEST SIDE STORY.

ACTIVITY 3

Complex Sentences

Use the directions in Activity 2 to complete lines 25 through 36. For lines 25 through 32, key the subject and predicate of the independent clause and of the dependent clause for each sentence.

 **Save as:** *CS1-ACT3*

A **complex** sentence contains only one independent clause and one or more dependent clauses.

Learn 25 The book that you gave Juan for his birthday is lost.

Learn 26 If I were you, I would speak to Paula before I left.

Learn 27 Miss Gomez, who chairs the department, is currently on leave.

Learn 28 Students who use their time wisely usually succeed.

The subject of a complex sentence may consist of more than one noun or pronoun; the predicate may consist of more than one verb.

Learn 29 All who were invited to the party also attended the game.

Learn 30 If you are to join, you should sign up and pay your dues.

Learn 31 After she and I left, Cliff and Pam sang and danced.

Learn 32 Although they don't know it yet, Fran and Brett were elected.

Apply 33 My PSAT and SAT scores are high. I may not get into Yale.

Apply 34 They attended the symphony. They then had a light supper.

Apply 35 Mindy is to audition for the part. She should apply now.

Apply 36 You are buying a computer. You should also get software.

ACTIVITY 4

Composing

Key each line once SS. In place of the blank line at the end of each sentence, key the word(s) that correctly complete(s) the sentence.

 **Save as:** *CS1-ACT4*

1. A small mass of land surrounded by water is a/an _________.
2. A large mass of land surrounded by water is a/an _________.
3. The earth rotates on what is called its _________.
4. When the sun comes up over the horizon, we say it _________.
5. When the sun goes down over the horizon, we say it _________.
6. A device used to display temperature is a/an _________.
7. A device used to display atmospheric pressure is a/an _________.

LESSON 64 | IMPROVE TABLE FORMATTING SKILLS

Objectives:

1. To improve table formatting skills.
2. To format tables with enhanced borders and shading.

64A • 5' Conditioning Practice

Key each line twice SS; key a 1' writing on line 3; determine *gwam*.

alphabet 1 Chuck said Dr. Webber plans on requiring just five zoology exams.

fig/sym 2 After deducting the 20% discount, Invoice #14380 totaled $597.60.

speed 3 Orlando may make an official bid for the antique enamel fishbowl.

gwam 1' | 1 | 2 | 3 | 4 | 5 | 6 | 7 | 8 | 9 | 10 | 11 | 12 | 13 |

64B • 45' Table Editing

Table 1

Key the table at the right; insert each of the following three names next to the individual's accomplishments.

Alex Haley
Thurgood Marshall
Colin Powell

Use the table formatting features that you have learned to arrange the data attractively on the page. Use a border similar to the one shown.

 **Save as:** *TBL64B1*

History Bits

"I have learned that success is to be measured not so much by the position that one has reached in life as by the obstacles which he has overcome while trying to succeed. Out of the hard and unusual struggle through which he is compelled to pass, he gets a strength, a confidence, that one misses whose pathway is comparatively smooth by reason of birth and race."

—Booker T. Washington

FAMOUS AMERICANS

Name	Significant Accomplishments
Charles Drew	Developed a means for preserving blood plasma for transfusion.
	First black officer to hold the highest military post in the U.S., Chairman of the U.S. Joint Chiefs of Staff.
Shirley Chisholm	First black woman to be elected to the U.S. Congress.
	First black member of the U.S. Supreme Court.
Booker T. Washington	Organized a teaching and industrial school for African Americans—Tuskegee Institute.
Benjamin Banneker	First African American to receive a presidential appointment. Famous for his role as a planner for Washington, D.C.
W. E. B. Du Bois	Cofounder of the organization that became the National Association for the Advancement of Colored People (NAACP).
Alice Walker	Pulitzer Prize-winning writer and poet. Novels include *The Color Purple* and *In Love and Trouble.*
	Pulitzer Prize-winning author. Wrote *Roots*, which was made into the highest-rated television miniseries of all time.
Frederick Douglass	Eminent human rights leader of the 19th century; the first black citizen to hold a high rank in the U.S. government.

Source: "Black History Innovators." USA Today. **http://www.usatoday.com** (15 February 2000).

UNIT 3

LESSONS 13-14

Review Figure Keys

LESSON 13

REVIEW FIGURE KEYS (8, 1, 9, 4, AND 0)

Objectives:

1. To review reach technique for **8, 1, 9, 4,** and **0**.
2. To improve skill on script, and rough-draft copy.

13A • 5' Conditioning Practice

Key each line twice SS; then key a 1' writing on line 3; determine *gwam.*

alphabet 1 The exquisite prize, a framed clock, was to be given to Jay.

spacing 2 They may try to be at the dorm in time to eat with the team.

easy 3 The maid was with the dog and six girls by the field of hay.

gwam 1' | 1 | 2 | 3 | 4 | 5 | 6 | 7 | 8 | 9 | 10 | 11 | 12 |

13B • 8' Review 8 and 1

Key each line twice SS (slowly, then faster); DS between 2-line groups.

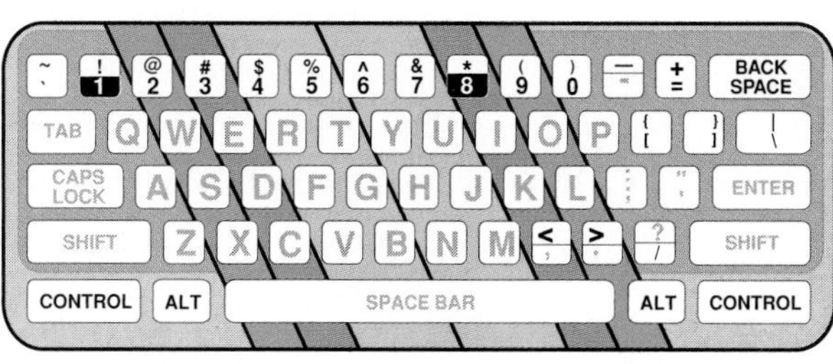

Review 8

1 k k 8k 8k kk 88 k8k k8k 88k 88k Reach up for 8, 88, and 888.

2 Key the figures 8, 88, and 888. Please open Room 88 or 888.

Review 1

3 a a 1a 1a aa 11 a1a a1a 11a 11a Reach up for 1, 11, and 111.

4 Add the figures 1, 11, and 111. Only 1 out of 111 finished.

Combine 8 and 1

5 Key 11, 18, 81, and 88. Just 11 of the 18 skiers have left.

6 Reach with the fingers to key 18 and 188 as well as 1 and 8.

7 The stock person counted 11 coats, 18 slacks, and 88 shirts.

Table 2
Format the table at the right. Use the table formatting features that you have learned to arrange the information attractively on the page. Use a border and shading similar to the illustration. Bold all text. DS between data entries.

 **Save as:** *TBL63B2*

THE CONSTITUTION		
The Executive Branch	**The Legislative Branch**	**The Judicial Branch**
• President administers and enforces federal laws • President chosen by electors who have been chosen by the states	• A bicameral or two-house legislature • Each state has equal number of representatives in the Senate • Representation in the House determined by state population • Simple majority required to enact legislation	• National court system directed by the Supreme Court • Courts to hear cases related to national laws, treaties, the Constitution; cases between states, between citizens of different states, or between a state and citizens of another state

Source: Matthew T. Downey, et al. United States History, 1997, p. 158.

Table 3
Format the table at the right. Use the table formatting features that you have learned to arrange the information attractively on the page. Use a border similar to the one shown.

 **Save as:** *TBL63B3*

MOST IMPORTANT PROBLEM		
Question: What do you think is the most important problem facing this country today?		
Year	**Problem**	**Percent**
1961	Unemployment	25
	Threat of war	19
	Threat of Communism	14
	Foreign relations/getting along with other people/nations	10
	Relations with Russia (no mention of war threat)	8
	Domestic economic problems - general	8
	Racial problems	6
1977	Inflation/high cost of living	58
	Unemployment/recession	39
	Energy shortage	23
	International problems/national defense	18
	Crime/courts	18
	Dissatisfaction with government/corruption	7
	Moral decline	6
1989	Economy	35
	Drug abuse	27
	Poverty	10
	Crime	6
	Moral decline	5

Source: Matthew T. Downey, et al. United States History, 1997, pp. 875, 1001, 1050.

13C • 7' Keyboard Reinforcement

Key each line twice SS (slowly, then faster); DS between 2-line groups.

Figures

1 May 1-8, May 11-18, June 1-8, and June 11-18 are open dates.

2 The quiz on the 18th will be on pages 11 to 18 and 81 to 88.

3 He said only 11 of us got No. 81 right; 88 got No. 81 wrong.

Home/1st

4 ax jab gab call man van back band gala calf cabman avalanche

5 small man | can mask | lava gas | hand vase | lack cash | a small vase

6 Ms. Maas can call a cab, and Jan can flag a small black van.

13D • 9' Review 9, 4, and 0

Key each line twice SS (slowly, then faster); DS between 2-line groups.

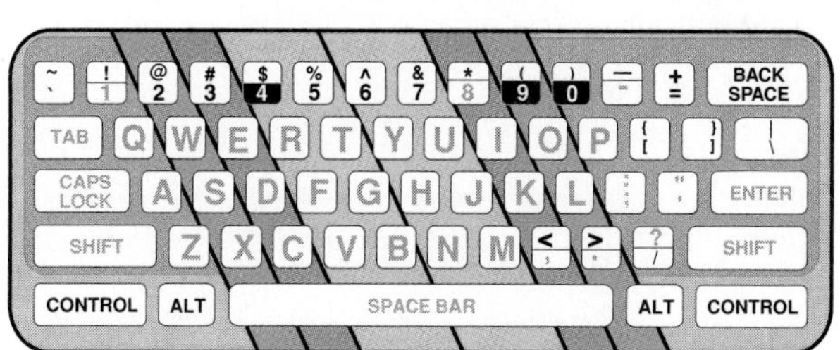

Note: Use the letter l in line 1. Use the figure 1 in line 2.

Review 9

1 l l 9l 9l ll 99 l9l l9l 99l 99l Reach up for 9, 99, and 999.

2 The social security number was 919-99-9191, not 191-99-1919.

Review 4

3 f f 4f 4f ff 44 f4f f4f 44f 44f Reach up for 4, 44, and 444.

4 Add the figures 4, 44, and 444. Please study pages 4 to 44.

Review 0

5 ; ; 0; 0; ;; 00 ;0; ;0; 00; 00; Reach up for 0, 00, and 000.

6 Snap the finger off the 0. I used 0, 00, and 000 sandpaper.

Combine 9, 4, and 0

7 Flights 904 and 490 left after Flights 409A, 400Z, and 940X.

8 My ZIP Code is 40099, not 44099. Is Tanya's 09094 or 90904?

13E • 11' Speed Check

1. Key a 30" writing on each line. Determine *gwam* on each writing.
2. Key another 30" writing on each line—at a faster pace.
3. Key two 2' writings on 12E, p. 26.

2	4	6	8	10	12	14	16	18	20	22

1 Suzy may fish off the dock with us.

2 Pay the girls for all the work they did.

3 Quen is due by six and may then fix the sign.

4 Janie is to vie with six girls for the city title.

5 Duane is to go to the lake to fix the auto for the man.

30" | 2 | 4 | 6 | 8 | 10 | 12 | 14 | 16 | 18 | 20 | 22 |

LESSON 63 APPLY BORDERS TO TABLES

Objectives:

1. To improve table formatting skills.
2. To format tables with enhanced borders and shading.

63A • 5' Conditioning Practice

Key each line twice SS; key a 1' writing on line 3; determine *gwam*.

alphabet 1 Karla justified a very low quiz score by explaining her problems.

fig/sym 2 My property tax increased by 12.7% ($486); I paid $3,590 in 2001.

speed 3 They may work with us to make a profit for the eighty auto firms.

gwam 1' | 1 | 2 | 3 | 4 | 5 | 6 | 7 | 8 | 9 | 10 | 11 | 12 | 13 |

FORMATTING

63B • 45' Table Formatting

Table 1

Format the table at the right. Use the table formatting features that you have learned to arrange the information attractively on the page. Use a table border and shading similar to the illustration. Adjust column widths so that each data entry fits on a single line.

 **Save as:** *TBL63B1*

PRESIDENTS 1945 - 2001				
President	**Years in Office**	**Profession**	**Elected from**	**Vice President**
Harry S. Truman	1945 - 1953	Businessman	Missouri	Alben W. Barkley
Dwight D. Eisenhower	1953 - 1961	Soldier	Kansas	Richard M. Nixon
John F. Kennedy	1961 - 1963	Author	Massachusetts	Lyndon B. Johnson
Lyndon B. Johnson	1963 - 1969	Teacher	Texas	Hubert H. Humphrey
Richard M. Nixon	1969 - 1974	Lawyer	California	Spiro T. Agnew Gerald R. Ford
Gerald R. Ford	1974 - 1977	Lawyer	Michigan	Nelson A. Rockefeller
James E. Carter, Jr.	1977 - 1981	Businessman	Georgia	Walter F. Mondale
Ronald W. Reagan	1981 - 1989	Actor	California	George H. W. Bush
George H. W. Bush	1989 - 1993	Businessman	Texas	J. Danforth Quayle
William J. Clinton	1993 - 2001	Lawyer	Arkansas	Albert Gore, Jr.
Blue = Republican Party Affiliation		Red = Democratic Party Affiliation		

Source: Matthew T. Downey, et al. United States History, 1997, pp. 1132–1133.

History Bits

"Ask not what your country can do for you—ask what you can do for your country."

—John F. Kennedy

13F • 10'
Script and Rough-Draft Copy

1. Key each line once DS (2 hard returns between lines).
2. Key the rough-draft lines again if time permits.

≡ = capitalize
∧ = insert
∼ = transpose
(with delete mark) = delete space
= add space
/lc = lowercase
⁀ = close up

Script

1 *Proofread: Compare copy word for word with the original.*
2 *Compare all figures digit by digit with your source copy.*
3 *Be sure to check for spacing and punctuation marks, also.*
4 *Copy in script or rough draft may not show exact spacing.*
5 *It is your job to insert correct spacing as you key copy.*
6 *Soon you will learn how to correct your errors on screen.*

Rough draft

7 cap the first word an all proper nouns in every sentence.
8 For example: pablo Mendez is from San juan,Puerto rico.
9 Ami Qwan and parents will return to Taiple this summer.
10 our coffee is from Columbia; tea, fromEngland or china.
11 How many of you have Ethnic origins ina for eign country?
12 did you know which of the states once were part of mexico?

LESSON 14 — REVIEW FIGURE KEYS (5, 7, 3, 6, AND 2)

Objectives:

1. To review reach technique for **5**, **7**, **3**, **6**, and **2**.
2. To improve skill transfer and build speed.

14A • 5'
Conditioning Practice

Key each line twice SS; then key a 1' writing on line 3; determine *gwam*.

alphabet 1 Zelda might fix the job growth plans very quickly on Monday.
spacing 2 He will go with me to the city to get the rest of the tapes.
easy 3 The six men with the problems may wish to visit the tax man.

gwam 1' | 1 | 2 | 3 | 4 | 5 | 6 | 7 | 8 | 9 | 10 | 11 | 12 |

14B • 5'
Review [5] and [7]

Key each line twice SS (slowly, then faster); DS between 2-line groups.

Review 5

1 f f 5f 5f ff 55 f5f f5f 55f 55f Reach up for 5, 55, and 555.
2 Reach up to 5 and back to f. Did he say to order 55 or 555?

Review 7

3 j j 7j 7j jj 77 j7j j7j 77j 77j Reach up for 7, 77, and 777.
4 Key the figures 7, 77, and 777. She checked Rooms 7 and 77.

62D • 30'
Table Formatting

Table 1

Key the table at the right using the information given below.

Column headings: row height 0.4"; center vertical alignment; bold text.

Data rows: row height 0.4"; bottom vertical alignment.

Table placement: center horizontally and vertically.

 **Save as:** *TBL62D1*

Table 2

Format the table shown below right using the information below.

Column headings: row height 0.4"; center vertical alignment; bold text; 15% gray shading.

Data rows: row height 0.4"; bottom vertical alignment; 15% gray shading where shown.

Table placement: center horizontally and vertically.

 **Save as:** *TBL62D2*

History Bits

"Under the command of Gen. Eisenhower, Allied naval forces supported by strong air forces began landing Allied armies this morning on the northern coast of France."

—**Communiqué No. 1**

Table 3

Note that Table 2 contains the same information as Table 1, but arranged in a different way. Use your decision-making skills to create a third table from the information, arranging it in still another way. Insert a row for the source note.

 **Save as:** *TBL62D3*

WHAT AMERICANS REMEMBER

Top Five Events

Rank	Age Group			
	18-35	35-54	55-64	65 and Over
1	Oklahoma City Bombing	Oklahoma City Bombing	JFK Death	JFK Death
2	Challenger	JFK Death	Moon Walk	Pearl Harbor
3	Gulf War Begins	Challenger	Oklahoma City Bombing	WWII Ends
4	Reagan Shot	Moon Walk	Challenger	Moon Walk
5	Berlin Wall Falls	Gulf War Begins	MLK Death	FDR Death

Source: The Pew Research Center, "Public Perspectives on the American Century." http://www.people-press.org/mill1sec4.htm (20 August 1999).

WHAT AMERICANS REMEMBER

Top Five Events

Event	**Age Group**			
	18-35	**35-54**	**55-64**	**65+**
■ Berlin Wall Falls	5	*	*	*
■ Challenger	2	3	4	*
■ Franklin D. Roosevelt Death	*	*	*	5
■ Gulf War Begins	3	5	*	*
■ John F. Kennedy Death	*	2	1	1
■ Martin Luther King, Jr., Death	*	*	5	*
■ Moon Walk	*	4	2	4
■ Oklahoma City Bombing	1	1	3	*
■ Pearl Harbor	*	*	*	2
■ Reagan Shot	4	*	*	*
■ World War II Ends	*	*	*	3
1 = Ranked First, 2 = Ranked Second, etc.; * = Not ranked in top five by this age group.				

Source: The Pew Research Center, "Public Perspectives on the American Century." http://www.people-press.org/mill1sec4.htm (20 August 1999).

14C • 8' Figure-Key Mastery

Key each line twice SS (slowly, then faster); DS between 2-line groups.

Straight copy

1 She moved from 819 Briar Lane to 4057 Park Avenue on May 15.

2 The 50-point quiz on May 17 covers pages 88-94, 97, and 100.

3 The meeting will be held in Room 87 on March 19 at 5:40 p.m.

Script

4 *The 495 representatives met from 7:00 to 8:40 p.m. on May 1.*

5 *Social Security Nos. 519-88-7504 and 798-05-4199 were found.*

6 *My office is at 157 Main, and my home is at 4081 92d Avenue.*

Rough draft

7 Runners 180,90 and 507 were schedule for August 15.

8 her tele phone number was changde to 194-5009 on July 1.

9 Re view Rules 1- on pages 89-90 and rules 15-19 no page 174.

14D • 8' Review 3, 6, and 2

Key each line twice SS (slowly, then faster); DS between 2-line groups.

Review 3

1 d d 3d 3d dd 33 d3d d3d 33d 33d Reach up for 3, 33, and 333.

2 Add the figures 3, 33, and 333. Read pages 3 to 33 tonight.

Review 6

3 j j 6j 6j jj 66 j6j j6j 66j 66j Reach up for 6, 66, and 666.

4 Key the figures 6, 66, and 666. Did just 6 of 66 finish it?

Review 2

5 s s 2s 2s ss 22 s2s s2s 22s 22s Reach up for 2, 22, and 222.

6 Reach up to 2 and back to s. Ashley reviewed pages 2 to 22.

Combine 3, 6, and 2

7 Only 263 of the 362 flights left on time on Monday, July 26.

8 Read Chapter 26, pages 263 to 326, for the exam on April 23.

62B • 8' Timed Writings

1. Take two 1' writings for speed; determine *gwam* on each writing.
2. Key one 3' writing for speed; determine *gwam*.

  all letters used

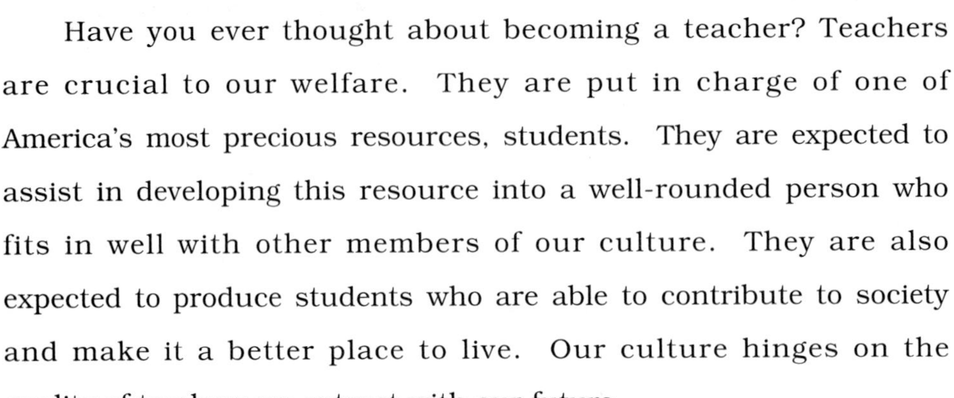

	gwam 1'	3'
Have you ever thought about becoming a teacher? Teachers	12	4
are crucial to our welfare. They are put in charge of one of	24	8
America's most precious resources, students. They are expected to	37	12
assist in developing this resource into a well-rounded person who	51	17
fits in well with other members of our culture. They are also	63	21
expected to produce students who are able to contribute to society	77	26
and make it a better place to live. Our culture hinges on the	89	30
quality of teachers we entrust with our future.	99	33
Being a teacher is quite a challenge. Teachers work with a	111	37
broad range of individuals with a variety of interests, back-	123	41
grounds, and abilities. Teachers try to help all students realize	136	45
their potential and be able to cope with a world that is changing	149	50
very rapidly every day. A teacher's job is to try to equip stu-	162	54
dents with the skills necessary to be lifelong learners, to keep	175	58
pace with changes, and to be productive. In order to be success-	188	63
ful at teaching, a person must like working with people and enjoy	201	67
learning.	203	68

 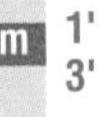    

gwam 1' | 1 | 2 | 3 | 4 | 5 | 6 | 7 | 8 | 9 | 10 | 11 | 12 | 13 |
3' | 1 | 2 | 3 | 4 |

62C • 7' Table Editing

Open *TBL61C3* (61C, Table 3) and make the following changes.

1. Delete *John Wilkes Booth* and *Thomas Jefferson* from the table.
2. Add the three names shown at the right (alphabetical order).
3. Make any adjustments necessary to make the table fit on one page.

 **Save as:** *TBL62C*

Tisquantum	Taught the Pilgrims farming techniques; helped them establish treaties with native tribes.	1580-1622 (approx.)
Sir Walter Raleigh	English adventurer who settled the region from South Carolina north to present-day New York City under a charter from Queen Elizabeth I of England.	1554-1618
John D. Rockefeller	Oil magnate and philanthropist; founded Standard Oil Company in 1870.	1839-1937

14E • 10'
Skill Transfer

1. Key a 1' writing on each ¶; determine *gwam* on each.
2. Compare rates. On which ¶ did you have highest *gwam*?
3. Key two 1' writings on each of the slower ¶s, trying to equal your highest *gwam* in Step 1.

Note:

Relative speeds on different kinds of copy:

- highest—straight copy
- next highest—script copy
- lowest—statistical copy

To determine *gwam*, use the 1' *gwam* scale for partial lines in ¶s 1 and 2, but count the words in ¶ 3.

all letters/figures used

	gwam 1'
You should try now to transfer to other types of copy	11
as much of your straight-copy speed as you can. Handwritten	23
copy and copy in which figures appear tend to slow you down.	35
You can increase speed on these, however, with extra effort.	47
An immediate goal for handwritten copy is at least 90 per-	11
cent of the straight-copy rate; for copy with figures, at	23
least 75 percent. Try to speed up balanced-hand figures such	35
as 26, 84, and 163. Key harder ones such as 452 and 980 more	48
slowly.	49
Copy that is written by hand is often not legible, and	11
the spelling of words may be puzzling. So give major attention	23
to unclear words. Question and correct the spacing used	35
with a comma or period. you can do this even as you key.	47

gwam 1' | 1 | 2 | 3 | 4 | 5 | 6 | 7 | 8 | 9 | 10 | 11 | 12 |

14F • 14'
Speed Building

1. Key a 1' writing on each ¶; determine *gwam* on each writing.
2. Add 2–4 *gwam* to better rate in Step 1 for a new goal.
3. Key three 1' writings on each ¶ trying to achieve new goal.

all letters used

	gwam 2'
When you need to adjust to a new situation in which new	6
people are involved, be quick to recognize that at first it	12
is you who must adapt. This is especially true in an office	18
where the roles of workers have already been established. It	24
is your job to fit into the team structure with harmony.	30
Learn the rules of the game and who the key players are;	35
then play according to those rules at first. Do not expect	41
to have the rules modified to fit your concept of what the	47
team structure and your role in it should be. Only after you	53
become a valuable member should you suggest major changes.	59

gwam 2' | 1 | 2 | 3 | 4 | 5 | 6 |

Table 3
Key the table at the right and insert the following three names beside the individual's accomplishments.

Albert Einstein
Thomas Alva Edison
Andrew Carnegie

Key the source note outside the table, below the last row. Use the table format features that you have learned to arrange the information attractively on the page.

 **Save as:** *TBL61C3*

History Bits

"I am the better writer, she (Susan B. Anthony) the better critic . . . and together we have made arguments that have stood unshaken by the storms of thirty long years; arguments that no man has answered."

—Elizabeth Cady Stanton

Table 4
Open *TBL60C1* (60C, Table 1). Shade Confederate officer rows in 10% gray shading and Union officer rows in light blue shading (or 5% gray).

 **Save as:** *TBL61C4*

KEY PEOPLE IN AMERICAN HISTORY

Name	Accomplishment	Life
Alexander Grayam Bell	Invented the telephone in 1976.	1847-1922
John Wilkes Boothe	Actor; Assassin of President Lincoln, April 14, 1865	1838-1865
	Scotish immigrant who built a fortune by building steel mills.	1835-1919
Crazy Horse	Sioux Indian chief who resisted government demands for his tribe to leave the Black Hills.	18421877
Jefferson David	President of the confederate States of America.	1808-1889
	American physicist; theory of relativity led to harnessing nuclear energy.	1879-1955
Thomas Jefferson	Third president of the United States; author of the Declaration of Independence.	1743-1826
Martin Luther King	Civil rights leader; belief in nonviolence was patterned after Mohandas Gandi.	1929-1968
Eleanor Roosevelt	President Franklin D. Roosevelt's wife and a major champoin for civil rights and humanitarian issues.	1884-1962
Elizabeth stanton	American socail reformer; led the struggle for women sufferage with Susan B. Anthony.	1815-1902
	American inventor of the incandescent light bulb and the phonograph.	*1847-1931*

Source: James R. Giese, et al. The American Century, 1999, pp. 929-935.

Select one of the names listed in the table. Use the Internet to find out more about the individual you select. Compose a paragraph or two telling about this person's contribution to American history.

LESSON 62 PRESENT INFORMATION IN TABLES

Objectives:

1. To improve table formatting skills.
2. To use decision-making skills to organize information in a table.

62A • 5'
Conditioning Practice

Key each line twice SS; key a 1' writing on line 3; determine *gwam*.

alphabet 1 Jung expects the twelve banks to formalize a few details quickly.
figures 2 The 10 a.m. meeting on May 29 will be in Rooms 360, 247, and 458.
speed 3 Orlando and the neighbor may go downtown to sign the audit forms.

gwam 1' | 1 | 2 | 3 | 4 | 5 | 6 | 7 | 8 | 9 | 10 | 11 | 12 | 13 |

UNIT 4

LESSONS 15-16

Build Keyboarding Skill

LESSON 15 SKILL BUILDING

Objectives:

1. To improve technique on individual letters.
2. To improve keying speed on 1' and 2' writings.

15A • 5' Conditioning Practice

Key each line twice SS; then key a 1' writing on line 3; determine *gwam.*

alphabet 1 Jack Faber was amazingly quiet during the extensive program.
spacing 2 it has | it will be | to your | by then | in our | it may be | to do the
easy 3 Jan may make a big profit if she owns the title to the land.
gwam 1' | 1 | 2 | 3 | 4 | 5 | 6 | 7 | 8 | 9 | 10 | 11 | 12 |

SKILL BUILDING

15B • 18' Technique: Individual Letters

Key each line twice SS (slowly, then faster); DS between 2-line groups.

Goal:
To keep keystroking action limited to the fingers.

Emphasize continuity and rhythm with curved, upright fingers.

A 1 Anna Haas ate the meal, assuming that her taxi had departed.
B 2 Bobby Barber bribed Bart to buy the baseball, bat, and base.
C 3 Chuck Cusack confiscated a raccoon and a cat from my clinic.
D 4 Donald doubted that Todd could decide on the daily dividend.
E 5 Ellen and Steven designed evening dresses for several years.

F 6 Felicia and her friend split their fifer's fees fifty-fifty.
G 7 Garn Taggart haggled with Dr. Gregg over the geography exam.
H 8 The highest honors for Heath were highlighted on each sheet.
I 9 Heidi Kim is an identical twin who idolizes her twin sister.
J 10 Janet and Jody joined Jay in Jericho in West Jordan in July.

K 11 Karl kept Kay's knickknack in a knapsack in the khaki kayak.
L 12 Molly filled the small holes in the little yellow lunch box.
M 13 Mr. Mark murmured about the minimal number of grammar gains.
gwam 1' | 1 | 2 | 3 | 4 | 5 | 6 | 7 | 8 | 9 | 10 | 11 | 12 |

LESSON 61 APPLY SHADING TO TABLES

Objectives:

1. To improve table formatting skills.
2. To enhance tables with shading.
3. To enhance table decision-making skills.

61A • 5' Conditioning Practice

Key each line twice SS; key a 1' writing on line 3; determine *gwam*.

alphabet 1 Hazel saw five or six people jumping quickly over the gray board.

figures 2 They picked up yard waste at 842 Lake, 1073 Park, and 3596 Cedar.

speed 3 The soggy field by the dog kennels was good for a big tug of war.

gwam 1' | 1 | 2 | 3 | 4 | 5 | 6 | 7 | 8 | 9 | 10 | 11 | 12 | 13 |

61B • 8' Table Editing

1. Open *TBL60C1* (60C, Table 1). At the end of the table, include the generals' names shown at the right.
2. Sort the table to arrange the new entries alphabetically with the rest of the entries.

 **Save as:** *TBL61B*

McClellan, George B.	Union Army General
Forrest, Nathan Bedford	Confederate Army General
Johnston, Albert Sidney	Confederate Army General
McDowell, Irvin	Union Army General

FORMATTING

61C • 37' Table Formatting

Table 1

1. Combine the three tables at the right into one. Use **FAMOUS AMERICANS** for the main title.
2. Include the following source note.
   "Black History Innovators." USA Today. http://www.usatoday.com (15 February 2000).
3. Format the table attractively. Adjust row height, column width, alignment, placement, etc. Use 10% shading for the top column headings and 20% shading for the bottom column headings.

 **Save as:** *TBL61C1*

Table 2

With *TBL61C1* (Table 1) open, alphabetize the entries in each column.

 **Save as:** *TBL61C2*

Thinkers and Innovators	
Name	Life
George W. Carver	1864-1943
W. E. B. Du Bois	1868-1963
Madam C. J. Walker	1867-1919
Booker T. Washington	1856-1915
Benjamin Banneker	1731-1806
Mary McLeod Bethune	1875-1955
Charles Drew	1904-1950

Politics	
Name	Life
Frederick Douglass	1817-1895
Rosa Parks	1913-
Harriet Tubman	1823-1913
Thurgood Marshall	1908-1993
Colin Powell	1937-
Shirley Chisholm	1924-
Martin Luther King, Jr.	1929-1968

Arts and Entertainment	
Name	Life
Louis Armstrong	1901-1971
Billie Holiday	1915-1959
Duke Ellington	1899-1974
Ella Fitzgerald	1917-1996
Bill Cosby	1937-
Alex Haley	1921-1992
Oprah Winfrey	1954-

15C • 12'
Technique: Tab

1. Key each short story title and opening line shown at the right.
2. Key the copy again at a faster pace.

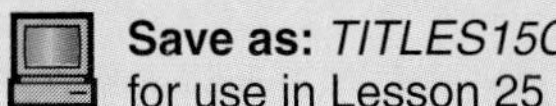

Save as: *TITLES15C* for use in Lesson 25

Technique **C • U • E**

- Reach up to the TAB key without moving the left hand away from you.
- Strike the TAB key firmly and release it quickly.

Optional Activity

Can you match each short story with its author?

Benjamin Franklin
Helen Keller
Katherine Mansfield
John Steinbeck
James Thurber
Mark Twain

"The Scotty Who Knew Too Much"

Tab → Several summers ago there was a Scotty who went to the country for a visit.

"Roughing It"

Tab → After leaving the Sink, we traveled along the Humboldt River a little way.

"The Autobiography Moral Perfection"

Tab → It was about this time that I conceived the bold and arduous project of arriving at moral perfection.

"The Chrysanthemums"

Tab → The high grey-flannel fog of winter closed off the Salinas Valley from the sky and from all the rest of the world.

"The Story of My Life"

Tab → The most important day I remember in all my life is the one on which my teacher, Anne Mansfield Sullivan, came to me.

"The Doll's House"

Tab → When dear old Mrs. Hay went back to town after staying with the Burnells, she sent the children a doll's house.

15D • 15'
Speed Building: Guided Writing

1. Key one 1' unguided and two 1' guided writings on each ¶, using the procedure on p. 22; determine *gwam*.
2. Key two 2' unguided writings on ¶s 1–2 combined; determine *gwam*.

Quarter-Minute Checkpoints				
gwam	1/4'	1/2'	3/4'	1'
20	5	10	15	20
24	6	12	18	24
28	7	14	21	28
32	8	16	24	32
36	9	18	27	36
40	10	20	30	40
44	11	22	33	44
48	12	24	36	48
52	13	26	39	52
56	14	28	42	56

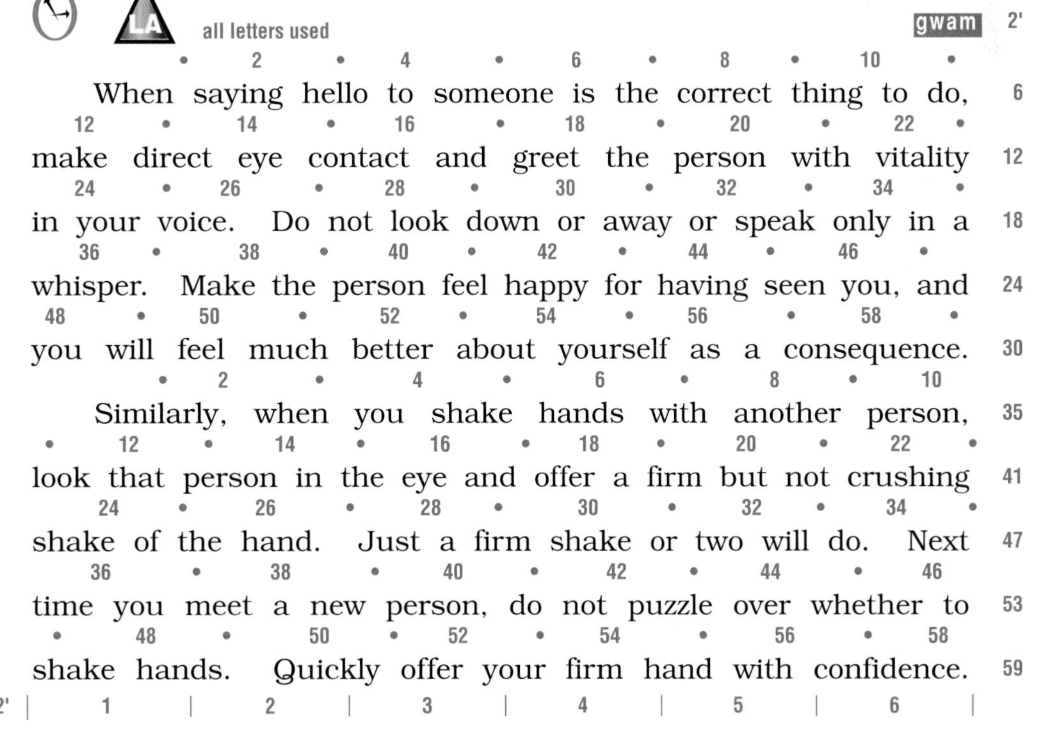

all letters used — gwam 2'

When saying hello to someone is the correct thing to do, 6
make direct eye contact and greet the person with vitality 12
in your voice. Do not look down or away or speak only in a 18
whisper. Make the person feel happy for having seen you, and 24
you will feel much better about yourself as a consequence. 30

Similarly, when you shake hands with another person, 35
look that person in the eye and offer a firm but not crushing 41
shake of the hand. Just a firm shake or two will do. Next 47
time you meet a new person, do not puzzle over whether to 53
shake hands. Quickly offer your firm hand with confidence. 59

2' | 1 | 2 | 3 | 4 | 5 | 6 |

Table 1, cont.

2. Create a table and fill in the information. Adjust column widths as needed.
3. Center and bold the main title and column headings.
4. Change the row height to 0.3" for all rows.
5. Change vertical alignment to *Center* for the column headings and to *Bottom* for all other rows.
6. Center the table horizontally and vertically.

 **Save as:** *TBL60C1*

Table 2
Create the table shown at the right using the information given below.

Main title: row height 0.9"; center vertical alignment; bold text.

Column headings: row height 0.4"; center vertical alignment; bold text.

Data rows: row height 0.3"; bottom vertical alignment; Column B center horizontal alignment.

Table placement: center horizontally and vertically.

 **Save as:** *TBL60C2*

Table 3
Create the table shown at the right using the information given below.

Main title: row height 0.7"; center vertical alignment; bold text.

Column headings: row height 0.4"; center vertical alignment; bold text.

Data rows: row height 0.35"; bottom vertical alignment.

Note:
The source note may be keyed outside the table as shown, or a new row may be inserted for it.

 **Save as:** *TBL60C3*

CIVIL WAR
Eastern Theater Campaigns

Campaign	**Dates**
First Bull Run (Manassas)	July 1861
Peninsular Campaign	April-July 1862
Jackson's Valley Campaign	March-June 1862
Second Bull Run (Manassas)	July-September 1862
Antietam (Sharpsburg) Campaign	September 1862
Fredericksburg Campaign	October-December 1862
Chancellorsville Campaign	April-May 1863
Gettysburg Campaign	June-July 1863
Wilderness Campaign	May 1864
Spotsylvania Campaign	May 1864
Petersburg Campaign	May 1864-April 1865
Grant's Pursuit of Lee	April 3 and 9, 1865
Sherman's March to the Sea	November-December 1864
Sherman's Pursuit of Johnston	December 1864-April 1865

Source: Collier's Encyclopedia, 1991.

THE CONFEDERATE STATES OF AMERICA

State	**Seceded from Union**	**Readmitted to Union**[1]
South Carolina	December 20, 1860	July 9, 1868
Mississippi	January 9, 1861	February 23, 1870
Florida	January 10, 1861	June 25, 1868
Alabama	January 11, 1861	July 13, 1868
Georgia	January 19, 1861	July 15, 1870[2]
Louisiana	January 26, 1861	July 9, 1868
Texas	March 2, 1861	March 30, 1870
Virginia	April 17, 1861	January 26, 1870
Arkansas	May 6, 1861	June 22, 1868
North Carolina	May 20, 1861	July 4, 1868
Tennessee	June 8, 1861	July 24, 1866

[1]Date of readmission to representation in U.S. House of Representatives.
[2]Second readmission date. First date was July 21, 1868, but the representatives were unseated March 5, 1869.

Source: The 1996 Information Please Almanac, pp. 748-781.

LESSON 16 SKILL BUILDING

Objectives:

1. To improve technique on individual letters.
2. To improve keying speed on 1'and 2' writings.

16A • 5' Conditioning Practice

Key each line twice SS; then key a 1' writing on line 3; determine *gwam.*

alphabet 1 Jim quickly realized that the beautiful gowns are expensive.
spacing 2 did go | to the | you can go | has been able | if you can | to see the
easy 3 Dick and the girls may go downtown to pay for the six signs.

gwam 1' | 1 | 2 | 3 | 4 | 5 | 6 | 7 | 8 | 9 | 10 | 11 | 12 |

16B • 18' Technique Mastery: Individual Letters

Key each line twice SS (slowly, then faster); DS between 2-line groups.

Goal:

To keep keystroking action in the fingers.

Emphasize continuity and rhythm with curved, upright fingers.

N 1 Neither John nor Ned wanted a no-nonsense lesson on manners.
O 2 One out of four people openly oppose our opening more docks.
P 3 Phillip chomped on apples as the puppy slept by the poppies.
Q 4 Quin quickly questioned the queen about the quarterly quota.
R 5 Ray arrived at four for a carriage ride over the rural road.

S 6 Steve sold six pairs of scissors in East Sussex on Saturday.
T 7 The tot toddled into the store to pet a cat and two kittens.
U 8 Usually you use undue pressure to persuade us to use quotas.
V 9 Vivian survived the vivacious vandal who wore a velvet veil.
W 10 When will the worker be allowed to wash the new west window?

X 11 The tax expert explained the extensive excise tax exemption.
Y 12 You usually yearn to play with Mary day after day after day.
Z 13 Zoro's zippy zigzags dazzled us but puzzled a zealous judge.

gwam 1' | 1 | 2 | 3 | 4 | 5 | 6 | 7 | 8 | 9 | 10 | 11 | 12 |

16C • 5' Skill Building

Key each line twice SS; DS between 2-line groups.

Space Bar

1 is it to go me see was you she pool turn they were next best
2 I will be able to try to fix the computer next week for you.

Word response

3 they did may auto form make both them soap held the ham busy
4 I may make a big sign to hang by the door of the civic hall.

Double letters

5 school butter took sell hood green foot current room stubborn
6 Will was a little foolish at the football assembly this week.

gwam 1' | 1 | 2 | 3 | 4 | 5 | 6 | 7 | 8 | 9 | 10 | 11 | 12 |

LESSON 60 IMPROVE TABLE FORMATTING SKILLS

Objectives:

1. To improve table formatting skills.
2. To improve language skills.

60A • 5' Conditioning Practice

Key each line twice SS; key a 1' writing on line 3; determine *gwam.*

alphabet 1 Zachary enjoyed picking six bouquets of vivid flowers at my home.
figures 2 I bought my first cards on July 25, 1980; I now have 3,467 cards.
speed 3 Dixie owns the six foals and the cow in the neighbor's hay field.
gwam 1' | 1 | 2 | 3 | 4 | 5 | 6 | 7 | 8 | 9 | 10 | 11 | 12 | 13 |

LANGUAGE SKILLS

60B • 8' Language Skills: Word Choice

1. Study the spelling/ definitions of the words at the right.
2. For each set of sentences, key the Learn line, then the Apply lines. Choose the correct word in parentheses.
3. Check your work; correct lines containing word-choice errors.

Save as: *CHOICE60B*

do (vb) to bring about; to carry out
due (adj) owed or owing as a debt; having reached the date for payment

for (prep/conj) used to indicate purpose; on behalf of; because; because of
four (n) the fourth in a set or series

Learn 1 **Do** you know when the three library books are **due**?
Apply 2 The next payment will be (do, due) on Tuesday, March 24.
Apply 3 I (do, due) not know when I will be available to meet again.

Learn 1 The **four** men asked for a salary increase **for** the next **four** years.
Apply 2 The manager left (for, four) an hour just before (for, four) o'clock.
Apply 3 The (for, four) coaches were mad after waiting (for, four) an hour.

FORMATTING

60C • 37' Review Table Formatting

1. Review the format guides for tables on p. 172 and the word processing features on pp. 169–171 as needed.
2. Key Tables 1–3 shown at the right and on p. 174.

Table 1

1. Determine the number of rows and columns needed to create a table for the data at the right. (Key the main title above the table, as shown.)

(continued on next page)

CIVIL WAR PERSONALITIES

Name	Position
Davis, Jefferson	Confederate Commander in Chief
Grant, Ulysses S.	Union Army Commanding General
Jackson, Stonewall	Confederate Army General
Johnston, Joseph E.	Confederate Army General
Lee, Robert E.	Confederate Army Commanding General
Lincoln, Abraham	Union Commander in Chief
Longstreet, James	Confederate Army General
Mead, George	Union Army General
Sheridan, Philip H.	Union Army General
Sherman, William T.	Union Army General
Stuart, J. E. B. (Jeb)	Confederate Army General
Thomas, George H.	Union Army General

Source: Encyclopedia Americana, 1998.

16D • 10' Handwritten Copy (Script)

Each sentence at the right is from a U.S. president's inaugural address. Key each sentence; then key it again at a faster pace.

Optional Activity

Can you match each quotation at the right with the president who said it?

George Bush
Dwight D. Eisenhower
John F. Kennedy
Franklin D. Roosevelt
Theodore Roosevelt

"How far have we come in man's long pilgrimage from darkness toward light?"

* * * * *

"We must hope to give our children a sense of what it means to be a loyal friend, a loving parent, a citizen who leaves his home, his neighborhood and town better than he found it."

* * * * *

"If we fail, the cause of free self-government throughout the world will rock to its foundations."

* * * * *

"Ask not what your country can do for you—ask what you can do for your country."

* * * * *

"So, first of all, let me assert my firm belief that the only thing we have to fear is fear itself."

16E • 12' Speed Building

1. Key one 1' unguided and two 1' guided writings on ¶ 1.
2. Key ¶ 2 in the same way.
3. Key two 2' unguided writings on ¶s 1–2 combined; determine *gwam*.

Quarter-Minute Checkpoints				
gwam	1/4'	1/2'	3/4'	1'
20	5	10	15	20
24	6	12	18	24
28	7	14	21	28
32	8	16	24	32
36	9	18	27	36
40	10	20	30	40
44	11	22	33	44
48	12	24	36	48
52	13	26	39	52
56	14	28	42	56

all letters used — *gwam* 2'

It is okay to try and try again if your first efforts do 6
not bring the correct results. If you try but fail again and 12
again, however, it is foolish to plug along in the very same 18
manner. Rather, experiment with another way to accomplish the 24
task that may bring the skill or knowledge you seek. 30

If your first attempts do not yield success, do not quit 35
and merely let it go at that. Instead, begin again in a bet- 41
ter way to finish the work or develop more insight into your 47
difficulty. If you recognize why you must do more than just 54
try, try again, you will work with purpose to achieve success. 60

gwam 2' | 1 | 2 | 3 | 4 | 5 | 6 |

UNIT 18

LESSONS 60-64

Improving Letter Formatting Skills

Format Guides: Tables

WHAT AMERICANS REMEMBER

Top Five Events

Event	Age Group			
	18-35	35-54	55-64	65+
■ Berlin Wall Falls	5	*	*	*
■ Challenger	2	3	4	*
■ Franklin D. Roosevelt Death	*	*	*	5
■ Gulf War Begins	3	5	*	*
■ John F. Kennedy Death	*	2	1	1
■ Martin Luther King, Jr., Death	*	*	5	*
■ Moon Walk	*	4	2	4
■ Oklahoma City Bombing	1	1	3	*
■ Pearl Harbor	*	*	*	2
■ Reagan Shot	4	*	*	*
■ World War II Ends	*	*	*	3
1 = Ranked First, 2 = Ranked Second, etc.; * = Not ranked in top five by this age group.				

Source: The Pew Research Center, "Public Perspectives on the American Century." http://www.people-press.org/mill1sec4.htm (20 August 1999).

Table with Joined and Split Cells

PRESIDENTS 1945 - 2001				
President	Years in Office	Profession	Elected from	Vice President
Harry S. Truman	1945 - 1953	Businessman	Missouri	Alben W. Barkley
Dwight D. Eisenhower	1953 - 1961	Soldier	Kansas	Richard M. Nixon
John F. Kennedy	1961 - 1963	Author	Massachusetts	Lyndon B. Johnson
Lyndon B. Johnson	1963 - 1969	Teacher	Texas	Hubert H. Humphrey
Richard M. Nixon	1969 - 1974	Lawyer	California	Spiro T. Agnew
				Gerald R. Ford
Gerald R. Ford	1974 - 1977	Lawyer	Michigan	Nelson A. Rockefeller
James E. Carter, Jr.	1977 - 1981	Businessman	Georgia	Walter F. Mondale
Ronald W. Reagan	1981 - 1989	Actor	California	George H. W. Bush
George H. W. Bush	1989 - 1993	Businessman	Texas	J. Danforth Quayle
William J. Clinton	1993 - 2001	Lawyer	Arkansas	Albert Gore, Jr.
Blue = Republican Party Affiliation		Red = Democratic Party Affiliation		

Source: Matthew T. Downey, et al. United States History, 1997, pp. 1132–1133.

Table with Shading and Borders

Note:
When you complete a table in this unit, check your work. Correct all spelling, keying, and formatting errors before closing or printing the file.

Format Guides: Tables

Tables are used to organize and present information in a concise, logical way to make it easy for the reader to understand and analyze information. The table format can make information easier or more difficult to understand.

You will be required to use the Table word processing features presented in Word Processing 4 (pp. 90-93) and Word Processing 8 (pp. 169-171) to format the tables in this unit. Most of the tables are already organized; you simply need to create them to look like the examples in the text. However, some of the tables will require you to use your decision-making skills to organize the information before formatting and keying the tables. To complete this unit successfully, you will need to understand the format features given below.

Table Format Features

Vertical placement. Center tables vertically. The top and bottom margins will be equal.

Horizontal placement. Center tables horizontally. The left and right margins will be equal.

Column width and row height. Adjust column width and row height to put more white space around data in the rows and columns. Additional white space makes data easier to read.

Vertical alignment. Within cells, data may be aligned at the top, center, or bottom. Title rows most often use center alignment. Data rows usually are either center- or bottom-aligned.

Horizontal alignment. Within columns, words may be left-aligned or center-aligned. Whole numbers are right-aligned if a column total is shown; decimal numbers are decimal-aligned. Other figures may be center-aligned.

Delete/Insert rows and/or columns. Delete empty rows or columns wherever they occur in a table. Also, insert a row(s) as needed above or below an existing row. Insert a column(s) to the left or right of an existing column as needed.

Join/Split cells. To make a table attractive and easy to read, join two or more cells into one cell for the main title, source note, and other data as needed. Any existing cell can be split (divided) into two or more smaller cells if necessary.

Shading. Use shading to enhance table appearance and to highlight selected columns, rows, or individual cells.

Borders. Borders may be applied around an entire table or around cells, rows, or columns within a table. Borders improve appearance as well as highlight the data within the borders.

Sort. In a table column, text can be sorted alphabetically in ascending (A to Z) or descending (Z to A) order. Also, numbers and dates can be sorted numerically (chronologically), in either ascending or descending order.

Communication Skills 2

ACTIVITY 1

Capitalization

1. Key lines 1–10 at the right, supplying capital letters as needed.
2. Check the accuracy of your work with the instructor; correct any errors you made.
3. Note the rule number at the left of each sentence in which you made a capitalization error.
4. Using the rules below the sentences and on p. 39, identify the rule(s) you need to review/practice.
5. **Read**: Study each rule.
6. **Learn**: Key the Learn line(s) beneath it, noting how the rule is applied.
7. **Apply**: Key the Apply line(s), supplying the needed capitalization.

 **Save as:** *CS2-ACT1*

Proofread & Correct

Rules		
1,6	1	has dr. holt moved his offices to hopewell medical center?
1,3,5	2	pam has made plans to spend thanksgiving day in fort wayne.
1,2,8	3	j. c. hauck will receive a d.d.s. degree from usc in june.
1,4,6	4	is tech services, inc., located at fifth street and elm?
1,2,7	5	i heard senator dole make his acceptance speech on thursday.
1,3,6	6	did mrs. alma s. banks apply for a job with butler county?
1,3	7	she knew that albany, not new york city, is the capital.
1,3	8	eldon and cindy marks now live in santa fe, new mexico.
1,6	9	are you going to the marx theater in mount adams tonight?
1,2,6	10	on friday, the first of july, we move to keystone plaza.

Capitalization

Rule 1: Capitalize the first word of a sentence, personal titles, and names of people.

Learn 1 Ask Ms. King if she and Mr. Valdez will sponsor our club.
Apply 2 did you see mrs. watts and gloria at the school play?

Rule 2: Capitalize days of the week and months of the year.

Learn 3 He said that school starts on the first Monday in September.
Apply 4 my birthday is on the third thursday of march this year.

Rule 3: Capitalize cities, states, countries, and specific geographic features.

Learn 5 When you were recently in Nevada, did you visit Lake Tahoe?
Apply 6 when in france, we saw paris from atop the eiffel tower.

Rule 4: Capitalize names of clubs, schools, companies, and other organizations.

Learn 7 The Voices of Harmony will perform at Music Hall next week.
Apply 8 lennox corp. owns the hyde park athletic club in boston.

Rule 5: Capitalize historic periods, holidays, and events.

Learn 9 The Fourth of July celebrates the signing of the Declaration of Independence.
Apply 10 henri asked if memorial day is an american holiday.

(continued on next page)

ACTIVITY 5

Borders

1. Read the copy at the right.
2. Learn how to use the Border feature of your software.
3. Open file CD-*WP8TBL5*. Complete the table so that it appears as shown at the right.

 **Save as:** *WP8ACT5*

Optional Activity 1

Open the Activity 5 file (*WP8ACT5*). Apply a different style border with a *Box* setting.

 **Save as:** *WP8ACT5-1*

Optional Activity 2

Open the Optional Activity 1 file (*WP8ACT5-1*). Apply a border around the cells of the three games Bruce's 6th-grade team plays. Also apply a border around the times they play the games.

 **Save as:** *WP8ACT5-2*

Use the Border feature to enhance the appearance and readability of tables. The **Border** feature allows a border to be added around an entire table or only selected parts of a table.

FIFTH & SIXTH GRADE TOURNAMENT SCHEDULE Altoona February 26				
Middle School Gym 5th Grade		Time	High School Gym 6th Grade	
Score	Teams		Teams	Score
	Bruce Somerset	9:00	Bruce Somerset	
	St. Croix Central St. Croix Falls		St. Croix Central St. Croix Falls	
	Menomonie Rice Lake	10:10	Menomonie Rice Lake	
	Altoona Eau Claire		Altoona Eau Claire	
	St. Croix Falls Bruce	11:20	St. Croix Falls Bruce	
	St. Croix Central Somerset		St. Croix Central Somerset	
	Rice Lake Eau Claire	12:30	Rice Lake Eau Claire	
	Menomonie Altoona		Menomonie Altoona	
	St. Croix Falls Somerset	1:40	St. Croix Falls Somerset	
	St. Croix Central Bruce		St. Croix Central Bruce	
	Rice Lake Altoona	2:50	Rice Lake Altoona	
	Menomonie Eau Claire		Menomonie Eau Claire	
	3rd and 4th place games	4:00	3rd and 4th place games	
	1st and 2nd place games	5:10	1st and 2nd place games	

ACTIVITY 6

Gridlines

1. Read the copy at the right.

When you remove table borders (*No Border* or *None*), light gray lines, called **gridlines**, replace the borders. These gridlines give you a visual guide as you work with the table; they do not print. The gray gridlines can be turned off by activating the **Hide Gridlines** option. This allows you to see what the table will look like when it is printed.

2. Learn how to use the Gridlines feature of your software.
3. Open the Activity 5 file (*WP8ACT5*). Apply the *None* border setting; then hide the gridlines.

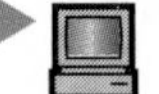 **Save as:** *WP8ACT6*

Rule 6: Capitalize streets, buildings, and other specific structures.

Learn 11 Jemel lives at Bay Shores near Golden Gate Bridge.
Apply 12 dubois tower is on fountain square at fifth and walnut.

Rule 7: Capitalize an official title when it precedes a name and elsewhere if it is a title of high distinction.

Learn 13 In what year did Juan Carlos become King of Spain?
Learn 14 Masami Chou, our class president, made the scholastic awards.
Apply 15 did the president speak to the nation from the rose garden?
Apply 16 mr. chavez, our company president, chairs two major panels.

Rule 8: Capitalize initials; also, letters in abbreviations if the letters would be capitalized when the words are spelled out.

Learn 17 Does Dr. R. J. Anderson have an Ed.D. or a Ph.D.?
Learn 18 She said that UPS stands for United Parcel Service.
Apply 19 we have a letter from ms. anna m. bucks of washington, d.c.
Apply 20 m.d. means Doctor of Medicine, not medical doctor.

ACTIVITY 2

Listening

Complete the listening activity as directed at the right.

 **Save as:** *CS2-ACT2*

1. Listen carefully to the sounds around you for 3'.
2. As you listen, key a numbered list of every different sound you hear.
3. Identify with asterisks the three loudest sounds you heard.

ACTIVITY 3

Composing

1. Key items 1 and 2 at the right as ¶ 1 of a short composition; supply the information needed to complete each sentence (in parentheses).
2. Key item 3 as ¶ 2, supplying the information noted in the parentheses.
3. Key item 4 as ¶ 3, supplying information noted in the parentheses.
4. Proofread, revise, and correct your composition. Look for improper capitalization, inaccurate information, misspelled words, and weak sentence structure.

Save as: *CS2-ACT3*

1 My name, (first/last), is (African/Asian/European/Hispanic, etc.) in origin.

2 My mother's ancestors originated in (name of country); my father's ancestors originated in (name of country).

3 I know the following facts about the country of my (mother's/father's) ancestors:

1. (enter first fact here)
2. (enter second fact here)
3. (enter third fact here)

4 If I could visit a country of my choice, I would visit (name of country) because (give two or three reasons).

ACTIVITY 3

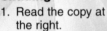

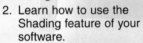

Split Cells/ Join Cells

1. Read the copy at the right.
2. Learn/review how to use the Split Cells and Join Cells features for your software.
3. Open the *CD-WP8TBL3* file.
4. Finish keying any columns that are incomplete.
5. Use the Split Cells and Join Cells features to complete the formatting. (You will shade the table as part of Activity 4.)
6. Center the table vertically and horizontally.

Save as: *WP8ACT3*

Use the Split Cells table feature to **split** (divide) cells horizontally or vertically.

Use the Join Cells table feature to **join** (merge) cells horizontally or vertically.

ACCOUNTING MAJOR					
General Electives (40 credits)				Business Core (32 credits)	Accounting Requirements (28 credits)
Category I (9 Credits)	**Category II** (9 Credits)	**Category III** (11 Credits)	**Category IV** (11 Credits)	Acct 201 Acct 202 Bcom 206 Bcom 207 MIS 240 Bsad 300 Bsad 305 Fin 320 Mktg 330 Mgmt 340 Mgmt 341 Mgmt 449	Acct 301 Acct 302 Acct 314 Acct 315 Acct 317 Acct 321 Acct 450 Acct 460 Fin 326 Fin 327
CJ 202 Math 111 Math 245	Biol 102 Chem 101 Geog 104	Econ 103 Econ 104 Psyc 100 Soc 101	No specific courses required.		
Category I - Communications and Analytical Skills Category II - Natural Sciences Category III - Social Sciences Category IV - Humanities					

ACTIVITY 4A-C

Shading

1. Read the copy at the right.
2. Learn how to use the Shading feature of your software.
3. Open *CD-WP8TBL4*. Shade alternate lines of the table as shown at the right. Use 10% shading except for the last line; use 25% shading on it.

Save as: *WP8ACT4A*

4. Open *WP8ACT2* (Activity 2 file). Shade *National League* with red (or 10% gray). Shade *American League* blue (or 20% gray).
5. For both the National and American Leagues, shade *East* yellow (or 5% gray); *West* green (or 10% gray); and *Central* purple (or 15% gray).

Save as: *WP8ACT4B*

6. Open the Activity 3 file (*WP8ACT3*). Apply 20% shading as shown in Activity 3, above.

Save as: *WP8ACT4C*

Use the **Shading** feature to enhance the appearance of tables to make them easier to read. The Shading feature allows you to fill in areas of the table with varying shades of gray or with color. Shading covers the selected area. It may be the entire table or a single cell, column, or row within a table.

TOP 10 USA BOX OFFICE FILMS*		
Movie	Year of Release	Total Gross
Titanic	1997	$600,743,440
Star Wars	1977	$460,935,655
Star Wars: Episode One—The Phantom Menace	1999	$430,984,033
E.T., the Extra-Terrestrial	1982	$399,804,539
Jurassic Park	1993	$356,763,175
Forrest Gump	1994	$329,452,287
The Lion King	1994	$312,775,367
Return of the Jedi	1983	$309,064,373
Independence Day	1996	$305,400,800
The Empire Strikes Back	1980	$290,158,751
*Box office listing in unadjusted 1999 U.S. dollars.		

Source: "Top 100 All-Time Films at the USA Box Office." Hollywood News. http://www.Hollywood.com (5 February 2000).

UNIT 5

LESSONS 17-19

Learn/Review Symbol Keys

LESSON 17 LEARN/REVIEW SYMBOL KEYS (/, $, !, %, <, AND >)

Objectives:

1. To learn or review control of **/**, **$**, **!**, **%**, **<**, and **>**.
2. To combine **/**, **$**, **!**, **%**, **<**, and **>** with other keys.

17A • 5' Conditioning Practice

Key each line twice SS; then key a 1' writing on line 3; determine *gwam.*

alphabet 1 Jackie will budget for the most expensive zoology equipment.

figures 2 I had 50 percent of the responses--3,923 of 7,846--by May 1.

easy 3 The official paid the men for the work they did on the dock.

gwam 1' | 1 | 2 | 3 | 4 | 5 | 6 | 7 | 8 | 9 | 10 | 11 | 12 |

17B • 15' Learn/Review /, $, and !

Key each line twice SS (slowly, then faster); DS between 2-line groups.

Spacing CUE

Do not space between a figure and the / or the $ sign.

The / is the shift of the question mark. Strike it with the right little finger.

The $ is the shift of 4. Control it with the left index finger.

The ! is the shift of 1 and is controlled by the left little finger.

Learn/Review / (diagonal or slash) Reach down with the right little finger.

1 ; ; /; /; ;; // ;/; ;/; 2/3 4/5 and/or We keyed 1/2 and 3/4.

2 Space between a whole number and a fraction: 5 2/3, 14 6/9.

3 Do not space before or after the / in a fraction: 2/3, 7/8.

Learn/Review $ (dollar sign) Reach up with the left index finger.

4 f F $f $F fF $$ f$f F$F $4 $4 for $4 Shift for $ and key $4.

5 A period separates dollars and cents: $4.50, $6.25, $19.50.

6 I earned $33.50 on Mon., $23.80 on Tues., and $44.90 on Wed.

Learn/Review ! (exclamation point) Reach up with the left little finger.

7 a A !a !A aA !! a!a A!A 1! 1! I am excited! I won the game!

8 On your mark! Get ready! Get set! Go! Go faster! I won!

9 Great! You made the team! Hurry up! I am late for school!

WORD PROCESSING 8

ACTIVITY 1

Review Table Formatting Features

Open the file *CD-WP8TBL1* and make the following changes to the table to make it look like the table at right.

1. Insert a new column to the right of the first column. Use **Department** for the column heading. Move the department names from Column A to Column B.
2. Merge the cells of the first row (main title).
3. Adjust column widths so the entire ZIP Code fits on one line with the city and state and all column headings fit on one line.
4. Delete the blank row.
5. Change the row height for all rows to 0.5".
6. Change the vertical alignment to *center* for the column heading row and to *bottom* for all entry rows.
7. Center the table horizontally and vertically.

Save as: *WP8ACT1*

DIRECTORY OF DEPARTMENT MANAGERS			
Manager	Department	Address	Home Phone
Michael Ross	Accounting	310 Flagstaff Ave. Saint Paul, MN 55124-3811	555-0102
Tanisha Santana	Finance	4123 Lakeview Rd. Minneapolis, MN 55438-3317	555-0189
Preston Foster	Marketing	376 Norwood Ave. Anoka, MN 55303-7742	555-0156
Natasha Ashford	Personnel	812 Dartmouth Dr. Hopkins, MN 55345-5622	555-0137
Jamal Richards	Purchasing	55 Wyndham Bay Saint Paul, MN 55125-0052	555-0176
Brianne Bostwick	Publications	927 Prestwick Ter. Minneapolis, MN 55443-4747	555-0123

ACTIVITY 2

Review Table Formatting Features

Open the file *CD-WP8TBL2* and change the table format to make it appear as shown at the right. Center the table horizontally and vertically on the page.

Save as: *WP8ACT2*

MAJOR LEAGUE BASEBALL					
National League			American League		
East	West	Central	East	West	Central
Atlanta Florida Montreal New York Philadelphia	Arizona Colorado Los Angeles San Diego San Francisco	Chicago Cincinnati Houston Milwaukee Pittsburgh St. Louis	Baltimore Boston New York Tampa Bay Toronto	Anaheim Oakland Seattle Texas	Chicago Cleveland Detroit Kansas City Minnesota

17C • 12'
Learn/Review %, <, and >

Key each line twice SS (slowly, then faster); DS between 2-line groups.

Spacing **CUE**

Do not space between a figure and the % sign.

The % is the shift of 5. Strike it with the left index finger.

The < is the shift of , and is controlled by the right middle finger.

The > is the shift of . and is controlled by the right ring finger.

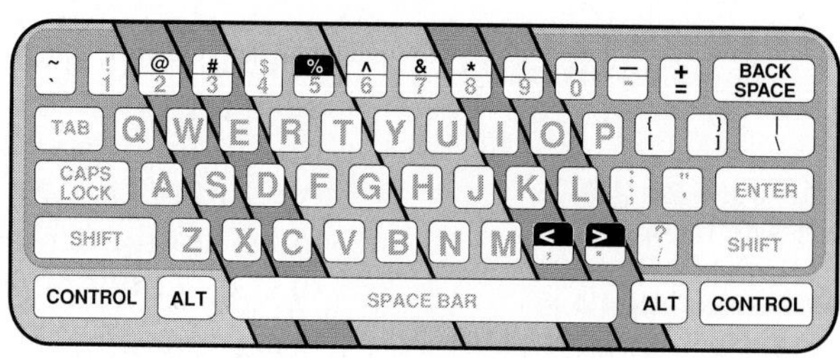

Learn/Review % (percent sign) Reach up with the left index finger.

1 f F %f fF % % f%F f%F 5%f 5%f Shift for the % in 5% and 15%.

2 Do not space between a number and %: 5%, 75%, 85%, and 95%.

3 Prices fell 10% on May 1, 15% on June 1, and 20% on July 15.

Learn/Review < ("less than" sign) Reach down with the right middle finger.

4 k K <k <K kK << k<K K<K <, <, <k, <k, <K< 10 < 18; 95 , 120.

5 If a < b, and c < d, and e < f, and a < c and e, then a < d.

Learn/Review > ("greater than" sign) Reach down with the right ring finger.

6 l L >l >L lL >> l>L L>L >. >. >l. >l. >L> 20 > 17; 105 > 98.

7 If b > a, and d > c, and f > e, and c and e > a, then f > a.

17D • 10'
Skill Building: Symbols

Key each line twice SS (slowly, then faster); DS between 2-line groups.

Combine /, $, and !

1 Only 2/3 of the class remembered to bring the $5 on Tuesday!

2 I was really excited! I received 1/2 of the $50 door prize!

3 Only 1/10 of the sellers earned more than $100! I felt bad!

Combine % and < >

4 Only 25% of the students got the answer to 5x > 10 but < 20.

5 Yes, 90% of the students scored > 75%, and 10% scored < 75%.

6 Only about 15% of the class understood the < and > concepts!

17E • 8'
Speed Building

1. Key three 1' writings on the ¶; determine *gwam* on each writing.
2. Key two 2' writings on the ¶; determine *gwam*.

all letters used — gwam 2'

When you key copy that contains both words and numbers, 6
it is best to key numbers using the top row. When the copy 12
consists primarily of figures, however, it may be faster to 18
use the keypad. In any event, keying figures quickly is a 24
major skill to prize. You can expect to key figures often 29
in the future, so learn to key them with very little peeking. 36

gwam 2' | 1 | 2 | 3 | 4 | 5 | 6 |

Letter 2

Key the letter at the right in block format. Remember to include a heading on the second page.

Date: **June 28, 200-**
Letter address:
Ms. Lindsay Grimaldi
3647 Greenpoint Ave.
Long Island City, NY 11101-4534

The letter is from **Jon A. Richardson, Instructor**.

Supply a salutation and complimentary closing.

 **Save as:** *LTR59B2*

Insert List

- The Film & More
- Special Features
- Timelines
- Maps
- People & Events
- Instructor's Guide

INTERNET ACTIVITY

Search the Web to learn more about Lindbergh, Roosevelt, or MacArthur. Key a couple of paragraphs about the individual, including what you learned from the Web search.

History Bits

"She walked in the slums and ghettos of the world, not on a tour of inspection, but as one who could not feel contentment when others were hungry."

—Adlai Stevenson about Eleanor Roosevelt

Last month while attending the history convention in Los Angeles, I went to a session titled "How to Bring History to Life." I thoroughly enjoyed the session and have since corresponded with the speaker, Mr. Martin Anderson. He led me to PBS's Web site titled "The American Experience." ¶ Three of the feature sites would integrate nicely into what we have planned for the last nine weeks of the school year. Each site includes:

Insert list here.

I've listed the sites below along with the description provided by PBS. Hopefully, you have access to the Internet at your summer home and will be able to take a quick look at the sites.

Lindbergh www.pbs.org/wgbh/amex/lindbergh/filmmore/index.html *At 25, Charles A. Lindbergh—handsome, talented, and brave—arrived in Paris, the first man to fly across the Atlantic. But the struggle to wear the mantle of legend would be a consuming one. Crowds pursued him; reporters invaded his private life. His marriage, travels with his wife, and the kidnapping and murder of their first child were all fodder for the front page.*

Eleanor Roosevelt www.pbs.org/wgbh/amex/eleanor/filmmore/index.html *Eleanor Roosevelt struggled to overcome an unhappy childhood, betrayal in her marriage, a controlling mother-in-law, and gripping depressions—all the while staying true to her passion for social justice. This biography includes rare home movies, contemporary footage, and . . . brings to vibrant life one of the century's most influential women.*

MacArthur www.pbs.org/wgbh/amex/macarthur/filmmore/index.html *No soldier in modern history has been more admired—or more reviled. Douglas MacArthur, liberator of the Philippines, shogun of occupied Japan, mastermind of the Inchon invasion, was an admired national hero when he was suddenly relieved of his command. A portrait of a complex, imposing, and fascinating American general.*

After reviewing the sites, let me know if you are interested in including them in your American History sections. I will arrange with the media center to have an Internet connection and large monitor available for all our sections on Friday of Weeks 5, 7, and 9. ¶ I enjoyed spending two months back on Utah State's campus. I decided to pursue my Master's degree. After summer school, I made a quick trip to the Grand Canyon and Zion National Park. What beautiful country! ¶ I hope you are enjoying the final days of your summer vacation on Long Island.

59C • 10' Editing Business Letters

Letters 1 and 2

Open 58B Letter 1 (*LTR58B1*); address it to the New Jersey and Georgia state presidents with the information shown at the right.

 **Save as:** *LTR59C1* and *LTR59C2*

Letter address:
Ms. Judith Cruz, President
7632 Stanworth Ln.
Princeton, NJ 08540-0032

New Jersey
Capital: Trenton
State Nickname: The Garden State
Admitted to the Union: No. 3 on December 18, 1787

Letter address:
Mr. Warren Courtier, President
1650 Kensington Dr.
Marietta, GA 30066-1375

Georgia
Capital: Atlanta
State Nickname: The Peach State
Admitted to the Union: No. 4 on January 2, 1788

LESSON 18 LEARN/REVIEW SYMBOL KEYS (#, &, +, @, AND ( ))

Objectives:

1. To learn or review control of **#**, **&**, **+**, **@**, and **( )**.
2. To combine **#**, **&**, **+**, **@**, and **( )** with other keys.

18A • 5' Conditioning Practice

Key each line twice SS; then key a 1' writing on line 3; determine *gwam.*

alphabet 1 Zack Gappow saved the job requirement list for the six boys.
figures 2 Jay Par's address is 3856 Ash Place, Houston, TX 77007-2491.
easy 3 I may visit the big chapel in the dismal town on the island.

gwam 1' | 1 | 2 | 3 | 4 | 5 | 6 | 7 | 8 | 9 | 10 | 11 | 12 |

18B • 15' Learn/Review #, &, and +

Key each line twice SS (slowly, then faster); DS between 2-line groups.

Spacing **C • U • E**

- Do not space between # and a figure.
- Space once before and after & used to join names.

The # is the shift of 3. The left middle finger controls it.

The & is the shift of 7. Control it with the right index finger.

The + is to the right of the hyphen. Depress the left shift; strike + with the right little finger.

Learn/Review # (number/pounds) Reach up with the left middle finger.

1 d d #d #d dd ## d#d d#d 3# 3# Shift for # as you enter #33d.
2 Do not space between a number and #: 3# of #633 at $9.35/#.
3 Jerry recorded Check #38 as #39, #39 as #40, and #40 as #41.

Learn/Review & (ampersand) Reach up with the right index finger.

4 j j &j &j jj && j&j j&j 7& 7& Have you written to Poe & Son?
5 Do not space before or after & in initials, e.g., CG&E, B&O.
6 She will interview with Johnson & Smith and Jones & Beckett.

Learn/Review + ("plus" sign) Reach up with the right little finger.

7 ; + ; + ;+; ;+; +;+ +;+ 7 + 7, a + b + c < a + b + d, 12 + 3
8 If you add 3 + 4 + 5 + 6 + 7, you will get 25 for an answer.
9 If you add 2 + 3 + 4 + 5 + 6, you will get 20 for an answer.

18C • 15' Skill Building

1. Review the procedure for setting speed goals (Guided Writing Procedure, p. 22).
2. Use this procedure as you key the unguided and guided writings in **15D** (p. 35).
3. Compare your *gwam* today (the better 2' writing) with your previous rate on these paragraphs.

58C • 8' Letter Editing

Open the file *LTR57B1* (Letter 1 of 57B) and make the changes shown at the right. Include a subject line: **KEYNOTE SPEAKERS**. Leave the rest of the letter as it is.

 **Save as:** *LTR58C*

. . . When you contact them, please ~~share with~~ tell them the theme of our convention and determine what they ~~would~~ propose as an opening or closing session ~~for our convention~~. ~~Of course, we need to be concerned with the budget; please determine what they would charge.~~

¶ As I am sure you are aware, we have a very limited budget. The budget often determines whom we invite. As you discuss fees with them, make sure they are aware that we are an educational institution. Oftentimes, professional presenters are willing to give "educational discounts."

¶ The speaker information will be needed before June 15 for our meeting. . . .

LESSON 59 IMPROVE BUSINESS LETTER FORMATTING

Objectives:

1. To increase proficiency at processing letters.
2. To format two-page business letters.

59A • 5' Conditioning Practice

Key each line twice SS; then key a 1' writing on line 3; determine *gwam*.

alphabet 1 Vicky acquired a sizable check from the next big jewelry company.

fig/sym 2 Item #4562 will cost Anderson & Sons $639.87 (less 10% for cash).

speed 3 Their big social for their neighbor may also be held in the city.

gwam 1' | 1 | 2 | 3 | 4 | 5 | 6 | 7 | 8 | 9 | 10 | 11 | 12 | 13 |

FORMATTING

59B • 35' Business Letters

Key in block format the business letter shown at the right.

Letter 1

Date: **May 28, 200-**

Letter address:

Mr. Jon A. Richardson
283 Mount Pleasant Dr.
Oklahoma City, OK 73110-6661

The letter is from **Martin G. Anderson, Professor**. Supply an appropriate salutation and complimentary closing.

 **Save as:** *LTR59B1*

Thank you for your kind letter. I'm glad you enjoyed my presentation at last week's convention. It is always nice to receive positive feedback from colleagues.

As I mentioned in my presentation, integrating the Internet into my class has made learning history more interesting for students. Having students just read about history from a textbook wasn't getting the results I wanted. Students were bored, and quite frankly so was I. Now, after students read the chapters, I integrate Internet activities with my lectures. I further enliven my class with electronic presentations, newspapers, speakers, and field trips. This combination brings to life for the students the events and individuals that have shaped our history. As a result, student motivation has increased and so has mine.

One of the Internet addresses that you will find particularly beneficial is PBS's "The American Experience" (www.pbs.org/wgbh/amex/whoweare.html). It has been active since November 1995 and has received excellent reviews. The 35 feature sites contain stories of people and events that shaped our country. These sites definitely help bring to life some of the incredible men and women who made this country what it is today.

Check out the site and let me know what you think. I'll look forward to seeing you again at next year's convention.

18D • 15' Learn/Review @, (, and)

Key each line twice SS (slowly, then faster); DS between 2-line groups.

Note:
Use the letter l in lines 4 and 5.

Spacing **C • U • E**

Do not space between a left or right parenthesis and the copy enclosed.

The @ is the shift of 2. Control it with the left ring finger.

The (is the shift of 9 and is controlled by the right ring finger.

The) is the shift of 0; use the right little finger to control it.

Learn/Review @ ("at" sign) Reach up with the left ring finger.

1 s s @s @s ss @@ s@ s@ @ @ The @ is used in e-mail addresses.
2 Change my e-mail address from myers@cs.com to myers@aol.com.
3 I bought 50 shares of F @ $53 1/8 and 100 of USB @ $58 7/16.

Learn/Review ((left parenthesis) Reach up with the right ring finger.

4 l l (l (l ll ((l(l l(l 9(9(Shift for the (as you key (9.
5 As (is the shift of 9, use the l finger to key 9, (, or (9.

Learn/Review) (right parenthesis) Reach up with the right little finger.

6 ; ;);); ;;)) ;); ;); 0) 0) Shift for the) as you key 0).
7 As) is the shift of 0, use the ; finger to key 0,), or 0).

Combine (and)

8 Hints: (1) depress shift; (2) strike key; (3) release both.
9 Tab steps: (1) clear tabs, (2) set stops, and (3) tabulate.

LESSON 19 LEARN/REVIEW SYMBOL KEYS (=, _, *, \, AND [ ])

Objectives:

1. To learn or review control of =, _, \, * , and [ ].
2. To combine =, _, \, * , and [ ] with other keys.

19A • 5' Conditioning Practice

Key each line twice SS; then key a 1' writing on line 3; determine *gwam.*

alphabet 1 Bobby Klun awarded Jayme sixth place for her very high quiz.
figures 2 The rate on May 14 was 12.57 percent; it was 8.96 on May 30.
easy 3 The haughty man was kept busy with a problem with the docks.

gwam 1' | 1 | 2 | 3 | 4 | 5 | 6 | 7 | 8 | 9 | 10 | 11 | 12 |

19B • 15' Skill Building

1. Review the procedure for speed level practice on p. 22 (Guided Writing Procedure).
2. Use this procedure as you key the unguided and guided writings in **16E** (p. 37).
3. Compare your *gwam* today (the better 2' writing) with your previous rate on these paragraphs.

58B • 37'
Business Letters

Key in block format the business letters shown at the right.

Letter 1

Date: **March 14, 200-**

Letter address:

Ms. Gwen English, President
3801 Wedgewood Rd.
Wilmington, DE 19805-9921

The letter is from **Marsha J. Johnson, Display Coordinator**. Supply an appropriate salutation and complimentary closing.

 **Save as:** *LTR58B1*

Letter 2

Revise Letter 1; address it to the Pennsylvania State President:

Mr. Todd Woodward, President
810 Lexington Cr.
State College, PA 16801-3452

The letter should be changed to reflect the Pennsylvania information given below:

Capital: **Harrisburg**

State Nickname: **The Keystone State**

Admitted to the Union: **No. 2 on December 12, 1787**

 **Save as:** *LTR58B2*

Letter 3

Use the Insert Date feature to insert the current date.

Letter address:

Attention Special Collections Director
University of Virginia Library
Alderman, 2 East
Charlottesville, VA 22903-0011

Supply an appropriate salutation and complimentary closing. The letter is from **Gregg G. Elway, Doctoral Candidate**.

 **Save as:** *LTR58B3*

At last year's national convention, our displays highlighted the U.S. Presidents. This year's exhibits will spotlight the states. Each delegation will have a table to display items relating to their state. Exhibits will be in the order the states were admitted to the Union. State presidents are being asked to coordinate the display for their states. If you are not able to coordinate your state exhibit, please arrange for another state officer to do it.

Each display area will include a backdrop, a table, and two chairs for representatives from your state. The table (2' x 6') will be covered with a white cloth. Your state flag will be displayed in front of the backdrop on the far right. The 10-foot wide backdrop will have a cutout of your state, along with the following information.

Delaware
Capital: Dover
State Nickname: The Diamond State
Admitted to the Union: No. 1 on December 7, 1787

Each delegation can decide what they want to exhibit on the table. We hope you will include something to give to the people attending the convention. You know how attendees like freebies. We anticipate about eight hundred people at the convention.

We are excited about the state exhibits and hope that you and your officers will make **Delaware's** display the best one at the convention.

I'm doing my dissertation on the Civil War generals and their families. Of course, it is easy to gather the needed information on U. S. Grant and Robert E. Lee. So much has been written about these icons of the Civil War that the problem is deciding what to include.

However, I'm not having as much luck with some of the other generals. I'm particularly interested in Galusha Pennypacker, who was claimed to be the youngest general of the Civil War, and in John E. Wool, who was claimed to be the oldest Civil War general. I believe Pennypacker was from Pennsylvania and Wool from New York. From the little I've been able to gather, I believe Pennypacker didn't reach voting age until after the war and Wool was on active duty at the age of 77 when the war began.

I'm going to be in Washington, D.C., next month. Would it be worth my time to drive to Charlottesville to have access to the archives at the University of Virginia? Since I have very limited time on this trip, I want to use it in the best way possible. If you don't feel that your library would be the best place to visit, could you suggest where my time might be better spent?

19C • 15'
Learn/Review =, _, and \

Key each line twice SS (slowly, then faster); DS between 2-line groups.

The = is the same key as + and is controlled by the right little finger.

The _ is the shift of the - and is controlled by the right little finger.

The \ is above ENTER. Use the right little finger to control it.

Learn/Review = (equals sign) Reach up with the right little finger.

1 ; ; =; =; ;; == ;= ;= += += The = is used in math equations.
2 Solve the following: 3a = 15, 5b = 30, 3c = 9, and 2d = 16.
3 If a = b + c and c = 5 and a = 9, can you determine what b=?

Learn/Review _ (underline) Reach up with the right little finger.

4 ; ; _; _; ;; __ ;_; ;_; -_ -_ Shift for the _ as you key _-.
5 The _ is used in some Internet locations, e.g., http_data_2.
6 My property has _____ parking spaces and _____ storage bins.

Learn/Review \ (backslash) Reach up with the right little finger.

7 ;; \; \; ;; \\ \;\ \;\ \;\; \;\; Do not shift for the \ key.
8 Use the \ key to map the drive to access \\sps25\deptdir556.
9 Map the drive to \\global128\coxjg$, not \\global127\coxjg$.

19D • 15'
Learn/Review *, [, and]

Key each line twice SS (slowly, then faster); DS between 2-line groups.

The * is the shift of 8. Control it with the right middle finger.

The [is to the right of p. Strike it with the right little finger.

The] is to the right of [and also is controlled by the right little finger.

Learn/Review * (asterisk) Reach up with the right middle finger.

1 k k *k *k *k* *k* * She used the * for a single source note.
2 Put an * before (*Gary, *Jan, and *Jay) to show high scores.
3 Asterisks (*) can be used to replace unprintable words ****.

Learn/Review [(left bracket) Reach up with the right little finger.

4 ; ; [; [; [;[[;[[[[[[a [B [c [D [e [F [g [H [i [J [k [L.
5 [m [N [o [P [q [R [s [T [u [V [w [X [y [Z [1 [2 [3 [4 [5 [6.

Learn/Review] (right bracket) Reach up with the right little finger.

6 ; ;];];];]];]]]]] A] b] C] d] E] f] G] h] I] j]]K]l.
7 M] n] O] p] Q] r] S] t] U] v] W] x] Y] z] 7] 8] 9] 10] 11]].

Combine [and]

8 Brackets ([]) are used in algebra: x = [5(a+b)] - [2(d-e)].
9 Use [ ] within quotations to indicate alterations [changes].

57C • 12'
Timed Writings

1. Key a 3' writing on ¶s 1 and 2 combined; determine *gwam* and number of errors.
2. Key a 1' writing on each ¶; determine *gwam* and number of errors.
3. Key another 3' writing on ¶s 1 and 2 combined; determine *gwam* and number of errors.

A all letters used

	gwam 3'	5'	
A college education is one of the best investments a person will	4	3	50
ever make. Acquiring an education takes an investment of time,	9	5	53
effort, and money. As with all investments, the investor must	13	8	55
realize that a definite degree of risk is involved. However, an	17	10	58
investment in a college education does not bear the degree of risk	22	13	61
that you will find with investments in such things as stocks, land,	26	16	63
or precious metals. Even though there is no guaranteed rate of	30	18	66
return on an education, a person will benefit in a variety of ways.	35	21	69
Usually, those with a college degree can expect to earn higher	39	23	71
salaries during their lifetime than those who do not have a college	44	26	74
degree.	44	26	74
What else can a person who has a college degree expect to gain?	49	29	77
One of the most common answers is that they would have more op-	53	31	79
tions than they would have if they did not have the degree. Most	57	34	82
colleges seek to foster the intellectual, social, personal, and	61	37	85
cultural growth of the student. As a result, those who have a	66	39	87
college degree can anticipate greater opportunities with more op-	70	42	90
tions than those who do not have a degree. For example, job, eco-	74	45	92
nomic, social, as well as travel options are all expanded for col-	79	47	95
lege graduates.	80	48	96

gwam 3' | 1 | 2 | 3 | 4 |
5' | 1 | 2 | 3 |

LESSON 58 FORMAT LETTERS WITH SPECIAL PARTS

Objectives:

1. To increase skill at formatting business letters.
2. To format business letters with special parts.

58A • 5'
Conditioning Practice

Key each line twice SS; then key a 1' writing on line 3; determine *gwam*.

alphabet 1 Bart can relax if he passed the major quiz with a very high mark.

figures 2 Crowds of 48,216 and 53,079 attended the final games of the year.

speed 3 Dianna and the visitor may handle the problems with the city bus.

gwam 1' | 1 | 2 | 3 | 4 | 5 | 6 | 7 | 8 | 9 | 10 | 11 | 12 | 13 |

UNIT 6

LESSONS 20-21

Build Keyboarding Skill

LESSON 20 SKILL BUILDING

Objectives:

1. To improve technique on individual letters.
2. To improve keying speed on 1' and 2' writings.

20A • 5' Conditioning Practice

Key each line twice SS; then key a 1' writing on line 3; determine *gwam*.

alphabet 1 Jack liked reviewing the problems on the tax quiz on Friday.
figures 2 Check #365 for $98.47, dated May 31, 2001, was not endorsed.
easy 3 The auditor may work with vigor to form the bus audit panel.

gwam 1' | 1 | 2 | 3 | 4 | 5 | 6 | 7 | 8 | 9 | 10 | 11 | 12 |

SKILL BUILDING

20B • 18' Technique Mastery: Individual Letters

Key each line twice SS (slowly, then faster); DS between 2-line groups. Take 30" writings on selected lines.

Technique Goals:

- curved, upright fingers
- quick-snap keystrokes
- quiet hands and arms

Emphasize continuity and rhythm with curved, upright fingers.

A 1 Aaron always ate a pancake at Anna's annual breakfast feast.
B 2 Bobby probably fibbed about being a busboy for the ballroom.
C 3 Cody can check with the conceited concierge about the clock.
D 4 The divided squad disturbed Dan Delgado, who departed today.
E 5 Pete was better after he developed three new feet exercises.

F 6 Jeff Keefer officially failed four of five finals on Friday.
G 7 Her granddaughter, Gwen, gave me eight gold eggs for a gift.
H 8 Hans helped her wash half the cheap dishes when he got home.
I 9 I investigate the significance of insignias to institutions.
J 10 Judge James told Jon to adjourn the jury until June or July.

K 11 Knock, khaki, knickknack, kicks, and kayak have multiple Ks.
L 12 Lillian left her landlord in the village to collect dollars.
M 13 The minimum amount may make the mission impossible for many.

gwam 1' | 1 | 2 | 3 | 4 | 5 | 6 | 7 | 8 | 9 | 10 | 11 | 12 |

57B • 33' Business Letters

Key in block format the business letters shown at the right.

Letter 1

Date: **May 23, 200-**

Letter address:

Mr. Jamison Cooper
882 Elderberry Dr.
Fayetteville, NC 28311-0065

The letter is from **Susanne J. Warrens**, who is the **Program Chair**. Supply an appropriate salutation and complimentary closing. Send a copy of the letter to **Marsha Edinburgh, President**.

 **Save as:** *LTR57B1*

Letters 2 and 3

Date (Letter 2): **June 4, 200-**

Date (Letter 3): **June 10, 200-**

Letter address:

Ms. Susanne J. Warrens
Program Chair
8367 Brookstone Ct.
Raleigh, NC 27615-1661

The letters are from **Jamison R. Cooper,** who is a **Program Committee Member**. Supply an appropriate salutation and complimentary closing. Be sure to include an Enclosure notation on each letter.

 **Save as:** *LTR57B2* and *LTR57B3*

Last week at our meeting, you mentioned several individuals you thought would be excellent presenters for the opening and closing sessions of next year's convention. I accept your offer to contact them. When you contact them, please share with them the theme of our convention and determine what they would propose as an opening or closing session for our convention. Of course, we need to be concerned with the budget; please determine the fee they would charge.

The information will be needed before June 15 for our meeting. Your willingness to serve on this committee is greatly appreciated. I'll look forward to seeing you in a couple of weeks.

Here is the information you requested. The presenter's name, the title of the presentation, a brief description of the presentation, and the fees charged are included. I've heard Kai Westmoreland and Steve Harmon present; they were excellent.

Kai Westmoreland—*The Great Depression.* Dr. Westmoreland explores the Great Depression in terms of the stock market crash, the economy, income distribution, and international and federal factors. The suffering that millions of American families endured during the depression is brought to life by Dr. Westmoreland's captivating style of presenting. ($500 plus expenses)

Steve Harmon—*World War II.* What better person to speak about World War II than one of the 156,000 Allied soldiers who crossed the English Channel in the D-Day invasion of France in June 1944? Harmon's presentation depicts the grim realities of a world war through the eyes of a young soldier. ($350 plus expenses)

Members who attended this year's convention recommended two other presenters—Tayt McCauley and Judith Earnhardt. McCauley's presentations deal with the Kennedy years; Earnhardt is well known for her presentations on women's suffrage. I have contacted them, but I've not yet heard from them. As soon as I do, I will get the information to you.

Here is the information on Judith Earnhardt and Tayt McCauley that I said I would send to you. Only a brief sketch on each person is given below; their complete resumes (enclosed) are very impressive. Evidently these two as well as the two I previously sent would be excellent choices for our convention. It's just a matter of deciding which two we want to go with and then contacting them to make sure they are available. We will want to do that as quickly as possible, as I'm sure all four are in high demand.

Judith Earnhardt—*Women's Suffrage.* Dr. Earnhardt explores the women's movement and the impact of such organizations as the American Woman Suffrage Association and the National Woman Suffrage Association. The presentation brings to life the early advocates of women's rights—Elizabeth Cady Stanton, Susan B. Anthony, Lucy Stone, and Julia Ward Howe. ($500 plus expenses)

Tayt McCauley—*The Kennedy Years.* Dr. McCauley recounts the events that touched the nation during the years of John F. Kennedy's administration. Included in the presentation are the Bay of Pigs, the Cuban Missile Crisis, the Moon Landing, Civil Rights, and the Kennedy Assassination. ($450 plus expenses)

If you think we need to identify additional presenters, I will be happy to do so. Please let me know if you want me to take care of anything else before our next meeting.

20C • 12' Handwritten Copy (Script)

Key each quotation twice (slowly, then faster); DS between 2-line groups.

Optional Activity

Can you match the quotation with the writer who is being quoted?

Henry B. Adams
Ralph Waldo Emerson
Thomas Jefferson
John Locke
Katherine Whitehorn
Oscar Wilde

1. "Every man I meet is in some way my superior."
2. "Find out what you like doing best and get someone to pay you for doing it."
3. "I can resist everything except temptation."
4. "I have always thought the actions of men the best interpreters of their thoughts."
5. "A teacher affects eternity; he can never tell, where his influence stops."
6. "I'm a great believer in luck, and I find the harder I work the more I have of it."

SKILL BUILDING

20D • 15' Speed Building: Guided Writing

1. Key one 1' unguided and two 1' guided writings on each ¶; determine *gwam*.
2. Key two 2' unguided writings on ¶s 1–2 combined; determine *gwam*.

Quarter-Minute Checkpoints				
gwam	1/4'	1/2'	3/4'	1'
20	5	10	15	20
24	6	12	18	24
28	7	14	21	28
32	8	16	24	32
36	9	18	27	36
40	10	20	30	40
44	11	22	33	44
48	12	24	36	48
52	13	26	39	52
56	14	28	42	56

A all letters used — gwam 2'

To move to the next level of word processing power, you must 6
now demonstrate certain abilities. First, you must show that you 13
can key with good technique, a modest level of speed, and a limit 19
on errors. Next, you must properly apply the basic rules of lan- 26
guage use. Finally, you must arrange basic documents properly. 32

If you believe you have already learned enough, think of the 38
future. Many jobs today require a higher level of keying skill 45
than you have acquired so far. Also realize that several styles 51
of letters, reports, and tables are in very common use today. As 58
a result, would you not benefit from another semester of training? 64

gwam 2' | 1 | 2 | 3 | 4 | 5 | 6 |

56C • 30' Business Letters

Letter 1

Format and key the text at the right as a business letter in block format. Use the USPS letter address style. Date the letter **February 20, 200-** and supply an appropriate salutation and complimentary closing. The letter is from **William P. Shea**. Don't forget the Enclosure notation.

Letter address:

MR AND MRS ERIC RUSSELL
PO BOX 215
MOORCROFT WY 82721-2152

 **Save as:** *LTR56C1*

Wyoming women were the first women in the United States to have the right to vote (1869). Ester Morris of South Pass City became the first woman judge in 1870. Wyoming was the first state to elect a woman to state office when Estelle Reel was elected State Superintendent of Public Instruction in 1894. Nellie Tayloe Ross became the first female governor in the United States when she was elected governor of Wyoming in 1925.

It is time to honor women such as these for the roles they played in shaping Wyoming and U.S. history. A Wyoming Women's Historical Museum is being planned. With your help, the museum can become a reality.

Our community would benefit from the increased tourist activity. Thousands of tourists visit the nation's first national monument, Devil's Tower, each year. Since Moorcroft is only 30 miles from Devil's Tower, a museum would draw many of them to our city as they travel to and from the Tower.

National and state funds for the project are being solicited; however, additional funding from the private sector will be required. Please look over the enclosed brochure and join the Wyoming Women's Historical Museum Foundation by making a contribution.

Letter 2

Format and key the text at the right as a business letter in block format.

 **Save as:** *LTR56C2*

Letter 3

Format and key the letter in 56B as a personal-business letter in block format.

 **Save as:** *LTR56C3*

August 10, 200- | Ms. Dorothy Shepard | P.O. Box 275 | Moorcroft, WY 82721-2342

Dear Ms. Shepard

GROUNDBREAKING CEREMONY

The planning committee is thrilled to announce the groundbreaking ceremony for the **Wyoming Women's Historical Museum:** Saturday, August 25.

As one who played an important role in reaching this milestone, you are invited to a luncheon before the ceremony. The luncheon will be held at the Mead House at 11:30. The groundbreaking will begin at 1:30.

The museum will be a source of great pride for Wyoming residents. Visitors will be reminded of the part Wyoming women played in the history of the state and nation.

Sincerely | William P. Shea | Committee Chair | xx

LESSON 57 FORMAT BUSINESS LETTERS

Objectives:

1. To format business letters.
2. To increase straight-copy keying skill.

57A • 5' Conditioning Practice

Key each line twice SS; then key a 1' writing on line 3; determine *gwam*.

alphabet 1 A poor joke by the cowardly young boxers left David quite amazed.

figures 2 Pages 386-457 in Chapters 29 and 30 will be reviewed on April 12.

speed 3 I own both the antique bottle and the enamel bottle on the shelf.

gwam 1' | 1 | 2 | 3 | 4 | 5 | 6 | 7 | 8 | 9 | 10 | 11 | 12 | 13 |

LESSON 21 SKILL BUILDING

Objectives:

1. To improve technique on individual letters.
2. To improve keying speed on 1' and 2' writings.

21A • 5' Conditioning Practice

Key each line twice SS; then key a 1' writing on line 3; determine *gwam.*

alphabet 1 Wayne gave Zelda exact requirements for taking the pulp job.

fig/sym 2 Add tax of 5.5% to Sales Slip #86-03 for a total of $142.79.

easy 3 The six girls at the dock may blame the man with their keys.

gwam 1' | 1 | 2 | 3 | 4 | 5 | 6 | 7 | 8 | 9 | 10 | 11 | 12 |

21B • 18' Technique Mastery: Individual Letters

Key each line twice SS (slowly, then faster); DS between 2-line groups. Take 30" writings on selected lines.

Technique Goals:

- curved, upright fingers
- quick-snap keystrokes
- quiet hands and arms

Emphasize continuity and rhythm with curved, upright fingers.

N 1 Ann wants Nathan to know when negotiations begin and finish.

O 2 Robert bought an overcoat to go to the open house on Monday.

P 3 Philippi purchased a pepper plant from that pompous peddler.

Q 4 Quincy quickly questioned the adequacy of the quirky quotes.

R 5 Our receiver tried to recover after arm surgery on Thursday.

S 6 Russ said it seems senseless to suggest this to his sisters.

T 7 Tabetha trusted Tim not to tinker with the next time report.

U 8 She was unusually subdued upon returning to our summerhouse.

V 9 Vivian vacated the vast village with five vivacious vandals.

W 10 Warren will work two weeks on woodwork with the wise owners.

X 11 Six tax experts expect to expand the six extra export taxes.

Y 12 Yes, by year's end Jayme may be ready to pay you your money.

Z 13 Zelda quizzed Zack on the zoology quiz in the sizzling heat.

gwam 1' | 1 | 2 | 3 | 4 | 5 | 6 | 7 | 8 | 9 | 10 | 11 | 12 |

21C • 5' Skill Building

Key each line twice SS; DS between 2-line groups.

Space Bar

1 day son new map cop let kite just the quit year bay vote not

2 She may see me next week to talk about a party for the team.

Word response

3 me dye may bit pen pan cow sir doe form lamb lake busy their

4 The doorman kept the big bushel of corn for the eight girls.

Double letters

5 Neillsville berry dollar trees wheels sheep tomorrow village

6 All three of the village cottonwood trees had green ribbons.

gwam 1' | 1 | 2 | 3 | 4 | 5 | 6 | 7 | 8 | 9 | 10 | 11 | 12 |

LANGUAGE SKILLS

55C • 8'
Language Skills: Word Choice

1. Study the spelling/definitions of these words.
2. For each set of sentences, key the Learn line; then the Apply lines. Choose the correct word in parentheses.
3. Check your work; rekey lines containing word-choice errors.

Save as: *CHOICE55C*

to (prep/adj) used to indicate action, relation, distance, direction
too (adv) besides; also; to excessive degree
two (pron/adj) one plus one in number

cents (n) specified portion of a dollar
sense (n/vb) meaning intended or conveyed; perceive by sense organs; ability to judge
since (adv/conj) after a definite time in the past; in view of the fact; because

Learn 1 If you are going **to** either of the **two** plays, I would like to go **too**.
Apply 2 (To, Too, Two) of the students are going (to, too, two) play on the team.
Apply 3 (To, Too, Two) much practice made the (to, too, two) players (to, too, two) tired.

Learn 1 **Since** I changed the dollars and **cents** columns, the figures make **sense**.
Apply 2 (Cents, Sense, Since) you bought the stock, it has gone up 77 (cents, sense, since).
Apply 3 The whole thing just doesn't make (cents, sense, since) to me.

LESSON 56 FORMAT BUSINESS LETTERS

Objectives:
1. To learn to format business letters.
2. To increase proficiency in keying opening and closing lines of letters.

56A • 5'
Conditioning Practice

Key each line twice SS; then key a 1' writing on line 3; determine *gwam*.

alphabet 1 Zack just saw five prime quail and a big fox by the old railroad.
figures 2 Only 168 of the 573 seniors had voted by 12:40 on Friday, May 29.
speed 3 The heir to the endowment may work on the problems with the firm.
gwam 1' | 1 | 2 | 3 | 4 | 5 | 6 | 7 | 8 | 9 | 10 | 11 | 12 | 13 |

56B • 15'
Drill: Personal-Business Letter

1. Take a 3' writing on the letter to determine *gwam*.
2. Key two 1' writings on opening lines through first ¶ of letter. If you finish before time is called, QS and start over. Try to key four more words on the second writing.
3. Key two 1' writings on ¶ 3 through closing lines. If you finish before time is called, QS and start ¶ 3 again. Try to key four more words on the second writing.
4. Key another 3' writing on the letter. Try to increase *gwam* by 4–8 words over your rate in Step 1.

words

622 Main St. | Moorcroft, WY 82721-7514 | January 5, 200- 11

Ms. Dorothy Shepard | P.O. Box 275 | Moorcroft, WY 82721-2342 22

Dear Ms. Shepard 26

Are you interested in serving on a planning committee for a women's 39
historical museum in Wyoming? The state's nickname (Equality State) 53
stems from the fact that Wyoming women were the first women in the 67
U.S. to achieve voting rights (1869). 74

Since then, many women have played an important part in shaping 87
the history of Wyoming. Are you aware that the first woman governor 101
in the U.S. came from Wyoming? Nellie Tayloe Ross became governor 114
of Wyoming in 1925. 119

Let's build a museum to recognize these women--a place for people to 132
reflect on events of the past and contemplate the future. I will call you 147
next week to see if you are willing to serve on the committee. 160

Sincerely | William P. Shea 165

21D • 10'
Handwritten Copy (Script)

Key each quotation twice (slowly, then faster); DS between 2-line groups.

Optional Activity

Can you match the quotation with the person who is being quoted?

Helen Keller
Ralph Waldo Emerson
Adlai Stevenson
Henry David Thoreau
Margaret Thatcher
Oscar Wilde

1. "No man is rich enough to buy back his past."

* * * * *

2. "Nothing great was ever achieved without enthusiasm."

* * * * *

3. "Keep your face to the sunshine and you cannot see the shadow."

* * * * *

4. "It is the greatest of all advantages to enjoy no advantage at all."

* * * * *

5. "If you want something said, ask a man; if you want something done, ask a woman."

* * * * *

6. "Man does not live by words alone, despite the fact that sometimes he has to eat them."

SKILL BUILDING

21E • 12'
Speed Building

1. Key one 1' unguided and two 1' guided writings on each ¶.
2. Key two 2' unguided writings on ¶s 1–2 combined; determine *gwam*.

Quarter-Minute Checkpoints				
gwam	1/4'	1/2'	3/4'	1'
20	5	10	15	20
24	6	12	18	24
28	7	14	21	28
32	8	16	24	32
36	9	18	27	36
40	10	20	30	40
44	11	22	33	44
48	12	24	36	48
52	13	26	39	52
56	14	28	42	56

all letters used — gwam 2'

As you build your keying power, the number of errors you 6
make is not very important because most of the errors are 12
accidental and incidental. Realize, however, that documents 18
are expected to be without flaw. A letter, report, or table 24
that contains flaws is not usable until it is corrected. So 30
find and correct all errors. 33

The best time to detect and correct errors is immediately 38
after you finish keying the copy. Therefore, just before you 45
print or close a document, proofread and correct any errors you 51
have made. Learn to proofread carefully and to correct all 57
errors quickly. To do the latter, know ways to move the 63
pointer and to select copy. 65

gwam 2' | 1 | 2 | 3 | 4 | 5 | 6 |

LESSON 55 REVIEW PERSONAL-BUSINESS LETTER FORMAT

Objectives:

1. To review personal-business letter format.
2. To improve language skills.

55A • 5' Conditioning Practice

Key each line twice SS; then key a 1' writing on line 3; determine *gwam*.

alphabet 1 A man in the park saw a fat lizard quickly devour six juicy bugs.

figures 2 Please revise pages 360, 492, and 578 for the August 21 deadline.

speed 3 Eight girls may sit with the maid in the wheelchair by the docks.

gwam 1' | 1 | 2 | 3 | 4 | 5 | 6 | 7 | 8 | 9 | 10 | 11 | 12 | 13 |

FORMATTING

55B • 37' Personal-Business Letters

Letter 1

Review the model personal-business letter on p. 83. Key in block format the letter shown at the right. Use the return address, date, and letter address shown below. Supply an appropriate salutation and complimentary closing. The letter is from **Suzanne E. Salmon, History Student**. Include a blind copy notation to your instructor.

Return address and date:

1116 Tiffany St.
Bronx, NY 10459-2276
May 3, 200-

Letter address:

Mr. Mitchell R. Clevenger
325 Manhattan Ave.
New York, NY 10025-3827

 **Save as:** *LTR55B1*

For one of the assignments in my U.S. history class, I have to interview a person who is knowledgeable about an event included in our history book. It didn't take long for me to decide whom I was going to contact.

Who better to talk about ***Operation Desert Storm*** than a newsperson assigned to the region to cover the news during this period? Would you be willing to meet with me for about an hour to discuss the Persian Gulf War? I would like to learn more about the following topics:

- The events that led up to the confrontation
- The confrontation
- The impact on the people of Iraq
- The impact on the environment in the region
- The role of General Colin Powell, Chairman of the Joint Chiefs of Staff
- The role of General Norman Schwarzkopf, U.S. Field Commander

Of course, if there are other things you would like to discuss to help me describe this event to the class, I would appreciate your sharing those topics with me also. I will call you next week to see if you will be available to meet with me.

Letter 2

Key in block format the letter shown at the right. Use the return address and date given below. Supply an appropriate complimentary closing for the letter from **Mitchell Clevenger, Reporter**.

Return address and date:

325 Manhattan Ave.
New York, NY 10025-3827
May 7, 200-

 **Save as:** *LTR55B2*

Ms. Suzanne E. Salmon | 1116 Tiffany St. | Bronx, NY 10459-2276 | Dear Ms. Salmon

I would be more than happy to meet with you to discuss my experiences during my assignment in the Persian Gulf region. It was one of the most, if not the most, exciting assignments I've worked on. The night the attack on Baghdad began will be with me for the rest of my life.

Also I will share with you the events in Kuwait that precipitated the war and the war's impact on the Kurd and Shi'ite refugees.

Please call me at 212-183-8211 so we can arrange a time and location to meet. I'm looking forward to meeting you.

ACTIVITY 1

Number Expression

1. Key lines 1–10 at the right, expressing numbers correctly (words or figures).
2. Check the accuracy of your work with the instructor; correct any errors you made.
3. Note the rule number at the left of each sentence in which you made a number expression error.
4. Using the rules below the sentences and on p. 50, identify the rule(s) you need to review/practice.
5. **Read**: Study each rule.
6. **Learn**: Key the Learn line(s) beneath it, noting how the rule is applied.
7. **Apply**: Key the Apply line(s), expressing the numbers correctly.

 **Save as:** *CS3-ACT1*

Proofread & Correct

Rules

1 1 20 members have already voted, but 15 have yet to do so.

2 2 Only twelve of the hikers are here; six have not returned.

3 3 Do you know if the eight fifteen Klondike flight is on time?

3,4 4 We should be at 1 Brooks Road no later than eleven thirty a.m.

5 5 This oriental carpet measures eight ft. by 10 ft.

5 6 The carton is two ft. square and weighs six lbs. eight oz.

6 7 Have you read pages 45 to 62 of Chapter two that he assigned?

7 8 She usually rides the bus from 6th Street to 1st Avenue.

8 9 Nearly 1/2 of the team is here; that is about 15.

8 10 A late fee of over 15 percent is charged after the 30th day.

Number Expression

Rule 1: Spell a number that begins a sentence even when other numbers in the sentence are shown in figures.

Learn 1 Twelve of the new shrubs have died; 48 are doing quite well.
Apply 2 14 members have paid their dues, but 89 have not done so.

Rule 2: Use figures for numbers above ten, and for numbers from one to ten when they are used with numbers above ten.

Learn 3 She ordered 8 word processors, 14 computers, and 4 printers.
Apply 4 Did he say they need ten or 14 sets of Z18 and Z19 diskettes?

Rule 3: Use figures to express date and time (unless followed by o'clock).

Learn 5 He will arrive on Paygo Flight 418 at 9:48 a.m. on March 14.
Apply 6 Candidates must be in Ivy Hall at eight forty a.m. on May one.

Rule 4: Use figures for house numbers except house number One.

Learn 7 My home is at 8 Vernon Drive; my office, at One Weber Plaza.
Apply 8 The Nelsons moved from 4059 Pyle Avenue to 1 Maple Circle.

Rule 5: Use figures to express measures and weights.

Learn 9 Glenda Redford is 5 ft. 4 in. tall and weighs 118 lbs. 9 oz.
Apply 10 This carton measures one ft. by nine in. and weighs five lbs.

(continued on next page)

UNIT 17

LESSONS 55-59

Improving Letter Formatting Skills

Format Guides: Business Letter, Block Style

GREGG G. ELWAY
18950 Bonanza Way • Gaithersburg, MD 20879-1211
301-555-1256 • elway@aol.com

May 15, 200-

Attention Special Collections Director
University of Virginia Library
Alderman, 2 East
Charlottesville, VA 22903-0011

Ladies and Gentlemen

I'm doing my dissertation on the Civil War generals and their families. Of course, it is easy to gather the needed information on U. S. Grant and Robert E. Lee. So much has been written about these icons of the Civil War that the problem is deciding on what to include.

However, I'm not having as much luck with some of the other generals. I'm particularly interested in Galusha Pennypacker who was claimed to be the youngest general of the Civil War and in John E. Wool who was claimed to be the oldest general of the Civil War. I believe Pennypacker was from Pennsylvania and Wool from New York. From what little I've been able to gather, I believe Penneypacker didn't reach voting age until after the war and Wool was on active duty at the age of 77 when the war began.

I'm going to be in Washington, D.C., next month. Would it be worth my time to drive to Charlottesville to have access to the archives at the University of Virginia? Since I have very limited time on this trip, I want to use it in the best way possible. If you don't feel that your library would be the best place to visit, could you offer a suggestion as to where my time might be better spent?

Sincerely

Gregg G. Elway
Doctoral Candidate

xx

Business Letter with Attention Line

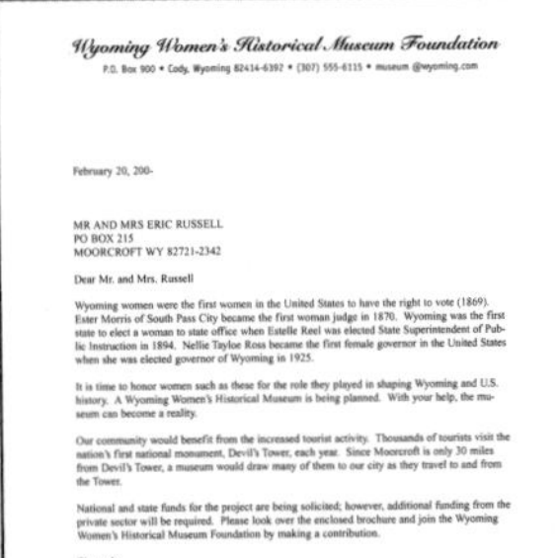

Wyoming Women's Historical Museum Foundation
P.O. Box 900 • Cody, Wyoming 82414-6397 • (307) 555-6115 • museum @wyoming.com

February 20, 200-

MR AND MRS ERIC RUSSELL
PO BOX 215
MOORCROFT WY 82721-2342

Dear Mr. and Mrs. Russell

Wyoming women were the first women in the United States to have the right to vote (1869). Ester Morris of South Pass City became the first woman judge in 1870. Wyoming was the first state to elect a woman to state office when Estelle Reel was elected State Superintendent of Public Instruction in 1894. Nellie Tayloe Ross became the first female governor in the United States when she was elected governor of Wyoming in 1925.

It is time to honor women such as these for the role they played in shaping Wyoming and U.S. history. A Wyoming Women's Historical Museum is being planned. With your help, the museum can become a reality.

Our community would benefit from the increased tourist activity. Thousands of tourists visit the nation's first national monument, Devil's Tower, each year. Since Moorcroft is only 30 miles from Devil's Tower, a museum would draw many of them to our city as they travel to and from the Tower.

National and state funds for the project are being solicited; however, additional funding from the private sector will be required. Please look over the enclosed brochure and join the Wyoming Women's Historical Museum Foundation by making a contribution.

Sincerely

Business Letter with Address in USPS Style

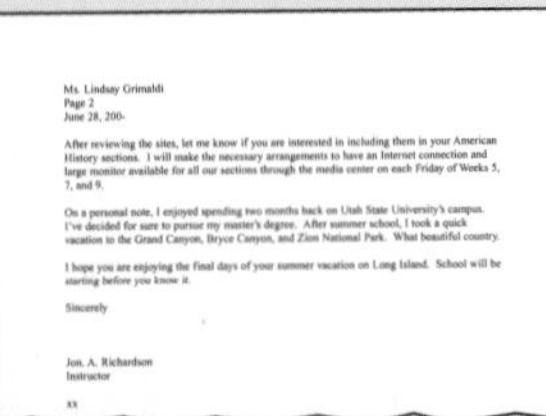

Ms. Lindsay Grimaldi
Page 2
June 28, 200-

After reviewing the sites, let me know if you are interested in including them in your American History sections. I will make the necessary arrangements to have an Internet connection and large monitor available for all our sections through the media center on each Friday of Weeks 5, 7, and 9.

On a personal note, I enjoyed spending two months back on Utah State University's campus. I've decided for sure to pursue my master's degree. After summer school, I took a quick vacation to the Grand Canyon, Bryce Canyon, and Zion National Park. What beautiful country.

I hope you are enjoying the final days of your summer vacation on Long Island. School will be starting before you know it.

Sincerely

Jon. A. Richardson
Instructor

xx

Business Letter (Page 2) with Second-Page Heading

In Unit 9 you learned to format personal-business letters. In this unit you will learn to format business letters. The only difference between the two is that a business letter is almost always printed on letterhead that includes the return address. Therefore, the return address does not need to be keyed.

Special Parts of Business Letters

In addition to the basic letter parts, business letters may include the special letter parts described below.

Attention line. An attention line should be used only when the writer does not know the name of the person who should receive the letter. For example, if a writer wants a letter to go to the director of special collections of a library but doesn't know the name of that person, *Attention Special Collections Director* or *Attention Director of Special Collections* could be used. When an attention line is used in a letter addressed to a company, key it as the first line of the letter and envelope addresses. When using an attention line, the correct salutation is *Ladies and Gentlemen*.

Subject line. The subject line specifies the topic discussed in the letter. Key the subject line in ALL CAPS, a DS below the salutation.

Reference initials. If someone other than the originator of the letter keys it, key the keyboard operator's initials in lowercase letters at the left margin a DS below the writer's name, title, or department.

Attachment/Enclosure notation. If another document is clipped or stapled to a letter, the word "Attachment" is keyed at the left margin a DS below the reference initials. If another document is included but not attached, the word "Enclosure" is used. If reference initials are not used, *Attachment* or *Enclosure* is keyed a DS below the writer's name.

Copy notation. A copy notation indicates that a copy of a letter is being sent to someone other than the addressee. Use "c" followed by the name of the person(s) to receive a copy. Place a copy notation a DS below the enclosure notation or the reference initials if there is no enclosure:

```
c Hector Ramirez
  Ursula O'Donohue
```

Blind copy notation. When a copy of a letter is to be sent to someone without disclosing to the addressee of the letter, a blind copy (bc) notation is used. When used, *bc* and the name of the person receiving the blind copy are keyed at the left margin a DS below the last letter part on all copies of the letter *except* the original.

```
bc Arlyn Hunter
   Miguel Rodriguez
```

USPS Letter Address Style

The letter address for any letter format may be keyed in uppercase and lowercase letters, or it may be keyed in ALL CAPS with no punctuation (USPS style). See illustration at left.

Second-Page Heading

Occasionally, a letter (or memo) will be longer than one page. Only p. 1 is keyed on letterhead; all additional pages should be keyed on plain paper with a second-page heading. Key the heading 1" from the top of the page SS in block format at the left margin. Include the name of the addressee, the page number, and the date. DS below the date before continuing the letter. See illustration at left.

Rule 6: Use figures for numbers following nouns.

Learn 11 Review Rules 1 to 18 in Chapter 5, pages 149 and 150, today.
Apply 12 Case 1849 is reviewed in Volume five, pages nine and ten.

Rule 7: Spell (and capitalize) names of small-numbered streets (ten and under).

Learn 13 I walked several blocks along Third Avenue to 54th Street.
Learn 14 At 7th Street she took a taxi to his home on 43d Avenue.

Rule 8: Spell indefinite numbers.

Learn 15 Joe owns one acre of Parcel A; that is almost fifty percent.
Learn 16 Nearly seventy members voted; that is nearly a fourth.
Apply 17 Over 20 percent of the students are out with the flu.
Apply 18 Just under 1/2 of the voters cast ballots for the issue.

ACTIVITY 2

Reading

1. Open the file *CD-CS3READ.*
2. Read the document; close the file.
3. Key answers to the questions at the right.
4. Check the accuracy of your work with the instructor; correct any errors you made.

Save as: *CS3-ACT2*

1. Will at least one member of the cast not return for the next season?
2. Has a studio been contracted to produce the show for next season?
3. Does each cast member earn the same amount per episode?
4. Is the television show a news magazine or comedy?
5. How many seasons has the show been aired, not counting next season?
6. Do all cast members' contracts expire at the same time?
7. What did the cast do three years ago to get raises?

ACTIVITY 3

Composing

1. Read carefully the two creeds (mottos) at the right.
2. Choose one as a topic for a short composition, and make notes of what the creed means to you.
3. Compose/key one or two paragraphs indicating what the creed means to you and why you believe it would be (or would not be) a good motto for your own behavior.

Save as: *CS3-ACT3*

The following creeds were written by Edward Everett Hale:

Harry Wadsworth Club

I am only one,
But still I am one.
I cannot do everything
But I can still do something;
And because I cannot do everything,
I will not refuse to do the something
that I can do.

Lend-a-Hand Society

To look up and not down,
To look forward and not back,
To look out and not in, and
To lend a hand.

ACTIVITY 3

Macro

1. Read the copy at the right. Learn to use the Macro feature.
2. Define a macro for ***The state capital of***.
3. Key each sentence at the right, inserting the macro for the repeated text.

 **Save as:** *WP7ACT3*

The **Macro** feature of a software package allows the operator to save (record) keystrokes and/or commands for retrieval (playback) later. A macro can be as simple as a few words, such as a company name, or as complex as the commands to create a table that will be used over and over. By eliminating repetitive keying and formatting, a macro saves time.

1. **The state capital of** Alaska is Juneau.
2. **The state capital of** Arizona is Phoenix.
3. **The state capital of** Colorado is Denver.
4. **The state capital of** Delaware is Dover.
5. **The state capital of** Florida is Tallahassee.
6. **The state capital of** Hawaii is Honolulu.

ACTIVITY 4

Reinforce Use of Macro

1. Use the Macro feature to record the table shell at the right.
2. In a new file, use the Macro feature to insert (playback) the table shell. In the shell, key the data shown in Table 1.

Note:
Striking the TAB key after keying the first data row will automatically insert a new row below it.

 **Save as:** *WP7ACT4-1*

3. In a new file, use the Macro feature to insert a table shell. Key the data for Table 2 at the right.

 **Save as:** *WP7ACT4-2*

4. In a new file, use the Macro feature to insert a table shell. Key the data for Table 3 at the right.

 **Save as:** *WP7ACT4-3*

Table Shell

KNOW YOUR STATES		
State	Capital	Flower

Table 1

KNOW YOUR STATES		
State	Capital	Flower
Arkansas	Little Rock	Apple Blossom
Louisiana	Baton Rouge	Magnolia
New Hampshire	Concord	Purple Lilac
New York	Albany	Rose

Table 2

KNOW YOUR STATES		
State	Capital	Flower
California	Sacramento	Golden Poppy
Iowa	Des Moines	Wild Rose
New Jersey	Trenton	Purple Violet
Texas	Austin	Bluebonnet

Table 3

KNOW YOUR STATES		
State	Capital	Flower
Connecticut	Hartford	Mountain Laurel
Georgia	Atlanta	Cherokee Rose
North Carolina	Raleigh	Dogwood
Oregon	Salem	Oregon Grape

ACTIVITIES 1-3

Learn Numeric Keypad Operation

ACTIVITY 1 NUMERIC KEYPAD KEYS: 4/5/6/0

Objectives:

1. To learn key techniques for **4**, **5**, **6**, and **0**.
2. To key these home-key numbers with speed and ease.

1A • 5' Numeric Keypad Operating Position

1. Position yourself in front of the keyboard—body erect, both feet on floor.
2. Place this book for easy reading—at right of keyboard or directly behind it.

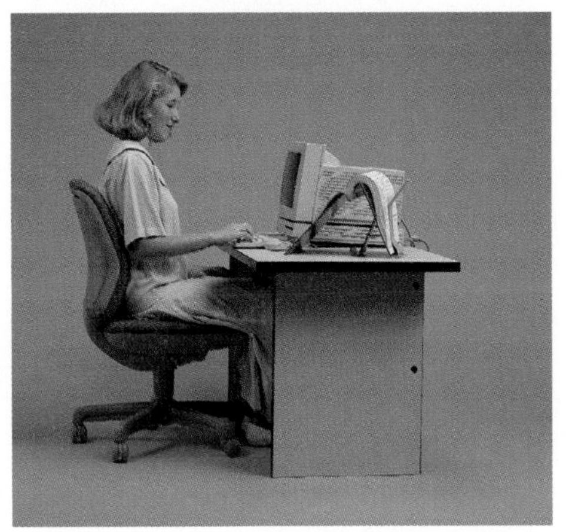

Input copy at right of (or behind) keypad

Proper position at keypad

1B • 5' Home-Key Position

Curve the fingers of the right hand and place them on the keypad:

- index finger on 4
- middle finger on 5
- ring finger on 6
- thumb on 0

Note:
To use the keypad, the Num (number) Lock must be activated.

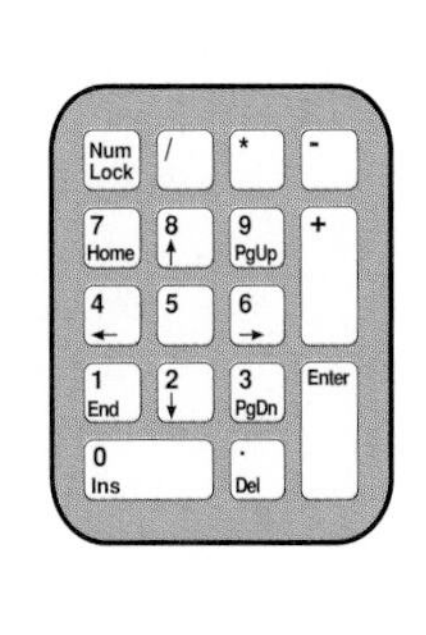

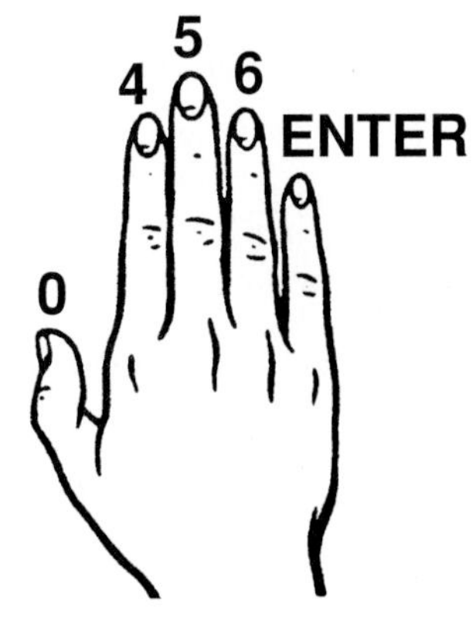

WORD PROCESSING 7

ACTIVITY 1

Insert Date, AutoComplete

1. Read the copy at the right.
2. Learn the Insert Date and Automatic Completion (AutoComplete) features of your wp software.
3. Key the information at the right using the Insert Date and AutoComplete features as indicated. If AutoComplete is not available with your software, use the Insert Date feature in place of it.

 **Save as:** *WP7ACT1*

Use the **Insert Date** feature to enter the date into a document automatically. Some software has an Update Automatically option along with Insert Date. When the Update option is used, the date is inserted as a date *field.* Each time the document is opened or printed, the current date replaces the previous date. The date on your computer must be current to insert the correct date in a document.

Some software provides an **Automatic Completion (AutoComplete)** feature, which also inserts the date automatically. When you start keying the month, AutoComplete *recognizes* the word and shows it in a tip box above the insertion point. By pressing the ENTER key, you enter the remainder of the month automatically, without keying it. When you press the Space Bar, the tip box shows the complete date. Striking the ENTER key enters the date.

Part I

<Insert Date>

Mr. Sean McCarthy
633 Country Club Dr.
Largo, FL 34641-5639

<Insert hard page break>

Part II

<Insert Date Field, Update Automatically>

Ms. Brittany Garcia
2130 Mt. Pleasant Dr.
Bridgeport, CT 06611-2301

<Insert hard page break>

Part III

1. Today is <AutoComplete>.
2. Your balance as of <Insert Date Field, Update Automatically> is $42.83.
3. I received your check today, <Insert Date>.
4. You will need to make sure that today's date, <Insert Date Field, Update Automatically>, is included on the form.

ACTIVITY 2

Navigate a Document

1. Read the copy at the right.
2. Learn to move the insertion point using Home, End, PageUp, PageDown, and Ctrl + arrow keys.
3. Key Sentence 1; edit as instructed in Sentences 2, 3, and 4, using *only* the insertion point move keys to navigate.

 **Save as:** *WP7ACT2*

The **Home**, **End**, **PageUp**, and **PageDown** keys can be used to *navigate* (move the insertion point quickly from one location to another) in a document.

The **CTRL** key in combination with the arrow keys can also be used to move the insertion point to various locations.

1. Key the following sentence.

   The basketball game is on Friday.

2. Make the following changes, using the insertion point move keys to navigate.

   The ^next *basketball game is on Friday,* ^February 20.

3. Make these additional changes, using the insertion point move keys to navigate.

   The next ^varsity *basketball game is on Friday, February 20,* at 7 p.m.

4. Make these changes.

   The next varsity basketball game is on ~~*Friday,*~~ ^Saturday, *February 20, at 7 p.m.* against Sundance.

1C • 40'
New Keys: 4, 5, 6, and 0 (Home Keys)

Use the calculator accessory on your computer to complete the drills at the right.

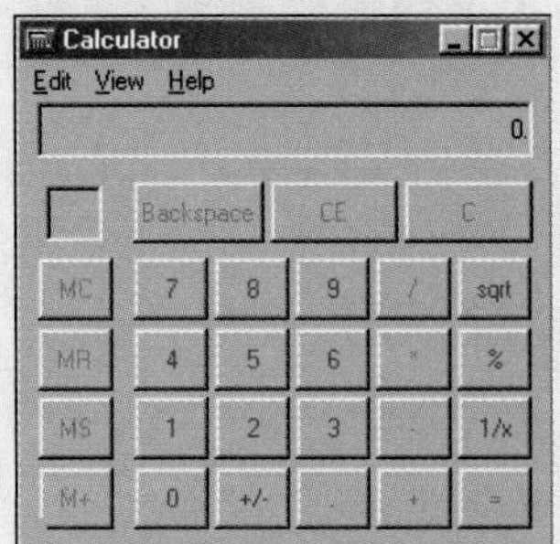

1. Curve the fingers of your right hand; place them upright on the keypad home keys:
   - index finger on 4
   - middle finger on 5
   - ring finger on 6
   - thumb on 0
2. Key/enter each number: Key the number and enter by pressing the + key with the little finger of the right hand.
3. After entering each number in the column, verify your answer with the answer shown below the column.
4. Press *ESC* on the main keyboard to clear the calculator; then enter numbers in the next column.
5. Repeat Steps 2–4 for Drills 1–6 to increase your input rate.

Technique C · U · E

Strike each key with a quick, sharp stroke with the *tip* of the finger; release the key quickly. Keep the fingers curved and upright, the wrist low, relaxed, and steady.

Strike *0* with the side of the right thumb, similar to the way you strike the Space Bar.

Drill 1

A	B	C	D	E	F
4	5	6	4	5	6
4	5	6	4	5	6
8	10	12	8	10	12

Drill 2

A	B	C	D	E	F
44	55	66	44	55	66
44	55	66	44	55	66
88	110	132	88	110	132

Drill 3

A	B	C	D	E	F
44	45	54	44	55	66
55	56	46	45	54	65
66	64	65	46	56	64
165	165	165	135	165	195

Drill 4

A	B	C	D	E	F
40	50	60	400	500	600
50	60	40	506	604	405
60	40	50	650	460	504
150	150	150	1,556	1,564	1,509

Drill 5

A	B	C	D	E	F
45	404	404	406	450	650
55	405	505	506	540	560
65	406	606	606	405	605
165	1,215	1,515	1,518	1,395	1,815

Drill 6

A	B	C	D	E	F
40	606	444	554	646	456
50	505	445	555	656	654
60	404	446	556	666	504
150	1,515	1,335	1,665	1,968	1,614

Rule 6: Use a comma to set off nonrestrictive clauses (not necessary to the meaning of the sentence); however, do not use commas to set off restrictive clauses (necessary to the meaning of the sentence).

Learn 17 The manuscript, which I prepared, needs to be revised.
Learn 18 The manuscript that presents banking alternatives is complete.
Apply 19 The movie which won top awards dealt with human rights.
Apply 20 The student who scores highest on the exam will win the award.

ACTIVITY 2

Reading

1. Open the file *CD-CS7READ* and read the document carefully.
2. Close the file.
3. Key the answers to the questions at the right.
4. Check the accuracy of your work with the instructor; correct any errors you made.

 **Save as:** *CS7-ACT2*

1. What was the final score of yesterday's soccer match?
2. Was the winning goal scored in the first or second half?
3. Will last year's City League champion be playing in this year's championship match?
4. Will the top-ranked team in the state be playing in this year's championship match?
5. Will the top-ranked team in the city be playing in the championship match?
6. Is the championship game to be played during the day or in the evening?
7. Has one or both of the teams playing in the championship match won a City League championship before?

ACTIVITY 3

Composing

1. Key the paragraph, correcting the word-choice errors it contains. (Every line contains at least one error; some lines contain two or more errors.)
2. Check the accuracy of your work with the instructor; correct any errors you made.
3. Compose a second paragraph to accomplish these goals:
   - Define what *respect* means to you.
   - Identify kinds of behavior that help one earn respect.
   - Identify kinds of behavior that cause the loss of respect.

 **Save as:** *CS7-ACT3*

That all individuals want others too respect them is not surprising. What is surprising is that sum people think their do respect even when there own behavior has been unacceptable or even illegal. Key two the issue is that we respect others *because* of certain behavior, rather then in spite of it. Its vital, than, to no that what people due and say determines the level of respect there given buy others. In that regard, than, respect has to be earned; its not hour unquestioned right to demand it. All of you hear and now should begin to chose behaviors that will led others to respect you. Its you're choice.

ACTIVITY 2 NUMERIC KEYPAD KEYS: 7/8/9

Objectives:

1. To learn reachstrokes for **7**, **8**, and **9**.
2. To combine the new keys with other keys learned.

2A • 5' Home-Key Review

Review the home keys by calculating totals for the problems at the right.

A	B	C	D	E	F
4	44	400	404	440	450
5	55	500	505	550	560
6	66	600	606	660	456
15	165	1,500	1,515	1,650	1,466

2B • 45' New Keys: 7, 8, and 9

Learn reach to 7

1. Locate 7 (above 4) on the numeric keypad.
2. Watch your index finger move up to 7 and back to 4 a few times without striking keys.
3. Practice striking *74* a few times as you watch the finger.
4. With eyes on copy, key/enter the data in Drills 1A and 1B. Do not worry about totals.

Learn reach to 8

1. Learn the middle-finger reach to 8 (above 5) as directed in Steps 1–3 above.
2. With eyes on copy, enter the data in Drills 1C and 1D.

Learn reach to 9

1. Learn the ring-finger reach to 9 (above 6) as directed above.
2. With eyes on copy, enter the data in Drills 1E and 1F.

Drills 2–5

1. Calculate the totals for each problem in Drills 2–5. Check your answers with the problem totals shown.
2. Repeat Drills 2–5 to increase your input speed.

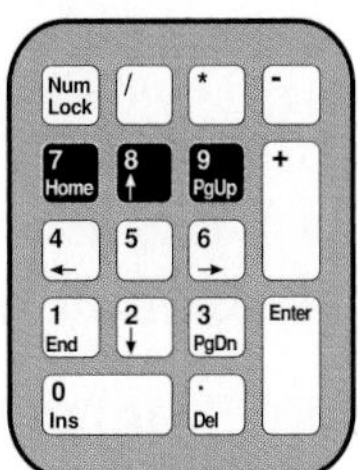

Drill 1

A	B	C	D	E	F
474	747	585	858	696	969
747	477	858	588	969	966
777	474	888	585	999	696
1,998	1,698	2,331	2,031	2,664	2,631

Drill 2

A	B	C	D	E	F
774	885	996	745	475	754
474	585	696	854	584	846
747	858	969	965	695	956
1,995	2,328	2,661	2,564	1,754	2,556

Drill 3

A	B	C	D	E	F
470	580	690	770	707	407
740	850	960	880	808	508
705	805	906	990	909	609
1,915	2,235	2,556	2,640	2,424	1,524

Drill 4

A	B	C	D	E	F
456	407	508	609	804	905
789	408	509	704	805	906
654	409	607	705	806	907
1,899	1,224	1,624	2,018	2,415	2,718

Drill 5

A	B	C	D	E	F
8	69	4	804	76	86
795	575	705	45	556	564
60	4	59	6	5	504
863	648	768	855	637	1,154

Communication Skills 7

ACTIVITY 1

Internal Punctuation: Comma

1. Key lines 1–10 at the right, supplying the needed commas.
2. Check the accuracy of your work with the instructor; correct any errors you made.
3. Note the rule number at the left of each sentence in which you made a comma error.
4. Using the rules below the sentences and on p. 157, identify the rule(s) you need to review/practice.
5. **Read**: Study each rule.
6. **Learn**: Key the Learn line(s) beneath it, noting how the rule is applied.
7. **Apply**: Key the Apply line(s), adding commas as needed.

 **Save as:** *CS7-ACT1*

Proofread & Correct

Rules		
1	1	My favorite sports are college football basketball and soccer.
1	2	If you finish your report before noon please give me a call.
1,2	3	I snacked on milk and cookies granola and some raisins.
3	4	Miss Qwan said "I was born in Taipei, Taiwan."
4	5	Mr. Sheldon the owner will speak to our managers today.
5	6	Why do you persist Kermit in moving your hands to the top row?
6	7	The report which Ted wrote is well organized and informative.
6	8	Only students who use their time wisely are likely to succeed.
3	9	Dr. Sachs said "Take two of these and call me in the morning."
6	10	Yolanda who is from Cuba intends to become a U.S. citizen.

Internal Punctuation: Comma

Rule 1: Use a comma after (a) introductory phrases or clauses and (b) words in a series.

Learn 1 When you finish keying the report, please give it to Mr. Kent.
Learn 2 We will play the Mets, Expos, and Cubs in our next home stand.
Apply 3 If you attend the play take Mary Jack and Tim with you.
Apply 4 The last exam covered memos simple tables and unbound reports.

Rule 2: Do not use a comma to separate two items treated as a single unit within a series.

Learn 5 Her favorite breakfast was bacon and eggs, muffins, and juice.
Apply 6 My choices are peaches and cream brownies or ice cream.
Apply 7 Trays of fresh fruit nuts and cheese and crackers awaited guests.

Rule 3: Use a comma before short direct quotations.

Learn 8 The man asked, "When does Flight 787 depart?"
Apply 9 Mrs. Ramirez replied "No, the report is not finished."
Apply 10 Dr. Feit said "Please make an appointment for next week."

Rule 4: Use a comma before and after a word or words in apposition (words that come together and refer to the same person or thing).

Learn 11 Coleta, the assistant manager, will chair the next meeting.
Apply 12 Greg Mathews a pitcher for the Braves will sign autographs.
Apply 13 The personnel director Marge Wilson will be the presenter.

Rule 5: Use a comma to set off words of direct address (the name of a person spoken to).

Learn 14 I believe, Tom, that you should fly to San Francisco.
Apply 15 Finish this assignment Mary before you start on the next one.
Apply 16 Please call me Erika if I can be of further assistance.

(continued on next page)

NUMERIC KEYPAD KEYS: 1/2/3

Objectives:

1. To learn reachstrokes for **1**, **2**, and **3**.
2. To combine the new keys with other keys learned.

3A • 5' Keypad Review

Review the keypad by calculating the totals for the problems at the right.

A	B	C	D	E	F	G
45	74	740	996	704	990	477
56	85	850	885	805	880	588
67	96	960	774	906	770	699
168	255	2,550	2,655	2,415	2,640	1,764

3B • 45' New Keys: 1, 2, and 3

Learn reach to 1

1. Locate 1 (below 4) on the numeric keypad.
2. Watch your index finger move down to 1 and back to 4 a few times without striking keys.
3. Practice striking *14* a few times as you watch the finger.
4. With eyes on copy, enter the data in Drills 1A and 1B. Do not worry about totals.

Learn reach to 2

1. Learn the middle-finger reach to 2 (below 5) as in Steps 1–3 above.
2. With eyes on copy, enter data in Drills 1C and 1D.

Learn reach to 3

1. Learn the ring-finger reach to 3 (below 6) as directed above.
2. With eyes on copy, enter data in Drills 1E–1G.

Drills 2–4

Calculate totals for each problem and check your answers.

Learn reach to . (decimal point)

1. Learn the ring-finger reach to the decimal point (.) located below the 3.
2. With eyes on copy, calculate the totals for each problem in Drill 5.
3. Repeat Drills 2–5 to increase your input speed.

Drill 1

A	B	C	D	E	F	G
144	114	525	252	363	636	120
141	414	252	552	363	366	285
414	141	225	525	336	636	396
699	669	1,002	1,329	1,062	1,638	801

Drill 2

A	B	C	D	E	F	G
411	552	663	571	514	481	963
144	255	366	482	425	672	852
414	525	636	539	563	953	471
969	1,332	1,665	1,592	1,502	2,106	2,286

Drill 3

A	B	C	D	E	F	G
471	582	693	303	939	396	417
41	802	963	220	822	285	508
14	825	936	101	717	174	639
526	2,209	2,592	624	2,478	855	1,564

Drill 4

A	B	C	D	E	F	G
75	128	167	102	853	549	180
189	34	258	368	264	367	475
3	591	349	549	971	102	396
267	753	774	1,019	2,088	1,018	1,051

Drill 5

A	B	C	D	E	F	G
1.30	2.58	23.87	90.37	16.89	47.01	59.28
4.17	6.90	14.65	4.25	3.25	28.36	1.76
5.47	9.48	38.52	94.62	20.14	75.37	61.04

SKILL BUILDING

54D • 12' Speed Forcing Drill

1. Key each line once at top speed.
2. Key two 15" timings on each line.

If you finish a line before time is called, start over. Your *gwam* is the figure at the end of the line PLUS the figure above or below the point at which you stopped.

Emphasis: high-frequency balanced-hand words

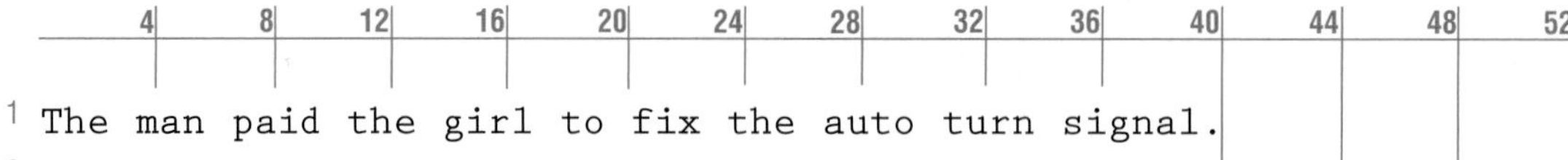

1 The man paid the girl to fix the auto turn signal.
2 Ellen bid for the antique chair and antique rifle.
3 Diana may make the title forms for big and small firms.
4 When did the auditor sign the audit forms for the city?
5 They kept the girls busy with the work down by the big lake.
6 Helen may go with us to the city to pay them for their work.
7 The man and I may dismantle the ancient ricksha in the big field.
8 Jay may suspend the men as a penalty for their work on the docks.

gwam 15" | 4 | 8 | 12 | 16 | 20 | 24 | 28 | 32 | 36 | 40 | 44 | 48 | 52

SKILL BUILDING

54E • 15' Skill Check

1. Take a 1' writing on ¶ 1; determine *gwam*.
2. Add 2–4 *gwam* to the rate attained in Step 1, and note quarter-minute checkpoints from the chart below.
3. Key two 1' guided writings on ¶ 1 to increase speed.
4. Practice ¶ 2 in the same way.
5. Take two 3' writings on ¶s 1 and 2 combined; determine *gwam* and find errors.

Quarter-Minute Checkpoints				
gwam	1/4'	1/2'	3/4'	1'
24	6	12	18	24
28	7	14	21	28
32	8	16	24	32
36	9	18	27	36
40	10	20	30	40
44	11	22	33	44
48	12	24	36	48
52	13	26	39	52
56	14	28	42	56
60	15	30	45	60

all letters used

	gwam 3'	5'	
Something that you can never escape is your attitude. It	4	2	44
will be with you forever. However, you decide whether your	8	5	47
attitude is an asset or a liability for you. Your attitude	12	7	49
reflects the way you feel about the world you abide in and	16	9	52
everything that is a part of that world. It reflects the way you	20	12	54
feel about yourself, about your environment, and about other peo-	25	15	57
ple who are a part of your environment. Oftentimes, people with	29	17	59
a positive attitude are people who are extremely successful.	33	20	62
At times we all have experiences that cause us to be	36	22	64
negative. The difference between a positive and a negative per-	41	24	66
son is that the positive person rebounds very quickly from a bad	45	27	69
experience; the negative person does not. The positive person is	49	30	72
a person who usually looks to the bright side of things and	53	32	74
recognizes the world as a place of promise, hope, joy, excite-	58	35	77
ment, and purpose. A negative person generally has just the	62	37	79
opposite view of the world. Remember, others want to be around	66	40	82
those who are positive but tend to avoid those who are negative.	70	42	84

gwam 3' | 1 | 2 | 3 | 4
5' | 1 | 2 | 3

WORD PROCESSING 

ACTIVITY 1

Insert and Typeover, Underline, Italic, and Bold

1. Read the information at the right; learn to use the word processing (wp) features described.
2. Key the lines given below right as shown.
3. Make the following changes in your lines:

line 1
Change "seven" to "eight."

line 2
Change "January" to "October."

line 9
Insert "new" before "car."
Insert "for college" after "left."

line 10
Insert "not" before "know."
Insert "the" after "know."

 **Save as:** *WP1ACT1*

Note:
Do not underline the punctuation after an underlined word, as shown in lines 8 and 10.

Insert
The **Insert** feature is active when you open a software program. Move the insertion point to where you want to insert copy; key the new text. Existing copy will move to the right.

Typeover
Typeover allows you to replace current copy with newly keyed text.

Underline
The **Underline** feature underlines text as it is keyed.

Italic
The **Italic** feature prints letters that slope up toward the right.

Bold
The **Bold** feature prints text darker than other copy as it is keyed.

1 Three of the seven dogs need to have their dog tags renewed.
2 His credit card bill for the month of January was $3,988.76.
3 Rebecca read *Little Women* by Louisa May Alcott for the test.
4 Yes, it is acceptable to *italicize* or underline book titles.
5 Patricia used the **bold** feature to **emphasize** her main points.
6 Their credit card number was **698 388 0054**, not 698 388 9954.
7 I have read both *The Firm* and *The Rainmaker* by John Grisham.
8 She overemphasized by ***underlining***, ***bolding***, and ***italicizing***.
9 I believe James bought a car before he left.
10 Sarah did know difference between affect and effect.

ACTIVITY 2

Alignment: Left, Center, Right

1. Read the copy at the right.
2. Learn the Alignment feature for your wp software.
3. Key the lines at the right. The page number will be right-aligned, the title will be center-aligned, and the last two lines will be left-aligned.

 **Save as:** *WP1ACT2*

Alignment (justification) refers to the horizontal position of a line of text. Use **left** alignment to start text at the left margin. Use **right** alignment to start text at the right margin. Use **center** alignment to center lines of text between the left and right margins.

Page 13

The Final Act

Just before dawn the policeman arrived at the home of Ms. Kennington.

All the lights were shining brightly. . . .

LESSON 54 — IMPROVE KEYING TECHNIQUE

Objectives:

1. To improve keying techniques.
2. To improve keying speed and control.

54A • 5' Conditioning Practice

Key each line twice SS; then key a 1' writing on line 3; determine *gwam*.

alphabet 1 Carl asked to be given just a week to reply to the tax quiz form.

figures 2 Rooms 268 and 397 were cleaned for the 10:45 meetings last night.

speed 3 Vivian burns wood and a small bit of coal to make an ample flame.

gwam 1' | 1 | 2 | 3 | 4 | 5 | 6 | 7 | 8 | 9 | 10 | 11 | 12 | 13 |

SKILL BUILDING

54B • 10' Technique: Letter Keys

1. Key lines 1-6 twice.
2. Take two 30" writings on line 7. If you complete the line, begin again.
3. Repeat Step 2 for lines 8 and 9.

> **Note:** Each word in this drill is among the 600 most-used words in the English language. Increase your keying rate by practicing them frequently.

One-hand words of 2-5 letters

1 no you was in we my be him are up as on get you only set see rate

2 few area no free you best date far tax case act fact water act on

3 card upon you few ever only fact after act state great as get see

4 you were | set rate | we are | at no | on you | at my best | get set | you were

5 as few | you set a date | my card | water tax | act on a | tax date | in case

6 my only date | water rate | my tax case | tax fact | my best date | my card

7 No, you are free only after I act on a rate on a state water tax.

8 Get him my extra database only after you set up exact test dates.

9 You set my area tax rate after a great state case on a water tax.

gwam 1' | 1 | 2 | 3 | 4 | 5 | 6 | 7 | 8 | 9 | 10 | 11 | 12 | 13 |

SKILL BUILDING

54C • 8' Technique: Number Keys/Tab

1. Set tabs at 2" and at 4".
2. Key the copy at the right.
3. Key three 1' writings, trying to key additional text on each writing.

Concentrate on figure location; quick tab spacing; eyes on copy.

530 Parkside Ave.	938 Merrimac Dr.	912 Santiago Rd.
4028 Hyde Cr.	665 Harbor Rd.	230 Palmetto St.
4039 Hazelwood Dr.	386 Granville Dr.	931 Columbia St.
901 Doverplum Ter.	216 Eastgate Dr.	856 Somerset St.
941 Scarborough St.	205 Salisbury St.	423 Janeway Ct.
497 Brookview Ln.	930 Ryecroft St.	734 Leemont Ct.
901 Phelps Rd.	283 Berkshire Dr.	925 Lovell Dr.
475 Beaver Rd.	601 Stanford St.	65 Vermont St.

ACTIVITY 3

Undo and Redo

1. Read the copy at the right.
2. Learn how to use the Undo and Redo features of your software.

Use the **Undo** feature to reverse the last change you made in text. Undo restores text to its original location, even if you have moved the insertion point to another position. Use the **Redo** feature to reverse the last Undo action.

3. Key the ¶ below DS using bold as shown.
4. Select and delete "San Francisco" and "Tchaikovsky's."
5. Use the Undo feature to reverse the changes.
6. Use the Redo feature to reverse the last Undo action.

Save as: *WP1ACT3*

The **San Francisco** Symphony Orchestra performed **Tchaikovsky's** 1812 Overture Op. 49 Waltz for their final number.

ACTIVITY 4

Hyphenation

1. Read the copy at the right.
2. Learn how to activate the Hyphenation feature in your wp software.
3. Key the text at the right DS, with hyphenation off. Print the text.
4. With hyphenation on, key the text again. Compare text on screen with the printout.

Save as: *WP1ACT4*

The **Hyphenation** feature automatically divides (hyphenates) words that would normally wrap to the next line.

This evens the right margin, making the text more attractive.

Use the Hyphenation feature to give text a professional look. With the Hyphenation feature on, the software divides long words between syllables at the end of lines. Using hyphenation makes the right margin less ragged. This feature is particularly helpful when keying in narrow columns.

ACTIVITY 5

Speller

1. Read the copy at the right.
2. Learn to use your wp software's Speller.
3. Key the ¶ exactly as it is shown.
4. Use the Speller to identify words spelled incorrectly or not in your Speller's dictionary. Correct all errors by editing or selecting a replacement. Proper names are correct.
5. Proofread after the Speller is used. Correct any errors found.

Save as: *WP1ACT5*

Use the **Speller** to check words, documents, or parts of documents for misspellings. A Speller checks a document by comparing each word in the document to words in its dictionary(ies). If the Speller finds a word in your document that is not identical to one in its dictionary(ies), the word is displayed in a dialog box. Usually the Speller lists words it "believes" are likely corrections (replacements) for the displayed word. When a word is displayed, you must select one of the following options:

- Retain the spelling displayed in the dialog box.
- Replace a misspelled word that is displayed with a correctly spelled word offered by the Speller.
- Edit a misspelled word that is displayed if the Speller does not list the correctly spelled replacement.
- Delete a word that is incorrectly repeated.

Dr. Lorentz met with the students on Friday to reviiw for for there test. He told the students that their would be three sections to the test. The first secction would be multiplee choice, the second sction would be true/false, and the last section would be short anser. He also said, "If you have spelling errors on you paper, you will have pionts deducted."

SKILL BUILDING

53D • 12' Speed Forcing Drill

1. Key each line once at top speed.
2. Key two 15" timings on each line.

If you finish a line before time is called, start over. Your *gwam* is the figure at the end of the line PLUS the figure above or below the point at which you stopped.

Emphasis: high-frequency balanced-hand words

```
1 Allene is to pay for the six pens for the auditor.
2 Henry is to go with us to the lake to fix the bus.
3 If the pay is right, Jan may make eight gowns for them.
4 They may be paid to fix the six signs down by the lake.
5 Enrique works with vigor to make the gowns for a big profit.
6 Pamela may hang the signs by the antique door of the chapel.
7 Dick and the busy man may work with vigor to fix the eight signs.
8 Did the firm bid for the right to the land downtown by city hall?
```

gwam 15" | 4 | 8 | 12 | 16 | 20 | 24 | 28 | 32 | 36 | 40 | 44 | 48 | 52 |

SKILL BUILDING

53E • 15' Skill Check

1. Key a 1' writing on ¶ 1; determine *gwam*.
2. Add 2–4 *gwam* to the rate attained in Step 1, and note quarter-minute checkpoints from the chart below.
3. Take two 1' guided writings on ¶ 1 to increase speed.
4. Practice ¶ 2 in the same way.
5. Take two 3' writings on ¶s 1 and 2 combined; determine *gwam* and count errors.

Quarter-Minute Checkpoints

gwam	1/4'	1/2'	3/4'	1'
24	6	12	18	24
28	7	14	21	28
32	8	16	24	32
36	9	18	27	36
40	10	20	30	40
44	11	22	33	44
48	12	24	36	48
52	13	26	39	52
56	14	28	42	56
60	15	30	45	60

A all letters used — gwam 3'

An education is becoming more important in our society. More	4	70
jobs will be open to the skilled person with fewer jobs open to	8	74
the unskilled or less educated person. Future jobs will require	13	79
people who can communicate and who have basic math and reading	17	83
skills. It is predicted that there will be a large number of new	21	87
jobs available to those with the appropriate training who want to	26	92
work in an office. These jobs will require the skills listed	30	96
above and an ability to process office documents.	33	99
To quickly process quality office documents will take a great	37	103
deal of training. A person must be able to key rapidly, format a	42	108
variety of documents, make decisions, follow directions, recognize	46	112
all types of errors, and apply language skills. In addition to	50	116
these skills, the best office workers will be willing to put forth	55	121
an extra effort. You should begin to put forth an extra effort	59	125
today to get the training needed to become one of the skilled	63	129
workers in the labor force of the future.	66	132

gwam 3' | 1 | 2 | 3 | 4 |

ACTIVITY 6

View and Zoom

1. Read the copy at right.
2. Learn how to use the View and Zoom features of your software.
3. Open the Activity 1 document (*WP1ACT1*). Follow the steps at the right.

Use the **View** and **Zoom** features to increase or decrease the amount of the page appearing on the screen. As you increase the amount of the page appearing on the screen, the print becomes smaller, but you will see a larger portion of the page. As you decrease the amount of the page appearing on the screen, you will see less of the page; but the print will be larger, making it easier to read.

Reducing the view enough to see the whole page allows you to check the appearance (margins, spacing, graphics, tables, etc.) prior to printing. Enlarging the view makes it easier to see and edit specific portions of the page.

Step 1: View the document as a whole page.
Step 2: View the document at 75 percent.
Step 3: View the document at 200 percent.
Step 4: Close the document (same filename).

ACTIVITY 7

Hard Page Break

1. Read the copy at right.
2. Learn how to insert and delete a hard page break.
3. Key the roster sign-up sheet for the Braves shown at the right. Start at about 2" from the top of the page. DS below the title and between the numbers; 12 players will be signing up for the team.
4. Insert a hard page break at the end of the Braves Roster page and create three more sign-up sheets: one for the Yankees, one for the Angels, and one for the Astros.

Save as: *WP1ACT7*

Word processing software has two types of page breaks: *soft* and *hard*. Both kinds signal the end of a page and the beginning of a new page. The software inserts a soft page break automatically when the current page is full. You insert hard page breaks manually when you want a new page to begin before the current one is full. When a hard page break is inserted, the software adjusts any following soft page breaks so that those pages will be full before a new one is started. Hard page breaks do not move unless you move them. To move a hard page break, you can (1) delete it and let the software insert soft page breaks, or (2) insert a new hard page break where you want it.

BRAVES ROSTER

1.

2.

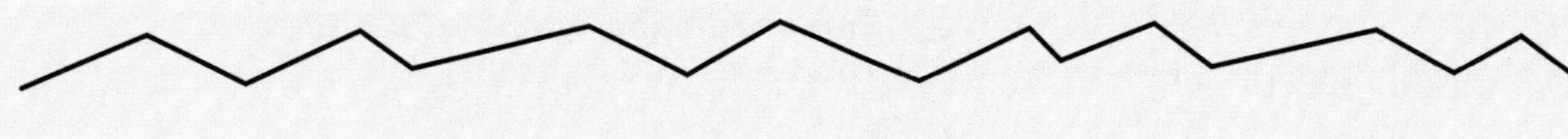

11.

12.

ACTIVITY 8

Tabs

1. Read the copy at the right.
2. Learn how to clear and set tabs (left, right, and decimal tabs) with your wp software.
3. Clear the preset tabs.

(continued on p. 58)

Most wp software has left tabs already set at half-inch (0.5") intervals from the left margin.

These preset tabs can be cleared and reset. Most wp software lets you set **left tabs**, **right tabs**, and **decimal tabs.**

Left tabs
Left tabs align all text evenly at the left by placing the text you key to the right of the tab setting. Left tabs are commonly used to align words.

Right tabs
Right tabs align all text evenly at the right by placing the text you key to the left of the tab setting. Right tabs are commonly used to align whole numbers.

Decimal tabs
Decimal tabs align all text at the decimal point or other character that you specify. If you key numbers in a column at a decimal tab, the decimal points will line up regardless of the number of places before or after the decimal point.

UNIT 16

LESSONS 53-54

Building Basic Skill

LESSON 53 IMPROVE KEYING TECHNIQUE

Objectives:

1. To improve keying techniques.
2. To improve keying speed and control.

53A • 5' Conditioning Practice

Key each line twice SS; then key a 1' writing on line 3; determine *gwam.*

alphabet 1 Next week Zelda Jacks will become a night supervisor for quality.

figures 2 Scores of 94, 83, 72, 65, and 100 gave Rhonda an average of 82.8.

speed 3 Kay paid the maid for the work she did on the shanty by the lake.

gwam 1' | 1 | 2 | 3 | 4 | 5 | 6 | 7 | 8 | 9 | 10 | 11 | 12 | 13 |

SKILL BUILDING

53B • 10' Keying Skill: Speed

1. Key lines 1-6 twice.
2. Take two 30" writings on line 7. If you complete the line, begin again.
3. Repeat Step 2 for lines 8 and 9.

Note: Each word in this drill is among the 600 most-used words in the English language. Increase your keying rate by practicing them frequently.

Balanced-hand words of 2-5 letters

1 or me go am do if so an us by to he it is big the six and but for

2 box did end due for may pay man own make also city with they when

3 them such than city they hand paid sign then form work both their

4 of it | it is | of such | paid them | such as | they work | go to | such a name

5 paid for | go to | pay for | big man | the forms | own them | and then | may go

6 is to go | make it for | pay for it | end to end | by the man | down by the

7 She may wish to go to the city to hand them the work form for us.

8 The city is to pay for the field work both of the men did for us.

9 The man may hand them the six forms when he pays for the big box.

gwam 1' | 1 | 2 | 3 | 4 | 5 | 6 | 7 | 8 | 9 | 10 | 11 | 12 | 13 |

SKILL BUILDING

53C • 8' Technique: Number Keys/Tab

1. Key each line twice (key number, depress TAB, key next number).
2. Take three 1' writings, trying to better your rate each time.

Concentrate on figure location; quick tab spacing; eyes on copy.

	930	792	556	938	394	282	737	889	1,901
	823	318	927	676	275	910	945	857	2,362
	714	640	801	544	651	720	104	262	5,435
gwam 1'		1	2	3		4	5	6	7

4. Set a left tab at 1.5", a right tab at 3.5", and a decimal tab at 4.5".
5. Key the first three lines at the right (DS) using these tab settings. Remember: Strike *Tab* to move to the next column on the same line. Strike ENTER to move to the next line.
6. Reset tabs: left tab at 2", right tab at 5", decimal tab at 6".
7. Key the last three lines (DS) using these tab settings (Step 6).

Save as: *WP1ACT8*

Left tab at 1.5"	**Right tab at 3.5"**	**Decimal tab at 4.5"**
↓	↓	↓
James Hill	6,750	88.395
Mark Johnson	863	1.38
Sue Chen	30	115.31
Left tab at 2"	**Right tab at 5"**	**Decimal tab at 6"**
↓	↓	↓
Juan Ortiz	142,250	0.25
Marsha Black	3,219	13.6
Kay Kent	56,873	297.312

ACTIVITY 9

Apply What You Have Learned

Team members for three teams are shown at the right. Using center alignment, key the information (DS) for each team on a separate page (use hard page breaks), starting at 2" from the top of the page.

The city and state should be bold and italic. The name of the team captain should be underlined.

Save as: *WP1ACT9*

TEAM 1	TEAM 2	TEAM 3
Beaver Meadows, PA	***Chapel Hill, TN***	***Scipio, UT***
Dustin Hedrington	Aaron Cain	Bradley Falkner
Keiko Koshuta	Susan Camacho	Lisa Friese
Sarah Martin	Nicole Stohlberg	Patric Sammuel
Zachary Ostmoe	Karen Xiong	Brent Wroblewski

ACTIVITY 10

Apply What You Have Learned

1. Set a left tab at 1", a right tab at 3.5", and a decimal tab at 5.5".
2. Beginning at about 2", key the text (DS) at the right.

Save as: *WP1ACT10*

Left tab at 1"	**Right tab at 3.5"**	**Decimal tab at 5.5"**
↓	↓	↓
one-eighth	1/8	.125
one-sixth	1/6	.1667
one-fourth	1/4	.25
one-third	1/3	.3333
one-half	1/2	.5
two-thirds	2/3	.6667
three-fourths	3/4	.75
one	1/1	1.0

FORMATTING

52C • 5' Table of Contents

In previous lessons, you keyed a report titled "Globalization." The headings in that report are shown at the right. Format and key a table of contents for the report.

Open the file (*RPT49B1*); verify that the page number for each heading is the same in your report. Change the table of contents as needed.

 **Save as:** *RPT52C*

TABLE OF CONTENTS

Causes of Globalization 1

Trade Agreements 2

GATT 2
The European Community 3
NAFTA 3

Growth in Developing Countries' Economies 4

Summary 5

SKILL BUILDING

52D • 8' Straight Copy

1. Key a 1' writing on ¶ 1, then on ¶ 2; determine *gwam* and number of errors on each writing.
2. Take a 3' writing on ¶s 1–2 combined; determine *gwam* and number of errors.

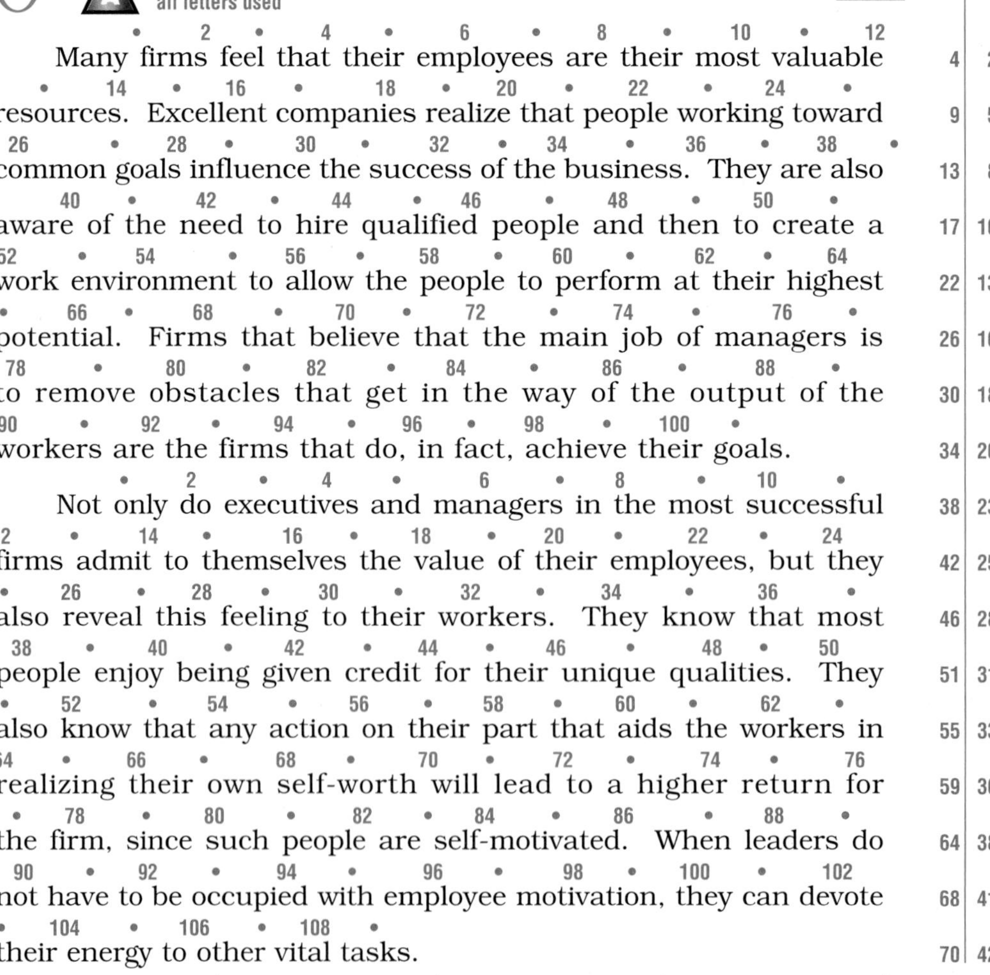

all letters used

Many firms feel that their employees are their most valuable resources. Excellent companies realize that people working toward common goals influence the success of the business. They are also aware of the need to hire qualified people and then to create a work environment to allow the people to perform at their highest potential. Firms that believe that the main job of managers is to remove obstacles that get in the way of the output of the workers are the firms that do, in fact, achieve their goals.

Not only do executives and managers in the most successful firms admit to themselves the value of their employees, but they also reveal this feeling to their workers. They know that most people enjoy being given credit for their unique qualities. They also know that any action on their part that aids the workers in realizing their own self-worth will lead to a higher return for the firm, since such people are self-motivated. When leaders do not have to be occupied with employee motivation, they can devote their energy to other vital tasks.

gwam 3'	5'	
4	2	45
9	5	47
13	8	50
17	10	53
22	13	55
26	16	58
30	18	60
34	20	63
38	23	65
42	25	68
46	28	70
51	31	73
55	33	75
59	36	78
64	38	81
68	41	83
70	42	85

UNIT 7

LESSONS 22-24

Learn to Format Memos and E-mail

Format Guides: Memos and E-mail

Interoffice Memo

Interoffice Memo

Memos (interoffice memorandums) are written messages used by employees within an organization to communicate with one another. A standard format (arrangement) for memos is presented below and illustrated on p. 60.

Memo margins.

Top margin (TM): 2"
Side margins (SM): default or 1"
Bottom margin (BM): about 1"

Memo heading. The memo heading includes who the memo is being sent to (TO:), who the memo is from (FROM:), the date the memo is being sent (DATE:), and what the memo is about (SUBJECT:). Begin all lines of the heading at the left margin and space as shown below.

TO: Tab twice to key name.
DS
FROM: Tab once to key name.
DS
DATE: Tab once to key date.
DS
SUBJECT: Tab once to key subject in ALL CAPS.
DS

Memo body. The paragraphs of the memo all begin at the left margin and are SS with a DS between paragraphs.

Reference initials. If someone other than the originator of the memo keys it, his/her initials are keyed in lowercase letters at the left margin, a DS below the body.

Attachment/Enclosure notations. If another document is attached to a memo, the word "Attachment" is keyed at the left margin a DS below the reference initials (or below the last line of the body if reference initials are not used). If a document accompanies the memo but is not attached to it, key the word "Enclosure."

E-mail

E-mail (electronic mail) is used in most business organizations. Because of the ease of creating and the speed of sending, e-mail messages have partially replaced the memo and the letter. Generally, delivery of an e-mail message takes place within minutes, whether the receiver is in the same building or in a location anywhere in the world.

The format used for e-mail is very similar to that used for memos. It may vary slightly, depending on the program used for creating e-mail. One commonly used format is shown on p. 62.

E-mail heading. The e-mail heading includes the same information as the memo (**To:**, **From:**, **Date:**, **and Subject:**). It may also include a **Cc:** line for sending a copy of the message to additional individuals, a **Bcc:** line for sending a copy of the message to someone without the receiver knowing, and an **Attachment:** line for attaching files to the e-mail message.

E-mail body. The paragraphs of an e-mail message all begin at the left margin and are SS with a DS between paragraphs.

EXTEND REPORT FORMATTING SKILLS

Objectives:

1. To complete formatting a bound report.
2. To format a references page, title page, and table of contents.

52A • 5' Conditioning Practice

Key each line twice SS; then key a 1' writing on line 3; determine *gwam*.

alphabet 1 Zack and our equipment manager will exchange jobs for seven days.

figures 2 If you call after 12:30 on Friday, you can reach him at 297-6854.

speed 3 The eight men in the shanty paid for a big bus to go to the city.

gwam 1' | 1 | 2 | 3 | 4 | 5 | 6 | 7 | 8 | 9 | 10 | 11 | 12 | 13 |

FORMATTING

52B • 32' Bound Report

Document 1 (Report Summary)

Complete the report "Delivering the Mail" that you began in Lesson 51.

1. Open the *CD-RPT52B* file. Make the corrections to the text shown at the right.
2. Copy the corrected text and paste at the end of the report keyed in 51B (*RPT51B1*).

Save as: *RPT52B1*

Summary

(now the U.S. Postal Service)

The Post Office has been the primary means for transporting written messages for many years. As the information age continues to emerge technologies will play a significant roll in getting written messages from the sender to the reciever. Again this change is directly attributable to speed Instead of talking in terms of months required for delivering a message from the east coast to the west coast, it now takes seconds. Today, e-mail and faxes as are just as important to a successful business operation as the Post Office.

we now talk in terms of

Document 2 (Title Page)

Review the guidelines for formatting a title page on p. 137. Format and key a title page for the report "Delivering the Mail."

Save as: *RPT52B2*

Document 3 (Table of Contents)

Review the guidelines for formatting a table of contents on p. 138. Format and key the information at the right as a table of contents for "Delivering the Mail."

Save as: *RPT52B3*

TABLE OF CONTENTS

Steamboats 1

Railroads 2

Pony Express 2

Automobiles 2

Airplanes 2

Summary 3

LESSON 22 FORMAT INTEROFFICE MEMOS

Objectives

1. To learn to format interoffice memos.
2. To process memos from arranged and semi-arranged copy.

22A • 5' Conditioning Practice

Key each line twice SS; then key a 1' writing on line 3; determine *gwam*.

alphabet 1 Darby and Jazmine gave a quick example of two helping verbs.

figures 2 The exam on May 28 for 50 points will test pages 396 to 471.

speed 3 Did the field auditor sign the amendment forms for the city?

gwam 1' | 1 | 2 | 3 | 4 | 5 | 6 | 7 | 8 | 9 | 10 | 11 | 12 |

2"

TO: Tab Tab Foreign Language Department Students
DS

FROM: Tab Mary Seville, Travel Abroad Coordinator
DS

DATE: Tab Tab November 2, 200-
DS

SUBJECT:Tab OPEN HOUSE
DS

1" Are you ready for a summer you will never forget? Then you will want to sign up for this year's Travel Abroad Program. You will travel to the country that famous writers like Virgil, Horace, and Dante called home. The music of Vivaldi, Verdi, and Puccini will come to life. You will visit art museums exhibiting the art of native sons such as Michelangelo Buonarotti and Giovanni Bellini. 1"
DS

By now you have probably guessed that we will be taking a trip to Italy this summer. Touring **Rome**, **Florence**, **Venice**, and **Naples** gives you the opportunity to experience firsthand the people, the culture, the history, and the cuisine of Italy.
DS

If you are interested in learning more about traveling to Italy this summer, attend our open house on November 15 at 3:30 in Room 314.
DS

xx

Shown in 12-point Times New Roman, with 2" top margin and 1" side margins, this memo appears smaller than actual size.

Interoffice Memo

Document 2 Endnotes (cont.)

[5]Albro Martin, Railroads Triumphant (New York: Oxford University Press, 1992), p. 94.

[6]Fred Reinfeld, Pony Express (Lincoln: University of Nebraska Press, 1973), p. 55.

[7]Carl H. Scheele, A Short History of the Mail Service (Washington, D.C.: Smithsonian Institution Press, 1970), p. 117.

[8]Fuller, p. 9.

[9]Leary, p. 29.

 Save as: *RPT51B2*

> No aspect of American life was untouched by the revolution that the trains brought in bringing mail service almost to the level of a free good. (For many years—ironically enough, until the depression called for an increase in the cost of a first-class letter to three cents—an ordinary first-class letter went for two cents.)[5]

Pony Express

The Pony Express was one of the most colorful means of transporting mail. This method of delivery was used to take mail from St. Joseph, Missouri, westward.

> April 3, 1860, remains a memorable day in the history of the frontier, for that was the day on which the Pony Express began its operations—westward from St. Joseph and eastward from San Francisco. Even in those days San Francisco had already become the most important city in California.[6]

With the East Coast being connected to the West Coast by railroad in 1869, the Pony Express had a relatively short life span.

Automobiles

The invention of the automobile in the late 1800s brought a new means of delivering mail in the United States.

> An automobile was used experimentally for rural delivery as early as 1902 at Adrian, Michigan, and in 1906 the Department gave permission for rural carriers to use their automobiles. The change from horse and wagon to the motor car paralleled improvements in highways and the development of more reliable automotive equipment. . . .[7]

Airplanes

The next major mode of transporting used by the Postal Service was airplanes. Speed was the driving force behind using airplanes. " . . . so closely has speed been associated with the mails that much of the world's postal history can be written around the attempts to send mail faster each day than it went the day before."[8]

The United States was the leader in transporting mail by air. In 1918 when the first air mail route took place (Washington to New York), no other nation in the world operated a scheduled air mail service.[9]

Note:
You will finish keying the report "Delivering the Mail" in Lesson 52.

22B • 45'
Memos

Study the format guides on p. 59 and the model that shows memo format on p. 60. Note the vertical and horizontal placement of memo parts and the spacing between them.

Memo 1

1. Key the model memo on p. 60.
2. Proofread your copy; correct all keying and formatting errors.

 **Save as:** *MEM022B1*

Memo 2

1. Format and key the text at the right in memo format. Use your initials as the keyboard operator.
2. Proofread your copy; correct all keying and formatting errors.

 **Save as:** *MEMO22B2*

Memo 3

1. Format and key the text at the right in memo format. Use your initials as the keyboard operator.
2. Proofread your copy; correct all keying and formatting errors.

 **Save as:** *MEMO22B3*

TO: Foreign Language Teachers

FROM: Mary Seville, Travel Abroad Coordinator

DATE: November 2, 200-

SUBJECT: OPEN HOUSE

I've enclosed copies of a memo announcing the open house for the Travel Abroad Program. Please distribute the memo to students in your classes.

Last year we had 25 students participate in the trip to England. If you have had the opportunity to talk with them about this experience, you know that the trip was very worthwhile and gave them memories that will last a lifetime. I am confident that the trip to Italy will be just as rewarding to those who participate. As you know, the experiences students gain from traveling abroad cannot be replicated in the classroom.

I appreciate your support of the program and your help in promoting it with your students.

xx

Enclosure

TO: Foreign Language Faculty

FROM: Karla A. Washburn

DATE: December 1, 200-

SUBJECT: TRAVEL ABROAD COORDINATOR

As you may have heard by now, Mary Seville announced her plans to retire at the end of next summer. In addition to hiring a new French teacher, we will need to replace Mary as our Travel Abroad Coordinator. This will be a very difficult task; Mary has done an excellent job.

If you are interested in this position, please let me know before you leave for the winter break. I would like to fill the position early next semester. This will allow the new coordinator to work with Mary as she plans this year's trip. The new coordinator would be expected to travel with Mary and the students to Italy this summer.

We also need to start thinking about a retirement party for Mary. If you are interested in being on a retirement party committee, please let me know.

LESSON 51 IMPROVE REPORT FORMATTING SKILLS

Objectives:

1. To format a bound report.
2. To format endnotes.

51A • 5' Conditioning Practice

Key each line twice SS; then key a 1' writing on line 3; determine *gwam*.

alphabet 1 Mack Walsh did quite a job to put an extravaganza on before July.

figures 2 Only 386 of the 497 students had completed the exam by 12:50 p.m.

speed 3 The visitor and I may handle all the problems with the amendment.

gwam 1' | 1 | 2 | 3 | 4 | 5 | 6 | 7 | 8 | 9 | 10 | 11 | 12 | 13 |

FORMATTING

51B • 45' Bound Report

Document 1 (Report Body)

1. Review the report format guides on pp. 137–138 as needed.
2. Format the copy at the right as a bound report with endnotes.
3. When you finish, use the Speller feature and proofread your copy.

 **Save as:** *RPT51B1*

Document 2 (Endnotes)

Prepare endnotes from the information below and on p. 149.

[1]Wayne E. Fuller, The American Mail (Chicago: University of Chicago Press, 1972), p. ix.

[2] William M. Leary, Aerial Pioneers (Washington, D.C.: Smithsonian Institution Press, 1985), p. 238.

[3]Richard Wormser, The Iron Horse: How Railroads Changed America (New York: Walker Publishing Company, Inc., 1993), p. 26.

[4]Leary, p. 238.

DELIVERING THE MAIL

For years, people have used written communication as one of their primary means of exchanging information. Those using this form of communicating have depended on the U.S. mail to transport their messages from one place to another.

> For much of American history, the mail was our main form of organized communication. Americans wanting to know the state of the world, the health of a friend, or the fate of their business anxiously awaited the mail. To advise a distant relative, to order goods, to pay a bill, to express views to their congressman or love to their fiancée, they used the mail. No American institution has been more intimately involved in daily hopes and fears.[1]

The history of the U.S. mail is not only interesting but also reflective of changes in American society, specifically transportation. A variety of modes of transporting mail have been used over the years. Speed, of course, was the driving force behind most of the changes.

Steamboats

Congress used inventions to move the mail from place to place. In 1813, five years after Robert Fulton's first experiments on the Hudson River, Congress authorized the Post Office to transport mail by steamboat.[2] Transporting mail to river cities worked very well. However, the efficiency of using steamboats to transport mail between New York and San Francisco was questionable. "The distance was 19,000 miles and the trip could take as long as six to seven months."[3]

Railroads

Although mail was carried by railroads as early as 1834, it was not until 1838 that Congress declared railroads to be post roads.[4] Trains eventually revolutionized mail delivery. The cost of sending a letter decreased substantially, making it more affordable to the public.

(*Report continued on next page*)

FORMAT E-MAIL MESSAGES

Objectives:

1. To learn to format e-mail messages.
2. To process e-mail messages from arranged and semi-arranged copy.

23A • 5' Conditioning Practice

Key each line twice SS; then key a 1' writing on line 3; determine *gwam*.

alphabet 1 Jordan placed first by solving the complex quiz in one week.

figures 2 The 389 members met on June 24, 2001, from 6:15 to 7:30 p.m.

speed 3 Jan paid the big man for the fieldwork he did for the firms.

gwam 1' | 1 | 2 | 3 | 4 | 5 | 6 | 7 | 8 | 9 | 10 | 11 | 12 |

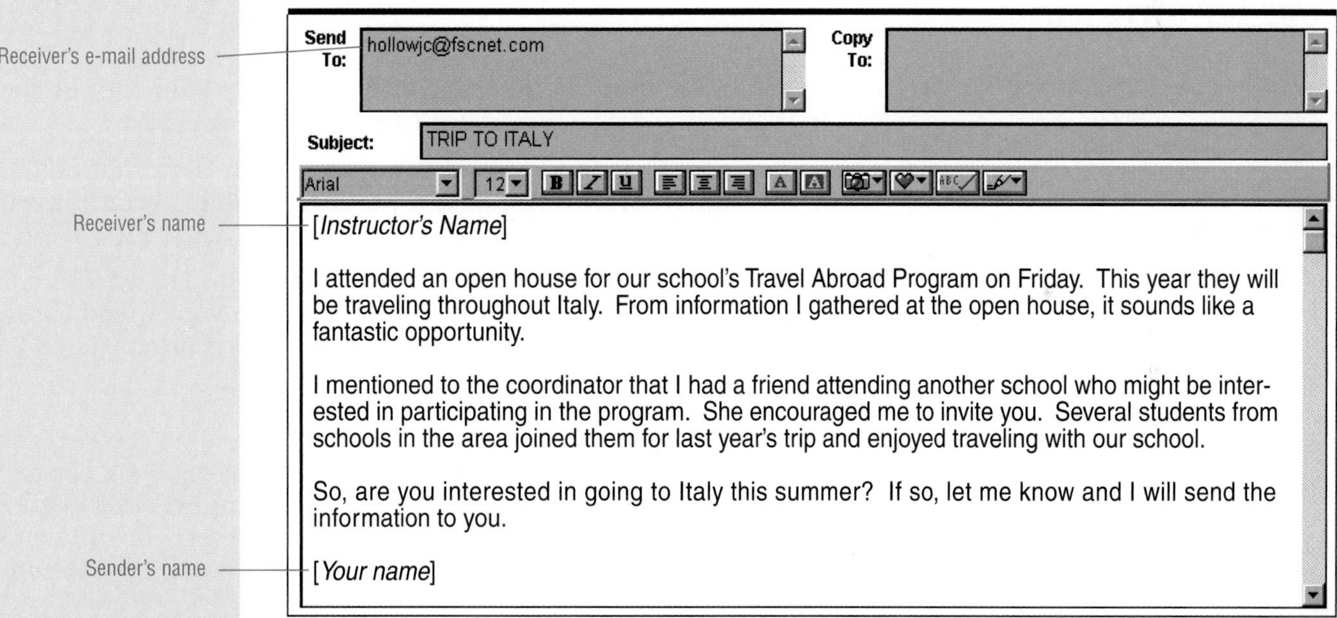

Receiver's e-mail address
Receiver's name
Sender's name
Send To:
hollowjc@fscnet.com
Copy To:
Subject:
TRIP TO ITALY
Arial
12
[Instructor's Name]
I attended an open house for our school's Travel Abroad Program on Friday. This year they will be traveling throughout Italy. From information I gathered at the open house, it sounds like a fantastic opportunity.
I mentioned to the coordinator that I had a friend attending another school who might be interested in participating in the program. She encouraged me to invite you. Several students from schools in the area joined them for last year's trip and enjoyed traveling with our school.
So, are you interested in going to Italy this summer? If so, let me know and I will send the information to you.
[Your name]

E-mail Message

Note:
In some e-mail software, the receiver's name may be keyed in the To: box along with the e-mail address. The date and time the message is sent will appear automatically above or below the message when the receiver gets it. Although no From: box is provided in this example, the sender's e-mail address will appear automatically also.

50C • 33'
Bound Report

Document 1 (Report Body)

1. Review the format guides for bound reports on pp. 137–138 as needed.
2. Format the copy at the right as a bound report with endnotes.
3. When you finish, use the Speller feature and proofread your copy.

Save as: *RPT50C1*

Document 2 (Endnotes)

Use the information below to prepare the endnotes.

[1]Robert J. Samuelson, "Lost on the Information Highway," Newsweek (December 20, 1993), p. 111.

[2]Laurence A. Canter and Martha S. Siegel, How to Make a FORTUNE on the Information Superhighway (New York: Harper-Collins Publishers, Inc., 1994), p. 1.

[3]"AOL Poised for Record Subscriber Growth," http://dailynews.yahoo.com/h/nm/19990921/wr/aol_3.html (21 September 1999).

Save as: *RPT50C2*

Document 3—Optional (References Page)

Use the endnotes information above to prepare a references page. See R45 for references format.

Note:
The entire Samuelson article is on p. 111 in *Newsweek*.

Save as: *RPT50C3*

INFORMATION SUPERHIGHWAY

Technology has a significant impact on our lives and will have an even greater impact in the future. During the early 1990s, the term "Information Highway" was first used to describe the next wave of technological advancements. As always there were those who were skeptical about what impact, if any, the "Information Highway" (also called the "Information Superhighway") would have on our lives.

One writer, as late as December 1993, indicated that he was not holding his breath. He doubted if the Information Superhighway would become a truly transforming technology; and if so, he felt, it may take decades. This writer went on to compare acceptance of the Information Superhighway to acceptance of the car.

> It takes time for breakthrough technologies to make their mark. Consider the car. In 1908 Henry Ford began selling the Model T. One early effort of low-cost cars was to rid cities of horses. A picture of a New York street in 1900 shows 36 horse carriages and 1 car; a picture of the same street in 1924 shows 40 cars and 1 carriage. This was a big deal. In 1900, horses dumped 2.5 million pounds of manure onto New York streets every day. Still, the car culture's triumph was slow.[1]

Other writers during the early 1990s were much more optimistic about the value of this superhighway and began predicting what it would mean to all of us in the near future.

> The Information Superhighway is going to affect your life, whether you want it to or not. In the very near future you will talk to your friends and family, send letters, go shopping, get news, find answers to your questions . . . .[2]

<u>What is the Information Superhighway?</u>

The Information Superhighway, more commonly called the **Internet**, is a large computer network made up of many smaller networks. By connecting to the Internet, an individual can access and exchange information with anyone else who is connected to the Internet. Currently, millions of individuals are connected; the number increases daily. In the fourth quarter of 1999, America Online Inc., an Internet service provider, added 685,000 new U.S. members.[3]

<u>What has been the Impact of the Superhighway?</u>

The development of the Information Superhighway since 1993 has been much faster than many expected and has even exceeded the visions of those who were predicting its widespread use.

Many individuals use the Information Superhighway daily to send **e-mail** messages and attachments; to participate in **chat groups**; to shop; and to get the latest news, weather, and sports. Taking the Internet away from them would impact them almost as much as taking away the telephone, television, and mail delivery service. The Information Superhighway has been constructed, and "road improvements" will make it even better in the future.

23B • 45'
E-mail Messages

Study the format guides on p. 59 and the model that illustrates e-mail on p. 62.

E-mail software users: Use your instructor's e-mail address for the TO: line of each message. Use your e-mail address for the FROM: line.

Word processing software users: Format each message as an interoffice memo, using the names given. Use the current date.

E-mail Message 1

1. Key the model e-mail on p. 62; replace the e-mail address given with your instructor's e-mail address.
2. Proofread your copy; correct all keying and formatting errors.

Save as: *EMAIL23B1**

*E-mail is saved automatically in the e-mail software. Use this filename only if your instructor directs you to save the message on disk.

E-mail Messages 2 and 3

1. Format and key the e-mail messages at the right.
2. Proofread your copy; correct all keying and formatting errors.

Save as: *EMAIL23B2* and *EMAIL23B3*

E-mail Message 2

TO: Margaret Simmons [On e-mail screen, key instructor's e-mail address.]

FROM: Erika Downey [On e-mail screen, use your e-mail address.]

DATE: February 25, 200- [On e-mail screen, date is inserted automatically.]

SUBJECT: HELP!!!

Hopefully, my sister told you that I would be e-mailing you. I'm writing a report on Mark Twain for my English class. Last weekend when Katherine was home, we were talking about this assignment. She mentioned that you were an English major and seemed to think that you had completed a course that focused on Mark Twain. She suggested that I contact you to see if you would be able to suggest some sources that I might use for this assignment.

As part of the report project, we have to read two of his books. I've already started reading *Life on the Mississippi.* Could you offer a suggestion as to what other book I should read for this assignment?

Katherine said that you are planning on coming home with her during spring break. I'll look forward to meeting you.

E-mail Message 3

TO: Marshall Sabin [Or instructor's e-mail address]

FROM: Tina Hansen [Or your e-mail address]

DATE: October 1, 200- [Inserted automatically on e-mail screen]

SUBJECT: INFORMATION FOR YOUR REPORT

I found a site on the World Wide Web at http://www.nytheatre-wire.com/PoorR.htm that lists the plays currently performed in New York City. It appears that there are five plays that were opened prior to 1990. Four of them were opened between 1980-1990. These include *Cats* (10/07/82), *Les Miserables* (03/12/87), *The Phantom of the Opera* (01/26/88), and *Tony n' Tina's Wedding* (02/06/88).

The only other play that I found that had opened prior to 1990 was *The Fantasticks*, which is New York's longest-running musical. It opened on May 3, 1960.

I scanned the information very quickly. You will want to check the Web site and verify the accuracy of the information before you include it in your report. If I find anything else that I think would add to your report, I will let you know.

LESSON 50 — FORMAT BOUND REPORTS WITH ENDNOTES

Objectives:

1. To format a bound report with endnotes.
2. To format a references page.

50A • 5' Conditioning Practice

Key each line twice SS; then key a 1' writing on line 3; determine *gwam*.

alphabet 1 Completing the five extra job requirements will keep Zelda happy.

figures 2 Check #97 was written for $3,525.16; Check #98 was for $3,785.40.

speed 3 Glen bid on the cornfield by the lake for land for the city hall.

gwam 1' | 1 | 2 | 3 | 4 | 5 | 6 | 7 | 8 | 9 | 10 | 11 | 12 | 13 |

SKILL BUILDING

50B • 12' Straight Copy

1. Key a 3' writing on ¶s 1–3 combined; determine *gwam* and number of errors.
2. Key a 1' writing on each ¶; determine *gwam* and number of errors on each ¶.
3. Take another 3' writing on ¶s 1–3 combined, trying to increase your *gwam* over the writing in Step 1.

A all letters used

	3'	5'	
Why are some people so amazingly productive while others are	4	2	47
not? Procrastination is the explanation offered in response to	8	5	49
this query. Productive people do not waste time. They maintain	13	8	52
that you should not put off till the next day what you can do	17	10	54
today. People who are successful tend to be those who manage	21	13	57
time rather than let time manage them.	24	14	59
A number of things can be done to combat procrastination.	28	17	61
First, prepare a listing of each task that needs to be accomplished.	32	19	64
Many of the tasks that appear on the list will take minimal time,	37	22	66
while others on the list may take a substantial amount. As each	41	25	69
task is achieved, it should be deleted from the list. This gives	45	27	72
a person a sense of accomplishment and increases the likelihood	50	30	74
of additional tasks being completed.	52	31	76
The next suggestion is to divide a big job into several smaller	56	34	78
parts. By doing so, the job will not appear so overwhelming. Along	61	37	81
with breaking the job down, set deadlines for completing each	65	39	83
part of the job. The probability of completing a large job is much	70	42	86
greater when it is divided into parts that have assigned deadlines.	74	44	89

gwam 3' | 1 | 2 | 3 | 4 |
5' | 1 | 2 | 3 |

FORMAT MEMOS AND E-MAIL

Objectives:

1. To check knowledge of e-mail and memo formats.
2. To check the level of your e-mail and memo processing skill.

24A • 5' Conditioning Practice

Key each line twice SS; then key a 1' writing on line 3; determine *gwam*.

alphabet 1 Dixie quickly gave him two big prizes for completing a jump.

fig/sym 2 I think the textbook (ISBN #0-538-64892-9) sells for $41.70.

speed 3 Helen is to go downtown to do the map work for the auditors.

gwam 1' | 1 | 2 | 3 | 4 | 5 | 6 | 7 | 8 | 9 | 10 | 11 | 12 |

FORMATTING

24B • 45' Memo and E-mail Processing

Memo 1

1. Format and key the memo at the right.
2. Use Speller and proofread your copy; correct all keying and formatting errors.

Save as: *MEMO24B1*

Note:
Use italic instead of underlines for the play titles.

TO: Drama Students

FROM: Ms. Fairbanks

DATE: November 1, 200-

SUBJECT: SELECTION OF SPRING PLAY

There are three plays that I would like you to consider for next semester's performance. They include:

The Importance of Being Earnest, a comedy written by Oscar Wilde. In the play Jack Worthing has a complicated courtship with Lady Bracknell's daughter, Gwendolen. His ward, Cecily, has fallen in love with his friend Algernon.

A Delicate Balance, a comedy written by Edward Albee. The play is a funny look at love, compassion, and the bonds of friendship and family.

A Comedy of Errors, a comedy written by William Shakespeare. The play is about mistaken identities of twins.

I have placed copies of the plays in the library on reserve. Please look them over by November 25 so that we can discuss them in class that day. We will need to make a decision before December 1 so that I can order the playbooks.

Document 1 (cont.)

Complete the Globalization report. Format and key the text at the right at the end of the report (*RPT48B*). The information for footnotes 9 and 10 is given below.

[9]Jacob, p. 74.

[10]Pete Engardio, "Third World Leapfrog," Business Week (May 18, 1994), p. 47.

 **Save as:** *RPT49B1*

Document 2 (Title Page)

Review the "Title Page" section of the format guides, p. 137. Prepare a title page for the Globalization report.

 **Save as:** *RPT49B2*

Document 3 (References Page)

Review the format guides for preparing a references page, p. 138. Using the information from the footnotes and the additional information below, prepare a references page for the Globalization report.

Engardio article, **pp. 47–49**

"Fact Sheet" article, **pp. 87–93**

Harris article, **pp. 755–776**

Jacob article, **pp. 74–90**

Richman article, **p. 14**

 **Save as:** *RPT49B3*

According to the U.S. Department of Commerce, the world's ten biggest emerging markets include:

- Argentina
- Brazil
- China
- India
- Indonesia
- Mexico
- Poland
- South Africa
- South Korea
- Turkey

Of these emerging markets, the most dramatic increase is in the East Asian countries. Estimated per capita incomes rose at an annual rate of 6.5 percent from 1983 to 1993. In China alone, incomes grew 8.5 percent annually.[9]

Recent technological developments have also contributed to globalization. Because of these developments, the world is a smaller place; communication is almost instant to many parts of the world. The extent of the technological developments can be sensed in Engardio's comments:[10]

> Places that until recently were incommunicado are rapidly acquiring state-of-the-art telecommunications that will let them foster both internal and foreign investment. It may take a decade for many countries in Asia, Latin America, and Eastern Europe to unclog bottlenecks in transportation and power supplies. But by installing optical fiber, digital switches, and the latest wireless transmission systems, urban centers and industrial zones from Beijing to Budapest are stepping into the Information Age. Videoconferencing, electronic data interchange, and digital mobile-phone services already are reaching most of Asia and parts of Eastern Europe.
>
> All of these developing regions see advanced communications as a way to leapfrog stages of economic development.

Summary

The world continues to become more globalized. The trend will continue because of three main factors: new and improved trade agreements, rapid growth rates of developing countries' economies, and technological advances. All of these factors foster globalization.

Memo 2

1. Format and key the memo at the right.
2. Use the Speller and proofread your copy; correct all keying and formatting errors.

 **Save as:** *MEMO24B2*

TO: Office Staff

FROM: Jennifer Green, General Manager

DATE: March 15, 200-

SUBJECT: NEW BOX OFFICE COORDINATOR

Rebecca Dunwoody has been hired to replace DeWayne Hughes as our box office coordinator. DeWayne has decided to return to school to start work on a Master of Business Administration degree. As you are aware, DeWayne has been a valuable asset to our organization for the past five years.

It was not easy finding a person with similar qualifications to replace DeWayne. His enthusiasm and love of music combined with a degree in music as well as a minor in business administration made the job particularly difficult. However, we believe we were successful when we were able to hire Ms. Dunwoody. She is a recent graduate of NYC's music program. While completing her degree, she worked as an assistant for the business manager of one of our competitors.

Please extend your appreciation and best wishes to DeWayne before he leaves on March 30 and welcome Rebecca when she arrives on March 25.

E-mail/Memo 3

1. Key the message at the right. If you are using e-mail software, send the message to your instructor. If you are using wp software, format it as an interoffice memo, using the headings provided.
2. Use the Speller and proofread your copy; correct all keying and formatting errors.

 **Save as:** *MEMO24B3*

Gather information about a play or concert you would like to attend. Send e-mail inviting a friend to go with you. Include all the necessary details. Several sites are listed below.

www.sfsymphony.org/

www.nytheatre.com/

www.theatreticket.com/

www.ticketmaster.com/

www.osscs.org/

TO: Mission Statement Committee

FROM: Jason R. Roberts, Chair

DATE: Current

SUBJECT: MISSION STATEMENT

As we develop our mission statement, we may want to review some of the mission statements of other symphonies. I have already looked at several on the Web. San Francisco's was one that I felt we could model ours after.

They have an overall mission statement followed by specific artistic, community, and organizational goals. I felt their community goals were particularly good, three of them being most appropriate for our organization:

1. Provide musical enrichment to the widest possible audiences.
2. Develop music education for a culturally diverse community.
3. Strengthen orchestra training for young musicians.

To view the complete mission statement, go to http://www.sfsymphony.org/info/mission.htm. I'll look forward to working with you at our next committee meeting.

LESSON 49 | IMPROVE REPORT FORMATTING

Objectives:

1. To format a bound report with footnotes.
2. To format a references page and title page.

49A • 5' Conditioning Practice

Key each line twice SS; then key a 1' writing on line 3; determine *gwam*.

alphabet 1 Jacques Zhukov played an excellent baseball game for the winners.

figures 2 Since 1987, 450 of our guests were from Maine; 362 from New York.

speed 3 The big city bus was downtown by the signs of the ancient chapel.

gwam 1'	1	2	3	4	5	6	7	8	9	10	11	12	13

FORMATTING

49B • 45' Bound Report

Document 1

Continue the Globalization report begun in Lesson 48. Insert the file *CD-GLOBAL* after the last sentence of the document created in 48B (*RPT48B*). Make the changes shown at the right. The information for footnotes 6–8 is given below.

[6]"Fact Sheet: European Community," Vol. 4, No. 7, Washington, D.C.: U.S. Department of State Dispatch (February 15, 1994), p. 89.

[7]Mario Bognanno and Kathryn J. Ready, eds., North American Free Trade Agreement (Westport, CT: Quorum Books, 1993), p. xiii.

[8]Rahul Jacob, "The Big Rise," Fortune (May 30, 1994), pp. 74-75.

The first step was ~~done~~ accomplished by the Paris and Rome treaties, which established the european community and consequently removed the economic barriers. The treaties called for members to establish a common market; a common customs tariff; and common economic, agricultural, transport, and nuclear policies.[6]

NAFTA. A trade agreement that will have a~~n~~ significant impact on the way business is conducted in the United States is the North American Free Trade Agreement. This trade agreement involves Canada, the United States, and Mexico. Proponents of NAFTA claim that the accord will not only increase trade throughout the Americas, but it will also moderate product prices and create jobs in all three of the countries.[7]

Over the years a number of trade agreements have been enacted that promote trade. The result of these agreements has been an ~~better~~ enhanced quality of life because of the increased access to goods and services produced in other countries.

Growth in Developing Countries' Economies

The growth in developing countries' economies is another major reason for globalizaiton. According to Jacob, the global surge means more consumers who need goods and servicse.[8] These needs appear because of the increase in percapita incomes of the developing countries.

(Report continued on next page)

SKILL BUILDER 1

Keyboard Review

1. Key each line twice SS; DS between 2-line groups.
2. If time permits, rekey lines that were awkward or difficult for you.

A/Z 1 Zoe had a pizza at the plaza by the zoo on a lazy, hazy day.

B/Y 2 Abby may be too busy to buy me a book for my long boat trip.

C/X 3 Zeno caught six cod to fix lunch for his six excited scouts.

D/W 4 Wilda would like to own the wild doe she found in the woods.

E/V 5 Evan will give us the van to move the five very heavy boxes.

F/U 6 All four of us bought coats with faux fur collars and cuffs.

G/T 7 Eight guys tugged the big boat into deep water to get going.

H/S 8 Marsha wishes to show us how to make charts on the computer.

I/R 9 Ira will rise above his ire to rid the firm of this problem.

J/Q 10 Quen just quietly quit the squad after a major joint injury.

K/P 11 Kip packed a backpack and put it on an oak box on the porch.

L/O 12 Lola is to wear the royal blue skirt and a gold wool blouse.

M/N 13 Many of the men met in the main hall to see the new manager.

figures 14 I worked from 8:30 to 5 at 1964 Lake Blvd. from May 7 to 26.

fig/sym 15 I quote, "ISBN #0-651-24876-3 was assigned to them in 1995."

Timed Writings

1. Key two 1' writings on each ¶; determine *gwam* on each writing.
2. Key two 2' writings on ¶s 1–2 combined; determine *gwam* on each writing.
3. Key two 3' writings on ¶s 1–2 combined; determine *gwam* and circle errors on each writing.
4. If time permits, key 1' guided writings on each ¶. To set a goal, add 2 to the *gwam* achieved in Step 1.

Quarter-Minute Checkpoints				
gwam	1/4'	1/2'	3/4'	1'
24	6	12	18	24
28	7	14	21	28
32	8	16	24	32
36	9	18	27	36
40	10	20	30	40
44	11	22	33	44
48	12	24	36	48
52	13	26	39	52
56	14	28	42	56

all letters used

	gwam 2'	3'
As you work for higher skill, remember that how well you	8	4
key fast is just as important as how fast you key. How well	12	8
you key at any speed depends in major ways upon the technique	18	12
or form you use. Bouncing hands and flying fingers lower the	24	16
speed, while quiet hands and low finger reaches increase speed.	31	20
Few of us ever reach what the experts believe is perfect	36	24
technique, but all of us should try to approach it. We must	42	28
realize that good form is the secret to higher speed with	48	32
fewer errors. We can then focus our practice on the improve-	54	36
ment of the features of good form that will bring success.	60	40

2' | 1 | 2 | 3 | 4 | 5 | 6

3' | 1 | 2 | 3 | 4

48B • 45' Bound Report

1. Review the report format guides on pp. 137–138; study the model report on p. 142. Note the format of the footnotes.
2. Key the first page of the Globalization report from the model on p. 142; continue keying the report from the rough-draft copy shown at the right. The information for footnotes 3, 4, and 5 is given below.

[3]Harris, p. 763.

[4]Encyclopedia Americana, Vol. 26 (Danbury, CT: Grolier Incorporated, 1993), p. 915.

[5]Louis S. Richman, "Dangerous Times for Trade Treaties," Fortune (September 20, 1993), p. 14.

3. When you finish, proofread your copy and correct any errors.

Save as: *RPT48B*

Note:

You will finish keying the Globalization report in Lesson 49.

- The reduction in trade and investment barriers in the post-world war II period.

- The rapid growth and increase in the size of developing countries' economies.

- Changes in technologies.[3]

Trade Agreements

Unfair Originally, each nation established its own rules governing foreign trade. Regulations and tariffs were often the out come, leading to the tariff wars of the 1930s.

> Nations have found it convenient . . . to agree to rules that limit their own freedom of action in trade matters, and generally to work toward removal of artificial and often arbitrary barriers to trade.[4]

Many trade agreements exist in the world today. Three of those agrements (General Agreement on Tariffs and Trade [GATT], the European Community, and the North American Free Trade Agreement [NAFTA]) have had or will have a significant impact on the UnitedStates.

GATT. The first trade agree ment of major significance was the General Agreement on Tariffs and Trade. The purpose of GATT was aimed at to lower tariff barriers among its members. The success of the organization is evidenced by its membership. Originally signed by 23 countries in 1947, the number of participating countries continues to grow.

> The Uruguay Round of GATT is the most ambitious trade agreement ever attempted. Some 108 nations would lower tariff and other barriers on textiles and agriculture goods; protect one another's intellectual property; and open their borders to banks, insurance companies, and purveyors of other services.[5]

The European Community. The European Community is another example of how trade agreements impact the production, distribution, and marketing of goods and services. The 12 member nations of the European Community have dismantled the internal borders of its members to enhance trade relations.

Dismantling the borders was only the first step toward an even greater purpose—the peaceful union of European countries.

(See Note at left.)

WORD PROCESSING 2

ACTIVITY 1

Margins

1. Read the copy at the right.
2. Learn how to set margins.
3. Set the left and right margins at 1.5". Key the first paragraph SS.
4. Change the left and right margins to 2". Key the second paragraph SS.

Save as: *WP2ACT1*

Use the **Margins** feature to change the amount of blank space at the top, bottom, right, and left edges of the paper.

The default margin settings are not the same for all software.

A person returning to the office environment after a 25-year absence would have a difficult time coping with the changes that have taken place during that time. Changing technology would best describe the challenges facing today's office worker.

Computers have replaced typewriters. Duplication methods have changed. Shorthand is an endangered skill with fewer and fewer office workers possessing it. And who had heard of the Internet 25 years ago?

ACTIVITY 2

Line Spacing

1. Read the copy at the right.
2. Use 1" right and left margins.
3. Learn how to change the line spacing for your wp software.

Use the **Line Spacing** feature of the software to change the amount of white space left between lines of text. The default setting for most wp software is single space. One-and-a-half spacing and double spacing are also common to most wp software.

4. Key the four lines (include numbers) below using the default line space setting. QS below the last line.
5. Change the line spacing to DS and key the four lines again.

Save as: *WP2ACT2*

1. Click the I-beam where you want the line spacing changed.
2. Select the option to change line spacing.
3. Specify the line spacing.
4. Begin or continue keying.

ACTIVITY 3

Widow/Orphan

1. Read the copy at the right.
2. Learn the Widow/Orphan feature for your software.
3. Open file *CD-WP2ACT3*. Notice that an orphan line appears at the top of p. 4.
4. Turn on the **Widow/ Orphan** feature at the beginning of that line. Notice how the feature reformats the text to prevent an orphan line.

Save as: *WP2ACT3*

The **Widow/Orphan** feature ensures that the first line of a paragraph does not appear by itself at the bottom of a page (**orphan line**) or that the last line of a paragraph does not appear by itself at the top of a page (**widow line**).

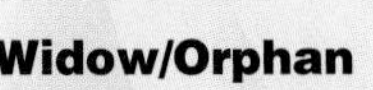

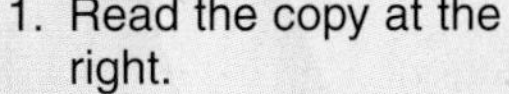

2

well organized, and easy to read.

Finally, support your report with a list of references from which you paraphrased or directly quoted. Quoting or paraphrasing without giving

Example of widow line

2"

Main heading

GLOBALIZATION

QS

We live in a time of worldwide change. What happens in one part of the world impacts people on the other side of the world. People around the world are influenced by common developments.[1]

Footnote superscript

The term "globalization" is used to describe this phenomenon. According to Harris, the term is being used in a variety of contexts.[2] In a very broad context, media use it almost daily to refer to a wide variety of political, sociological, environmental, and economic trends.

Footnote superscript

1.5" LM

1" RM

The business world, however, uses this term in a much narrower context to refer to the production, distribution, and marketing of goods and services at an international level. Everyone is impacted by the continued increase of globalization in a variety of ways. The types of food we eat, the kinds of clothes we wear, the variety of technologies that we utilize, the modes of transportation that are available to us, and the types of jobs we pursue are directly linked to "globalization." Globalization is changing the world we live in.

Causes of Globalization

Harris indicates that there are three main factors contributing to globalization. These factors include:

Footnotes

---

[1]Robert K. Schaeffer, Understanding Globalization (Lanham, MD: Rowman & Littlefield Publishers, Inc., 1997), p. 1.

[2]Richard G. Harris, "Globalization, Trade, and Income," Canadian Journal of Economics (November 1993), p. 755.

Bound Report with Footnotes

ACTIVITY 4

Indentation

1. Read the information at the right.
2. Learn how to change indentations for your wp software.
3. Key the three paragraphs at the right, indenting them as indicated.

 **Save as:** *WP2ACT4*

Use the **Indent** feature to move text away from the margin. A **left indent** (**paragraph indent**) moves the text one tab stop to the right, away from the left margin. A **hanging indent** moves all but the first line of a paragraph one tab stop to the right.

No indent

This example shows text that is not indented from the left margin. All lines begin at the left margin.

Left (paragraph) indent 0.5"

This example shows text that is indented from the left margin. Notice that each line begins at the indentation point.

Hanging indent 0.5"

This example shows hanging indent. Notice that the first line begins at the left margin, but the remaining lines begin at the indentation point.

ACTIVITY 5

Page Numbers

1. Read the copy at the right.
2. Learn how to number pages (and hide page numbers) with your wp software.
3. Open the document created in Activity 3 (*WP2ACT3*).
4. Number all five pages with the page number at bottom center of the page. Hide the number on p. 1.
5. Use View to verify that the page numbers have been added (pp. 2–5) or hidden (p. 1).

 **Save as:** *WP2ACT5*

Use the **Page Numbers** feature to place page numbers in specific locations on the printed page. Most software allows you to select the style of number or letter (Arabic numerals—1, 2, 3; lowercase Roman numerals—i, ii, iii; uppercase Roman numerals—I, II, III; uppercase letters—A, B, C; or lowercase letters—a, b, c). You can place numbers at the top or bottom of the page, aligned at the left margin, center, or right margin. Use the **Hide** or **Suppress** option to keep the page number from appearing on a page.

1

example). Finally, check the list to see that the items are tied together and related to the core idea. When appropriate, use tables, charts, or graphs to condense data; then list only summaries of what the visuals reveal in greater detail.
Draft the Message
To draft or compose the message, pretend that the reader is sitting before you. Write (at the keyboard) as you would talk with that person (level of vocabulary, degree of formality, and so on). Focus on the core of your message as you follow your listed items. Ignore for now such things as grammar, spelling, and style. Complete the entire report in one work session, if possible. If that is not possible, finish at least a major section without stopping (to gain continuity).
Revise the Copy
To revise, read and study what you wrote. Try to read the text as the reader will—without knowing what you meant to say. Ask again and again: Does it do what I set out to do—to get the message from my mind into the reader's mind in a favorable way? If not, why not? Check for and eliminate clichés, faulty logic, irrelevant facts or ideas, lack of examples, or vague statements. Revise the message until it cannot be misunderstood.
Edit the Text
To edit, study the revised draft and analyze how you said what you wrote, looking at each word, phrase, and sentence.

2

3

4

5

6

Page numbering positions

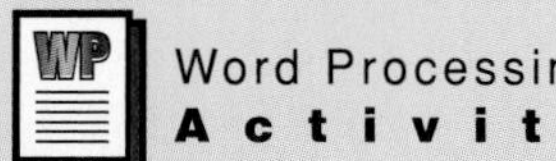

Open *CD-SPOTTAIL*. Make the corrections shown at the right, and copy/paste the text to the end of the PLAINS INDIANS report.

Document 2 (References Page)

Prepare a separate references page from the information at the right. Proofread; correct any errors.

Save as: *RPT47B2*

Use the Internet to learn about a person named in the report. Compose a paragraph about the person.

Spotted Tail

Spotted Tail (?1833-1881) was born along the White River either in present-day South Dakota or near present-day Laramie, Wyoming. He be came the leader of the Brulé Sioux and was one of the signers of the Fort Laramie Treaty of 1868. Eventually, he became the government-appointed chief of the agency Sioux andmade frequent trips to Washington, D.C. in that capacity. (Bowman, 1995, 688) Starting in 1870 spotted Tail became the statesman that made him the greatest chief the Brulés ever new. (Fielder, 1975, p. 29)

Bowman, John S. (ed). The Cambridge Dictionary of American Biography. Cambridge: Cambridge University Press, 1995.

Fielder, Mildred. Sioux Indian Leaders. Seattle: Superior Publishing Company, 1975.

Utley, Robert M. The Lance and the Shield: The Life and Times of Sitting Bull. New York: Henry Holt and Company, 1993.

LANGUAGE SKILLS

47C • 8' Language Skills: Word Choice

1. Study the spelling/definitions of these words.
2. For each set of sentences, key the Learn line; then the Apply lines. Choose the correct word in parentheses.
3. Check your work; correct lines containing word-choice errors.

Save as: *CHOICE47C*

some (n/adv) unknown or unspecified unit or thing; to a degree or extent

sum (n/vb) the whole amount; the total; to find a total; summary of points

hour (n) the 24th part of a day; a particular time

our (adj) of or relating to ourselves as possessors

Learn 1 The large **sum** awarded did not satisfy **some** of the people.
Apply 2 The first grader said, "The (some, sum) of five and two is seven."
Apply 3 (Some, Sum) students were able to find the correct (some, sum) for the problem.

Learn 1 The first **hour** of **our** class will be used for going over the next assignment.
Apply 2 What (hour, our) of the day would you like to have (hour, our) group perform?
Apply 3 Minutes turned into (hours, ours) as we waited for (hour, our) turn to perform.

LESSON 48 FORMAT BOUND REPORT WITH FOOTNOTES

Objectives:

1. To format a bound report with footnotes.
2. To format a references page.

48A • 5' Conditioning Practice

Key each line twice SS; then key a 1' writing on line 3; determine *gwam*.

alphabet 1 Bob Writz quickly thanked them for giving excellent jury reports.
fig/sym 2 The order (No. 3972) for 16 pies and 20 cakes ($385.34) was late.
speed 3 Make the panel suspend the pay of their officials as the penalty.

gwam 1' | 1 | 2 | 3 | 4 | 5 | 6 | 7 | 8 | 9 | 10 | 11 | 12 | 13 |

ACTIVITY 6

Apply What You Have Learned

1. Key the text at the right.
2. Center the heading in ALL CAPS 2" from the top; QS below title.
3. DS the first paragraph.
4. SS the second paragraph; indent it from the left margin, using the Paragraph Indent feature.
5. Center and key **REFERENCE** a QS below the second paragraph; QS below REFERENCE and key the reference.
6. Use the Hanging Indent feature to key the reference lines.
7. Use the Speller, then proofread.

 **Save as:** *WP2ACT6*

FAMOUS SPEECHES

Many famous speeches have been delivered over the years. The content of these speeches continues to be used to inspire, motivate, and unify us today. Winston Churchill and Abraham Lincoln delivered two great examples of such speeches.

> Winston Churchill served his country as soldier, statesman, historian, and journalist. His military career and work as a reporter took him to India, Cuba, and the Sudan. He was elected to Parliament in 1900, again from 1906-1908, and from 1924-1945. He held dozens of other key posts, including that of Prime Minister. (LaRocco and Johnson, 1997, 49)

REFERENCE

LaRocco, Christine B., and Elaine B. Johnson. British & World Literature for Life and Work. Cincinnati: South-Western Publishing Co., 1997.

ACTIVITY 7

Apply What You Have Learned

1. Set the left and right margins at 2".
2. Center and key each name (bold) and quotation on a separate page, with a QS between the name and quote.
3. Place page numbers at bottom center on each page.

 **Save as:** *WP2ACT7*

Nathan Hale

"I only regret that I have but one life to lose for my country."

Golda Meir

"A leader who doesn't hesitate before he sends his nation into battle is not fit to be a leader."

Jacqueline Kennedy Onassis

"If you bungle raising your kids, I don't think whatever else you do well matters very much."

Oscar Wilde

"Life is too serious to be taken seriously."

ACTIVITY 8

Review Tabs

1. Set a left tab at 1", a right tab at 3.5", and a decimal tab at 4.5".
2. Using these tabs, key lines 2–6 at the right.
3. Clear tabs; reset: left tab, 0.75"; right tab, 3.75"; decimal tab, 5".
4. Key lines 2–6 again.

 **Save as:** *WP2ACT8*

Player	**Hits**	**Average**
Walker, Colorado	166	.379
Gonzalez, Arizona	206	.336
Abreu, Philadelphia	183	.335
Casey, Cincinnati	197	.332
Cirillo, Milwaukee	198	.326

Crazy Horse

(?1842-1877)

Crazy Horse was also born near the Black Hills. His father was a medicine man;his mother wasthe sister of Spotted Tail. He was recognized as a skilled hunter and fighter. Crazy Horse believed he was imune from battle injury and took part in all the major Sioux battles to protect the Black Hills. He was named war supreme and peace chief of the Oglalas in 1876 and led the Sioux and Cheyenne to victory at the battle of Rosebud in January that year. Perhaps he is remembered most for leading the Sioux and Cheyenne in the battle of the Bighorn where his warriors defeated Custers forces. Crazy Horse is regarded at the greatest leader of the Sioux and a symbol of there heroic resistance. (Bowman, 1995, 160-161)

m · # · # · against white intrusion · Little · ' · , · as · ir

Red Cloud

Red Cloud (1822-1909) was born near the Platte River in present-day Nebraska. Because of his intelligence, strength, and bravery, he became the the chief of the Oglala Sioux. Red Cloud's War took place between 1865 and 1868. These battles forced the closing of the Bozeman trail and the sining of the Fort Laramie Treaty in 1868. In exchange for peace, the U.S. government accepted the territorial claims of the sioux. (Bowman, 1995, 601)

" · " · g

Sitting Bull

Sitting Bull (?1831-1890) was born on the Grand River in South Dakota. He was nown among the Sioux as a war rior even during his youth. He was bitterly opposed to white encroachment but made peace in 1868 when the U.S. government gave him a large reservation free of white settlers. When gold was discovered, he joined the Arapaho to fight the invaders. (Bowman, 1995, 673) According to fellow tribesmen, the name Sitting Bull, suggested an animal possessed of great endurance that planted immovably on its haunches to fight on to the death. (Utley, 1993, 15)

k · , · guaranteed · in the Black Hills

and Cheyenne

![WP] Word Processing Activity

Open file *CD-REDCLOUD*. Make the corrections shown at the right. Then copy/paste the text in the PLAINS INDIANS report (Document 1) where indicated.

History Bits

"Impossible!" easterners scoffed. "Herds of bison so immense they stretched as far as the eye could see? Half-mile-deep canyons carved by rivers through solid rock? Winter temperatures so bitter expectorations froze? Preposterous. Unbelievable."

—Bill Vossler

(Report continued on next page)

UNIT 8

LESSONS 25-27

Learn to Format Unbound Reports

Format Guides: Unbound Reports

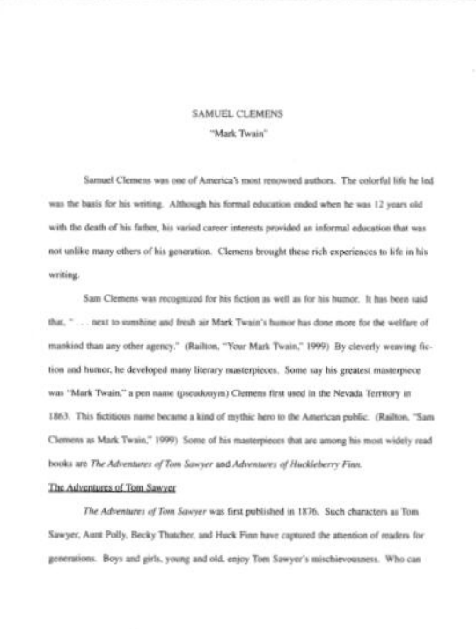

SAMUEL CLEMENS

"Mark Twain"

Samuel Clemens was one of America's most renowned authors. The colorful life he led was the basis for his writing. Although his formal education ended when he was 12 years old with the death of his father, his varied career interests provided an informal education that was not unlike many others of his generation. Clemens brought these rich experiences to life in his writing.

Sam Clemens was recognized for his fiction as well as for his humor. It has been said that, " . . . next to sunshine and fresh air Mark Twain's humor has done more for the welfare of mankind than any other agency." (Railton, "Your Mark Twain," 1999) By cleverly weaving fiction and humor, he developed many literary masterpieces. Some say his greatest masterpiece was "Mark Twain," a pen name (pseudonym) Clemens first used in the Nevada Territory in 1863. This fictitious name became a kind of mythic hero to the American public. (Railton, "Sam Clemens as Mark Twain," 1999) Some of his masterpieces that are among his most widely read books are *The Adventures of Tom Sawyer* and *Adventures of Huckleberry Finn.*

The Adventures of Tom Sawyer

The Adventures of Tom Sawyer was first published in 1876. Such characters as Tom Sawyer, Aunt Polly, Becky Thatcher, and Huck Finn have captured the attention of readers for generations. Boys and girls, young and old, enjoy Tom Sawyer's mischievousness. Who can

Page 1

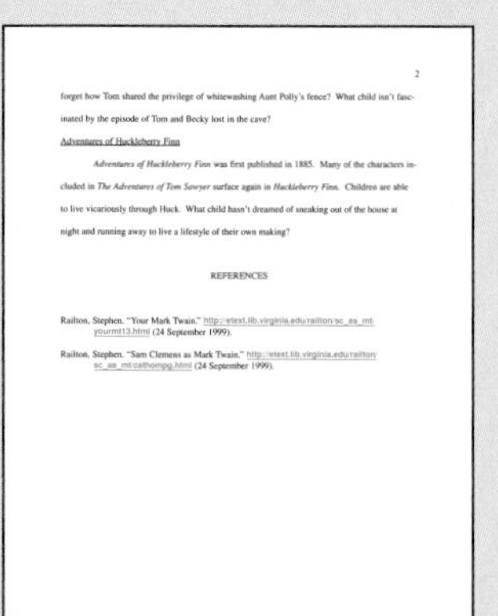

2

forget how Tom shared the privilege of whitewashing Aunt Polly's fence? What child isn't fascinated by the episode of Tom and Becky lost in the cave?

Adventures of Huckleberry Finn

Adventures of Huckleberry Finn was first published in 1885. Many of the characters included in *The Adventures of Tom Sawyer* surface again in *Huckleberry Finn.* Children are able to live vicariously through Huck. What child hasn't dreamed of sneaking out of the house at night and running away to live a lifestyle of their own making?

REFERENCES

Railton, Stephen. "Your Mark Twain." http://etext.lib.virginia.edu/railton/sc_as_mt/yourmt13.html (24 September 1999).

Railton, Stephen. "Sam Clemens as Mark Twain." http://etext.lib.virginia.edu/railton/sc_as_mt/cathompg.html (24 September 1999).

Page 2

Short reports are often prepared without covers or binders. If they consist of more than one page, the pages are usually fastened together in the upper-left corner by a staple or paper clip. Such reports are called **unbound** reports.

Standard Margins

The standard margins for unbound reports are presented below.

First page:	
Side margins:	1"
Top margin:	2"
Bottom margin:	about 1"
Page number:	optional; bottom at center if used
Second and subsequent pages:	
Side margins:	1"
Top margin:	1"
Bottom margin:	about 1"
Page number:	top; right-aligned

Internal Spacing

A QS is left between the report title and the first line of the body. Multiple-line titles are DS.

A DS is left above and below side headings and between paragraphs. Paragraphs may be SS or DS. *The reports you key in this unit will have DS paragraphs.*

Page Numbers

The first page of an unbound report may or may not include a page number. *The reports keyed for this unit will not include a page number on the first page.* On the second and subsequent pages, the page number should be right-aligned at the top of the page. Your software will automatically place the page number in the location you specify.

Textual (Within Text) Citations

References used to give credit for quoted or paraphrased material—called **textual citations**—are keyed in parentheses in the report body. Textual citations include the name(s) of the author(s), year of publication, and page number(s) of the reference material. **Note:** For electronic references (from the Internet), textual citations include the name(s) of the author(s) and the year of publication.

Quotations of up to three keyed lines are enclosed in quotation marks. Long quotations (four lines or more) are left indented (or left and right indented). Paraphrased material is not enclosed in quotation marks, nor is it indented.

An **ellipsis** (. . .) is used to indicate material omitted from a quotation. An ellipsis is three periods, each preceded and followed by a space. If the omitted material occurs at the end of a sentence, include the period or other punctuation before the ellipsis.

```
In ancient Greece, plays were
performed only a few times a
year. . . . The festivals were
held to honor Dionysus in the hope
that he would bless the Greeks. .
. . (Prince and Jackson, 1997, 35)
```

Reference List

All references used in a report are listed at the end under the heading REFERENCES (or BIBLIOGRAPHY or WORKS CITED). QS between the heading and the first reference. References are listed alphabetically by authors' last names. SS each reference; DS between references. Begin first line of each reference at left margin; indent other lines 0.5".

If the reference list appears on the last page of the report body, QS between the last line of text and REFERENCES. If the reference list appears on a separate page, use the same margins as for the first page of the report and include a page number.

LESSON 47 | IMPROVE REPORT FORMATTING SKILLS

Objectives:

1. To format a bound report with textual citations and references.
2. To improve word choice skills.

47A • 5'
Conditioning Practice

Key each line twice SS; then key a 1' writing on line 3; determine *gwam*.

alphabet 1 Jack Fitzgerald always competed in the six big equestrian events.

figures 2 Only 6,398 of the 14,652 men scored above 70 percent on the test.

speed 3 Dick is to make a turn to the right at the big sign for downtown.

gwam 1' | 1 | 2 | 3 | 4 | 5 | 6 | 7 | 8 | 9 | 10 | 11 | 12 | 13 |

FORMATTING

47B • 37'
Bound Report

Document 1 (Report Body)

1. Review the format guides for bound reports on pp. 137–138 as needed.
2. Format the text at the right and on pp. 140 and 141 as a bound report with textual citations.
3. When you finish, proofread your copy and correct any errors.

Save as: *RPT47B1*

History Bits

"I will return to you in stone."

—Crazy Horse

"My fellow chiefs and I would like the white man to know the red man has great heroes, too."

—Lakota Chief Henry Standing Bear

PLAINS INDIANS

The American Plains Indians are among the ~~most~~ best known of all Native Americans. These Indians played a significant role in shaping the history of the West. Some of the more noteworthy Plains Indians were big Foot, Black Kettle, Crazy Horse, Red Cloud, Sitting Bull, and Spotted Tail.

Big Foot

Big Foot (?1825-1890) was also known as Spotted Elk. Born in the northern Great Plains, he eventually became a Minneconjou Teton Sioux chief. He was part of a tribal delegation that traveled to Wash ington, D.C., and worke d to establish schools throughout the Sioux territory. He was one of those massacred at Wounded Knee in December 1890. (Bowman, 1995, 63)

Black Kettle

Black Kettle (?1803-1868) was born near the Black Hills in present-day South Dakota. He was recognized as a Southern Cheyenne peace chief for his efforts to bring peace to the region. However, his attempts at accommodation ~~failed~~ were not successful, and his band was massacred at sand creek in 1864. Even though he continued to seek peace, he was killed with the remainder of his tribe in the Washita Valley of Oklahoma in 1868. (Bowman, 1995, 67)

(Report continued on next page)

2" TM

Title

EFFECTIVE COMMUNICATORS

QS

Report body

Communication is the thread that binds our society together. Effective communicators are able to use the thread (communication skills) to shape the future. To be an effective communicator, one must know how to put words together that communicate thoughts, ideas, and feelings. These thoughts, ideas, and feelings are then expressed in writing or delivered orally. Some individuals are immortalized because of their ability to put words together. A few examples of those who have been immortalized are Patrick Henry, Nathan Hale, and Abraham Lincoln.

DS

Side heading

Patrick Henry

DS

1" LM

1" RM

Words move people to action. Patrick Henry's words ("I know not what course others may take; but as for me, give me liberty or give me death!") helped bring about the Revolutionary War in 1775.

DS

Side heading

Nathan Hale

DS

Words show an individual's commitment. Who can question Nathan Hale's commitment when he said, "I only regret that I have but one life to lose for my country."

DS

Side heading

Abraham Lincoln

DS

Words can inspire. The Gettysburg Address (Abraham Lincoln, 1863) inspired the Union to carry on its cause. Today many Americans, still inspired by Lincoln's words, have memorized at least part of his address. "Four score and seven years ago, our fathers brought forth on this continent a new nation, . . . dedicated to the proposition that all men are created equal. . . ."

About 1"

Unbound Report, page 1

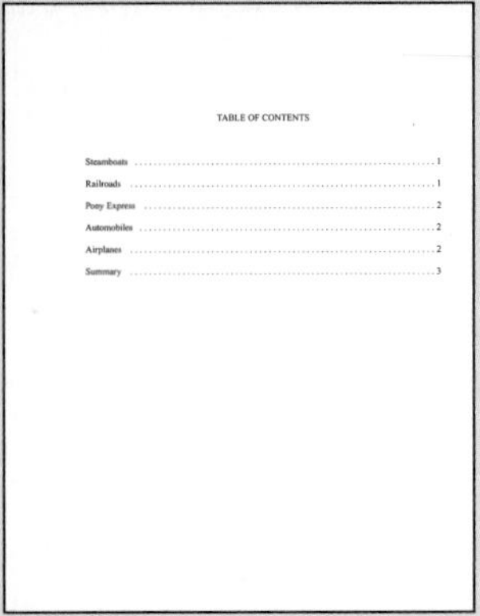

Table of Contents

Table of Contents

A table of contents lists the headings of a report and the page numbers where those headings can be found in the report. The side and top margins for the table of contents are the same as those used for the first page of the report. Include TABLE OF CONTENTS (centered, 2" from top) as a heading. Then QS before listing side and paragraph headings (if included). Side headings are DS beginning at left margin; paragraph headings are indented and SS with a DS above and below them. Page numbers for each entry are keyed at the right margin.

Documentation

Documentation is used to give credit for published material (electronic as well as printed) that is quoted or closely paraphrased (slightly changed). Three types of documentation will be used in this unit: textual citation, endnotes, and footnotes.

Textual citation. The textual citation method of documentation was used in Unit 8. This method includes the name(s) of the author(s), the date of the referenced publication, and the page number(s) of the material cited as part of the report text.

`(Wagner, 2001, 248)`

When the author's name is used in the text introducing the quotation, only the year of publication and the page number(s) appear in parentheses.

`Wagner (2001, 248) said that . . .`

For electronic references, include the author's name and the year.

Endnotes. The endnotes method of documentation identifies the reference cited by a superscript number. . . .[1]

The complete documentation for the reference is placed at the end of the report in a section titled ENDNOTES. The references listed in the endnotes section are placed in the same order they appear in the report. A corresponding superscript number identifies the reference in the text.

The endnotes page has the same top and side margins as the first page of the report, except that it has a page number 1" from the top at the right margin. Each endnote is SS, with a DS between endnotes. The first line of each endnote is indented 0.5" from the left margin (keyed to a superscript endnote number); all other lines begin at the left margin.

[1]Richard G. Harris, "Globalization, Trade, and Income," Canadian Journal of Economics (November 1993), p. 755.

Footnotes. The footnotes method of documentation also identifies the reference cited by a superscript number. . . .[1]

However, the complete documentation for the reference is placed at the bottom of the same page and is identified with the same superscript number (see model report on p. 142).

Each footnote is indented 0.5" and SS, with a DS between footnotes. Footnotes should be numbered consecutively throughout a report.

References page. Each of these three types of documentation (textual citation, endnotes, and footnotes) requires a references page. All references cited in the report are listed alphabetically by author surnames at the end of a report under the heading REFERENCES (or BIBLIOGRAPHY or WORKS CITED). QS between the heading and the first reference.

Use the same margins as for the first page of the report and include a page number. SS each reference; DS between references. Begin the first line of each reference at the left margin; indent other lines 0.5" (or to the paragraph indentation point).

LESSON 25 FORMAT UNBOUND REPORTS

Objectives:

1. To learn format features of unbound reports.
2. To process a one-page unbound report in proper format.

25A • 5' Conditioning Practice

Key each line twice SS; then key a 1' writing on line 3; determine *gwam.*

alphabet 1 Jack will help Mary fix the quaint old stove at the big zoo.
figures 2 Check Numbers 197, 267, 304, and 315 were cashed on June 28.
speed 3 Jan and Sydney may wish to make gowns for the civic socials.

gwam 1' | 1 | 2 | 3 | 4 | 5 | 6 | 7 | 8 | 9 | 10 | 11 | 12 |

FORMATTING

25B • 35' Unbound Report

Save as: *RPT25B*

1. Read the format guides on p. 70; study the model report on p. 71.
2. Key the model report using the spacing guides given on the model; run the Speller, proofread, and correct errors.
3. If time permits, key the report again at rough-draft speed to increase your input speed.

25C • 10' Report Formatting/ Editing

Open *TITLES15C*, which you created in Lesson 15. For each of the six stories, reformat the title, author, and first sentence in report format as shown at the right. Each entry should appear on a separate page.

Save as: *RPTS25C*

2" TM

(Title) THE SCOTTY WHO KNEW TOO MUCH
DS
(Author) by James Thurber
QS
(First sentence) Several summers ago there was a Scotty who went to the country for a visit.

Page number centered at the bottom of the page.

1

LESSON 26 FORMAT UNBOUND REPORT WITH TEXTUAL CITATIONS

Objectives:

1. To process a two-page unbound report in proper format.
2. To format textual citations in a report.
3. To process references.

26A • 5' Conditioning Practice

Key each line twice SS; then key a 1' writing on line 3; determine *gwam.*

alphabet 1 Jessica moved quickly to her left to win the next big prize.
figures 2 Mike used a comma in 3,209 and 4,146 but not in 769 and 805.
speed 3 The key is to name the right six goals and to work for them.

gwam 1' | 1 | 2 | 3 | 4 | 5 | 6 | 7 | 8 | 9 | 10 | 11 | 12 |

UNIT 15

LESSONS 47-52

Improve Report Formatting Skills

Format Guides: Bound Reports

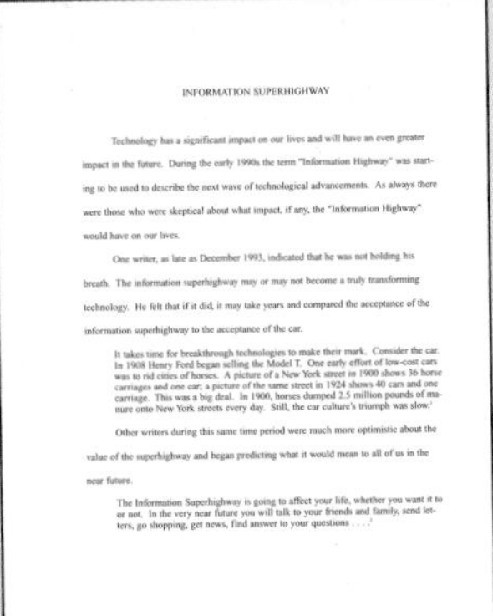

INFORMATION SUPERHIGHWAY

Technology has a significant impact on our lives and will have an even greater impact in the future. During the early 1990s the term "Information Highway" was starting to be used to describe the next wave of technological advancements. As always there were those who were skeptical about what impact, if any, the "Information Highway" would have on our lives.

One writer, as late as December 1993, indicated that he was not holding his breath. The information superhighway may or may not become a truly transforming technology. He felt that if it did, it may take years and compared the acceptance of the information superhighway to the acceptance of the car.

> It takes time for breakthrough technologies to make their mark. Consider the car. In 1908 Henry Ford began selling the Model T. One early effort of low-cost cars was to rid cities of horses. A picture of a New York street in 1900 shows 36 horse carriages and one car; a picture of the same street in 1924 shows 40 cars and one carriage. This was a big deal. In 1900, horses dumped 2.5 million pounds of manure onto New York streets every day. Still, the car culture's triumph was slow.[1]

Other writers during this same time period were much more optimistic about the value of the superhighway and began predicting what it would mean to all of us in the near future.

> The Information Superhighway is going to affect your life, whether you want it to or not. In the very near future you will talk to your friends and family, send letters, go shopping, get news, find answer to your questions . . . .[2]

Bound Report with Long Quotations, Endnotes

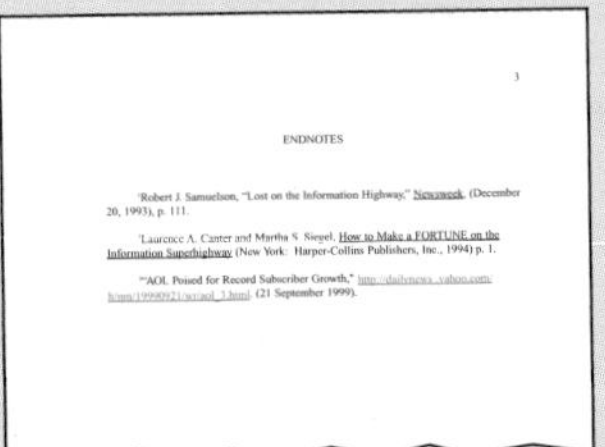

3

ENDNOTES

[1]Robert J. Samuelson, "Lost on the Information Highway," Newsweek, (December 20, 1993), p. 111.

[2]Laurence A. Canter and Martha S. Siegel, How to Make a FORTUNE on the Information Superhighway (New York: Harper-Collins Publishers, Inc., 1994) p. 1.

[3]"AOL Poised for Record Subscriber Growth," http://dailynews.yahoo.com/h/nm/19990921/wr/aol_1.html, (21 September 1999).

Endnotes Page

DELIVERING THE MAIL

Student Name

School Name

Current Date

Bound Report Title Page

In Unit 8 you learned to format short, **unbound** reports using the textual citation method of documentation. In this unit you will learn to format longer **bound** reports. The endnote and footnote methods of documentation are introduced in this unit.

Bound Reports

Longer reports are generally bound at the left margin. The binding takes about one-half inch (0.5") of space. To accommodate the binding, the left margin is increased to 1.5" on all pages.

Standard Margins

Except for the left margin (1" for unbound and 1.5" for bound), all margin settings are the same for unbound and bound reports. The right margin is 1". A top margin of 2" and a bottom margin of about 1" are customarily used on the first page of reports. All remaining pages are keyed with 1" top and bottom margins. Because an exact 1" bottom margin is not always possible, the bottom margin may be adjusted to prevent a side heading or first line of a paragraph from printing as the last line on a page (orphan); or the last line of a paragraph from occurring at the top of a new page (widow). The Widow/Orphan software feature (p. 67) also may be used to prevent these problems.

Page Numbering

The first page of a report usually is not numbered. However, if a page number is used on the first page, position it at the bottom of the page using center alignment. On the second and subsequent pages, position the page number at the top of the page using right alignment.

Internal Spacing

A QS is left between the report title and the first line of the body. Multiple-line titles are DS.

A DS is left above and below side headings and between paragraphs. The reports you key in this unit will have DS paragraphs. However, paragraphs may be SS or DS. The DS paragraphs are indented 0.5".

Long quotes. Quoted material of four or more lines should be SS and indented 0.5" from the left margin. DS above and below the quoted material. The first line is indented an additional 0.5" if the quotation starts at the beginning of a paragraph.

Enumerated items. Indent enumerated items 0.5" from the left margin; block the lines at that point. Single-space individual items; DS between items. Double-space above and below a series of items.

Headings and Subheadings

Main heading. Center the main heading in ALL CAPS.

Side headings. Begin side headings at the left margin. Capitalize the first letter of the first word and all other main words in each heading. Underline side headings.

Paragraph headings. Indent paragraph headings 0.5" from the left margin. Capitalize only the first letter of the first word and any proper nouns; underline the heading; and follow the heading with a period.

Title Page

A cover or title page is prepared for most bound reports. To format a title page, center the title in ALL CAPS 2" from the top. Center the writer's name in capital and lowercase letters 5" from the top. The school name is centered a DS below the writer's name. The date should be centered 9" from the top.

2" TM

Title

SAMUEL CLEMENS

DS

"Mark Twain"

QS

Report body

Samuel Clemens was one of America's most renowned authors. The colorful life he led was the basis for his writing. Although his formal education ended when he was 12 years old with the death of his father, his varied career interests provided an informal education that was not unlike many others of his generation. Clemens brought these rich experiences to life in his writing.

1" LM

1" RM

DS

Sam Clemens was recognized for his fiction as well as for his humor. It has been said that, " . . . next to sunshine and fresh air Mark Twain's humor has done more for the welfare of mankind than any other agency." (Railton, "Your Mark Twain," 1999) By cleverly weaving fiction and humor, he developed many literary masterpieces. Some say his greatest masterpiece was "Mark Twain," a pen name (pseudonym) Clemens first used in the Nevada Territory in 1863. This fictitious name became a kind of mythic hero to the American public. (Railton, "Sam Clemens as Mark Twain," 1999) Some of his masterpieces that are among his most widely read books are *The Adventures of Tom Sawyer* and *Adventures of Huckleberry Finn.*

Textual citation

Textual citation

DS

Side heading

The Adventures of Tom Sawyer

DS

The Adventures of Tom Sawyer was first published in 1876. Such characters as Tom Sawyer, Aunt Polly, Becky Thatcher, and Huck Finn have captured the attention of readers for generations. Boys and girls, young and old, enjoy Tom Sawyer's mischievousness. Who can

About 1"

Unbound Report with Textual Citations, page 1

(continued on next page)

ACTIVITY 7

Insert File

1. Read the information at the right; learn to use the Insert File feature for your software.
2. Leaving a 2" top margin, key the copy at the right (except words printed in red).
3. Insert the *CD-EXAM1* and *CD-EXAM2* files where indicated at the right.

 **Save as:** *WP6ACT7*

To insert an existing file into a file that you are currently working on, use the **Insert File** feature.

TABLE EXAMS

Here is a list of the software features you will need to know for the first exam on tables.

Insert ***CD-EXAM1*** file.

For the second exam on tables, you will need to know the following table formatting software features.

Insert ***CD-EXAM2*** file.

ACTIVITY 8

Dot Leader Tab

1. Read the information at the right; learn to use the Dot Leader Tab feature for your software.
2. Format and key the copy at the right, leaving a 2" TM and using the Dot Leader Tab feature. Leave a space before and after inserting the dot leader tab to enhance the appearance of the text.

 **Save as:** *WP6ACT8*

The **Dot Leader Tab** feature automatically places dot leaders (. . . .) between columns of designated text. The leaders lead the eyes from the text in the first column to the text in the second column. A *right* dot leader tab inserts the text to the left of the tab setting; a *left* dot leader tab inserts the text to the right of the tab setting.

TELEPHONE EXTENSIONS

Felix McDowell 1844

Ryan Smith 2915

Maria Sanchez 4895

Rebecca LaFrentz 4817

ACTIVITY 9

Apply What You Have Learned

1. Set a right dot leader tab at the right margin.
2. Key the text, leaving a 2" TM and using dot leaders.
3. Set a left dot leader tab 1.5" to the left of the right margin.
4. QS and key the text again. Notice how the names in the right column are aligned when a left dot leader tab is used versus a right tab.
5. Use the Sort feature to alphabetize by city.

 **Save as:** *WP6ACT9*

BRANCH MANAGERS

Phoenix Manager . . . . Sharon Tietz

Denver Manager . . . . Orlando Perez

Dallas Manager . . . . Karla Kwan

New York Manager . . . . Austin Alexander

Orlando Manager . . . . Chad Nowitzki

Minneapolis Manager . . . . Predrag DeWees

Page number

2

forget how Tom shared the privilege of whitewashing Aunt Polly's fence? What child isn't fascinated by the episode of Tom and Becky lost in the cave?

DS

Side heading

Adventures of Huckleberry Finn

DS

1" LM

Adventures of Huckleberry Finn was first published in 1885. Many of the characters included in *The Adventures of Tom Sawyer* surface again in *Huckleberry Finn.* Children are able to live vicariously through Huck. What child hasn't dreamed of sneaking out of the house at night and running away to live a lifestyle of their own making?

1" RM

QS

REFERENCES

QS

List of references

Railton, Stephen. "Your Mark Twain." http://etext.lib.virginia.edu/railton/sc_as_mt/yourmt13.html (24 September 1999).

DS

Railton, Stephen. "Sam Clemens as Mark Twain." http://etext.lib.virginia.edu/railton/sc_as_mt/cathompg.html (24 September 1999).

Unbound Report with Textual Citations, page 2

26B • 37' Unbound Report

 **Save as:** *RPT26B*

1. Review the format guides on p. 70; study the model report on pp. 73–74.
2. Key the model report; follow the spacing guides. Run the Speller, proofread, and correct errors.
3. If time permits, key the report again at rough-draft speed.

LANGUAGE SKILLS

26C • 8' Language Skills: Word Choice

1. Study the spelling/definitions of the words at the right.
2. Key line 1, noting the proper choice of words.
3. Key lines 2–3, choosing the right words.
4. Check your work; correct lines with errors.

 **Save as:** *CHOICE26C*

know (vb) to be aware of the truth of; to have understanding of

no (adv/adj/n) in no respect or degree; not so; indicates denial or refusal

your (adj) of or relating to you or yourself as possessor

you're (contr) you are

Learn 1 Did she **know** that there are **no** exceptions to the rule?
Apply 2 I just (know, no) that this is going to be a great year.
Apply 3 (Know, No), she didn't (know, no) that she was late.

Learn 1 When **you're** on campus, be sure to pick up **your** schedule.
Apply 2 (Your, You're) mother left (your, you're) keys on the table.
Apply 3 When (your, you're) out of the office, (your, you're) supervisor should be informed.

ACTIVITY 4

Footnotes and Endnotes

1. Read the information at the right; learn to use the Footnote and Endnote feature in your software.
2. Open file *CD-TAXES.* Insert the two footnotes shown at the right where indicated in the file.
3. Delete *(Insert footnote No. x)* from the copy.

 **Save as:** *WP6ACT4*

Use the **Footnote and Endnote** feature to identify sources quoted in your text. WP software automatically positions and prints each footnote at the bottom of the same page as the reference to it. It automatically prints endnotes on a separate page at the end of the report. WP software lets you edit, add, or delete footnotes and endnotes and automatically makes the necessary changes in numbering and formatting.

[1]David J. Rachman and Michael H. Mescon, Business Today (New York: Random House, 1987), p. 529.

[2]Greg Anrig, Jr., "Making the Most of 1988's Low Tax Rate," Money (February 1988), pp. 56-57.

Optional Activity

1. Open *WP6ACT4.*
2. Change both footnotes to endnotes.
3. Print the Endnotes page only.
4. Save the file as *WP6ACT4OP.*

ACTIVITY 5

Superscript

1. Read the information at the right; learn to use the Superscript feature.
2. Open file *CD-VOICEMAIL.* Change the three endnote numbers to superscripts.
3. Delete *(Apply superscript . . .)* from the copy.
4. Format endnotes 2 and 3 (at the right) on page 2 of the file, below endnote 1.

 **Save as:** *WP6ACT5*

Text may be placed slightly higher than other text on a line by using the **Superscript** feature. The superscript is commonly used for footnotes and endnotes not inserted with the Footnote and Endnote feature, and for mathematical formulas and equations.

ENDNOTES

[1]John Grove, "New Media for Your Messages," The Secretary (March 1993), p. 6.

[2]Grove, p. 7.

[3]Amy Gage, "Voice Mail Technology Can Be a Source of Frustration, Irritation," St. Paul Pioneer Press (August 3, 1994), p. 1C.

ACTIVITY 6

Bullets and Numbering

1. Read the information at the right; learn to use the Bullets and Numbering features in your software.
2. Format and key the text at the right using the Bullets and Numbering features. Use bullets of your choice.

 **Save as:** *WP6ACT6*

Bullets (special characters) are used to enhance the appearance of text. Bullets are often used to add visual interest or emphasis. Examples of bullets: ❖ ➢ ✓ •

Numbering is used to show the proper order of a series of steps. Use numbers instead of bullets whenever the order of items is important.

Please contact the following freshmen to determine if they would like to try out for the play next week: (*insert bulleted list*) Anita Rawlins, Roberto Jimanez, Ho Chi.

Then do the following:

1. Check files for names of freshmen in last year's play.
2. Contact them to see if they will participate this year.
3. Contact these sophomores to see if they are still interested: (*insert bulleted list*) Ted Roberts, Marsha Mallory, Clint Hernandez.

FORMAT UNBOUND REPORT WITH REFERENCES

Objectives:

1. To process a two-page unbound report in proper format.
2. To process a references page.

27A • 5' Conditioning Practice

Key each line twice SS; then key a 1' writing on line 3; determine *gwam*.

alphabet 1 Jacob Lutz made the very quick trip to France six weeks ago.

figures 2 Only 1,359 of the 6,487 members were at the 2001 convention.

speed 3 They may turn down the lane by the shanty to their big lake.

1' | 1 | 2 | 3 | 4 | 5 | 6 | 7 | 8 | 9 | 10 | 11 | 12 |

FORMATTING

27B • 45' Unbound Reports

Report 1

Format the text at the right as a DS unbound report. Include the references given below on a separate page of the report. Correct errors as you key.

Save as: *RPT27B1*

REFERENCES

***Encyclopedia Americana*, Vol. 25. "Statue of Liberty." Danbury, CT: Grolier Incorporated, 1998.**

Luedtke, Luther S., ed. *Making America*. Chapel Hill: University of North Carolina Press, 1992.

Search the Web for additional information about immigration.

Be prepared to make a few comments to your classmates about what you found.

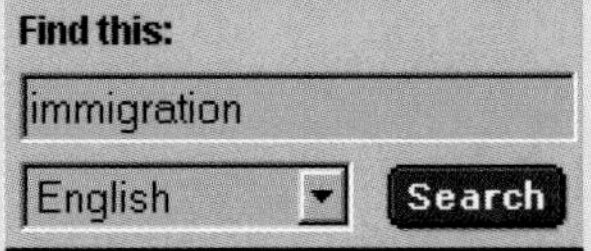

IMMIGRATION TO AMERICA

America has often been called the "melting pot." The name is derived from America's rich tradition of opening its doors to immigrants from all over the world. These immigrants came to the United States looking for something better. Most of them did not possess wealth or power in their home countries. Most were not highly educated. Other than these few commonalities of what they didn't possess, their backgrounds were vastly different. The thread, however, that bound these immigrants together was their vision of improving their current situation.

Emma Lazarus, in a poem entitled "The New Colossus," which is inscribed on the pedestal of the Statue of Liberty, tells of the invitation extended to those wanting to make America their home. ". . . Give me your tired, your poor, your huddled masses yearning to breathe free, ..." (*Encyclopedia Americana*, 1998, Vol. 25, 637)

Immigration Before 1780

Many have accepted the invitation to make America their home. Most of the immigrants before 1780 were from Europe.

The "melting pot" concept can be better understood by the following quote. "I could point out to you a family whose grandfather was an Englishman, whose wife was Dutch, whose son married a French woman, and whose four sons have wives of different nations." (Luedtke, 1992, 3)

Recent Immigration

Recent immigration patterns have changed; the reasons have not. Individuals and families still come to the United States with a vision of improving their lives. The backgrounds of today's immigrants expand beyond the European borders. Today they come from all over the world. At a 1984 oath-taking ceremony in Los Angeles, there were nearly a thousand individuals from the Philippines, 890 from Mexico, 704 from Vietnam, 110 from Lebanon, 126 from the United Kingdom, and 62 from Israel. Although not as large a number, there were also individuals from Lithuania, Zimbabwe, and Tanzania. (Luedtke, 1992, 3)

WORD PROCESSING 6

ACTIVITY 1

Review WP Features: Margins, Spacing, and Left (Paragraph) Indent

1. Format and key the copy at the right, using a 1.5" left margin and a 1" right margin. DS ¶ 1; SS ¶ 2.
2. Use the Left (Paragraph) Indent feature to indent the long quotation (¶ 2) 0.5" from the left margin.

 **Save as:** *WP6ACT1*

Another speech of significant magnitude was delivered by Winston Churchill. (1940, 572) His words not only lifted the spirits of the British but also were motivational to those committed to the Allied cause.

> We shall go on to the end, we shall fight in France, we shall fight on the seas and oceans, we shall fight with growing confidence and growing strength in the air, we shall defend our island, whatever the cost may be, we shall fight on the beaches, we shall fight on the landing grounds, we. . . .

ACTIVITY 2

Review WP Features: Margins, Alignment, and Hanging Indent

1. Set a 1.5" left margin and a 1" right margin. Use the Align Right feature to place the page number (**6**) 1" from the top at the right margin.
2. Center and key REFERENCES 2" from the top of the paper; QS. Use the Hanging Indent feature to format and key the references shown at the right.

 **Save as:** *WP6ACT2*

6

REFERENCES

Churchill, Winston. "We Shall Fight in the Fields and in the Streets." London, June 4, 1940. Quoted by William J. Bennett, The Book of Virtues. New York: Simon & Schuster, 1993.

Henry, Patrick. "Liberty or Death." Richmond, VA, March 23, 1775. Quoted in North American Biographies, Vol. 6. Danbury, CT: Grolier Education Corporation, 1994.

Lincoln, Abraham. "The Gettysburg Address." Gettysburg, PA, November 19, 1863. Quoted by Joseph Nathan Kane, Facts About the President, 5th ed. New York: The H. W. Wilson Company, 1989.

ACTIVITY 3

Review WP Feature: Copy Text from File to File

The text shown at the right completes the Winston Churchill quote in Activity 1.

1. Open file *CD-CHURCHILL* and copy the text.
2. Open *WP6ACT1* (the file created in Activity 1 above).
3. Paste the copied text at the ellipsis; then delete the ellipsis.

 **Save as:** *WP6ACT3*

> shall fight in the fields and in the streets, we shall fight in the hills; we shall never surrender, and even if, which I do not for a moment believe, this island or a large part of it were subjugated and starving, then our Empire beyond the seas, armed and guarded by the British fleet, would carry on the struggle, until in God's good time, the New World, with all its power and might, steps forth to the rescue and the liberation of the old.

Report 2
Process the play review shown at the right as a DS unbound report. Correct errors as you key.

 **Save as:** *RPT27B2*

PLAY REVIEW

by

Denise Jackson

Carousel, the Rodgers and Hammerstein classic musical, has been revived in a stunning new production at Omnibus University.

Students of Rodgers and Hammerstein's work will note the fresh approach from the opening curtain. Gone is the traditional park scene. In its stead is a cleverly staged "mill" workroom complete with a gigantic loom. The scene rapidly changes to an amusement park with a modern multicolored spinning carousel. Also new in this production are nonspecific ethnic casting, streamlined musical numbers, and updated dialogue.

Carousel is one of the genre's first to use a serious theme. The story recounts the life of Billy Bigelow, a "barker" for the carousel. Billy falls in love with Julie Jordan, a worker at the mill, shunning the advances of the aging carousel owner, Nellie Fowler. Billy then loses his job, marries Julie, and becomes a "worthless bum," in the opinion of Julie's friends. Julie's pregnancy, the turning point in the plot, forces Billy to evaluate his worthiness for parenthood.

Billy decides to turn to thievery rather than to work to get money to support his family. An ill-fated robbery attempt ends with Billy killing himself to avoid being arrested. The next scene finds Billy in heaven, repentant and determined to return to earth to undo some of the harm he has caused. Upon his surrealistic return, he awkwardly but effectively touches the lives of Julie and his daughter.

Critics have called this musical "out of date and out of touch" because of its treatment of women. Most notable is that Billy actually strikes his wife and his daughter. Their reaction to being hit is that "it's only his way of showing affection." In spite of this apparent flaw, *Carousel* has found new life in this newly staged, artfully performed production.

ACTIVITY 2

Listening

Complete the listening activity as directed at the right.

 **Save as:** *CS6-ACT2*

1. Open the sound file (*CD-CS6LISTN*), which contains directions for driving to Mansfield Soccer Field.
2. Take notes as you listen to the directions.
3. Close the file.
4. Using your notes, key the directions in sentence form.
5. Check the accuracy of your work with the instructor.

ACTIVITY 3

Write to Learn

Complete the Write-to-Learn activity as directed at the right.

 **Save as:** *CS6-ACT3*

1. Using word processing or speech recognition software, write a paragraph explaining how you would copy text from one place in a document to another.
2. Write a second paragraph explaining how to merge cells in a table.

ACTIVITY 4

Composing

1. Read the paragraph at the right.*
2. On the basis of your experience in viewing movies and TV, compose a paragraph indicating whether you agree or disagree with the young people who responded to the poll. Give reasons.

 **Save as:** *CS6-ACT4*

*Source: *USA Today*, March 1995.

A poll of young people revealed that U.S. youths thought current TV and movie fare glamorizes violence and sex without portraying the negative consequences of immoral behavior. Over sixty percent of youths surveyed said that such glamorizations on the screen influenced them to engage in such behavior.

27C • Optional Timed Writings

1. Key a 1' writing on each ¶; determine *gwam* on each writing.
2. Key a 2' writing on ¶s 1–2 combined; determine *gwam.*
3. Key a 3' writing on ¶s 1–3 combined; determine *gwam.*

A all letters used

	gwam 2'	3'	
What is a job? In its larger sense, a job is a regular duty,	6	4	60
role, or function that one performs for pay. Therefore, when you	13	8	64
apply for and accept a job, you accept responsibility for complet-	19	13	69
ing a series of specified tasks such as data entry, recordkeeping,	26	17	73
and word processing.	28	19	74
What is a career? A career is a broad field in business, pro-	34	23	78
fession, or public life that permits one to progress in successive	41	27	83
steps up the job ladder. Whatever the tasks performed, one may	47	31	87
have a career in law, in health services, in education, or in busi-	54	36	92
ness, for example.	56	37	93
It should be very clear that a career may include many jobs,	62	41	97
each with different ability requirements. Realize, however, that	69	46	101
many of the jobs leading to increasing success in most careers are	75	50	106
better done with greater ease by people who have built a high level	82	55	110
of keying skill.	84	56	112

gwam 2' | 1 | 2 | 3 | 4 | 5 | 6
3' | 1 | 2 | 3 | 4

Word Processing Activity

LS: DS

Center the poem shown at the right vertically and horizontally on the page. QS below the author's name. Bold the title and italicize the body.

Source: Encyclopedia Americana, Vol. 25. Danbury, CT: Grolier Incorporated, 1998, p. 637.

THE NEW COLOSSUS

By Emma Lazarus

Not like the brazen giant of Greek fame,
With conquering limbs astride from land to land;
Here at our sea-washed, sunset gates shall stand
A mighty woman with a torch, whose flame
Is the imprisoned lightning, and her name
Mother of Exiles. From her beacon-hand
Glows world-wide welcome; her mild eyes command
The air-bridged harbor that twin cities frame.
"Keep ancient lands, your storied pomp!" cries she
With silent lips. "Give me your tired, your poor,
Your huddled masses yearning to breathe free,
The wretched refuse of your teeming shore.
Send these, the homeless, tempest-tost to me,
I lift my lamp beside the golden door!"

Communication Skills 6

ACTIVITY 1

Terminal Punctuation: Period, Question Mark, Exclamation Point

1. Key the paragraph at the right, using the correct punctuation.
2. Check the accuracy of your work with the instructor; correct any errors you made.
3. Note the rule number at the left of each line in which you made a punctuation error.
4. Using the rules at the right, identify the rule(s) you need to review/practice.
5. **Read**: Study each rule.
6. **Learn**: Key the Learn line(s) beneath it, noting how the rule is applied.
7. **Apply**: Key the Apply line(s), adding the correct terminal punctuation.

Save as: *CS6-ACT1*

Proofread & Correct

Rules
5 "Jump" the fireman shouted to the young boy frozen with
1 fear on the window ledge of the burning building "Will you
3 catch me" the young boy cried to the men and women holding a
1,5,1 safety net forty feet below "Into the net" they yelled
Mustering his courage, the boy jumped safely into the net and
1 then into his mother's outstretched arms

Terminal Punctuation: Period

Rule 1: Use a period at the end of a declarative sentence (a sentence that is not regarded as a question or exclamation).

Learn 1 I wonder why *Phantom of the Opera* has always been so popular.
Apply 2 Fran and I saw *Cats* in London We also saw *Sunset Boulevard*

Rule 2: Use a period at the end of a polite request stated in the form of a question but not intended as one.

Learn 3 Matt, will you please collect the papers at the end of each row.
Apply 4 Will you please call me at 555-0140 to set up an appointment

Terminal Punctuation: Question Mark

Rule 3: Use a question mark at the end of a sentence intended as a question.

Learn 5 Did you go to the annual flower show in Ault Park this year?
Apply 6 How many medals did the U.S.A. win in the 1996 Summer Games

Rule 4: For emphasis, a question mark may be used after each item in a series of interrogative expressions.

Learn 7 Can we count on wins in gymnastics? in diving? in soccer?
Apply 8 What grade did you get for technique for speed for accuracy

Terminal Punctuation: Exclamation Point

Rule 5: Use an exclamation point after emphatic (forceful) exclamations and after phrases and sentences that are clearly exclamatory.

Learn 9 The lady screamed, "Stop that man!"
Learn 10 "Bravo!" many yelled at the end of the Skate America program.
Apply 11 "Yes" her gym coach exclaimed when Kerri stuck the landing.
Apply 12 The burglar stopped when he saw the sign, "Beware, vicious dog"

Communication Skills 4

ACTIVITY 1

Pronoun Agreement

1. Key lines 1–10 at the right, using the correct pronouns.
2. Check the accuracy of your work with the instructor; correct any errors you made.
3. Note the rule number at the left of each sentence in which you made a pronoun agreement error.
4. Using the rules below the sentences, identify the rule(s) you need to review/practice.
5. **Read**: Study each rule.
6. **Learn**: Key the Learn line(s) beneath it, noting how the rule is applied.
7. **Apply**: Key the Apply line(s), choosing the correct pronouns.

 **Save as:** *CS4-ACT1*

Proofread & Correct

Rules

1 1 Suzy knew that (he, she, they) should do her best at all times.
3 2 People who entered the contest say (he, she, they) are confident.
3 3 As soon as class is over, I like to transcribe (our, my) notes.
3 4 Mrs. Kelso gave (her, his, their) lecture in Royce Hall.
2 5 The yacht moved slowly around (her, his, its) anchor.
1 6 As you practice the drills, (his, your) skill increases.
1 7 I played my new clarinet in (my, their, your) last recital.
3 8 The editors planned quickly for (its, their) next luncheon.
4 9 The women's volleyball team won (its, their) tenth game today.
4 10 Our family will take (its, their) annual trip in August.

Pronoun Agreement

Rule 1: A personal pronoun (*I, we, you, he, she, it, their*, etc.) agrees in **person** (first, second, or third) with the noun or other pronoun it represents.

Learn 1 We can win the game if we all give each play our best effort. (1st person)
Learn 2 You may play softball only after you finish all your homework. (2nd person)
Learn 3 Andrea said that she will drive her car to the shopping mall. (3rd person)
Apply 4 Those who saw the exhibit said that (he, she, they) were impressed.
Apply 5 After you run for a few days, (my, your) muscles will be less sore.
Apply 6 Before I take the test, I want to review (our, my) class notes.

Rule 2: A personal pronoun agrees in **gender** (feminine, masculine, or neuter) with the noun or other pronoun it represents.

Learn 7 Miss Kimoto will give her talk after the announcements. (feminine)
Learn 8 The small boat lost its way in the dense fog. (neuter)
Apply 9 Each winner will get a corsage as she receives (her, its) award.
Apply 10 The ball circled the rim before (he, it) dropped through the hoop.

Rule 3: A personal pronoun agrees in **number** (singular or plural) with the noun or other pronoun it represents.

Learn 11 Celine drove her new car to Del Rio, Texas, last week. (singular)
Learn 12 The club officers made careful plans for their next meeting. (plural)
Apply 13 All workers must submit (his, their) vacation requests.
Apply 14 The sloop lost (its, their) headsail in the windstorm.

Rule 4: A personal pronoun that represents a collective noun (*team, committee, family*, etc.) may be singular or plural, depending on the meaning of the collective noun.

Learn 15 Our men's soccer team played its fifth game today. (acting as a unit)
Learn 16 The vice squad took their positions in the square. (acting individually)
Apply 17 The jury will render (its, their) verdict at 1:30 today.
Apply 18 The Finance Committee had presented (its, their) written reports.

Memo 2

1. Format the text at the right as a memo to **Kara Hundley, Chair,** from **Richard Ashmore, Committee Member**. Use the current date and this subject line: **RECOMMENDATION FOR CORPORATE GIVING**.
2. Correct all spelling, keying, and formatting errors.

 **Save as:** *MEMO46B2*

History Bits

"I am determined to sustain myself as long as possible and die like a soldier who never forgets what is due to his own honor and that of his country. . . ."

—William Barret Travis
Commander of the Alamo
February 24, 1836

Memo 3

1. Open the file *CD-MEMO46B3*; make the corrections shown at the right.
2. Add a copy notation: **Spencer Schultz**.

 **Save as:** *MEMO46B3*

46C • 7'
Drill: Memo Format

Key two 2' writings on Memo 3, using information below for the headings.

Try to key at least four additional words on the second 2' timing.

TO: Manuel Lopez, Convention Chair

FROM: Marsha Johnson, Display Coordinator

DATE: ***Current Date***

SUBJECT: GRAPHIC ARTIST

Remember the Alamo!!! As part of our annual corporate giving program, I am recommending that we make a contribution to The Alamo, managed by the Daughters of the Republic of Texas. They depend entirely on donations and proceeds from the gift shop for covering operating costs.

I believe it is important for us to honor those who played integral roles in the history of our state. Our children need to be reminded of the lives of James Bowie, David Crockett, and William Barret Travis, who made the ultimate sacrifice for freedom. And, who can forget the role Sam Houston played as the commander in chief of the Texan army in the revolution against Mexico? Memories of Texan legends are preserved at the Alamo.

Please list the Alamo as a potential recipient in our corporate giving program next year. Of course, we will discuss it when we meet.

Thank you for recomending the graphics artist The graphics for our state history displays at this year s convention were excellent

From the beginning of the project we knew we were going be pleased with the artwork The artist attended to a of our brain storming sessions His enthusiasm for the project motivated the entire committee His suggestions for implementing graphic arts into our display met all of our expectations The quantity of work completed by the artist was superb and on those rare occasions where an error was found he always made timely corrections

As you are well aware the displays were one of the things participants liked best about this year's convention Much of the success can be attributed to our graphic artist who we hired on the basis of your recommendation Again thank you

ACTIVITY 2

Listening

1. Open the file *CD-CS4LISTN.* This sound file contains a weather forecast.
2. Listen to the forecast; then close the file.
3. Key answers to the questions at the right. Check the accuracy of your work.

Save as: *CS4-ACT2*

1. What were the high and low temperatures for today?
2. What are the predicted high and low temperatures for tomorrow?
3. Is it likely to rain tomorrow?
4. How many days are likely to have rain in the five-day forecast?
5. What is the highest temperature predicted in the five-day forecast?
6. What is the lowest temperature predicted in the five-day forecast?

ACTIVITY 3

Write to Learn

Complete the Write-to-Learn activity as directed at the right.

Save as: *CS4-ACT3*

1. Using word processing or speech recognition software, write a paragraph explaining how to bold and italicize a paragraph after it is keyed.
2. Write a second paragraph explaining how to set the left and right margins of a document in your word processing software.

ACTIVITY 4

Composing

1. Read the paragraph at the right. Was the student's action right or wrong (legally, ethically, or morally)?
2. Can stealing be justified for any reason? Compose a paragraph stating your views and giving your reasons.
3. Revise, proofread, and correct your paragraph.
4. Key the paragraph at the right as ¶ 1; key your corrected paragraph as ¶ 2.

Save as: *CS4-ACT4*

A student sees a designer jacket hanging over the door of a locker. No one seems to be around. The student tries it on; it looks great. He likes it and wants it. He reasons that if the owner can afford an expensive jacket, he can afford another one. So quickly the student puts it in his gym bag and walks away.

Memo 3

1. Format and key the text at the right as a memo.
2. Send copies to **Timothy Gerrard** and **Maria Valdez**.
3. Check the memo; correct all formatting, spelling, and keying errors.

 **Save as:** *MEMO45B3*

TO: Andrew Nelson, Manager; Amy McDonald, Assistant Manager; Judith Smythe, Assistant Manager | FROM: Malcolm McKinley, Travel Agent | DATE: May 3, 200- | SUBJECT: CIVIL WAR BUS TOUR

Yes, I think there would be an interest in a bus tour of some of the battle campaigns of the Civil War. My recommendation would be to start with a six-day tour that includes some of the most famous battlefields.

Of course, the one that comes to mind right away is Gettysburg, where over 158,000 Union (George G. Meade) and Confederate (Robert E. Lee) soldiers fought courageously for their causes. This battle (July 1-3, 1863) resulted in an estimated 51,000 lives being lost. Being able to visit the place where President Lincoln delivered the Gettysburg Address would also be of real interest to those considering the trip. I've looked at several Web sites, and evidently something of interest is always going on in or near Gettysburg.

The other battlefields that I recommend including on the tour are Manassas (Virginia) and Antietam (Maryland). Both of these battlefields were key encounters of the Civil War.

Within the next week, I will provide you with more details on a tour such as the one I've briefly presented.

LESSON 46 — IMPROVE E-MAIL AND MEMO FORMATTING SKILLS

Objectives:

1. To increase proficiency in formatting and keying memos.
2. To increase proficiency in formatting and keying e-mail.

46A • 5' Conditioning Practice

Key each line twice SS; then key a 1' writing on line 3; determine *gwam*.

alphabet 1 Gavin Zahn will buy the exquisite green jacket from the old shop.

figures 2 Check No. 183 was used to pay Invoices 397 and 406 on October 25.

speed 3 Glen may pay the haughty neighbor if the turn signals work right.

gwam 1' | 1 | 2 | 3 | 4 | 5 | 6 | 7 | 8 | 9 | 10 | 11 | 12 | 13 |

FORMATTING

46B • 38' E-mail and Memos

Document 1 (E-mail)

Key the text as e-mail to your instructor and a classmate. (If e-mail software is not available, format/key a memo to **John Ewing**. Use the current date.) Send a blind courtesy copy to a classmate OR key a blind copy notation on the memo: **Sally Enders**. Check your work.

 **Save as:** *MAIL46B1* (or *MEMO46B1*)

SUBJECT: FIELD TRIP PROPOSAL | In our American history class, my students are studying the American Revolution. To bring this unit to life, I would like to take the class on a field trip to the Valley Forge Historical Society Museum.

According to their Web site, the museum ". . . offers visitors to Valley Forge the opportunity to understand the value of the sacrifice made by the 12,000 men who camped here during the winter of 1777-78. The spirit of Valley Forge is chronicled through galleries and displays that present the letters, weapons, and personal effects of the great and everyday Continental soldier."

I believe this would be an excellent educational experience for our students. When would you be available to meet with me to discuss a field trip of this nature?

WORD PROCESSING 

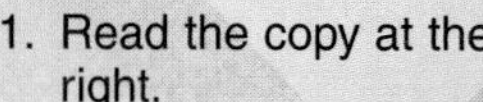

ACTIVITY 1

Select

1. Read the copy at the right.
2. Learn how to select text using your wp software.
3. Open file *CD-WP3ACT1*.
4. Select text and italicize, underline, and bold the copy as shown at the right.
5. Select and delete the semicolon and last six words of line 4.

 **Save as:** *WP3ACT1*

Use the mouse and/or various key combinations to **select** (highlight) text, on which various operations may be performed.

Once selected, the text can be bolded, italicized, underlined, deleted, copied, moved, printed, saved, etc.

1. You will need to know how to **bold**, *italicize*, and <u>underline</u> for the exam.
2. Have you read *The Grapes of Wrath* by **John Steinbeck**?
3. <u>Rebecca Smith</u> is employed in the office of **Market & Johnson**.
4. Henry W. Longfellow wrote *Ballads*; Oliver Wendell Holmes wrote *Old Ironsides*.
5. Tanya misspelled *congratulations* and *italicized* on the quiz.

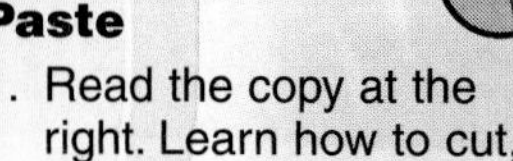

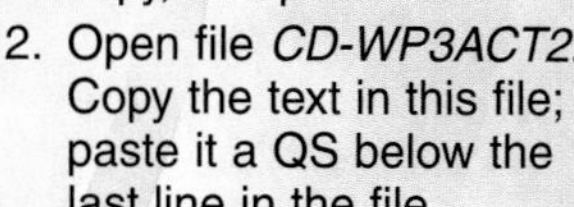

ACTIVITY 2

Cut, Copy, and Paste

1. Read the copy at the right. Learn how to cut, copy, and paste text.
2. Open file *CD-WP3ACT2*. Copy the text in this file; paste it a QS below the last line in the file.
3. In the second set of steps, use Cut and Paste to arrange the four steps in order.

 **Save as:** *WP3ACT2*

After you have selected text, you can use the Cut, Copy and Paste features. The **Cut** feature removes selected text from the current location; the **Paste** feature places it at another location. The **Copy** feature copies the selected text so it can be placed in another location (paste), leaving the original text unchanged.

Step 1 Select text to be cut (moved).

Step 2 Click **Cut** to remove text from the current location.

Step 3 Move the insertion point to the desired location.

Step 4 Click **Paste** to place the cut text at the new location.

ACTIVITY 3

Center Page

1. Read the copy at the right. Learn how to center copy vertically.
2. Key the copy DS; center the copy horizontally and vertically.
3. Use the View feature to see how it will look on a printed page.

 **Save as:** *WP3ACT3*

Use the **Center Page** feature to center lines of text between the top and bottom margins of the page. This feature leaves an equal (or nearly equal) amount of white space above and below the text. Inserting two hard returns below the last keyed line gives the document a better appearance.

Pot of Gold

by Dianna Vermillion

Together we chased after the rainbow

to find the pot of gold; but in each other,

we found our own treasure to unfold.

[Insert two hard returns]

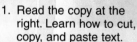

IMPROVE MEMO FORMATTING SKILLS

Objectives:

1. To increase proficiency in formatting memos.
2. To format memo distribution lists.

45A • 5' Conditioning Practice

Key each line twice SS; then take a 1' writing on line 3; determine *gwam*.

alphabet 1 Rebecca enjoyed explaining her vast knowledge of the zoo marquee.

figures 2 Flight 784 is scheduled to leave at 10:35 from Gate 96 on May 20.

speed 3 The maid may make the usual visit to the dock to work on the map.

gwam 1' | 1 | 2 | 3 | 4 | 5 | 6 | 7 | 8 | 9 | 10 | 11 | 12 | 13 |

FORMATTING

45B • 45' Memos

Memo 1

1. Format and key the copy at the right as an inter-office memo.
2. Check the memo; correct all formatting, spelling, and keying errors.

Save as: *MEMO45B1*

TO: American History Students | FROM: Professor Perry | DATE: January 20, 200- | SUBJECT: NEXT EXAM

Here is the information about next week's exam. It will cover Chapter 22, pp. 702-727, and Chapter 23, pp. 740-769.

The main emphasis of Chapter 22 is the New Deal. You will be expected to explain what the New Deal was, why some people criticized it while others praised it, and the impact of the New Deal on the U.S. economy.

Between 1933 and 1937, many pieces of legislation associated with the New Deal were passed. Make sure you know the purpose of each of the following acts.

* Emergency Banking Act
* Agricultural Adjustment Act
* Federal Emergency Relief Act
* Home Owners Refinancing Act
* National Industrial Recovery Act
* Emergency Relief Appropriation Act
* National Labor Relations Act
* Social Security Act

Chapter 23 covers World War II. We thoroughly discussed this chapter in class. Make sure you review your notes carefully.

If you are knowledgeable about these topics, you should do well on the exam.

Memo 2

1. Format and key the copy at the right as a memo to **Marsha Hanson, Director**. The memo is from **Alison Sadecki**. Use the current date and this subject line: **ANTHONY AND STANTON DISCUSSION**.
2. Include a blind copy notation: **Kevin Hefner**.
3. Check the memo; correct all errors.

Save as: *MEMO45B2*

Even though the Virginia Women's Museum is primarily for recognizing those women who contributed greatly to Virginia's history, I think it appropriate to recognize some early leaders of the women's movement on a national level.

Susan B. Anthony and Elizabeth Cady Stanton are two women who led the struggle for women's suffrage at the national level. They organized the National Woman Suffrage Association. Shouldn't they be recognized for their gallant efforts in our museum as well?

Please include a discussion of this issue on the next agenda.

ACTIVITY 4

Envelopes

1. Read the copy at the right.
2. Learn how to prepare envelopes using your wp software.
3. Use the Envelopes feature to format a small envelope (No. 6 3/4) for Envelope 1 and a large envelope (No. 10) for Envelope 2.
4. Key the delivery address in ALL CAPS without punctuation, as shown.

 **Save as:** *WP3ACT4*

Use the **Envelopes** feature to format envelopes for the documents you create. This feature allows you to select the size of the envelope, enter the **sender's return address** and the **receiver's delivery (mailing) address**, and print the envelope. Some wp software contains an option for printing the delivery point bar code on the envelope.

Sender's return address:	**Receiver's delivery (mailing) address:**
Envelope 1 Robert Frederick 1520 Janewood Way Pittsburgh, PA 15220-7623	MS JUANITA LOPEZ 2113 KENMORE TER BROOKLYN NY 11226-9253
Envelope 2 Laura A. Jefferson 76 Livingston Ave. Fort Worth, TX 76110-0021	MR DENNIS BENTON 861 LEDBETTER PL S KENNEWICK WA 99337-6520

ACTIVITY 5

Apply What You Have Learned

1. Open file *CD-WP3ACT5*. Make the changes shown at the right.
2. At the end of each line, key (bold and italicize) the state nickname.
3. **Bold** the names of the states; *italicize* the state flower.
4. Use the Cut and Paste features to arrange the lines alphabetically by state.
5. Center the text vertically.

 **Save as:** *WP3ACT5*

Vermont, Montpelier - *Red Clover* - ***Green Mountain State***

New Jersey, Trenton - *Purple Violet* - ***Garden State***

Washington, Olympia - *Rhododendron* - ***Evergreen State***

Georgia, Atlanta - *Cherokee Rose* - ***Peach State***

Massachusetts, Boston - *Mayflower* - ***Bay State***

Iowa, Des Moines - *Wild Rose* - ***Hawkeye State***

New York, Albany - *Rose* - ***Empire State***

Missouri, Jefferson City - *Hawthorn* - ***Show Me State***

Texas, Austin - *Bluebonnet* - ***Lone Star State***

Hawaii, Honolulu - *Hibiscus* - ***Aloha State***

ACTIVITY 6

Apply What You Have Learned

Prepare a No. 10 envelope for each address at the right.

 **Save as:** *WP3ACT6-1* and *WP3ACT6-2*

Sender's return address:	**Receiver's delivery (mailing) address:**
Envelope 1 Roger J. Essex 564 Glencreek Ln. Cleveland, OH 44136-3625	MS LANESSA HOWARD 310 EISENHOWER ST CASPER WY 82604-0032
Envelope 2 Harold Baxter Autumn Forest Dr. Memphis, TN 38125-0013	MR KENT BOZEMAN 382 LOOKOUT MTN RAPID CITY SD 57702-5643

Document 2 (E-mail)

Key the text as e-mail to four classmates. Send a copy to your instructor. Attach Document 1 (*MAIL44B1*). Check your work.

 **Save as:** *MAIL44B2*

SUBJECT: AMERICAN HISTORY | Attached is the list of the five Americans who I feel had the greatest impact on our history. A few notes about the individuals are provided after each name. Narrowing the list to five was very difficult. (¶) I've reserved a room in the library for us to meet on Thursday, March 25, at 3 p.m. By then we should have received and reviewed each other's lists. Be prepared to decide on the final ten individuals to include in the report for Ms. Graham. (¶) I look forward to receiving each of your lists.

Document 3 (Attachment)

TM: 2" **LS:** 1.5

Key the list centered on the page. Center a two-line title in bold: **RECOMMENDATIONS FOR OUTSTANDING AMERICANS REPORT.** Check your work.

 **Save as:** *MAIL44B3*

Susan B. Anthony	Martin Luther King, Jr.
Neil Armstrong	Abraham Lincoln
Alexander Graham Bell	Douglas MacArthur
Thomas Alva Edison	Thomas Paine
Albert Einstein	Sir Walter Raleigh
Benjamin Franklin	Eleanor Roosevelt
Samuel Gompers	Franklin Roosevelt
Ulysses S. Grant	Harriet Beecher Stowe
Patrick Henry	Henry David Thoreau
Thomas Jefferson	George Washington

Document 4 (E-mail)

Key the text as e-mail to the same four classmates as Document 2. Attach Document 3 (*MAIL44B3*). Check your work.

When you receive this e-mail from classmates, forward one message to your instructor.

 **Save as:** *MAIL44B4*

SUBJECT: OUTSTANDING AMERICANS LIST | Don't forget our meeting tomorrow. Since the librarian wouldn't give me a specific room ahead of time, let's plan on meeting at the front desk at 3 p.m. (¶) I went ahead and created a combined list of all the names you sent me via e-mail. A total of 20 individuals were named at least once. The alphabetical list is attached. (¶) See you tomorrow at 3.

LANGUAGE SKILLS

44C • 8'
Language Skills: Word Choice

1. Study the spelling/definitions of the words at the right.
2. Key line 1, noting the proper choice of words.
3. Key lines 2–3, choosing the right words to complete the lines correctly.
4. Repeat Steps 2 and 3.
5. Check your work; correct word-choice errors.

 **Save as:** *CHOICE44C*

hole (n) an opening in or through something
whole (adj/n) having all its proper parts; a complete amount or sum

peak (n) pointed end; top of a mountain; highest level
peek (vb) to glance or look at for a brief time

Learn 1 The **whole** group helped dig a **hole** to bury the time capsule.
Apply 2 They ate the (hole, whole) cake before going to the water (hole, whole).
Apply 3 He told us, "The (hole, whole) is greater than the sum of its parts."

Learn 1 If you **peek** out the window, you will see the **peak** of the iceberg.
Apply 2 The (peak, peek) of the mountain came into view as they drove around the curve.
Apply 3 Students were told not to (peak, peek) at the keyboard in order to reach (peek, peak) skill.

UNIT 9

LESSONS 28-30

Learn to Format Personal-Business Letters

Format Guides: Personal-Business Letter, Block Style

230 Glendale Ct.
Brooklyn, NY 11234-3721
February 15, 200-

Ms. Julie Hutchinson
1825 Melbourne Ave.
Flushing, NY 11367-2351

Dear Julie

It seems like years since we were in Ms. Gerhig's keyboarding class. Now I wish I would have paid more attention. As I indicated on the phone, I am applying for a position as box office co-ordinator for one of the theaters on Broadway. Of course, I know the importance of having my letter of application and resume formatted correctly, but I'm not sure that I remember how to do it.

Since you just completed your business education degree, I knew where to get the help I needed. Thanks for agreeing to look over my application documents; they are enclosed. Also, if you have any suggestions for changes to the content, please share those with me too. This job is so important to me; it's the one I really want.

Thanks again for agreeing to help. If I get the job, I'll take you out to one of New York's finest restaurants.

Sincerely

Rebecca Dunworthy

Enclosures

Personal-Business Letter

A letter written by an individual to deal with business of a personal nature is called a **personal-business letter**. Block format (shown at the left) is commonly used for formatting personal-business letters.

Letters arranged in block format have all parts of the letter beginning at the left margin. The paragraphs are not indented.

Letter Margins

Side margin: 1" (or default)
Top margin: 2"
Bottom margin: about 1"

Instead of a 2" top margin, letters may be centered vertically with the Center Page feature. Inserting two hard returns below the last keyed line places the letter in reading position.

Basic Parts of Personal-Business Letters

The basic parts of the personal-business letter are described below in order of placement.

Return address. The return address consists of a line for the street address and one for the city, state, and ZIP Code.

Date. Key the month, day, and year on the line below the city, state, and ZIP Code.

Letter address. Key the first line of the letter (delivery) address a QS below the date. A personal title (*Miss, Mr., Mrs., Ms.*) or professional title (*Dr., Lt., Senator*) is keyed before the receiver's name.

Salutation. Key the salutation (greeting) a DS below the letter address.

Body. Begin the letter body (message) a DS below the salutation. SS and block the paragraphs with a DS between them.

Complimentary close. Key the complimentary close (farewell) a DS below the last line of the body.

Name of the writer. Key the name of the writer (originator of the message) a QS below the complimentary close. The name may be preceded by a personal title (*Miss, Mrs., Ms.*) to indicate how a female prefers to be addressed in a response. If a male has a name that does not clearly indicate his gender (*Kim, Leslie, Pat,* for example), the title *Mr.* may precede his name.

Special Parts of Letters

In addition to the basic letter parts, letters may include the special letter parts described below.

Reference initials. If someone other than the originator of the letter keys it, key the keyboard operator's initials in lowercase letters at the left margin, a DS below the writer's name.

Attachment/Enclosure notation. If another document is attached to a letter, the word "Attachment" is keyed at the left margin, a DS below the reference initials. If the additional document is not attached, the word "Enclosure" is used. If reference initials are not used, "Attachment" or "Enclosure" is keyed a DS below the writer's name.

LESSON 44 IMPROVE E-MAIL FORMATTING SKILLS

Objectives:

1. To process e-mail messages with attachments and copy notations.
2. To improve language skills.

44A • 5' Conditioning Practice

Key each line twice SS; then key a 1' writing on line 3; determine *gwam*.

alphabet 1 Tom saw Jo leave quickly for her job after my dog won six prizes.

fig/sym 2 Check No. 203 ($1,486.17) and Check No. 219 ($57.98) are missing.

speed 3 Did their auditor sign the key element of the forms for the firm?

gwam 1' | 1 | 2 | 3 | 4 | 5 | 6 | 7 | 8 | 9 | 10 | 11 | 12 | 13 |

FORMATTING

44B • 37' Send/Receive E-mail

Document 1 (Attachment)

TM: 2"

LS: SS (Do not indent paragraphs)

1. Format and key the text at the right.
2. Bold all names. DS the heading; QS below the date.
3. Correct all spelling, keying, and formatting errors.

 **Save as:** *MAIL44B1*

AMERICAN HISTORY
your Name
March 18, 200-

Albert Einstein: American physicist whose theory of relativity led to the harnessing of nuclear energy.

Benjamin Franklin: A leading American stateman, inventor, philanthropist, publisher, author, revolutionary, and thinker.

Abraham Lincoln: The sixteenth President of the United States; helped keep the Union together during the Civil War which led to the abolishment of slavery; recognized for his honesty and compassion.

Franklin Roosevelt: Thirty-second President of the United States; led the country during two critical periods in United States history (the Great Depression and World War II).

George Washington: Commander in Chief of the Continental Army during the American Revolution; first President of the United States.

History Bits

"If A equals success, then the formula is:

A = X + Y + Z.

X is work. Y is play. Z is keep your mouth shut."

—Albert Einstein

INTERNET  ACTIVITY

Search the Web to learn more about one of the individuals whose name appears at the right or one of those listed in Document 3 (p. 128).

Compose a paragraph or two about the individual.

2" TM

Return address 230 Glendale Ct.
Brooklyn, NY 11234-3721
Date February 15, 200-
QS

Letter address Ms. Julie Hutchinson
1825 Melbourne Ave.
Flushing, NY 11367-2351

Salutation Dear Julie

Body It seems like years since we were in Ms. Gerhig's keyboarding class. Now I wish I would have paid more attention. As I indicated on the phone, I am applying for a position as box office co-ordinator for one of the theaters on Broadway. Of course, I know the importance of having my letter of application and resume formatted correctly, but I'm not sure that I remember how to do it.
DS

1" LM Since you just completed your business education degree, I knew where to get the help I needed. Thanks for agreeing to look over my application documents; they are enclosed. Also, if you have any suggestions for changes to the content, please share those with me too. This job is so important to me; it's the one I really want. 1" RM
DS

Thanks again for agreeing to help. If I get the job, I'll take you out to one of New York's finest restaurants.
DS

Complimentary close Sincerely
QS

Writer Rebecca Dunworthy
DS

Enclosure notation Enclosures

Shown in 12-point Times New Roman, with 2" top margin and 1" side margins, this letter appears smaller than actual size.

Personal-Business Letter in Block Format

UNIT 14

LESSONS 44-46

Improving E-mail and Memo Formatting Skills

Format Guides: Memos and E-mail

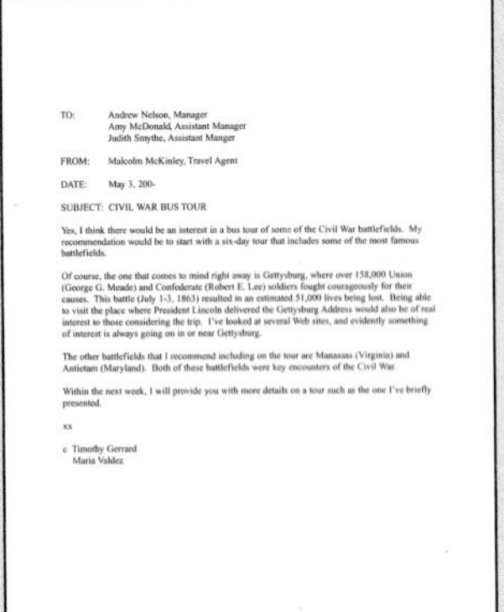

TO: Andrew Nelson, Manager
Amy McDonald, Assistant Manager
Judith Smythe, Assistant Manger

FROM: Malcolm McKinley, Travel Agent

DATE: May 3, 200-

SUBJECT: CIVIL WAR BUS TOUR

Yes, I think there would be an interest in a bus tour of some of the Civil War battlefields. My recommendation would be to start with a six-day tour that includes some of the most famous battlefields.

Of course, the one that comes to mind right away is Gettysburg, where over 158,000 Union (George G. Meade) and Confederate (Robert E. Lee) soldiers fought courageously for their causes. This battle (July 1-3, 1863) resulted in an estimated 51,000 lives being lost. Being able to visit the place where President Lincoln delivered the Gettysburg Address would also be of real interest to those considering the trip. I've looked at several Web sites, and evidently something of interest is always going on in or near Gettysburg.

The other battlefields that I recommend including on the tour are Manassas (Virginia) and Antietam (Maryland). Both of these battlefields were key encounters of the Civil War.

Within the next week, I will provide you with more details on a tour such as the one I've briefly presented.

xx

c Timothy Gerrard
Maria Valdez

Interoffice Memo with Distribution List

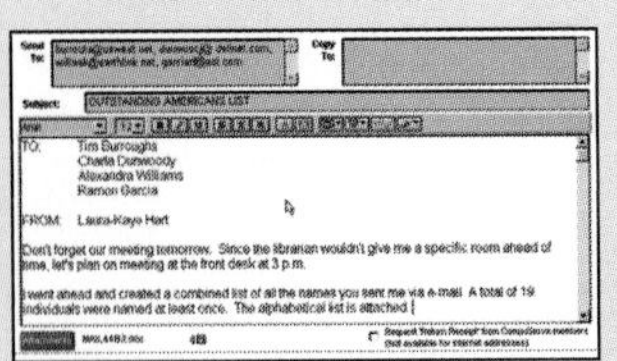

Subject: OUTSTANDING AMERICANS LIST

TO: Tim Burroughs
Charla Dunwoody
Alexandra Williams
Ramon Garcia

FROM: Laura-Kaye Hart

Don't forget our meeting tomorrow. Since the librarian wouldn't give me a specific room ahead of time, let's plan on meeting at the front desk at 3 p.m.

I went ahead and created a combined list of all the names you sent me via e-mail. A total of 19 individuals were named at least once. The alphabetical list is attached.

E-mail Message with Distribution List

Special E-mail Software Features

Several software features make communicating through e-mail fast and efficient.

E-mail address list. Names and e-mail addresses of persons you correspond with often may be kept in an address list. An address can be entered on the TO: line by selecting it from the list.

E-mail copies. Copies of e-mail can be sent to additional addresses at the same time you send the original message. The **Cc:** (courtesy copy) and **Bcc:** (blind courtesy copy) features of e-mail software are used to send copies.

Cc: If you want the recipient to know that you have sent the message to others, key the e-mail address of the other individuals on the **Cc:** line in the e-mail heading.

Bcc: If you do NOT want the recipient to know that you have sent the message to others, key their e-mail addresses on the **Bcc:** line in the e-mail heading.

Attachments. Documents, such as reports, tables, spreadsheets, and databases, may be attached electronically to e-mail. Common names of the software feature are **Attachments**, **Attached**, and **Attach File**.

Forward. The Forward feature allows you to forward a copy of an e-mail message you received to other individuals.

Reply. The Reply feature is used to respond quickly to incoming e-mail. The incoming message (unless deleted) and reply are sent to the sender of the original message. The originator's address does not have to be keyed. The original message quickly reminds the originator what the reply is about, so a brief reply is sufficient.

E-mail distribution list. When e-mail is sent to several addresses at once, use a distribution list:

To: burrouta@uswest.net, dunwoocj@dellnet.com, williaak@earthlink.net, garciarf@aol.com

For sending e-mail often to the same group of people, the Recipient List feature (on most e-mail software) saves time. All addresses in a group can be entered on the TO: line at once when the name of the recipient list is selected.

Special Memo Parts

In addition to the standard memo parts, several parts enhance communicating with memos.

Copy notations. A copy notation indicates that a copy of a memo is being sent to someone other than the addressee. Use "c" followed by the name of the person(s) to receive a copy. Place a copy notation a double space below the last line of the enclosure notation or the reference initials if there is no enclosure. If you do not want the person to know you are sending it to others, use the "bc" (blind copy) notation on the copy only.

Attachment/Enclosure notation. If another document is attached to a memo, the word *Attachment* is keyed at the left margin a DS below the reference initials. If a document is included but not attached, the word *Enclosure* is used instead. If reference initials are not used, the notation is keyed a DS below the body of the memo.

Memo distribution list. When a memo is sent to several individuals, a distribution list is used. Format the memo distribution list as shown below:

To: Tim Burroughs
Charla Dunwoody
Alexandra Williams
Ramon Garcia

LESSON 28 FORMAT PERSONAL-BUSINESS LETTERS

Objectives:

1. To learn to format personal-business letters in block format.
2. To improve word-choice skills.

28A • 5' Conditioning Practice

Key each line twice SS; then key a 1' writing on line 3; determine *gwam.*

alphabet 1 Before leaving them, Jessie quickly swam a dozen extra laps.

fig/sym 2 Kimberly ordered 37 1/2 yards of #804 linen at $6.59 a yard.

speed 3 Six firms may bid for an authentic map of an ancient island.

gwam 1' | 1 | 2 | 3 | 4 | 5 | 6 | 7 | 8 | 9 | 10 | 11 | 12 |

FORMATTING

28B • 37' Personal-Business Letters in Block Format

Letter 1

Study the format guides on p. 82 and the model letter on p. 83. Note the placement of letter parts and spacing between the parts.

Format/key Letter 1 (the model) on p. 83. Proofread and correct errors.

Save as: *LTR28B1*

Letter 2

Format/key Letter 2 shown at the right. Place letter parts properly and space correctly. Refer to the model on p. 83 as needed. Proofread and correct errors.

Save as: *LTR28B2*

words

2832 Primrose St. 4
Eugene, OR 97402-1716 8
November 20, 200- 12

Mr. Andrew Chaney 15
324 Brookside Ave. NW 20
Salem, OR 97304-9008 24

Dear Mr. Chaney 27

Thank you for taking time out of your busy schedule to speak to our **A**spiring **M**usicians **C**lub. It was great learning more about the "Masters" from you. 57

I particularly enjoyed learning more about the German composers. It is amazing that so many of the great musicians (Johann Sebastian Bach, Ludwig van Beethoven, Robert Schumann, Felix Mendelssohn, and Richard Wagner) are all from Germany. It is my goal to continue my study of music at the **Staatliche Hochschule fur Musik Rheinland** in Germany once I graduate from college. 133

Your insights into what it takes to make it as a professional musician were also enlightening for our members. Those of us who want to become professional musicians know we have to rededicate ourselves to that goal if we are going to be successful. 183

Thank you again for sharing your expertise with our club. 195

Sincerely 197

Stephen R. Knowles 200
AMC Member 202

ACTIVITY 4

Reinforce Copying Files

Open the files *CD-GETTYS1*, *CD-GETTYS2*, and *CD-GETTYS3*.

Create a copy of the Gettysburg Address as directed at the right.

 **Save as:** *WP5ACT4*

The initial words of each of the three paragraphs of the Gettysburg Address are shown at the right. The names of the files where these paragraphs can be found are shown in parentheses.

Copy the paragraphs from *GETTYS2* and *GETTYS3* and place them in the correct order in *GETTYS1*. Leave a DS between paragraphs.

Paragraph 1: Four score and seven years ago, our fathers brought forth on this continent . . . (*GETTYS1*)

Paragraph 2: Now we are engaged in a great civil war, testing . . . (*GETTYS2*)

Paragraph 3: But in a large sense we cannot dedicate, we cannot consecrate, we cannot hallow this ground. The brave . . . (*GETTYS3*)

ACTIVITY 5

Review WP Features

1. Read line 1 at the right and choose the correct word in parentheses.
2. Key the sentence with the correct word choice underlined and bolded.
3. Repeat Steps 1 and 2 for the remaining sentences.

 **Save as:** *WP5ACT5*

1. I will be (their/there) on Friday.
2. Do you (know/no) the answer?
3. Let me know when (your/you're) available to have (your/you're) picture taken.
4. Which (cite/sight/site) did he choose for the new studio?
5. She (knew/new) his (knew/new) telephone number.

ACTIVITY 6

Review WP Features

1. Open the file *CD-WP5ACT6*.
2. Delete the incorrect word choice and parentheses from each sentence; bold and underline the correct word choice.
3. Copy lines 6–10; open the file created in Activity 5 (*WP5ACT5*); paste copied text a DS below line 5.

 **Save as:** *WP5ACT6*

ACTIVITY 7

Review WP Features

1. Set a left tab at 0.5", a right tab at 3.5", and a decimal tab at 5.5".
2. Key data (DS) at the right; omit column headings.

 **Save as:** *WP5ACT7*

Player/Team	Free Throws	Free Throw %
Hornacek, Utah	109 of 113	.964602
Miller, Indiana	223 of 239	.933054
Armstrong, Orlando	135 of 148	.912162
Brandon, Minnesota	121 of 133	.909774
Allen, Milwaukee	215 of 239	.899582
Cassell, Milwaukee	229 of 260	.880769

LANGUAGE SKILLS

28C • 8'
Language Skills: Word Choice

1. Study the spelling/definitions of the words at the right.
2. Key line 1, noting the proper choice of words.
3. Key lines 2–3, choosing the right words in each line.
4. Check your work; correct lines containing word-choice errors.

Save as: *CHOICE28C*

knew (vb) past tense of know; to have understood; to have recognized the truth or nature of

new (adj) novel; fresh; having existed for a short time; created in recent past

hear (vb) to gain knowledge of by the ear

here (adv) in or at this place; at this point; in this case; on this point

Learn 1 Katie **knew** she needed to buy a **new** computer for college.
Apply 2 Robert (knew, new) a (knew, new) car was out of the question.
Apply 3 All (knew, new) students (knew, new) the orientation schedule.

Learn 1 Did you **hear** the speech President Smith gave when he was **here**?
Apply 2 Liz said she couldn't (hear, here) the jazz singer from (hear, here).
Apply 3 (Hear, Here) is the address you wanted when you were (hear, here).

LESSON 29 FORMAT PERSONAL-BUSINESS LETTERS

Objectives:

1. To review format of personal-business letters in block style.
2. To learn to format/key envelopes.

29A • 5'
Conditioning Practice

Key each line twice SS; then key a 1' writing on line 3; determine *gwam.*

alphabet 1 Six boys quickly removed the juice from a sizzling stew pot.
fig/sym 2 The 2001 profit was $97,658 (up 34% from the previous year).
speed 3 Their neighbor may pay for half the land for the big chapel.

gwam 1' | 1 | 2 | 3 | 4 | 5 | 6 | 7 | 8 | 9 | 10 | 11 | 12 |

FORMATTING

29B • 35'
Personal-Business Letters in Block Format

Letter 1

Review the model personal-business letter on p. 83. Format and key in block style the letter shown at the right.

Save as: *LTR29B1*

Note:
Line endings for opening and closing lines are indicated by color verticals. Insert a hard return at these points.

words

610 Grand Ave. | Laramie, WY 82070-1423 | October 10, 200- | 11
Elegant Treasures | 388 Stonegate Dr. | Longview, TX 75601-0132 | 23
Dear Armani Dealer 27

Last week I noticed that you had Giuseppe Armani figurines in your 40
window. Do you have other figurines? 48

A friend gave me a pamphlet showing three Armani millennium 60
sculptures: **Stardust** (Years 1-999), **Silver Moon** (Years 1000-1999), 74
and **Comet** (Year 2000 and beyond). I want to buy all three sculptures. 88
Do you have them in stock, or could you order them? If not, could you 102
refer me to a nearby dealer? 108

I look forward to adding these exquisite pieces to my collection. 122

Sincerely | Cynthia A. Maustin 127

WORD PROCESSING 5

ACTIVITY 1

Review WP Features

Key sentences 1–5; underline, *italicize*, and **bold** text as you key. Use the Hanging Indent feature to align the second line of text under the first line as shown.

 **Save as:** *WP5ACT1*

1. **Benjamin Britten's** *Four Sea Interludes* include ***Dawn***, ***Sunday Morning***, ***Moonlight***, and ***Storm***.
2. Chris O'Donnell, Renee Zellweger, Brooke Shields, and Mariah Carey star in ***The Bachelor***.
3. The titles of **books** and **movies** should be underlined or *italicized.*
4. Any Given Sunday is a **drama**; Magnolia is a **comedy**; and Supernova is a **sci-fi**.
5. Henry Wadsworth **Longfellow** wrote *Success*; Samuel **Longfellow** wrote *Go Forth to Life.*

ACTIVITY 2

Review WP Features

1. Open the file *CD-WP5ACT2.*
2. Underline, *italicize*, and **bold** text as shown at the right.

 **Save as:** *WP5ACT2*

6. During the first week of February, *The Testament* by **John Grisham** was No. 1 on the Best Sellers list.
7. Time and Newsweek featured articles on the tragic deaths of John F. Kennedy, Jr., and Carolyn Bessette Kennedy.
8. Margins were presented in **WP2**; Cut, Copy, and Paste were presented in **WP3**.
9. Do you know the difference between ***their*** and ***there***?
10. *The Village Blacksmith* (**Longfellow**) and *The Road Not Taken* (**Frost**) were discussed in class on Friday.

ACTIVITY 3

Copy Text to Another File

1. Read the copy at the right.
2. Open the file you created in Activity 2 (*WP5ACT2*); copy Sentences 6–10.
3. Open *WP5ACT1*, the file you created in Activity 1; place the copied text a DS below Sentence 5.

 **Save as:** *WP5ACT3*

Use the **Copy** and **Paste** features to copy text from one file to another.

Use the **Cut** and **Paste** features to move text from one file to another.

Steps to Copy, Cut, and Paste:

1. Select the text.
2. Copy or cut the selected text.
3. Open the document in which you want to place the copied (or cut) text.
4. Place the insertion point where you want to place the text.
5. Paste the text at the insertion point.

Letter 2
Format and key the text at the right as a personal-business letter in block format.

Save as: *LTR29B2*

words

117 Whitman Ave. | Hartford, CT 06107-4518 | July 2, 200- | Ms. 12
Geneva Everett | 880 Honeysuckle Dr. | Athens, GA 30606-9231 | 23
Dear Geneva 25

Last week at the Educational Theatre Association National Convention 39
you mentioned that your teaching assignment for next year included 53
an Introduction to Shakespeare class. I find the Internet to be a very 67
useful supplement for creating interest in many of the classes I teach. 82
Here are four Internet locations dealing with Shakespeare that you 95
may find helpful for your new class. 103

http://www.shakespeares-globe.org/Default.htm 112
http://www.wfu.edu/~tedforrl/shakesp.htm 120
http://www.jetlink.net/~massij/shakes/ 128
http://www.albemarle-london.com/map-globe.html 137

Another resource that I use is a booklet published by Thomson 150
Learning: *Introducing Shakespeare*. A copy of the title page is 163
attached. It includes scenes from some of Shakespeare's best-known 176
works. Scenes from my favorites (*Romeo and Juliet, A Midsummer* 189
Night's Dream, and *Julius Caesar*) are included. 199

As I come across other resources, I will forward them to you. Enjoy 213
the rest of the summer; another school year will be upon us before we 227
know it. 229

Sincerely | Marshall W. Cline | Attachment 236

FORMATTING

29C • 10' Envelopes

1. Study the guides at the right and the illustrations below. Specific keying details are provided for those choosing to format envelopes without the Envelopes feature because of printer issues.
2. Format a small (No. 6 3/4) envelope for Letter 1 in 29B and a large (No. 10) envelope for Letter 2 in 29B.

Save as: *ENV29C1* and *ENV29C2*

Sender's return address

Use block style, SS, and Initial Caps or ALL CAPS. If not using the Envelopes feature, begin as near to the top and left edge of the envelope as possible—TM and LM about 0.25".

Receiver's delivery address

Use USPS (postal service) style: block style, SS, ALL CAPS, no punctuation.

Place city name, two-letter state abbreviation, and ZIP Code +4 on last address line. One space precedes the ZIP Code.

If not using the Envelopes feature, tab over 2.5" for the small envelope and 4" for the large envelope. Insert hard returns to place the first line about 2" from the top.

Envelope 1

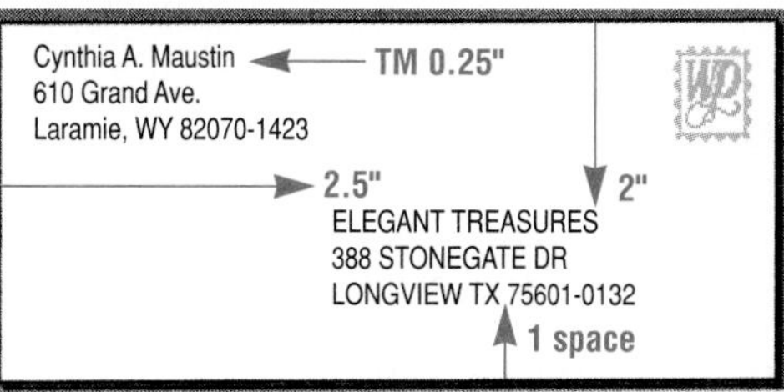

Envelope 2

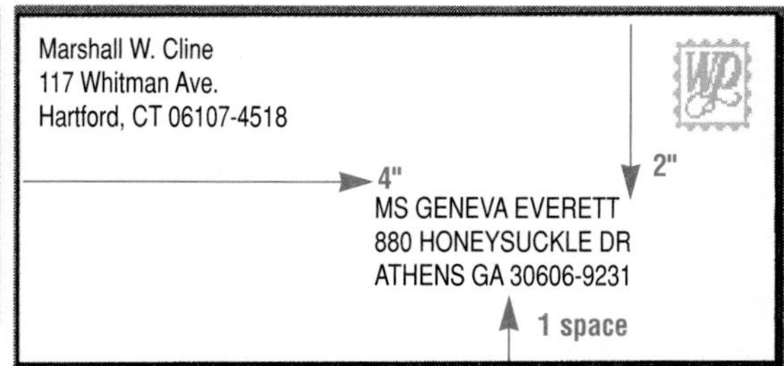

SKILL BUILDING

43D • 12'
Speed Forcing Drill

Key each line once at top speed. Then try to complete each sentence on the 15", 12", or 10" call, as directed by your instructor. Force speed to higher levels as you move from line to line.

Emphasis: high-frequency balanced-hand words

	gwam 15"	12"	10"
Glen and I may key the forms for the city auditor.	40	50	60
He may make a sign to hang by the door of the bus.	40	50	60
They may make a profit if they do all of the busy work.	44	55	66
Six of the boys may bid for the land on the big island.	44	55	66
If he pays for the bus to the social, the girls may go also.	48	60	72
The neighbor paid the maid for the work she did on the dock.	48	60	72
It is their civic duty to handle their problems with proficiency.	52	65	78
Helen is to pay the firm for all the work they do on the autobus.	52	65	78

SKILL BUILDING

43E • 15'
Skill Check

1. Key a 1' writing on ¶ 1; determine *gwam.*
2. Add 2–4 *gwam* to the rate attained in Step 1, and note quarter-minute checkpoints in the chart below.
3. Take two 1' guided writings on ¶ 1 to increase speed.
4. Practice ¶ 2 in the same way.
5. Take two 3' writings on ¶s 1 and 2 combined; determine *gwam* and find errors.

Quarter-Minute Checkpoints				
gwam	1/4'	1/2'	3/4'	1'
24	6	12	18	24
28	7	14	21	28
32	8	16	24	32
36	9	18	27	36
40	10	20	30	40
44	11	22	33	44
48	12	24	36	48
52	13	26	39	52
56	14	28	42	56
60	15	30	45	60

A all letters used

	gwam 3'	
Many options are available for people to ponder as they	4	64
invest their money. Real estate, savings accounts, money market	8	69
accounts, bonds, and stocks are but a few of the options that	12	73
are open to those who wish to invest their extra money. Several	17	77
factors will determine which type of investment a person will	21	81
choose. These factors pertain to the expected rate of return, the	25	86
degree of liquidity desired, and the amount of risk a person is	29	90
willing to take.	30	91
An investor who seeks a high rate of return and who is	34	95
willing to take a high degree of risk often considers the stock	38	99
market. Stock markets or stock exchanges are organizations that	43	103
bring investors together to buy and sell shares of stock. Stock	47	108
represents a share in the ownership of a company. Since more	51	112
risk is associated with an investment that has a high rate of	55	116
return, judgment must be exercised by those thinking about the	60	120
purchase of stock.	61	121

gwam 3' | 1 | 2 | 3 | 4 |

LESSON 30 FORMAT PERSONAL-BUSINESS LETTERS

Objectives:

1. To format personal-business letters in block format.
2. To format/key envelopes.

30A • 5' Conditioning Practice

Key each line twice SS; then key a 1' writing on line 3; determine *gwam.*

alphabet 1 Jack next placed my winning bid for the prized antique vase.

fig/sym 2 I deposited Lund & Lutz's $937.46 check (#2408) on April 15.

speed 3 Jan is to go to the city hall to sign the land forms for us.

gwam 1' | 1 | 2 | 3 | 4 | 5 | 6 | 7 | 8 | 9 | 10 | 11 | 12 |

FORMATTING

30B • 45' Personal-Business Letters in Block Format

Letter 1

Format and key the letter at the right in block format; check spelling, proofread, and correct the letter before you save it.

Save as: *LTR30B1*

words

1245 Park Ave. 3
New York, NY 10128-2231 8
October 28, 200- 11

Mrs. Tara Cruz 14
4221 Beekman St. 18
New York, NY 10038-8326 22

Dear Mrs. Cruz 25

Mrs. Kenningston's fifth grade class will be attending a production of 40
the Broadway musical *The Lion King* on March 25 to conclude their 53
study of the theater. As you are probably aware, the play is based on 67
the 1994 Disney film about a young lion's coming-of-age struggles. 80

Attending the play will give the fifth graders a real sense of New York 95
theater. The production will be at the New Amsterdam Theatre, built 109
in 1903 and for years considered the most majestic on 42d Street. 122
With its recent renovation, it has been restored almost to its original 136
grandeur. The theatre is best known as the home of the Ziegfeld 149
Follies (1913 through 1927) and George M. Cohan's *Forty-Five Minutes* 163
from Broadway. 166

This will be a great experience for the fifth graders. Mrs. Kenningston 181
would like four parents to help chaperone on the day of the 193
production. Are you interested and willing to assist? I will call you 207
next week to determine your availability and discuss details. 220

Sincerely 222

Marsha Rhodes 224
Parent Volunteer 228

SKILL BUILDING

42E • 12'
Speed Forcing Drill

Key each line once at top speed. Then try to complete each sentence on the 15", 12", or 10" call, as directed by your instructor. Force speed to higher levels as you move from line to line.

Emphasis: high-frequency balanced-hand words

	gwam 15"	12"	10"
The sign is on the mantle by the antique ornament.	40	50	60
Pamela kept the food for the fish by the fishbowl.	40	50	60
I paid the man by the dock for the six bushels of corn.	44	55	66
The box with a shamrock and an iris is by the car door.	44	55	66
He owns the chair in the shanty at the end of the cornfield.	48	60	72
Their auditor may work on the problems with the eight firms.	48	60	72
To the right of the lake is the dismal shanty with the six ducks.	52	65	78
The maid may go with them when they go to the city for the gowns.	52	65	78

LESSON 43 IMPROVE KEYING TECHNIQUE

Objectives:

1. To improve keying techniques.
2. To improve keying speed and control.

43A • 5'
Conditioning Practice

Key each line twice SS; then take a 1' writing on line 3; determine *gwam*.

alphabet 1 Jack Lopez will attend the quality frog exhibits over the summer.
figures 2 Tim's score was 79 percent; he missed numbers 18, 26, 30, and 45.
speed 3 Pamela may blame the men for the problem with the neighbor's dog.

gwam 1' | 1 | 2 | 3 | 4 | 5 | 6 | 7 | 8 | 9 | 10 | 11 | 12 | 13 |

SKILL BUILDING

43B • 10'
Technique: Letter Keys

1. Key each line twice.
2. Take a 30" writing on each line. If you complete the line, key it again.

Goals:

- To keep keystroking action limited to the fingers.
- Continuity and rhythm with curved, upright fingers.

R 1 The raindrops bore down on the robbers during the February storm.
S 2 The Mets, Astros, Reds, Twins, Jays, and Cubs sold season passes.
T 3 Trent bought the teal teakettle on the stove in downtown Seattle.
U 4 Ursula usually rushes to the music museum on Tuesday, not Sunday.
V 5 Vivacious Eve viewed seven vivid violets in the vases in the van.
W 6 We swore we would work with the two wonderful kids for two weeks.
X 7 Rex Baxter explained the extra excise tax to excited expatriates.
Y 8 Yes, Ty is very busy trying to justify buying the yellow bicycle.
Z 9 Dazed, Zelda zigzagged to a plaza by the zoo to see a lazy zebra.

gwam 1' | 1 | 2 | 3 | 4 | 5 | 6 | 7 | 8 | 9 | 10 | 11 | 12 | 13 |

SKILL BUILDING

43C • 8'
Technique: Number Keys/Tab

1. Set tabs at 2" and at 4".
2. Key the copy at the right.
3. Key three 1' writings, trying to key additional text on each writing.

313 Richards Rd.	842 Warner Rd.	8634 Pearl Blvd.
67 Simmons St.	7619 Stewart Ave.	129 Silk Oak Dr.
9057 Taurus Ct.	904 Tebbetts Dr.	55 Vineland Ave.
436 Seaton Hall Ln.	802 Mayflower St.	627 Kimball Ave.
4021 Phyllis Way	357 Garvin St.	2004 Huber St.
138 Truman St.	84 Talmadge Pl.	835 Knobloch Ln.

Letter 2
Format and key the letter at the right in block format; proofread and correct the letter before you save it.

Save as: *LTR30B2*

Letter 3
Format and key the letter at the right below in block format; proofread and correct the letter before you save it.

Save as: *LTR30B3*

Word Processing **Activity**

Prepare letters for the other three parents who helped chaperone the field trip. Their addresses are shown below.

Mr. Charles Chan
389 Wadsworth Ave.
New York, NY 10040-0025

Ms. Alesha Ramirez
175 Morningside Ave.
New York, NY 10027-8735

Ms. Gwendolyn Maas
1615 Henry Hudson Pky.
New York, NY 10034-6721

Save as:
LTR30B3CHAN
LTR30B3RAMI
LTR30B3MAAS

The Web address for Broadway theater information is shown at the right. Visit the site, select **Theatre Listings**, search for **New Amsterdam Theatre**, and find the information about educational discounts and wheelchair accessibility requested by Marsha Rhodes in Letter 2 (30B).

Compose a response to Ms. Rhodes as though you were the New Amsterdam's ticket manager. Prepare a No. 10 envelope.

Save as:
LTR30OPTIONAL

---

words

1245 Park Ave. | New York, NY 10128-2231 | January 5, 200- | 11
Ticket Manager | New Amsterdam Theatre | Broadway at Eighth Ave. 23
| New York, NY 10036 | Dear Ticket Manager 31

Mrs. Kenningston's fifth grade class from Washington Elementary 44
School will be studying theater during the month of March. To 56
conclude their study, Mrs. Kenningston would like for them to attend 70
a Broadway production of *The Lion King* on March 25. 81

Approximately twenty children would attend the performance along 94
with five chaperones. Does your theatre offer educational discounts 108
for the matinee performance? 114

One of our students needs wheelchair accessibility. What facilities do 128
you have to accommodate this student? 136

The students are very excited about the possibility of attending a live 150
Broadway production. Please provide me with the requested information 164
as soon as possible so that the necessary arrangements can be made. 178

Sincerely | Marsha Rhodes | Parent Volunteer 186

---

words

1245 Park Ave. | New York, NY 10128-2231 | April 1, 200- | Mrs. 12
Tara Cruz | 4221 Beekman St. | New York, NY 10038-8326 | Dear 23
Mrs. Cruz 25

Thank you for helping chaperone the fifth grade class on their field trip 40
to Broadway. When I visited Mrs. Kenningston's classroom yesterday, 53
the children were still excited about having attended the play. Their 68
thank-you note is enclosed. 73

Because of parents like you, educational experiences outside the 86
classroom are possible. These experiences bring to life what the 100
students learn in school. I'm glad our children have this enrichment. 114

Thank you again for accepting the challenge of watching over the fifth 128
graders on their exciting trip to Broadway. I know the task wasn't 142
easy, but I felt it was well worth our time. 151

Sincerely | Marsha Rhodes | Parent Volunteer | Enclosure 161

Web address:
http://www.theatre.com/

Return address (letter):
Broadway at Eighth Ave.
New York, NY 10036

Return address (envelope):
[Your name], Ticket Manager
New Amsterdam Theatre
Broadway at Eighth Ave.
New York, NY 10036

Letter (Delivery) address:
MS MARSHA RHODES
1245 PARK AVE
NEW YORK NY 10128-2231

LESSON 42 IMPROVE KEYING TECHNIQUE

Objectives:
1. To improve keying techniques.
2. To improve keying speed and control.

42A • 5' Conditioning Practice

Key each line twice SS; then key a 1' writing on line 3; determine *gwam*.

alphabet 1 Jake Lopez may give a few more racquetball exhibitions in Dallas.
figures 2 Ray quickly found the total of 8.16, 9.43, and 10.25 to be 27.84.
speed 3 Bob's neighbor may dismantle the ancient shanty in the big field.

gwam 1' | 1 | 2 | 3 | 4 | 5 | 6 | 7 | 8 | 9 | 10 | 11 | 12 | 13 |

SKILL BUILDING

42B • 10' Technique: Letter Keys

1. Key each line twice.
2. Take a 30" writing on each line. If you complete the line, key it again.

Goal:
To keep keystroking action limited to the fingers.

Emphasize continuity and rhythm with curved, upright fingers.

I 1 Michigan, Illinois, Indiana, and Missouri are all in the Midwest.
J 2 Jay juggled plans to join Jane for juice with the judge and jury.
K 3 Katie knocked the knickknacks off the kiosk with her knobby knee.
L 4 Please allow me to be a little late with all legal illustrations.
M 5 Mary is immensely immature; her mannerisms make me extremely mad.
N 6 Nancy knew she would win the nomination at their next convention.
O 7 Roberto opposed opening the store on Monday mornings before noon.
P 8 Pam wrapped the peppermints in purple paper for the photographer.
Q 9 Qwin quietly queried Quincy on the quantity and quality of quail.

gwam 1' | 1 | 2 | 3 | 4 | 5 | 6 | 7 | 8 | 9 | 10 | 11 | 12 | 13 |

SKILL BUILDING

42C • 8' Technique: Number Keys/Tab

1. Set tabs at 2" and at 4".
2. Key the copy at the right.
3. Key three 1' writings, trying to key additional text on each writing.

Concentrate on figure location; quick tab spacing; eyes on copy.

429 Piedmont Ct.	883 Northgate Rd.	801 Montana Ave.
9173 Salem Rd.	554 Taunton Ave.	129 Venturi Rd.
3928 Market St.	885 Kickapoo Trail	820 Scarlett Dr.
890 Richmond St.	910 Plymouth Dr.	856 Lakewood Dr.
830 Manzanita Ave.	819 Oakdale Way	102 Victoria St.
306 Beckett Ter.	282 Curnan Way	823 Brook Ter.

SKILL BUILDING

42D • 15' Skill Check

1. Key three 1' writings on ¶ 1 of 41E. Strive to increase your rate on each writing.
2. Repeat Step 1 using ¶ 2.
3. Key two 3' writings using both ¶s.
4. Determine better 3' *gwam* and record it for later use.

SKILL BUILDER 2

Speed Building

1. Key each line once SS; DS between 2-line groups.

Goal: No pauses between letters and words.

2. Key a 1' writing on each of lines 4, 6, 8, and 10; determine *gwam* on each.
3. If time permits, rekey the three slowest lines.

space bar
1 city then they form than body them busy sign firm duty turn proxy
2 Jan may do key work for the six men on the audit of the big firm.

shift keys
3 Lake Como | Hawaii or Alaska | Madrid and Bogota | Sparks & Mason, Inc.
4 Karl left for Bora Bora in May; Nan goes to Lake Worth in August.

adjacent keys
5 same wire open tire sure ruin said trim went fire spot lids walks
6 We opened a shop by the stadium to offer the best sporting goods.

long direct reaches
7 vice much many nice once myth lace cents under check juice center
8 Eunice brought a recorder to the music hall to record my recital.

word response
9 their right field world forms visit title chair spent towns usual
10 They wish to go with the girl to the city to make the visual aid.

gwam 1' | 1 | 2 | 3 | 4 | 5 | 6 | 7 | 8 | 9 | 10 | 11 | 12 | 13 |

Timed Writings

1. Key a 1' writing on each ¶; determine *gwam* on each one.
2. Key two 2' writings on ¶s 1–2 combined; determine *gwam* on each writing.
3. Key two 3' writing on ¶s 1–3 combined; determine *gwam* and count errors on each writing.
4. If time permits, key two 1' guided writings on each ¶; one for control and one for speed (add 4 to your rate in Step 1). Set quarter-minute goals using the chart below.

Quarter-Minute Checkpoints

gwam	1/4'	1/2'	3/4'	1'
24	6	12	18	24
28	7	14	21	28
32	8	16	24	32
36	9	18	27	36
40	10	20	30	40
44	11	22	33	44
48	12	24	36	48
52	13	26	39	52
56	14	28	42	56

A all letters used — gwam 2' | 3'

In deciding upon a career, learn as much as possible about 6 4 57
what individuals in that career do. For each job class, there are 12 8 62
job requirements and qualifications that must be met. Analyze 19 13 66
these tasks very critically in terms of your personality and what 25 17 70
you like to do. 27 18 71

A high percentage of jobs in major careers demand education or 33 22 76
training after high school. The training may be very specialized, 40 27 80
requiring intensive study or interning for two or more years. You 47 31 85
must decide if you are willing to expend so much time and effort. 53 35 90

After you have decided upon a career to pursue, discuss the 59 39 93
choice with parents, teachers, and others. Such people can help 66 44 97
you design a plan to guide you along the series of steps required 72 48 102
in pursuing your goal. Keep the plan flexible and change it when- 79 52 106
ever necessary. 80 53 107

gwam 2' | 1 | 2 | 3 | 4 | 5 | 6
3' | 1 | 2 | 3 | 4

SKILL BUILDING

41D • 12'
Speed Forcing Drill

Key each line once at top speed. Then try to complete each sentence on the 15", 12", or 10" call, as directed by your instructor. Force speed to higher levels as you move from line to line.

Emphasis: high-frequency balanced-hand words

	gwam 15"	12"	10"
Diane may go to the dock to visit the eight girls.	40	50	60
She is to go with them to the city to see the dog.	40	50	60
The sorority girls paid for the auto to go to the city.	44	55	66
She is to go to the city with us to sign the six forms.	44	55	66
Dick may go to the big island to fix the auto for the widow.	48	60	72
Glen and the big dog slept by the antique chair on the dock.	48	60	72
Nancy may pay the men for all the work they did down by the lake.	52	65	78
They held the big social for their neighbor downtown at the hall.	52	65	78

SKILL BUILDING

41E • 15'
Skill Check

1. Key a 1' writing on ¶ 1; determine *gwam*.
2. Add 2-4 *gwam* to the rate attained in Step 1, and note quarter-minute checkpoints in the chart below.
3. Key two 1' guided writings on ¶ 1 to increase speed.
4. Practice ¶ 2 in the same way.
5. Key two 3' writings on ¶s 1 and 2 combined; determine *gwam* and find errors.

Quarter-Minute Checkpoints				
gwam	1/4'	1/2'	3/4'	1'
24	6	12	18	24
28	7	14	21	28
32	8	16	24	32
36	9	18	27	36
40	10	20	30	40
44	11	22	33	44
48	12	24	36	48
52	13	26	39	52
56	14	28	42	56
60	15	30	45	60

A all letters used — gwam 3'

Quite a few of today's consumers buy on credit each day 4 67
without considering the consequences of the costs associated with 8 71
purchases made on credit. A decreased spending capacity in the 12 75
future is one of the main points that needs to be taken into 16 79
account prior to making a major credit purchase. Buyers who 21 83
utilize credit need to remember that earnings going toward the 25 87
repayment of a loan restrict funds that could be used to buy other 29 92
goods or services. 30 93

Buyers must also remember that credit can be expensive; there 35 97
are costs associated with it. One of those costs is interest. In- 39 102
terest is the sum charged for the use of money. Buyers who make 43 106
purchases via credit can also expect to be charged service fees or 48 111
finance charges. Perhaps the biggest cost of credit, however, is 52 115
the opportunity cost. The opportunity cost can be viewed as the 57 119
cost of not acquiring certain goods or services in order to ac- 61 124
quire other goods or services. 63 126

gwam 3' | 1 | 2 | 3 | 4 |

WORD PROCESSING 4

ACTIVITY 1

Insert Table

1. Read the copy at the right.
2. Learn how to create a table with your word processing software.
3. Create and fill in the table shown at the right.

 **Save as:** *WP4ACT1*

Use the **Table** feature to create a grid for arranging information in rows and columns. Tables consist of vertical columns and horizontal rows. Columns are labeled alphabetically from left to right; rows are labeled numerically from top to bottom. The crossing of columns and rows makes **cells**.

When text is keyed in a cell, it wraps around in that cell—instead of wrapping around to the next row. A line space is added to the cell each time the text wraps around.

To fill in cells, use the TAB key or Right arrow key to move from cell to cell in a row and from row to row. (Striking ENTER will simply insert a blank line space in the cell.) To move around in a filled-in table, use the arrow keys, TAB, or the mouse (click the desired cell).

NATIONAL LEAGUE CY YOUNG AWARD WINNERS

Year	Player	Team
1990	Doug Drabek	Pirates
1991	Tom Glavine	Braves
1992	Greg Maddux	Cubs
1993	Greg Maddux	Braves
1994	Greg Maddux	Braves
1995	Greg Maddux	Braves
1996	John Smoltz	Braves

ACTIVITY 2

Insert and Delete Rows and Columns

1. Read the copy at the right.
2. Open the table you created in Activity 1 (*WP4ACT1*).
3. Insert the information for 1997–1999 and make the other changes shown at the right.

 **Save as:** *WP4ACT2*

The Table feature can be used to edit or modify existing tables. Common modifications include the addition and deletion of rows and columns.

1997	*Pedro Martinez*	*Expos*
1998	*Tom Glavine*	*Braves*
1999	*Randy Johnson*	*Diamondbacks*

1. Delete the 1990–1992 award winners.
2. Delete the column showing the team the award winner played for.
3. Undo the last change made to restore the deleted column.

UNIT 13

LESSONS 41-43

Building Basic Skill

LESSON 41 IMPROVE KEYING TECHNIQUE

Objectives:

1. To improve keying techniques.
2. To improve keying speed and control.

41A • 5' Conditioning Practice

Key each line twice SS; then take a 1' writing on line 3; determine *gwam*.

alphabet 1 How will Joy pack a dozen big boxes of their expensive equipment?

figures 2 Math 458 had 239 students enrolled in Sections 9, 10, 16, and 17.

speed 3 My sick neighbor did the title work on the bus for the eight men.

gwam 1' | 1 | 2 | 3 | 4 | 5 | 6 | 7 | 8 | 9 | 10 | 11 | 12 | 13 |

SKILL BUILDING

41B • 10' Technique: Letter Keys

1. Key each line twice.
2. Take a 30" timing on each line. If you complete the line, key it again.

Goal:
To keep keystroking action limited to the fingers.

Emphasize continuity and rhythm with curved, upright fingers.

A 1 Alexandra made an appearance at the Alabama and Arkansas parades.

B 2 Bobby babysat both the bubbly Babbit brats at the baseball games.

C 3 Chad, the eccentric character with a classic crew cut, may catch.

D 4 David and Eddie dodged the duck as it waddled down the dark road.

E 5 Eileen elevated her desk eleven inches above all the other desks.

F 6 Before I left, Faye found forty to fifty feet of flowered fabric.

G 7 Greg groggily got up and gazed grudgingly at the haggard old dog.

H 8 She held the hooks for him while he helped her catch the hamster.

gwam 1' | 1 | 2 | 3 | 4 | 5 | 6 | 7 | 8 | 9 | 10 | 11 | 12 | 13 |

SKILL BUILDING

41C • 8' Technique: Number Keys/Tab

1. Key each line twice (key number, depress TAB, key next number).
2. Take three 1' writings, trying to better your rate each time.

Concentrate on figure location; quick tab spacing; eyes on copy.

30	927	565	389	943	828	377	898	901
23	183	279	766	752	109	459	578	623
14	406	180	445	516	207	140	626	354

gwam 1' | 1 | 2 | 3 | 4 | 5 | 6 | 7

ACTIVITY 3

Join Cells and Change Column Width

1. Read the information at the right.
2. Learn how to join cells.
3. Learn how to adjust column widths.
4. Open the file *CD-WP4ACT3.*
5. Join the cells of Row 1.
6. Adjust the column widths so that the name of each sales representative fits on one line, as shown at the right. Adjust the width of other columns as needed.

 **Save as:** *WP4ACT3*

Use the Table feature to **join** cells (merge two or more cells into one cell). This feature is useful when information in the table spans more than one column or row. The main title, for example, spans all columns.

In a newly created table, all columns are the same width. You can change the width of one or more columns to accommodate entries of unequal widths.

SALES REPORT				
Sales Rep.	Territory	Jan.	Feb.	March
Juan Ramirez	Washington	12,325	13,870	12,005
Shawn Hewitt	Oregon	15,680	17,305	7,950
Maria Hernandez	Idaho	9,480	16,780	14,600
Cheryl Updike	Washington	10,054	8,500	17,085
Tanya Goodman	Washington	19,230	11,230	15,780
Jason Graham	Oregon	15,900	16,730	9,290
Carolyn Plummer	Idaho	20,370	13,558	12,654
Scott Bowe	Idaho	15,750	14,560	16,218
Brandon Olson	Oregon	14,371	11,073	19,301
Laura Chen	Washington	17,320	9,108	18,730

ACTIVITY 4

Change Table Format

1. Read the information at the right.
2. Learn how to make formatting changes in a table.
3. Open *WP4ACT3*, created in Activity 3.
4. Make the formatting changes given below and shown at the right.
   a. Bold and center the main title.
   b. Center-align Column B.
   c. Right-align Columns C, D, and E.
   d. Bold and center the column headings.
   e. Bold and italicize the highest sales figure for each month.

 **Save as:** *WP4ACT4*

The formatting changes (bold, italicize, alignment, etc.) that you have learned to make to text can also be made to the text within a table. You can do this prior to keying the text into the table, or it can be done after the text has been entered. After the table is complete, make changes by selecting the cell (row or column) to be changed and then giving the software command to make the change.

SALES REPORT				
Sales Rep.	**Territory**	**Jan.**	**Feb.**	**March**
Juan Ramirez	Washington	12,325	13,870	12,005
Shawn Hewitt	Oregon	15,680	***17,305***	7,950
Maria Hernandez	Idaho	9,480	16,780	14,600
Cheryl Updike	Washington	10,054	8,500	17,085
Tanya Goodman	Washington	19,230	11,230	15,780
Jason Graham	Oregon	15,900	16,730	9,290
Carolyn Plummer	Idaho	***20,370***	13,558	12,654
Scott Bowe	Idaho	15,750	14,560	16,218
Brandon Olson	Oregon	14,371	11,073	***19,301***
Laura Chen	Washington	17,320	9,108	18,730

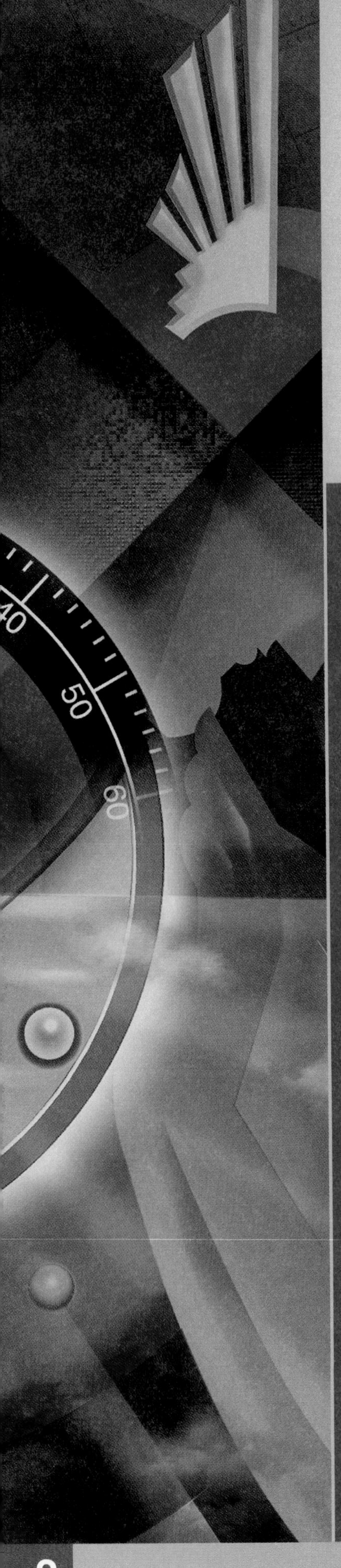

PART 2

UNITS 13-21

Computer Keyboarding: Improve & Extend

No matter what career you choose or what jobs you have along the way, a computer — and a computer keyboard — almost certainly will be at the center of your work. You will use new technology to build on existing keying skills.

You may have used, read about, or heard about *speech recognition technology (SRT)*. SRT is the ability of computers to understand spoken words and convert them into text. Using SRT, one can enter words and commands by talking to the computer and then watch the document appear on the screen.

Some people believe that SRT will make keyboarding a thing of the past, like the Pony Express or Henry Ford's Model T car. In fact, there is room for many versions of keyboarding technology, including computer keyboards and SRT. So instead of putting your keyboard in a museum, put it to work as you improve and extend your keying skills.

In Part 2 you will refine keying techniques, increase communication skills, and learn advanced word processing features. You will process e-mail with attachments, reports with footnotes, and tables with borders and shading, to name a few. And that's not all.

You will go to work in the home office of a growing organization with branches in five cities. Your work for the President/CEO often takes you to the company's Web page.

Let's get started!

ACTIVITY 5

Center Tables Horizontally and Vertically

1. Read the information at the right.
2. Learn to center tables horizontally and vertically.
3. Open the file you created in Activity 4 (*WP4ACT4*).
4. Center the table vertically.
5. Center the table horizontally.

 **Save as:** *WP4ACT5*

Use the **Center alignment** Table feature to center a table from left to right on a page.

Use the **Vertical alignment**, or **Center Page**, feature to center a table from top to bottom on a page.

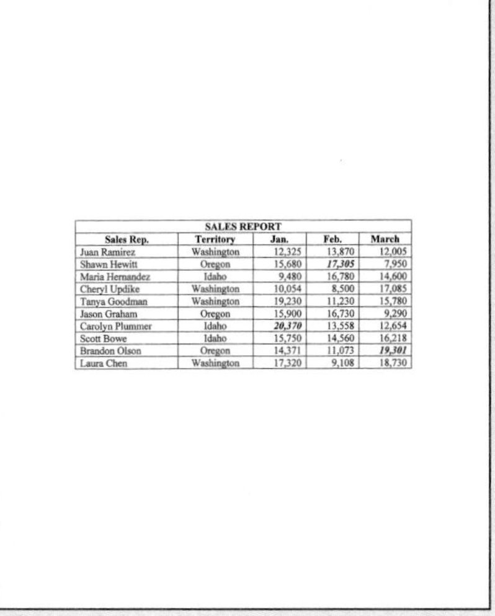

SALES REPORT				
Sales Rep.	**Territory**	**Jan.**	**Feb.**	**March**
Juan Ramirez	Washington	12,325	13,870	12,005
Shawn Hewitt	Oregon	15,680	***17,305***	7,950
Maria Hernandez	Idaho	9,480	16,780	14,600
Cheryl Updike	Washington	10,054	8,500	17,085
Tanya Goodman	Washington	19,230	11,230	15,780
Jason Graham	Oregon	15,900	16,730	9,290
Carolyn Plummer	Idaho	***20,370***	13,558	12,654
Scott Bowe	Idaho	15,750	14,560	16,218
Brandon Olson	Oregon	14,371	11,073	***19,301***
Laura Chen	Washington	17,320	9,108	18,730

ACTIVITY 6

Sort Tables

1. Read the information at the right; learn to use the Sort feature.
2. Open *WP4ACT5*, which you created in Activity 5.
3. Sort the table by Territory (Column B) in descending order as shown.
4. Sort the table by March sales (Column E) in descending order.

 **Save as:** *WP4ACT6*

The **Sort** feature arranges text in a table in a specific order. The feature sorts alphabetic or numeric text in ascending or descending order.

SALES REPORT				
Sales Rep.	**Territory**	**Jan.**	**Feb.**	**March**
Juan Ramirez	Washington	12,325	13,870	12,005
Cheryl Updike	Washington	10,054	8,500	17,085
Tanya Goodman	Washington	19,230	11,230	15,780
Brandon Olson	Oregon	14,371	11,073	***19,301***
Maria Hernandez	Idaho	9,480	16,780	14,600
Carolyn Plummer	Idaho	***20,370***	13,558	12,654
Scott Bowe	Idaho	15,750	14,560	16,218

ACTIVITY 7

Change Row Height and Vertical Alignment

1. Read the copy at the right; learn how to change row height.
2. Open the file created in Activity 6 (*WP4ACT6*). Change row height as follows: main title row, 0.6"; column headings, 0.5"; other rows, 0.4".
3. Change vertical alignment as follows: main title and column headings, **center**; data entry rows, **bottom** alignment.

 **Save as:** *WP4ACT7*

Use the Table feature to change the height of the rows in a table. The height of all the rows of the table can be changed to the same height, or each row can be a different height.

Use the Table feature to change the vertical alignment of text in cells. The text within a cell can be top-aligned, center-aligned, or bottom-aligned.

Top align - 0.3"	Center align - 0.3"	Bottom align - 0.3"
Top align - 0.4"	Center align - 0.4"	Bottom align - 0.4"
Top align - 0.5"	Center align - 0.5"	Bottom align - 0.5"

Your Perspective

A growing number of "fair trade" organizations provide artists, artisans, and farmers, often from developing countries, with a means of marketing their goods globally at a fair price. One such organization is PEOPLink. PEOPLink works with a network of Trading Partners, mostly nonprofit groups from Latin America, Asia, and Africa, that serve community artisan groups. PEOPLink gives its Trading Partners digital cameras to photograph products and markets those products in its online catalog. The organization also provides online information about the work and lives of the artisans, teaches them to build and maintain their own Web catalogs, gives them online training, and helps them develop their products. The table below shows fair trade products and their countries of origin.

FAIR TRADE ARTS AND CRAFTS

Product	Country
Sculptures	Cameroon
Baskets	Uganda
Molas	Panama
Pitchers	Guatemala
Brooches	Russia

Music has a rich cultural history. From ancient times, different cultures have developed their own styles of music and have invented different instruments with which to express them.

In music, the influence of one culture on another can be clearly seen and can produce exciting results. Take the American composer Aaron Copland, for example. Some of Copland's best-known compositions were based on American folk music, such as the ballets *Billy the Kid* (1938), *Rodeo* (1942), and *Appalachian Spring* (1944). His *El salon Mexico* was inspired by Mexican folk music.

Radio, television, the Internet, and high-quality sound and video recording have made music from many different cultures accessible to listeners worldwide. They have also helped to make music even more multicultural. For example, South Indian *cine*, or motion-picture music, uses both Indian and Western musical instruments and mixes classical Indian music with Western rock and jazz.*

*Source: David Butler, B.SC., M.A., Ph.D. "Music." *Microsoft® Encarta® Online Encyclopedia 2000* http://encarta.msn.com (16 July 2000).

Global Awareness

ACTIVITIES

1. Key and format the table at the left. Use the table formatting features that you have learned to arrange the information attractively on the page.
2. Form a group with some other students. Develop a plan for a school fair in which you could showcase the work of artists from your school and community. Include details such as the date of the fair, where it would be held, how you would invite participants, how many you could invite, and where and how you would advertise the event.

Cultural Diversity

ACTIVITIES

1. Pair up with another student who likes a musician that you also like. Talk about this musician. Address the following questions, taking notes on the answers.
   a. Does this musician's work show the influence of other musicians or other kinds of music? If so, in what way?
   b. Do you think people in another country might form perceptions of this musician's country based on his or her music? If so, what might they be?
   c. Think of the music you like to listen to and the music your parents like. How important is culture to being able to appreciate a particular kind of music?
2. Develop your notes and key them into a one-page essay in unbound report format.

ACTIVITY 8

Apply What You Have Learned

1. Open the file *CD-WP4ACT8*.
2. Insert a column for the dates, as shown at right.
3. Bold and center column headings.
4. Center the information in the Date column.
5. Adjust column widths to fit the information.
6. Sort the Date column in ascending order.
7. Insert a row for: **1807 - Steamboat - Robert Fulton**.
8. Insert a row above the column headings; merge the cells. Cut and paste the main title in the merged row.
9. Center the table on the page.

 **Save as:** *WP4ACT8*

INVENTIONS

Date	Invention	Inventor
1877	Phonograph	Thomas Edison
1805	Railroad locomotive	Richard Trevithick
1846	Sewing machine	Elias Howe
1867	Revolver	Samuel Colt
1820	Calculating machine	Charles Babbage
1867	Typewriter	Christopher Sholes

ACTIVITY 9

Apply What You Have Learned

1. Open the file CD-*WP4ACT9*. Insert a column for **Sale Price** as shown, and enter the amounts.
2. Insert a row at the end* with the following information in the cells: **Sandager, Rocky Mountain Road, 950**.
3. Adjust column widths to fit the information.
4. Sort the Artist column in ascending order.**
5. Change the row height for the main title to 0.6"; change the row height for the column headings to 0.5"; change the row height for the data rows to 0.4".
6. Change the vertical alignment for the main title and column headings to *center*; change the vertical alignment for the data rows to *bottom*.
7. Center the table on the page.

 **Save as:** *WP4ACT9*

***Note:**
To add a row at the end, place the insertion point in the last existing cell and press TAB.

****Note:**
The $ should precede the first entry in the Sale Price column after the sort ($1,139).

JUNE ART GALLERY SPECIALS		
Artist	**Art Print**	Sale Price
Richmond	*Summer Home*	$9,250
Du Bois	*City Lights*	165
Gennrich	*Brittany's Garden*	425
Sinclair	*Sunday Morning*	1,095
Shoji	*Christmas Morning*	350
Chen	*Coming Home*	1,139
Lindquist	*Dakota Country*	280
Hohenstein	*The Old Mill*	3,325
Debauche	*Campers' Delight*	150

Your Perspective

Nel mezzo del cammin di nostra vita
mi ritrovai per una selva oscura,
che la diritta via era smarrita.

Midway in the journey of our life
I found myself in a dark wood,
for the straight way was lost.

An image that you will find in the literature of many times and places is that of a person traveling through a forest. Dante Alighieri used it in the opening lines of *The Divine Comedy*, above (translation by Charles S. Singleton). So did Nathaniel Hawthorne in his short story "Young Goodman Brown" and Robert Frost in his poem "The Road Not Taken." In the late 1980s, Steven Sondheim and James Lapine wrote a successful musical on the theme of traveling through a forest called *Into the Woods*.

Into the Woods begins with wishes, the simple wishes of characters we know from fairy tales. Jack (of "Jack and the Beanstalk") wishes to sell his cow to get money for his mother. Cinderella wishes to go to the ball. Into the woods the characters go, in pursuit of their wishes. And then things start to get complicated.

Into the Woods explores two themes. One is the difficulty of making the right choices; the other is whether the end justifies the means. Is it right for someone to cheat Jack into trading his cow for "magic" beans? What are the risks of stealing a giant's gold to buy back the cow and be rich?

For some of the characters, the woods are where they begin to discover just who they are and who they want to be. Cinderella finds she doesn't want to marry a prince. Neither does she want to be a servant in her stepmother's house. She wants "something in-between."

One way of seeing the woods is as a journey through life, in which the right path can be difficult to find or choose. At the end of the play *Into the Woods*, the remaining characters have learned some lessons about making the right choices. Part of what they have learned is this:

You can't just act,
You have to listen.
You can't just act,
You have to think.

Ethics: The Right Thing to Do

ACTIVITIES

1. Read the material at the left.
2. As a warm-up, key the Italian and then the English lines from *The Divine Comedy*. As you key the English words, think about what they mean.
3. Why do you think woods appear in so many stories? Key a list of adjectives that describe the woods at different times of day.
4. Form a group with some other students. Think of recent movies in which the characters made difficult choices. Why do you think the characters chose as they did? Each person should contribute ideas.
5. Compose and key a paragraph describing a time when you had to make a tough decision. What did you consider in making your choice?

UNIT 10

LESSONS 31-34

Learn to Format Tables

Format Guides: Tables

TOP TEN ANCESTRY GROUPS OF U.S. POPULATION			
1990 Census			
Rank	**Ancestry**	**Number**	**Percent of Population**
1	German	57,947,873	23.3
2	Irish	38,735,539	15.6
3	English	32,651,788	13.1
4	African American	23,777,098	9.6
5	Italian	14,664,550	5.9
6	American	12,395,999	5.0
7	Mexican	11,586,983	4.7
8	French	10,320,935	4.1
9	Polish	9,366,106	3.8
10	Native American	8,708,220	3.5
Source: *The Information Please Almanac*. Boston: Houghton Mifflin Company, 1996.			

Four-Column Table with Source Note

TABLES		
Format Features		
Horizontal Alignment	**Vertical Alignment**	**Row Height**
Left	Top	0.7"
Center	Top	0.7"
Right	Top	0.7"
Left	Center	0.55"
Center	Center	0.55"
Right	Center	0.55"
Left	Bottom	0.4"
Center	Bottom	0.4"
Right	Bottom	0.4"
2"	1.5"	1"

Alignment in Tables

Format Guides: Tables

Although you will use a word processing feature to create tables, you will need these guidelines for making your tables easy to read and attractive.

Parts of a Table

A **table** is an arrangement of data (words and/or numbers) in rows and columns. Columns are labeled alphabetically from left to right; rows are labeled numerically from top to bottom. Tables range in complexity from those with only two columns and a title to those with several columns and special features. The tables in this unit are limited to those with the following parts:

1. Main title usually in ALL CAPS (centered in first row or placed above the table).
2. Secondary title in capital and lowercase letters (centered a DS below the main title).
3. Column heading (centered over the column).
4. Body (data entries).
5. Source note (bottom left).
6. Gridlines (may be hidden).*

---

*Some software prints the gridlines between columns and rows (as shown in the model, p. 95) or allows you to hide all or some of the lines before printing. **Note:** If your software prints gridlines by default, leave the lines in all your tables unless your instructor directs you to hide them. If gridlines do not print, column headings should be underlined. Also, the last entry in an amount column with a total should be underlined.

Table Format Features

The following features (illustrated on p. 95) can be used to make your tables attractive and easy to read.

Vertical placement. A table may be centered vertically (equal top and bottom margins), or it may begin 2" from the top edge of the page.

Horizontal placement. Tables are most attractive when centered horizontally (side to side) on the page.

Column width. Generally, each column should be only slightly wider than the longest data entry in the column. Table columns should be identical widths or markedly different widths. Columns that are only slightly different widths should be avoided.

Row height. All rows, including title rows, may be the same height. To enhance appearance, the main title row height may be slightly more than the secondary title row height, which may be more than the column heading row. The column heading row height may be more than the data entry rows.

Vertical alignment. Within rows, data entries can be aligned at the top, center, or bottom. Most often you will use center vertical alignment for the headings and bottom vertical alignment for data rows beneath the headings. If a source note is included, it should also be bottom-aligned.

Horizontal alignment. Within columns, words may be left-aligned or center-aligned. Whole numbers are right-aligned if a column total is shown; decimal numbers are decimal-aligned. Other figures may be center-aligned.

40C • 35' Assess Table Formatting Skills

Table 1

Create the table shown at the right using the information given below. Center the table horizontally and vertically.

Main title: row height 0.7"; center vertically

Column headings: row height 0.4"; center vertically

Data rows: row height 0.3"; bottom vertical alignment

Column widths: Adjust column widths to arrange material attractively on the page.

 **Save as:** *TBL40C1*

Table 2

Create the table shown at the right using the information given for Table 1. Center the table horizontally and vertically. Use **VAN NOY ART GALLERY** for the main title; use **June-August Exhibits** for the secondary title.

Adjust column widths to arrange material attractively on the page.

 **Save as:** *TBL40C2*

Table 3

Using the table formatting features that you have learned to arrange information attractively on a page, format and key the data at the right as a table. Use **THEATER VOCABULARY WORDS** for the main title and **April 7-25** for the secondary title.

 **Save as:** *TBL40C3*

AMERICA'S CASTLES **Eastern Region**	
Castle	**Location**
The Breakers	Newport, Rhode Island
Chesterwood	Stockbridge, Massachusetts
Drumthwacket	Princeton, New Jersey
George Eastman House	Rochester, New York
Hildene	Manchester, Vermont
Longwood	Kennett Square, Pennsylvania
Lyndhurst Mansion	Tarrytown, New York
Marble House	Newport, Rhode Island
Sunnyside	Tarrytown, New York

Source: A&E, "America's Castles." http://www.aetv.com/tv/shows/castles/index2.html (26 January 2000).

Exhibit	*Opening/Closing Dates*
Emerging Artists	*June 1 - June 10*
19th-Century European Paintings	*June 11 - June 20*
Colonial American Art	*June 21 - June 30*
Old Masters' Paintings	*July 1 - July 15*
American Oil Paintings	*July 16 - July 31*
19th-Century French Prints	*August 1 - August 15*
American Impressionists	*August 16 - 30*

Week of April 7	**Week of April 14**	**Week of April 21**
blackout	Callbacks	Choreography
Conflict	Critique	Cues
Dialogue	Ensemble	Feed back
Floorplan	Illusion	Imagination
Improvisation	intermission	Literary merit
Meladrama	Narrator	Playright
Run-throughs	Screen play	Soliloquy
Theme	Tragedy	Visualization

Vertical Centering (equal top and bottom margins)

Main title

Secondary title

Column headings

Body

TOP 10 BROADWAY GROSSES		
Week Ending September 12, 1999		
Production	***Gross This Week***	***Gross Last Week***
Annie Get Your Gun	$ 572,885	$ 671,363
Cabaret	466,670	515,787
Chicago	536,852	523,106
Death of a Salesman	351,082	NA
Fosse	566,644	605,993
Les Miserables	375,318	436,915
Miss Saigon	395,522	434,641
Ragtime	420,902	539,158
The Lion King	880,717	875,772
The Phantom of the Opera	601,218	594,636
Totals	$5,167,810	$5,197,371

Horizontal Centering (equal side margins)

Three-Column Table Centered Horizontally and Vertically

LESSON 40 — ASSESS TABLE FORMATTING SKILLS

Objectives:

1. To assess keying skills.
2. To assess table formatting skills.

40A • 5' Conditioning Practice

Key each line twice SS; then take a 1' writing on line 3; determine *gwam*.

alphabet 1 Peter was amazed at just how quickly you fixed the big vans.

fig/sym 2 Of 34,198 citizens, 25,648 (75%) voted in the 2000 election.

speed 3 Orlando may make a big map to hang by the door of city hall.

gwam 1' | 1 | 2 | 3 | 4 | 5 | 6 | 7 | 8 | 9 | 10 | 11 | 12 |

40B • 10' Assessment: Keying Skills

1. Key a 1' writing on each ¶; determine *gwam*.
2. Key two 3' writings on ¶s 1–2 combined; determine *gwam* and count errors.

Quarter-Minute Checkpoints				
gwam	1/4'	1/2'	3/4'	1'
24	6	12	18	24
28	7	14	21	28
32	8	16	24	32
36	9	18	27	36
40	10	20	30	40
44	11	22	33	44
48	12	24	36	48
52	13	26	39	52
56	14	28	42	56
60	15	30	45	60

all letters used

	gwam 3'	
Conflict resolution is a practical skill to learn. When	4	72
two people are involved in exchanging ideas, values, or beliefs,	8	76
the possibility for some type of problem exists. Those involved	12	80
with a conflict usually try winning while making the other per-	17	84
son lose. This often leads to winning the battle while losing	21	89
the war. A better way to deal with problems is to realize that	25	93
it is possible to come up with a solution where each person is	29	97
able to win.	30	98
There are quite a number of ideas for dealing with con-	34	102
flict. The next time you are in the middle of a conflict try	38	106
the following approach to solve it. First, step back from the	42	110
situation and try to be objective rather than exchanging per-	46	114
sonal attacks. Try to defuse the situation. Define exactly	50	118
what is causing the problem. Don't view the problem as a win or	55	122
lose situation. After defining the problem, come up with sev-	59	126
eral possible solutions. Discuss the merits of each solution.	63	131
Try to agree on a solution that works for each person who is in-	67	135
volved.	68	135

gwam 3' | 1 | 2 | 3 | 4 |

LESSON 31

FORMAT TWO-COLUMN TABLES WITH COLUMN HEADINGS

Objectives:

1. To learn placement/arrangement of basic table parts.
2. To format tables using the Table formatting features.

31A • 5' Conditioning Practice

Key each line twice SS; key a 1' writing on line 3; determine *gwam.*

alphabet 1 Meg saw an extra big jet zip quickly over the frozen desert.

fig/sym 2 My income tax for 2001 was $3,875.69--up 4% over 2000's tax.

speed 3 Dick may make a bid on the ivory gowns they got in the city.

gwam 1' | 1 | 2 | 3 | 4 | 5 | 6 | 7 | 8 | 9 | 10 | 11 | 12 |

FORMATTING

31B • 45' Two-Column Tables with Column Headings

1. Study the format guides for tables on p. 94.
2. Study the model on p. 95: vertical and horizontal centering, row height, alignment, and column width.
3. Key Tables 1–3 shown at right and on p. 97.

Table 1

1. Set a top margin of 2".
2. Center and bold the main title; DS.
3. Create a 2 by 9 table (2 columns, 9 rows) and fill in the data shown at the right above.
4. Center and bold the column headings.

 **Save as:** *TBL31B1*

Table 2

1. Center and bold the main title; DS.
2. Create a 2 by 13 table (2 columns, 13 rows) and fill in the data shown at the right.
3. Center and bold the column headings.
4. Center the table horizontally and vertically.

 **Save as:** *TBL31B2*

POEMS TO IMPROVE OUR LIVES

Poem	**Written By**
Great Men	Ralph Waldo Emerson
Success	Henry Wadsworth Longfellow
If	Rudyard Kipling
The Road Not Taken	Robert Frost
Will	Ella Wheeler Wilcox
The Sin of Omission	Margaret E. Sangster
Good and Bad Children	Robert Louis Stevenson
Lady Clare	Alfred Tennyson

THE SOUND OF MUSIC CAST

Character	**Cast Member**
Sister Margaretta	Rebecca Tewksberry
Sister Berthe	Teresa Pohlad
Maria Rainer	Britta Ventura
Captain Georg von Trapp	Mark Stottlemyre
Liesl von Trapp	Brett Hampton
Friedrich von Trapp	Steven Finley
Louisa von Trapp	Nancy Krause
Kurt von Trapp	Joel Lambrecht
Brigitta von Trapp	Laura McDowell
Marta von Trapp	Amy Ross
Gretl von Trapp	Beth Reeves
Admiral von Schreiber	Clayton Perry

Document 1 (continued)

Renaissance chateau started in 1889 took hundreds of workers five years to build. (A&E, Biltmore, 2000)

The Breakers

The Breakers is located in Newport, Rhode Island. It was built for Cornelius Vanderbilt II. The 70-room castle (Italian Renaissance) was started in 1895. Upon its completion, the castle was filled with antiques from France and Italy. (A&E, Breakers, 2000)

Marble House

Marble House is also located in Newport, Rhode Island. During the 1890s, Newport became the summer colony of New England's wealthiest families. Marble House was built for William K. Vanderbilt, who was a grandson of Cornelius Vanderbilt. Mrs. Vanderbilt intended for the summerhouse to be a "temple to the arts." (A&E, Marble, 2000)

Document 2 (References List)
Use the information at the right to create a references list on a separate page. Correct all spelling, keying, and formatting errors.

 **Save as:** *RPT39B2*

REFERENCES

A&E, "America's Castles--Biltmore House." http://www.aetv.com/tv/shows/castles/biltmore.html (26 January 2000).

A&E, "America's Castles--The Breakers." http://www.aetv.com/tv/shows/castles/breakers.html (26 January 2000).

A&E, "America's Castles--Marble House." http://www.aetv.com/tv/shows/castles/marble.html (26 January 2000).

Encyclopedia Americana, "Cornelius Vanderbilt." Danbury, CT: Grolier Incorporated, 1998.

Smith, Helen Ainslie. *One Hundred Famous Americans*. Reprint of 1886 ed. Freeport, New York: Books for Libraries Press, 1972.

39C • 10'
Assessment: Keying Skills

1. Key a 1' writing on each ¶ of 38B, p. 110; determine *gwam*.
2. Key two 3' writings on ¶s 1–2 combined (38B, p. 110); determine *gwam*, count errors.

Table 3

1. Center and bold the main title; DS.
2. Create a 2 by 11 table and fill in the data shown at the right.
3. Center and bold the column headings.
4. Center the table horizontally and vertically.

 **Save as:** *TBL31B3*

FAMOUS PAINTINGS

Artist	Painting
Claude Monet	The Boat Studio
Paul Cezanne	Riverbanks
Rembrandt	The Mill
Michelangelo	The Holy Family
Leonardo da Vinci	The Mona Lisa
Vincent van Gogh	The Starry Night
Raphael	The School of Athens
Berthe Morisot	Little Girl Reading
Pierre-Auguste Renoir	Girls at the Piano
Jan Vermeer	The Milkmaid

LESSON 32 FORMAT TWO-COLUMN TABLES WITH MAIN, SECONDARY, AND COLUMN HEADINGS

Objectives:

1. To use Table features to edit existing tables.
2. To format two-column tables with main, secondary, and column headings.

32A • 5' Conditioning Practice

Key each line twice SS; key a 1' writing on line 3; determine *gwam*.

alphabet 1 Jay was amazed at how quickly a proud man fixed the big van.
fig/sym 2 Review reaches: $70, $64, 95%, #20, 5-point, 1/8, B&O 38's.
speed 3 Lane is to fix the big signs by the chapel for the neighbor.
gwam 1' | 1 | 2 | 3 | 4 | 5 | 6 | 7 | 8 | 9 | 10 | 11 | 12 |

FORMATTING

32B • 45' Two-Column Tables

Table 1

1. Open file *CD-TBL32B1*.
2. Make the format changes given at the right.

 **Save as:** *TBL32B1*

1. Join the cells of Row 1; center and bold the main title.
2. Join the cells of Row 2; center the secondary title.
3. Bold and center column headings.
4. Change the row height of main title to 0.5"; secondary title to 0.4"; column headings to 0.35"; and data rows to 0.3".
5. Change the column width of Column A to 3.5", Column B to 2".
6. Change the vertical alignment for the first three rows to **center**; the data rows to **bottom**.
7. Change the horizontal alignment for Column B to **center**.
8. Center the table horizontally and vertically.

Table 2

1. Open file *CD-TBL32B2*.
2. Make the format changes given at the right.

 **Save as:** *TBL32B2*

1. Change the row height for all rows to 0.4".
2. Change the horizontal alignment for Column B to **center**.
3. Change vertical alignment for the column headings to **center**; the data rows to **bottom**.
4. Insert two rows at the end of the table and key the following:

Diego Velazquez — Juan de Pareja

Jean-Auguste-Dominique Ingres — Princess de Broglie

LESSON 39 ASSESS REPORT FORMATTING SKILLS

Objectives:

1. To assess keying skills.
2. To assess report formatting skills.

39A • 5' Conditioning Practice

Key each line twice SS; then key a 1' writing on line 3; determine *gwam*.

alphabet 1 Joey was quite amazed by his blocking of seven extra points.

figures 2 In 1990, we had only 345 computers; as of 2000 we owned 876.

speed 3 Diana paid for the antique ornament and the six enamel keys.

gwam 1' | 1 | 2 | 3 | 4 | 5 | 6 | 7 | 8 | 9 | 10 | 11 | 12 |

39B • 35' Assess Report Formatting Skills

Document 1 (Unbound Report)
Format and key the text at the right as an unbound report. Correct all spelling, keying, and formatting errors.

 **Save as:** *RPT39B1*

AMERICA'S CASTLES

The castles listed on A&E's "America's Castles" belonged to the rich and famous. By looking at the history of some of the families that owned these castles, it is easy to see why people say that America is the land of opportunity.

Cornelius Vanderbilt was a man who took advantage of the opportunities America had to offer. He was born on May 27, 1794, to a family of modest means. Cornelius ended his formal schooling by the age of 11. (Encyclopedia Americana, 1998, Vol. 27, 891) He achieved success because he was industrious. He knew how to work, and he knew the value of the money that came from hard work. Other qualities that made him successful were perseverance, enterprise, courage, and trustworthiness. Being trustworthy meant he could command better prices than others doing the same job. (Smith, 528, 1886) Because of these qualities, Cornelius Vanderbilt was able to amass one of the largest fortunes ever made in America from his shipping and railroad enterprises.

Three of America's castles were built by descendants of the man who came out of humble beginnings to amass such a large fortune. The Biltmore House, The Breakers, and Marble House were all built by Cornelius Vanderbilt's descendants.

Biltmore House

The Biltmore House (also known as America's largest home) is located on 8,000 acres near Asheville, North Carolina. It was built for George W. Vanderbilt. The 250-room French

(continued on next page)

Table 3

1. Determine the number of rows and columns needed to create a table for the data shown at the right.
2. Create a table and fill in the data.
3. Center and bold the main title, secondary title, and column headings.
4. Change the row height to 0.4" for all rows.
5. Use **center** vertical alignment for all rows.
6. Center text horizontally in Column B.
7. Center the table horizontally and vertically.

 **Save as:** *TBL32B3*

CHILDREN'S STORIES

by Laura Ingalls Wilder

Book	**Year Published**
Little House in the Big Woods	1932
Little House on the Prairie	1935
On the Banks of Plum Creek	1937
By the Shores of Silver Lake	1939
The Long Winter	1940
Little Town on the Prairie	1941
These Happy Golden Years	1943

Table 4

1. Determine the number of rows and columns needed for the data shown at the right.
2. Create a table and fill in the data.
3. Center and bold the main title, secondary title, and column headings.
4. Change the row height to 0.4" for all rows.
5. Use **center** vertical alignment for all title rows; **bottom**-align all data rows.
6. Center text horizontally in Column B.
7. Center the table on the page.

 **Save as:** *TBL32B4*

BROADWAY'S LONGEST RUNS

As of October 3, 1999

Broadway Show	**Number of Performances**
Cats	7,093
A Chorus Line	6,137
Oh! Calcutta (Revival)	5,962
*Les Miserables	5,175
*The Phantom of the Opera	4,905
*Miss Saigon	3,516
42nd Street	3,485
Grease	3,388
Fiddler on the Roof	3,242
Life With Father	3,224

Source: Theatre.com. http://www.BroadwayNow.com/public/longestruns.asp (5 October 1999).

*Shows marked with asterisk (*) were still running at the time of this publication.

Table 5

Update Table 4 with the information provided at the right.

 **Save as:** *TBL32B5*

As of May 28, 2000

Cats	7,365
Les Miserables	5,431
The Phantom of the Opera	5,181
Miss Saigon	3,788

Go to the News page of the Broadway Web site below. Update Table 5 to reflect Broadway's Longest Runs as of the most recent date listed at the site.

http://www.theatre.com/

38C • 35'
Assess Document Formatting Skills

Document 1 (E-mail)
Format and key the text at the right as an e-mail message if you have access to e-mail software. Send the e-mail to your instructor.

If you do not have access to e-mail software, format and key the text as an interoffice memo to **Miguel Martinez** from you.

DATE: **Current Date**

SUBJECT: **MACBETH QUOTE**

Correct all spelling, keying, and formatting errors.

 **Save as:** *EMAIL38C1*

I enjoyed our visit last week at the class reunion. How quickly time passes; it seems like only yesterday that we graduated. Of course, a class reunion is a quick reminder that it **wasn't** yesterday.

I was able to find the quote that we discussed with the group on Friday. Your memory definitely serves you better than mine; it was a quote from George Bernard Shaw. However, he was referring to Shakespeare's *Macbeth*. Here is the exact quote by Shaw: "Life is not a 'brief candle.' It is a splendid torch that I want to make burn as brightly as possible before handing it on to future generations."

I was glad to see that so many of our classmates are living lives as "splendid torches" rather than as "brief candles."

Document 2 (Letter)
Format and key the text at the right as a personal-business letter from **Elizabeth A. Ross**.

Supply an appropriate salutation and complimentary close. Be sure to include your reference initials and an attachment notation.

Return Address and Date:
183 Lennox St.
Portland, ME 04103-5282
May 3, 200-

Letter Address:
Ms. Suzzanne Hamlin, President
Portland Historical Society
1821 Island View Rd.
Portland, ME 04107-3712

Correct all spelling, keying, and formatting errors.

 **Save as:** *LTR38C2*

After doing research on possible historical destinations for our Annual Portland Historical Society trip, I narrowed our choices to the Hildene House in Manchester, Vermont, and The Breakers in Newport, Rhode Island. The Hildene House was built in 1902 for Robert Todd Lincoln, the son of Abraham Lincoln; The Breakers was built for Cornelius Vanderbilt II in 1895.

I met with our planning committee yesterday to share the information I was able to obtain. After discussing the merits of both places, our recommendation is The Breakers for this year's trip. Even though we liked both places, the committee felt that many of our members would have already visited the Hildene House since it is so close to Portland.

I've attached some information on The Breakers. As soon as I receive the additional information I requested about expenses, I will send it to you. You should have it in plenty of time for the June meeting.

Document 3 (Memo)
Format and key the text at the right as a memo to **Suzzanne Hamlin** from **Elizabeth A. Ross**. Date the memo **May 3, 200-**; use **SUMMER TRIP** for the subject line. Correct all spelling, keying, and formatting errors.

 **Save as:** *MEMO38C3*

Here are some of the costs that our group will incur on our trip to The Breakers.

The admission fee for The Breakers is $10. I'll check on group rates this week. Round-trip airfare from Portland to T. F. Green Airport is $235. Of course, you know that rates vary considerably during the summer months. My travel agent will inform me of any summer specials.

I'm still waiting for rates for the hotel accommodations. I've narrowed the list to Castle Hill Inn and Resort, Vanderbilt Hall, and Hotel Viking. Any of the three would provide excellent accommodations. As soon as they send the rates, I'll forward them to you.

LESSON 33 FORMAT THREE-COLUMN TABLES

Objectives:

1. To format three-column tables with main, secondary, and column headings.
2. To improve language skills (word choice).

33A • 5' Conditioning Practice

Key each line twice SS; key a 1' writing on line 3; determine *gwam*.

alphabet 1 Eight extra pizzas will be baked quickly for the jovial men.

fig/sym 2 Kaye said, "Can't you touch-key 45, 935, $608, and 17 1/2%?"

speed 3 Orlando and the girls may do the work for the big city firm.

gwam 1' | 1 | 2 | 3 | 4 | 5 | 6 | 7 | 8 | 9 | 10 | 11 | 12 |

LANGUAGE SKILLS

33B • 8' Language Skills: Word Choice

1. Study the spelling and definitions of the words at the right.
2. Key line 1 (Learn line), noting the proper choice of words.
3. Key lines 2–3 (the Apply lines), choosing the right words to complete the lines correctly.
4. Check your work; correct lines containing word-choice errors.

Save as: *CHOICE 33B*

cite (vb) to quote; to use as support; to commend; to summon

sight (n/vb) ability to see; something seen; a device to improve aim; to observe or focus

site (n) the place something is, was, or will be located or situated

their (pron) belonging to them

there (adv/pron) in or at that place or stage; word used to introduce a sentence or clause

they're (contr) a contracted form of *they are*

Learn 1 He will **cite** the article from the Web **site** about improving your **sight.**
Apply 2 You need to (cite, sight, site) five sources in the report due on Friday.
Apply 3 The (cite, sight, site) he chose for the party was a (cite, sight, site) to be seen.

Learn 1 **There** is the car **they're** going to use in **their** next play production.
Apply 2 (Their, There, They're) making (their, there, they're) school lunches.
Apply 3 (Their, There, They're) is the box of (their, there, they're) tools.

FORMATTING

33C • 37' Three-Column Tables

Table 1

Create and format the table shown at the right, using the information given below.

Main title: row height 0.5"; center vertical alignment

Secondary title: row height 0.45"; center vertical alignment

Column headings: row height 0.4"; center vertical alignment

Data rows: row height 0.3"; bottom vertical alignment

Table: center on page

Save as: *TBL33C1*

TOP 5 BROADWAY GROSSES		
Week Ending *September 12, 1999*		
Production	**Gross This Week**	**Gross Last Week**
Annie Get Your Gun	$ 572,885	*$ 671,363*
Chicago	536,852	*523,106*
Fosse	566,644	*605,993*
The Lion King	880,717	*875,772*
The Phantom of the Opera	601,218	*594,636*
Totals	$3,158,316	*$3,270,870*
Source: Theatre.com. http://www.BroadwayNow.com/public/boxoffice.asp (13 September 1999).		

UNIT 12

LESSONS 38-40

Assessing Document Formatting Skills

LESSON 38 ASSESS E-MAIL, MEMO, AND LETTER FORMATTING SKILLS

Objectives:

1. To assess keying skills.
2. To assess e-mail, memo, and letter formatting skills.

38A • 5' Conditioning Practice

Key each line twice SS; then take a 1' writing on line 3; determine *gwam.*

alphabet 1 Even Jack will be taking part of a history quiz next Monday.

fig/sym 2 Out of stock items (#7850*, #461A*, and #2093*) are in blue.

speed 3 Jana may hang the big sign by the antique door of city hall.

gwam 1' | 1 | 2 | 3 | 4 | 5 | 6 | 7 | 8 | 9 | 10 | 11 | 12 |

38B • 10' Assessment: Keying Skills

1. Key a 1' writing on each ¶; determine *gwam.*
2. Key two 3' writings on ¶s 1–2 combined; determine *gwam* and count errors.

Quarter-Minute Checkpoints				
gwam	1/4'	1/2'	3/4'	1'
24	6	12	18	24
28	7	14	21	28
32	8	16	24	32
36	9	18	27	36
40	10	20	30	40
44	11	22	33	44
48	12	24	36	48
52	13	26	39	52
56	14	28	42	56
60	15	30	45	60

A all letters used

	gwam 2'	3'	
As you build your keying skill, the number of errors you	6	4	45
make is not very important because most of the errors are acci-	12	8	49
dental. Realize, however, that documents are expected to be	18	12	53
without flaw. A letter, report, or table that has flaws is not	25	16	58
usable until it is corrected. So find and correct all errors.	31	20	62
The best time to detect and correct your errors is while	36	24	66
the copy is still on a monitor. Therefore, just before removing	43	29	70
the copy from the monitor, proofread it and correct any errors	49	33	74
you have made. Learn to proofread very carefully and to correct	56	37	78
all errors quickly. Improve your production skill in this way.	62	41	83

gwam 2' | 1 | 2 | 3 | 4 | 5 | 6 |
3' | 1 | 2 | 3 | 4 |

Table 2
Create the table shown at the right using the information given below.

Main title: row height 0.5"; center vertical alignment

Column headings: row height 0.4"; center vertical alignment

Data rows: row height 0.3"; bottom vertical alignment

Table: center on page

Column A: 2" wide

Column B: 1" wide

Column C: 2" wide

 **Save as:** *TBL33C2*

Selected Works by American Authors		
Author	**Life**	**Works**
Robert Lee Forst	1874-1963	West-Running Brook
Henry w. Longfellow	1807-1882	Balleds
Carl Sandburn	1878-1967	Smoke and Steel
Louisa May Ascott	1832-1888	Little Women
William Faulkner	1897-1962	The Sound and the Furry
Samuel L. Clemens	1833-1910	Adventures of Tom Sawyer
Scott F. Fitzgerald	1896-1940	All Sad Young Men

Table 3
Arrange the data at the right as a table. Use **WIMBLEDON SINGLES CHAMPIONS** for the main title; **1995–1999** for the secondary title; and **Women's Champion**, **Year**, **Men's Champion** for the three column headings. Arrange the data attractively on the page.

 **Save as:** *TBL33C3*

1995 Steffi Graf
1998 Jana Novotna
1997 Martina Hingis
1996 Steffi Graf
1999 Lindsay Davenport

1997 Pete Sampras
1999 Pete Sampras
1995 Pete Sampras
1998 Pete Sampras
1996 Richard Krajicek

Table 4
Open Table 2 (*TBL33C2*). Insert data shown at right. Delete the year author died; change column heading to **Year Born**. Sort data by Year Born in ascending order.

 **Save as:** *TBL33C4*

Arthur Miller	*1915*	*Death of a Salesman*
Oliver W. Holmes	*1809*	*Old Ironsides*

LESSON 34 FORMAT FOUR-COLUMN TABLES

Objectives:

1. To format four-column tables with main, secondary, and column headings.
2. To make independent decisions about table formatting features.

34A • 5' Conditioning Practice

Key each line twice SS; key a 1' writing on line 3; determine *gwam*.

alphabet 1 David will buy the six unique jackets from Grady for prizes.

fig/sym 2 Jerry's 2001 tax was $4,875, about 7% ($369) less than 2000.

speed 3 Glen works with vigor to dismantle the downtown city chapel.

gwam 1' | 1 | 2 | 3 | 4 | 5 | 6 | 7 | 8 | 9 | 10 | 11 | 12 |

Table 3
Format the data at the right as a table. Use the table formatting features that you have learned to arrange the data attractively on the page.

 **Save as:** *TBL37B3*

NEW YORK PLAYS		
Plays	**Theater**	**Date Opened**
Annie Get Your Gun	Marquis Theater	03/04/99
Beauty and the Beast	Palace Theatre	04/18/94
Cabaret	Studio 54	03/19/98
Cats	Winter Garden Theater	10/07/82
Chicago	Shubert Theatre	11/14/96
Death of a Salesman	Eugene O'Neill Theater	02/10/99
The Lion King	New Amsterdam Theatre	11/13/97
Les Miserables	Imperial Theater	03/12/87
Miss Saigon	Broadway Theater	04/11/91
The Phantom of the Opera	Majestic Theater	01/26/88

Source: Theatre.com. http://www.nytheatre-wire.com/PoorR.htm (1 October 1999).

SKILL BUILDING

37C • 10' Timed Writings

1. Key a 1' writing on each ¶; determine *gwam*.
2. Key a 2' writing on ¶s 1–3 combined; determine *gwam*.
3. Key a 3' writing on ¶s 1–3 combined; determine *gwam* and count errors.

all letters used

gwam 2' | 3'

There is a value in work, value to the worker as well as 6 4
to the employer for whom one works. In spite of the 11 7
stress or pressure under which many people work, gainful work 17 11
provides workers with a feeling of security and self-esteem. 23 15

Some people do not want to work unless they have a job of 29 19
prestige; that is, a job that others admire or envy. To obtain 35 24
such a position, one must be prepared to perform the tasks the 42 28
job requires. Realize this now; prepare yourself. 47 31

School and college courses are designed to help you to 52 35
excel in the basic knowledge and skills the better jobs demand. 59 39
Beyond all of this, special training or work experience may be 65 43
needed for you to move up in your chosen career. 70 47

gwam 2' | 1 | 2 | 3 | 4 | 5 | 6
3' | 1 | 2 | 3 | 4

34B • 45'
Four-Column Tables

Table 1
Format the data at the right as a table. Use **FAMOUS COMPOSERS** for the main title and **1756–1899** for the secondary title. Arrange the data attractively on the page. Use the Sort feature to arrange the composers in alphabetical order.

Save as: *TBL34B1*

Composer	**Nationality**	**Life**	**Music**
Mozart	Austrian	1756-1791	Don Giovanni
Beethoven	German	1770-1827	Ninth Symphony
Berlioz	French	1803-1869	Romeo and Juliet
Mendelssohn	German	1809-1847	Reformation
Chopin	Franco-Polish	1810-1849	Sonata in B Minor
Schumann	German	1810-1856	Rhenish Symphony
Wagner	German	1813-1883	Rienzi
Strauss	Austrian	1825-1899	Blue Danube

Table 2
Format the table at the right, arranging the data attractively.

Use **TOP TEN ANCESTRY GROUPS OF U.S. POPULATION** for the main title and **1990 Census** for the secondary title.

Save as: *TBL34B2*

Rank	Ancestry	Number	Percent of Population
1	German	57,947,873	23.3
2	Irish	38,735,539	15.6
3	English	32,651,788	13.1
4	Afro American	23,777,098	9.6
5	Italain	14,664,550	5.9
6	American	12,395,000	50
7	Mexican	11,586,983	4.7
8	French	10,320,935	4.1
9	Polish	9,366,106	3.8
10	American Indian	8,708,220	3.5

Source: *The Information Please Almanac*. Boston: Houghton Mifflin Company, 1996.

Table 3
Arrange the data at the right attractively in a table according to Rank (1–10). Use **TOP BASEBALL MOVIES** for the main title; **Fall 1999** for the secondary title; **Rank**, **Movie**, **Year**, and **Percent of Votes** for the column headings.

The tenth movie is **Fear Strikes Out** made in **1957**, **0.6** percent of votes. Include a source note: **Source: *USA Today.*** **http://www.usatoday.com/sports/baseball/mlbfs97.htm (17 September 1999).**

Save as: *TBL34B3*

4	Pride of the Yankees	1942	8.0
9	Damn Yankees	1958	1.0
8	Bad News Bears	1976	3.2
2	The Natural	1984	25.1
3	Bull Durham	1988	18.4
6	Eight Men Out	1988	4.4
1	Field of Dreams	1989	29.4%
5	Major League	1989	8.0
7	League of Their Own	1992	4.4

LESSON 37 PREPARE FOR ASSESSMENT: TABLES

Objective:

To prepare for assessment of table formatting skills.

37A • 5' Conditioning Practice

Key each line twice SS; then key a 1' writing on line 3; determine *gwam.*

alphabet 1 Joyce Savin fixed the big clock that may win a unique prize.

figures 2 Items marked * are out of stock: #785*, #461A*, and #2093*.

speed 3 The firm paid for the rigid sign by the downtown civic hall.

gwam 1' | 1 | 2 | 3 | 4 | 5 | 6 | 7 | 8 | 9 | 10 | 11 | 12 |

FORMATTING

37B • 35' Reinforce Table Formatting Skills

Table 1

Create the table shown at the right using the information given below. Center the table horizontally and vertically.

Main title: row height 0.5"; center vertical alignment

Column headings: row height 0.4"; center vertical alignment

Data rows: row height 0.3"; bottom vertical alignment

Adjust column widths to arrange material attractively on the page.

Save as: *TBL37B1*

AMERICAN LITERATURE - 1900s	
Literature	**Author**
A Rose for Emily (1930)	William Faulkner
The Grapes of Wrath (1939)	John Steinbeck
The Scotty Who Knew Too Much (1940)	James Thurber
House Made of Dawn (1968)	N. Scott Momaday
Everyday Use (1973)	Alice Walker
The Wife's Story (1932)	Ursula K. Le Guin
I Ask My Mother to Sing (1986)	Li-Young Lee
The Phone Booth at the Corner (1989)	Juan Delgado

Table 2

Create the table shown at the right using the information given for Table 1. Center the table horizontally and vertically.

Adjust column widths to arrange material attractively on the page.

Save as: *TBL37B2*

WILLIAM SHAKESPEARE		
Play	**Year Written**	**Category**
The Comedy of Errors	1590	Comedy
Richard II	1595	History
Romeo and Juliet	1595	Tragedy
Much Ado About Nothing	1599	Comedy
Julius Caesar	1599	Tragedy
Hamlet	1601	Tragedy
King Lear	1605	Tragedy
The Tempest	1611	Comedy

Communication Skills 5

ACTIVITY 1

Subject/Verb Agreement

1. Key lines 1–10 at the right, using the correct verb.
2. Check the accuracy of your work with the instructor; correct any errors you made.
3. Note the rule number at the left of each sentence in which you made a verb agreement error.
4. Using the rules below the sentences and on p. 103, identify the rule(s) you need to review/practice.
5. **Read**: Study each rule.
6. **Learn**: Key the Learn line(s) beneath it, noting how the rule is applied.
7. **Apply**: Key the Apply line(s), choosing the correct verb.

 **Save as:** *CS5-ACT1*

Proofread & Correct

Rules

1 1 Sandra and Rich (is, are) running for class secretary.
1 2 They (has, have) to score high on the SAT to enter that college.
2 3 You (doesn't, don't) think keyboarding is important.
2 4 Why (doesn't, don't) she take the test for advanced placement?
3 5 Neither of the candidates (meet, meets) the leadership criteria.
3 6 One of your art students (is, are) likely to win the prize.
5 7 The number of people against the proposal (is, are) quite small.
4 8 The manager, as well as his assistant, (is, are) to attend.
6 9 Neither the teacher nor her students (is, are) here.
3 10 All the meat (is, are) spoiled, but some items (is, are) okay.

Subject/Verb Agreement

Rule 1: Use a singular verb with a singular subject (noun or pronoun); use a plural verb with a plural subject and with a compound subject (two nouns or pronouns joined by *and*).

Learn 1 The speaker was delayed at the airport for over thirty minutes.
Learn 2 The players are all here, and they are getting restless.
Learn 3 You and your assistant are to join us for lunch.
Apply 4 The treasurer of the class (is, are) to introduce the speaker.
Apply 5 Dr. Cho (was, were) to give the lecture, but he (is, are) ill.
Apply 6 Mrs. Samoa and her son (is, are) to be on a local talk show.

Rule 2: Use the plural verb *do not* or *don't* with pronoun subjects *I, we, you*, and *they* as well as with plural nouns; use the singular verb *does not* or *doesn't* with pronouns *he, she,* and *it* as well as with singular nouns.

Learn 7 I do not find this report believable; you don't either.
Learn 8 If she doesn't accept our offer, we don't have to raise it.
Apply 9 They (doesn't, don't) discount, so I (doesn't, don't) shop there.
Apply 10 Jo and he (doesn't, don't) ski; they (doesn't, don't) plan to go.

Rule 3: Use singular verbs with indefinite pronouns (*each, every, any, either, neither, one*, etc.) and with *all* and *some* used as subjects if their modifiers are singular (but use plural verbs with *all* and *some* if their modifiers are plural).

Learn 11 Each of these girls has an important role in the class play.
Learn 12 Some of the new paint is already cracking and peeling.
Learn 13 All of the workers are to be paid for the special holiday.
Apply 14 Neither of them (is, are) well enough to start the game.
Apply 15 Some of the juice (is, are) sweet; some (is, are) quite tart.
Apply 16 Every girl and boy (is, are) sure to benefit from this decision.

(continued on next page)

Document 2 (References List)

Use the information below to create a references list on a separate page. Check and correct all keying and format errors.

REFERENCES

Berthold, Margot. The History of World Theater. New York: The Continuum Publishing Company, 1991.

Prince, Nancy, and Jeanie Jackson. Exploring Theatre. Minneapolis/St. Paul: West Publishing Company, 1997.

 **Save as:** *RPT36B2*

Roman Theatre

The Roman Theatre was the next widely recognized form of the theatre. The first Roman theatrical performance, historians believe, was performed around 365 B.C. Seneca, Plautus, and Terentius are the best known of the early Roman playwrights. Seneca was known for his tragedies, while the other two were known for their comedies.

The Roman plays were similar to those of the Greeks. Unlike the Greeks, however, the Romans did not limit the number of actors in each play. Another major difference between the Greek and Roman theatres was the theatre buildings. *The Romans were great engineers and architects. They built theatres that were unified, freestanding structures several stories high. (Prince and Jackson, 1997, 44)*

SKILL BUILDING

36C • 10' Timed Writings

1. Key a 1' writing on each ¶; determine *gwam.*
2. Key a 2' writing on ¶s 1–2 combined; determine *gwam.*
3. Key a 3' writing on ¶s 1–2 combined; determine *gwam* and count errors.

Quarter-Minute Checkpoints				
gwam	1/4'	1/2'	3/4'	1'
24	6	12	18	24
28	7	14	21	28
32	8	16	24	32
36	9	18	27	36
40	10	20	30	40
44	11	22	33	44
48	12	24	36	48
52	13	26	39	52
56	14	28	42	56
60	15	30	45	60

 all letters used

gwam 2' | 3'

The value of an education has been a topic discussed many 6 4
times with a great deal of zest. The value is often measured in 12 8
terms of costs and benefits to the taxpayer. It is also judged in 19 13
terms of changes in the individuals taking part in the educational 26 17
process. Gains in the level of knowledge, the development and 32 21
refinement of attitudes, and the acquiring of skills are believed 39 26
to be crucial parts of an education. 42 28

Education is a never-ending process. A person is exposed to for- 49 32
mal and informal education throughout his or her life. Formal learning 56 37
takes place in a structured situation such as a school or 62 41
a college. Informal learning occurs from the experience gained 68 45
from daily living. We are constantly educated from all the types 75 50
of media with which we come in contact each day as well as by each 81 54
person with whom we exchange ideas. 85 57

gwam 2' | 1 | 2 | 3 | 4 | 5 | 6
3' | 1 | 2 | 3 | 4

Rule 4: Use a singular verb with a singular subject that is separated from the verb by the phrase *as well as* or *in addition to*; use a plural verb with a plural subject so separated.

Learn 17 The letter, in addition to the report, has to be revised.
Learn 18 The shirts, as well as the dress, have to be pressed again.
Apply 19 The driver, as well as the burglar, (was, were) apprehended.
Apply 20 Two managers, in addition to the president, (is, are) to attend.

Rule 5: Use a singular verb if *number* is used as the subject and is preceded by *the*; use a plural verb if *number* is the subject and is preceded by *a*.

Learn 21 A number of them have already voted, but the number is small.
Apply 22 The number of jobs (is, are) low; a number of us (has, have) applied.

Rule 6: Use a singular verb with singular subjects linked by *or* or *nor*, but if one subject is singular and the other is plural, the verb agrees with the nearer subject.

Learn 23 Neither Ms. Moss nor Mr. Katz was invited to speak.
Learn 24 Either the manager or his assistants are to participate.
Apply 25 If neither he nor they (go, goes), either you or she (has, have) to.

ACTIVITY 2

Reading

1. Open the file *CD-CS5READ* and read the document carefully.
2. Close the file.
3. Key the answers to the questions at the right, using complete sentences.
4. Check the accuracy of your work with the instructor; correct any errors you made.

 **Save as:** *CS5-ACT2*

1. What kind of positions are being filled?
2. What is the minimum number of hours each employee must work each week?
3. Is weekend work available?
4. What benefit is offered to employees who have young children to care for?
5. Is the pay based only on performance?
6. When are the position openings available?
7. Do all telemarketing employees work during daytime hours?
8. How can you submit a resume?

ACTIVITY 3

Composing

1. Study the quotations at the right. Consider the relationship between honesty and truth.
2. Compose/key a paragraph to show your understanding of honesty and truth. Describe an incident in which honesty and truth *should* prevail but don't in real life.

 **Save as:** *CS5-ACT3*

Honesty's the best policy.
—Cervantes

Piety requires us to honor truth above our friends.
—Aristotle

To be honest . . . here is a task for all that a man has of fortitude.
—Robert Louis Stevenson

The dignity of truth is lost with protesting.
—Ben Jonson

PREPARE FOR ASSESSMENT: REPORTS

Objective:

To prepare for assessment of report formatting skills.

36A • 5' Conditioning Practice

Key each line twice SS; then take a 1' writing on line 3; determine *gwam.*

alphabet 1 Quincy just put back five azure gems next to the gold watch.

figures 2 Tim moved from 5142 Troy Lane to 936 - 23d Street on 8/7/01.

speed 3 He lent the field auditor a hand with the work for the firm.

gwam 1' | 1 | 2 | 3 | 4 | 5 | 6 | 7 | 8 | 9 | 10 | 11 | 12 |

FORMATTING

36B • 35' Reinforce Report Formatting Skills

Document 1 (Unbound Report)

Format and key the text at the right as an unbound report. Use **THEATRE** for the title of the report. Check and correct all keying and format errors.

 **Save as:** *RPT36B1*

Tonight the house lights will dim and another performance will begin on Broadway. Perhaps it will be another performance of *Cats*, a play that had accumulated 7,225 performances as of January 23, 2000. Or perhaps it will be the play that replaces *Cats*.

Somewhere, sometime today, another enactment of one of Shakespeare's plays will take place. It may be in a high school auditorium, or it may be at a professional Shakespearean playhouse.

Theatre has enriched the lives of people for many years. No one really knows when the first play production was performed. However, historians say, "Theatre is as old as mankind. There have been primitive forms of it since man's beginnings." (Berthold, 1991, 1) The more commonly recognized form of theatre, the play, dates back to what is referred to as "Greek Theatre" and "Roman Theatre."

Greek Theatre

Greek Theatre started around 500 B.C. Sophocles and Aristophanes are two of the well-known Greek playwrights whose works are still being performed today.

Religious festivals that honored the Greek god of wine and fertility (Dionysus) were part of the culture of Greece around this time. The Greeks felt that if they honored Dionysus, he would in turn bless them with many children, rich land, and abundant crops. Plays were performed as part of these festivals.

To accommodate the large number of people who attended the plays (as many as 14,000 to 17,000 people, according to historians), theatres were built into a hillside. The plays were staged in the morning and lasted until sunset, since there was no electricity for lighting. (Prince and Jackson, 1997, 35)

(continued on next page)

UNIT 11

LESSONS 35-37

Prepare for Document Formatting Assessment

LESSON 35 PREPARE FOR ASSESSMENT: E-MAIL, MEMOS, LETTERS

Objective:
To prepare for assessment of e-mail, memo, and letter formatting skills.

35A • 5' Conditioning Practice

Key each line twice SS; then key a 1' writing on line 3; determine *gwam.*

alphabet 1 Jacques paid a very sizeable sum for the meetings next week.

fig/sym 2 The desk (#539A28) and chair (#61B34) usually sell for $700.

speed 3 Helen did the work for us, but the neighbor will pay for it.

gwam 1' | 1 | 2 | 3 | 4 | 5 | 6 | 7 | 8 | 9 | 10 | 11 | 12 |

FORMATTING

35B • 45' Reinforce E-mail/Memo/Letter Formatting Skills

Document 1 (E-mail)
Format and key the text at the right. If you have e-mail software, format the message as e-mail (from you to your instructor). Format it as an interoffice memo if you do not have e-mail software.

Check your message; correct all errors.

 **Save as:** *EMAIL35B1*

Note: This message contains some *incomplete sentences;* for example, "Tournament started in 1877 at Wimbledon" and "Shakespeare plays in the open air." In an incomplete sentence, a nonessential word or words are missing. Some writers use them to save time when writing informal messages, such as e-mail or memos.

TO: Jessica Holloway

FROM: Barbara Knight

DATE: March 15, 200-

SUBJECT: LONDON EXCURSION

I've listed below several other events, along with a brief description, which are taking place in London while we are there. Please let me know which ones are of interest to you, and I'll get additional information on them.

Lawn Tennis Championship. Tournament started in 1877 at Wimbledon. It is now recognized as one of the premiere Grand Slam events.

Kenwood Lakeside Concerts. Fifty-year tradition of outdoor concerts. Includes fireworks and laser shows.

The Proms. Henry Wood Promenade Concerts started in 1895. Attracts devoted music lovers from around the world.

Outdoor Shakespeare Performances. Shakespeare plays in the open air. Bring a blanket and enjoy!

Royal Academy's Summer Exhibition. Founded in 1768. Over two centuries of summer exhibits of living painters.

Document 2 (Memo)
Format and key the text at the right as a memo. Check your copy; correct all keying and format errors.

 **Save as:** *MEMO35B2*

TO: Marguerite Mercedes, Director

FROM: Justin Mathews, Administrative Assistant

DATE: March 5, 200-

SUBJECT: BALLET COMPANY ADDRESSES

Attached is the address list for the ballet companies that you requested. I was unable to secure an address for the Bolshoi Ballet in Moscow.

I have seen the Royal Swedish Ballet, the American Ballet Theatre, and the Paris Opera Ballet perform. They were all excellent. The patrons of our Artist Series would be extremely pleased with any of the three performances.

Even though I have not personally seen performances by any of the other groups on the list, I have heard excellent comments by others who have been fortunate enough to see them perform. I don't think we can go wrong by inviting any of those on the list to be a part of next year's Artist Series.

xx

Attachment

Document 3 (Letter)
Format and key the text at the right as a personal-business letter. Replace *xx* with your reference initials. Check your copy; correct all keying and formatting errors.

 **Save as:** *LTR35B3*

Note:
Although the preferred spelling of *theater* (U.S.) ends with *er*, the word ends with *re* for several prominent institutions in this country, as in Britain; notably, American Ballet Theatre, New Amsterdam Theatre, Palace Theatre, and Shubert Theatre.

words

810 Lake Grove Ct. | San Diego, CA 92131-8112 | March 30, 200- 12
Ms. Barbara Knight | 2010 Rosewood Pl. | Riverside, CA 92506-6528 | 24
Dear Barbara 27

Can you believe that we will be in London in less than three months? 41
London is one of my favorite places to visit. 50

I've done some checking on London's theatres. Do any of the three 64
plays I've listed below interest you? If so, let me know, and I'll make the 78
arrangements. 82

Les Miserables: Story revolves around nineteenth-century French 95
Revolution with its struggles, passion, and love. 105

Amadeus: Story about the life of Mozart in eighteenth-century Vienna 119
and his rivalry with composer Sallieri. 127

Starlight Express: Musical by Andrew Lloyd Weber with lyrics by 140
Richard Stilgoe. 144

Les Miserables is being performed at the Palace Theatre, *Amadeus* at 158
the Old Vic, and *Starlight Express* at the Apollo Victoria. The Palace 172
Theatre and The Old Vic were both built in the 1800s. 183

I've confirmed our reservations at the Copthorne Tara. If there is 197
anything else that you would like me to check, let me know. 209

Sincerely | Jessica C. Holloway | xx 215

Resources

New-Key Learning R2-R33

Repetitive Stress Injury R34-R36

Windows Tutorial R37-R39

Internet Guide with Applications R40-R43

Basic Format Guides for Correspondence and Reports R44-R45

Software Features Index R46

Software Features Index

Align text (*see* Alignment)
Alignment
  Horizontal, 55
  In table cells, 92
  Vertical, 80
AutoComplete, 158
Automatic completion (*see* AutoComplete)

Bold, 55
Borders, 171
Bottom-aligned text (*see* Alignment, In table cells)
Bullets and Numbering, 135

Center, 55 (*see also* Alignment)
Center-aligned text (*see* Alignment, In table cells)
Center page, 80
Center table, 92
Column width (table), 91
Copy, 80
Copy text file to file, 124
Cut, 80

Decimal tabs (*see* Tabs)
Delete columns (table), 90
Delete rows (table), 90
Dot leader tab, 136 (*see also* Tabs)

Envelopes, 81

Footnote and Endnote, 135

Gridlines (table), 171

Hanging indent (*see* Indentation)
Hard page break, 57
Horizontal alignment (*see* Alignment)
Hyphenation, 56

Indentation, 68
Insert columns (table), 90
Insert date, 158
Insert date field, 158
Insert file, 136
Insert rows (table), 90
Insert table, 90
Insert text, 55
Italic, 55

Join cells (table), 91, 170
Justification, 55

Leader tab (*see* Dot leader tab)
Left alignment (*see* Alignment)
Left tabs (*see* Tabs)
Line spacing, 67

Macro, 159
Margins, 67

Navigation features, 158

Orphan (*see* Widow/Orphan)

Page break (*see* Hard page break)
Page numbers, 68
Paste, 80

Redo, 56
Right alignment (*see* Alignment)
Right tabs (*see* Tabs)
Row height (table), 92

Select, 80
Shading (table), 170
Sort (table), 92
Speller, 56
Split cells (table), 170 (*see also* Join cells)
Superscript, 135

Tables (various), 90
Tabs, 57, 136
Text alignment (*see* Alignment)
Top-aligned text (*see* Alignment, In table cells)
Typeover, 55

Underline, 55
Undo, 56
Update automatically (*see* Insert date field)

Vertical alignment (*see* Alignment)
View, 57

Widow/Orphan, 67

Zoom, 57

New-Key Learning

LESSONS 1-15

LESSON 1 HOME KEYS (fdsa jkl;)

Objectives:

1. To learn control of home keys (**fdsa jkl;**).

2. To learn control of **Space Bar** and **Enter** key.

1A • Work Area Arrangement

Arrange work area as shown at the right.

- alphanumeric (main) keyboard directly in front of chair; front edge of keyboard even with edge of table or desk
- monitor placed for easy viewing
- disk drives placed for easy access and disks within easy reach (unless using a network)
- book behind or at side of keyboard; top raised for easy reading

Properly arranged work area

1B • Keying Position

The features of proper position are shown at right and listed below:

- fingers curved and upright over home keys
- wrists low, but not touching keyboard
- forearms parallel to slant of keyboard
- body erect, sitting back in chair
- feet on floor for balance

Proper position at computer

DOCUMENT*	FORMAT GUIDES**
Memo (60)	**Margins:** TM—2″ | SM—default or 1″ | BM—about 1″ **LS:** DS headings; SS ¶s with DS between ¶s • Key headings at left margin in ALL CAPS—**TO:**, **FROM:**, **DATE:**, and **SUBJECT:**. Key receiver's name (title optional) at second default tab after **TO:** heading; key sender's name (title optional), date, and subject at first default tab after appropriate headings. • Key body (message) a DS below subject line, without indenting ¶s. **Special parts (in alphabetical order):** Attachment/Enclosure notation (other documents included with memo), keyed a DS below reference initials: *Attachment* (if other document is attached to memo) or *Enclosure* (if other document is enclosed but not attached). • Blind copy notation (when copy of memo is sent without disclosing to addressee), keyed (**bc** followed by name of person receiving copy) on copy ONLY, a DS below Attachment/Enclosure notation, if any, or reference initials. • Copy notation (when copy of memo is sent to someone other than addressee), keyed (**c** followed by name of person receiving copy) a DS below Attachment/Enclosure notation, if any, or reference initials. • Reference initials (when someone other than writer keys memo), keyed in lowercase a DS below last line of body. • Second-page heading (when memo exceeds one page), keyed on three lines (addressee's name, *Page #*, date), beginning at TM on each page after first.
References List (74)	**Margins (separate page):** TM—2″ | SM—default or 1″ | BM—about 1″ | Page #: top at RM **LS:** SS each reference; DS between references. • Center title (**REFERENCES**) in ALL CAPS at TM (if separate page) or a QS below last line of body (if on last page of report). • QS below title. • Begin first line of each reference at LM; indent other lines 0.5″ (hanging indent style).
Report, Bound (137)	**Margins: First page:** TM—2″ | LM—1.5″ | RM—1″ | BM—about 1″ | Page #—optional; centered at bottom if used. **Subsequent pages:** TM—1″ | LM—1.5″ | RM—1″ | BM—about 1″ | Page #—top at RM. **LS:** DS ¶s and between ¶s; DS above and below side headings. • *See* Report, Unbound. • Bind pages 0.5″ from left edge.
Report, Unbound (71, 73, 74)	**Margins: First page:** TM—2″ | SM—default or 1″ | BM—about 1″ | Page #—optional; bottom at center if used. **Subsequent pages:** TM—1″ | SM—default or 1″ | BM—about 1″ | Page #: top at RM. **LS:** SS or DS ¶s with DS between ¶s • Center title in ALL CAPS; DS multiple-line titles; QS below title. • If body is DS, indent first line of each ¶ 0.5″; if body is SS, begin all lines at LM. DS above and below side headings. • Document sources with *textual citations* (author name, publication year, page number in parentheses within body), endnotes, or footnotes. • Key long quotations (four or more lines) SS, indented 0.5″ from LM. DS above and below quotation. • *See also* References List.
Table of Contents (138)	**Margins:** Same as first page of report. *See* Report, Bound and Report, Unbound. **LS:** DS side headings; SS ¶ headings • Center title (**TABLE OF CONTENTS**) at TM; QS below title. • Begin side headings at LM; indent ¶ headings 0.5″ from LM. • Key page number for each heading at RM.
Title Page (137)	**Margins:** Same as first page of report. *See* Report, Bound and Report, Unbound. Center all lines horizontally. • Key report title (ALL CAPS) at TM. Key report writer's name (capitals and lowercase) 5″ from top edge. Key school name a DS below writer's name. Key date (month, day, and year or month and year) 9″ from top edge.

* Numbers in parentheses indicate location of a model document.
** Use Index to find more detailed format guides.

1C • Home-Key Position

1. Find the home keys on the chart: **f d s a** for left hand and **j k l ;** for right hand.
2. Locate and place your fingers on the home keys on your keyboard with your fingers well curved and upright (not slanting).
3. Remove your fingers from the keyboard; then place them in home-key position again, curving and holding them *lightly* on the keys.

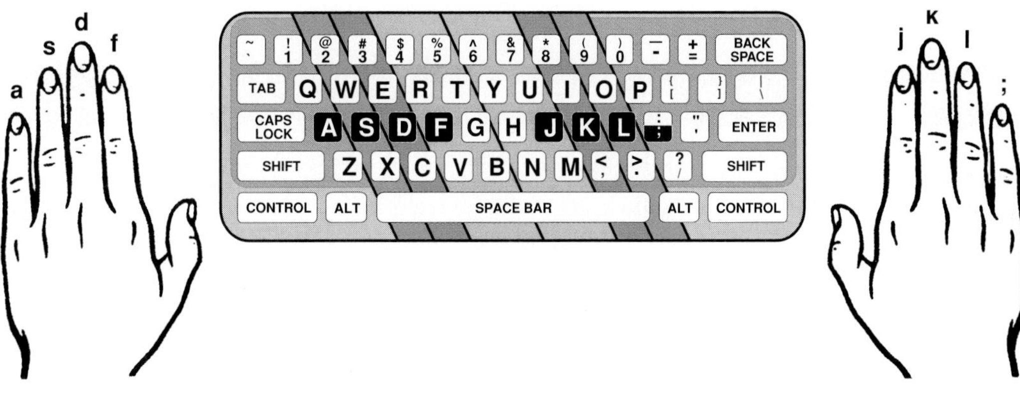

1D • Techniques: Home Keys and Spacebar

1. Read the hints and study the illustrations at the right.
2. Place your fingers in home-key position as directed in 1C above.
3. Strike the key for each letter in the first group below the illustration.
4. After striking *;* (semi-colon), strike the *Space Bar* once.
5. Continue to key the line; strike the *Space Bar* once at the point of each arrow.
6. Review proper position (1B); then repeat Steps 3–5 above.

Technique **H · I · N · T**

Keystroking: Strike each key with a light tap with the tip of the finger, snapping the fingertip toward the palm of the hand.

Spacing: Strike the Space Bar with the right thumb; use a quick down-and-in motion (toward the palm). Avoid pauses before or after spacing.

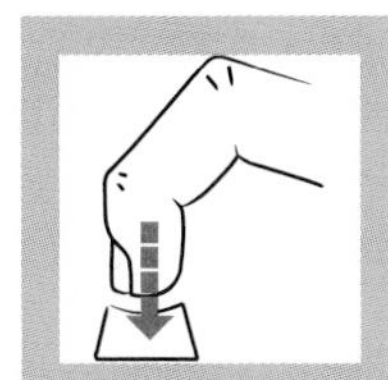

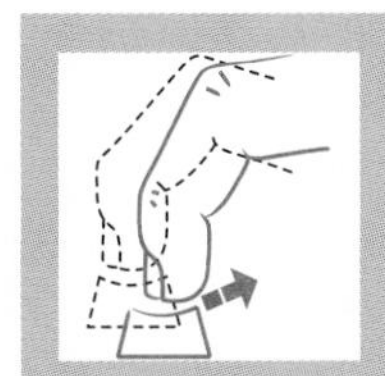

Space once.

```
fdsajkl; f d s a j k l ; ff jj dd kk ss ll aa ;;
```

1E • Technique: Hard Return at Line Endings

1. Read the information and study the illustration at the right.
2. Practice the ENTER key reach several times.

Hard Return
To return the insertion point to the left margin and move it down to the next line, strike ENTER.

This is called a **hard return**. Use a hard return at the end of all drill lines. Use two hard returns when directed to double-space.

Hard Return Technique
Reach the little finger of the right hand to the ENTER key, tap the key, and return the finger quickly to home-key position.

Basic Format Guides for Correspondence and Reports

DOCUMENT*	FORMAT GUIDES**
E-mail (62)	**Margins:** Key all lines at left edge of e-mail screen. **LS:** Key ¶s SS; DS between ¶s. • Insert receiver's e-mail address in **TO:** box. • Key receiver's name on first line of e-mail screen; DS below receiver's name. Key sender's name a DS below last line of message.
Endnotes Page (137)	**Margins:** Same as first page of report, except page # 1" from top edge at RM. *See* Report, Bound and Report, Unbound. **LS:** SS endnotes with DS between them. • Center title **ENDNOTES** in ALL CAPS at TM. • QS below title. • Indent first line of each endnote 0.5" from LM (keyed to a superscript endnote number). Begin all other lines at LM.
Envelope (86)	**Margins:** Margins similar to the following specifications are preset by Envelopes word processing feature. **Return address:** TM—0.25" | LM—0.25" **Delivery address: Small (No. 6¾) envelope:** TM—2" | LM—2.5" **Large (No. 10) envelope:** TM—2" | LM—4" **LS:** SS. • Key return address in caps and lowercase, beginning each line at LM. ***Note:*** Return address is often preprinted on envelopes used for business letters. Key delivery address in USPS style (left-aligned in ALL CAPS, with no punctuation). • Include three to six lines, with city, two-letter state abbreviation, and ZIP+4 on last line. Space once between state abbreviation and ZIP+4.
Letter in Block Format **Business (160)** **Personal Business (83)**	**Margins: First page:** TM—2" (One-page letters may be centered vertically.) | SM—default or 1" | BM—about 1" **Subsequent pages:** TM—1" | SM—default or 1" | BM—about 1" Begin all letter parts at LM. • **Personal-business letter:** Key first line of sender's (return) address at TM; SS address. Key date (month, day, year) below last line of return address (city, state, ZIP+4). • **Business letter:** Key date (month, day, year) at TM. • **Business and personal-business letter:** Key letter (delivery) address a QS below date, with personal (*Miss, Mr., Mrs., Ms.*) or professional (*Dr., Lt., Senator*) title before receiver's name. Letter address may be keyed in USPS (ALL CAPS, no punctuation) style. Key salutation (greeting) a DS below letter address. • Begin body (message) a DS below salutation; SS and block ¶s with DS between them. • Key complimentary close (farewell) a DS below last line of body. QS below complimentary close; key writer's (originator's) name. **Special parts (in alphabetical order):** Attachment/Enclosure notation (other documents included with letter), keyed a DS below reference initials: *Attachment* (if other document is attached to letter) or *Enclosure* (if other document is enclosed but not attached). • Attention line (when name of person who should receive letter is unknown), keyed as first line of letter address: *Attention Special Collections Director.* • Blind copy notation (when copy of letter is sent without disclosing to addressee), keyed (**bc** followed by name of person receiving copy) on copy ONLY, a DS below Attachment/Enclosure notation, if any, or reference initials. • Copy notation (when copy of letter is sent to someone other than addressee), keyed (**c** followed by name of person receiving copy) a DS below Attachment/Enclosure notation, if any, or reference initials. • Reference initials (when someone other than writer keys letter), keyed in lowercase a DS below writer's name. • Second-page heading (when letter exceeds one page), keyed on three lines (receiver's name, *Page #*, date), beginning at TM on each page after first. • Subject line (when description of letter content is desirable), keyed a DS below salutation in ALL CAPS.

* Numbers in parentheses indicate location of a model document.
** Use Index to find more detailed format guides.

1F • Home-Key and Spacebar Practice

1. Place your hands in home-key position (left-hand fingers on **f d s a** and right-hand fingers on **j k l ;**).
2. Key the lines once: single-spaced (SS) with a double space (DS) between 2-line groups. Do not key line numbers.

Fingers curved and upright

Down-and-in spacing motion

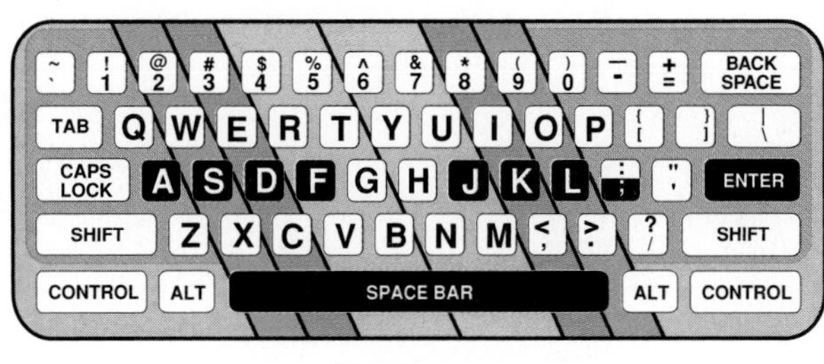

Strike Space Bar once to space.

1 j jj f ff k kk d dd l ll s ss ; ;; a aa jkl; fdsa
2 j jj f ff k kk d dd l ll s ss ; ;; a aa jkl; fdsa

Strike the ENTER key twice to double-space (DS).

3 a aa ; ;; s ss l ll d dd k kk f ff j jj fdsa jkl;
4 a aa ; ;; s ss l ll d dd k kk f ff j jj fdsa jkl;

DS

5 jf jf kd kd ls ls ;a ;a fj fj dk dk sl sl a; a; f
6 jf jf kd kd ls ls ;a ;a fj fj dk dk sl sl a; a; f

DS

7 a;fj a;sldkfj a;sldkfj a;sldkfj a;sldkfj a;sldkfj
8 a;fj a;sldkfj a;sldkfj a;sldkfj a;sldkfj a;sldkfj

Strike the ENTER key 4 times to quadruple-space (QS).

1G • Technique: Enter Key Practice

Key the lines once: single-spaced (SS) with a double space (DS) between 2-line groups. Do not key line numbers.

Spacing **C • U • E**

When lines are SS, strike ENTER twice to insert a DS between 2-line groups.

Reach with little finger; tap ENTER key quickly; return finger to home key.

1 a;sldkfj a;sldkfj
2 a;sldkfj a;sldkfj

DS

3 ff jj dd kk ss ll aa ;;
4 ff jj dd kk ss ll aa ;;

DS

5 fj dk sl a; a; as df ;l kj;
6 fj dk sl a; a; as df ;l kj;

DS

7 fj dk sl a; jf kd ls ;a fdsa jkl
8 fj dk sl a; jf kd ls ;a fdsa jkl

DS

9 k; fa kl ds ak dl fj s; lafj ksd; dlj
10 k; fa kl ds ak dl fj s; lafj ksd; dlj

DS

11 fa sd j; kl ak sj fl d; akdj s;lf sfk; djl
12 fa sd j; kl ak sj fl d; akdj s;lf sfk; djl

QS

starting with a resource like an encyclopedia (e.g., www.webopedia.com or www.britannica.com). You can then use a search engine to find highlights or recent news about the river.

Drill 3: Searching Savvy

In this drill, we'll use some of the methods just described to find information on the Web.

1. Let's find out if the Gap has a Web site by using the format *www.companyname.com*. Key www.gap.com.
2. Try finding the Web sites for Nike and another company that interests you. Add the last site to your list of bookmarks or favorites.
3. Find the Web sites for Fritos®, Coke®, or other products that interest you.
4. Find the Web sites for the USDA (the United States Department of Agriculture), MIT (the Massachusetts Institute of Technology), and a college or university that interests you. Add the last site to your list of bookmarks or favorites.
5. Select a search engine from your browser using the toolbar Search button.
6. You are going to take a class in martial arts and need a uniform. In the text box, key **martial arts**.
7. You will get results on many different aspects of martial arts, such as history, associations, and styles. You could weed through the site descriptions and find some sites that sell uniforms, but instead, let's add another keyword to narrow your search. Do a new search for *martial arts uniforms*.

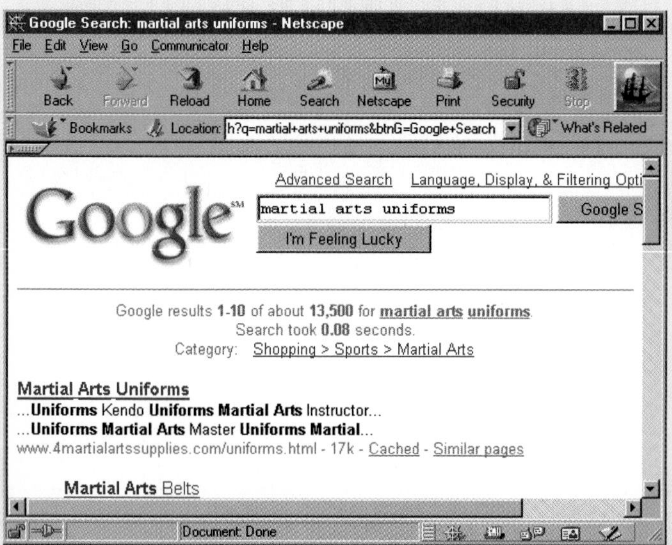

8. You will get some specific sites where you can purchase uniforms. Find two prices for uniforms in your size.

Drill 4: Scavenger Hunt

In this final drill, let's apply the skills you've learned to go on a scavenger hunt on the Web.

1. Find the date and time of the next space shuttle launch.
2. Get tomorrow's weather forecast for West Monroe, Louisiana.
3. Find the definition of the word *parterre*.
4. At the British Broadcasting Corporation Web site, find today's top story.
5. Find the current price per share of two stocks.
6. Find an astronomy Web site called something like *stardate* and print an interesting item from the site.
7. Shop for a good rate on a round-trip flight from Boston, Massachusetts, to San Diego, California, leaving three weeks from today and staying a week.
8. Find a recent news item about acid rain.
9. At the Web site for the Federal Reserve Bank of Minneapolis, find out how much a dollar's worth of goods bought in 1954 would cost this year.
10. Find a site that gives product reviews for DVD players.
11. Find three resources for financial aid for college.
12. Find some biographical information on Gary Soto. **Bonus:** Find a poem by Soto.

1H • Home-Key Mastery

1. Key the lines once (without the numbers); strike the ENTER key twice to double-space (DS).
2. Rekey the drill at a faster pace.

Technique **C • U • E**

Keep fingers curved and upright over home keys, right thumb just barely touching the Space Bar.

Spacing **C • U • E**

Space once after ; used as punctuation.

Correct finger alignment

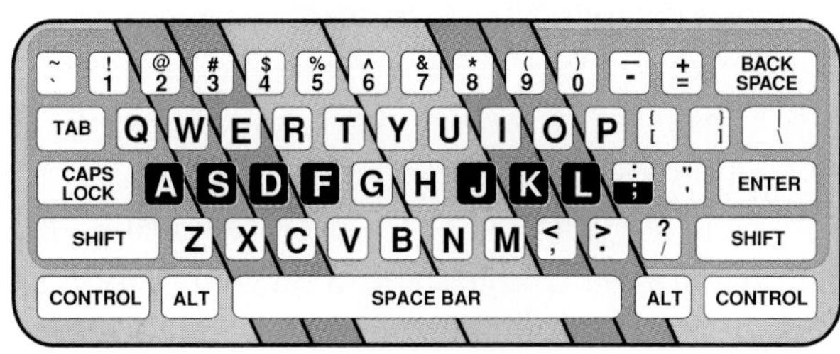

1 aa ;; ss ll dd kk ff jj a; sl dk fj jf kd ls ;a jf
DS
2 a a as as ad ad ask ask lad lad fad fad jak jak la
DS
3 all all fad fad jak jak add add ask ask ads ads as
DS
4 a lad; a jak; a lass; all ads; add all; ask a lass
DS
5 as a lad; a fall fad; ask all dads; as a fall fad;

1I • End-of-Lesson Routine

1. Exit the software.
2. Remove disk from disk drive.
3. Turn off equipment if directed to do so.
4. Store materials as the instructor directs.

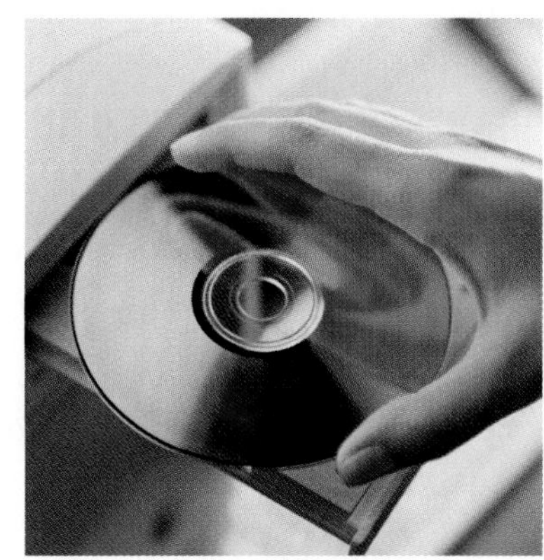

Disk removal

1J • Enrichment

1. Key the drill once as shown to improve control of home keys.
2. Key the drill again to quicken your keystrokes.

Spacing **C • U • E**

To DS between single-spaced lines, strike ENTER twice.

1 ja js jd jf f; fl fk fj ka ks kd kf d; dl dk dj a;
DS
2 la ls ld lf s; sl sk sj ;a ;s ;d ;f a; al ak aj fj
DS
3 jj aa kk ss ll dd ;; ff fj dk sl a; jf kd ls ;a a;
DS
4 as as ask ask ad ad lad lad all all fall fall lass
DS
5 as a fad; as a dad; ask a lad; as a lass; all lads
DS
6 a sad dad; all lads fall; ask a lass; a jak salad;
DS
7 add a jak; a fall ad; all fall ads; ask a sad lass

these links and your browser navigation features to answer the following questions:

a. When and why did Lassen become a national park?
b. How many of the four types of volcanoes in the world are found in the park?
c. How can you drive to the park from Red Bluff?
d. If you want to hike some of the best trails in Lassen, what is the minimum amount of time you should plan to visit?
e. How much will it cost to visit the park by car?
f. Does the park have campgrounds?

6. Explore the Park Service site further. Try *Links to the Past* or *Nature Net* or find a park you would like to visit.

NAME YOUR FAVORITES

As you travel the Web, you will find some pages that you will want to visit frequently. Browsers give you an easy way to do so. You can add the site to a list of **Favorites** or **Bookmarks** in your browser (the exact name depends on the browser). These sites stay in the list until you delete them. To go to one of these sites, simply choose it from the Favorites or Bookmarks list.

Many browsers offer alternatives to keying the *http* portion of a URL. Beginning in the next drill, try leaving out *http*. If this doesn't work, continue to key *http://* as you did in Drill 1.

Drill 2: Navigation and Bookmarks

In this drill, you'll hone your skills at finding information on a site and navigating to other sites.

1. Go to the Appaloosa Horse Club Web site at www.appaloosa.com.

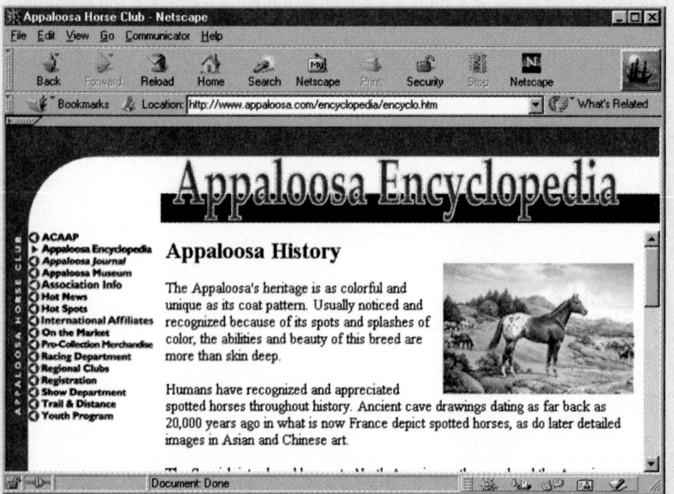

2. Use the site hyperlinks and your browser navigation features to answer the following questions:
   a. To be registered as an Appaloosa, what four distinguishing features must a horse have?
   b. Which of these features is unique to the Ap?
   c. What is the meaning of *sclera*?
   d. How did the Appaloosa get its name?
   e. How many Aps are registered with the Association today? (Use the most recent figure provided.)
3. Visit the following sites, adding two of them to your list of bookmarks or favorites.
   - www.cnn.com
   - www.ipl.org
   - www.m-w.com
   - www.espn.com
   - www.petersons.com
   - www.doughnet.com
   - www.weather.com
   - www.edmunds.com
4. Browse for two additional sites you like, and add them to your list of bookmarks or favorites.
5. Use the Bookmarks or Favorites feature to access three of the sites that you added in this drill.

SEARCH SMART

One of the main reasons people use the Web is to search for information about a certain topic. **Search engines** like Yahoo!, AltaVista, and Google search many Web sites for keywords you specify and show you the search results. In just a few seconds, search engines make available to you huge amounts of material that would be difficult, if not impossible, to access in any other way.

The more specific your keywords are, the better your search results are likely to be. You can access a selection of search engines by clicking the Search button in your browser, or you can key the URL of a search engine to go directly to it.

Search engines aren't always the most efficient choice. For instance, to find the Web site for a company, product, college or university, or government agency, you can often key the name directly, using this format:

www.companyname.com	→	www.corel.com
www.productname.com	→	www.whopper.com
www.schoolname.edu	→	www.nyu.edu
www.governmentagency.gov	→	www.epa.gov

To find general information about a topic (for example, for a report on the Rhine River), you are sometimes better off

LESSON 2 | NEW KEYS: h AND e

Objectives:

1. To learn reach technique for **h** and **e**.
2. To combine smoothly **h** and **e** with home keys.

2A • Get Ready to Key

At the beginning of each practice session, follow the *Standard Plan* given at the right to get ready to key the lesson.

Standard Plan for Getting Ready to Key

1. Arrange work area similar to the illustration on p. R2.
2. Check to see that the computer, monitor, and printer (if any) are plugged in.
3. Load the computer software specified by your instructor.
4. Align the front of the keyboard with the front edge of the desk or table.
5. Position the monitor and the textbook for easy reading.

2B • Plan for Learning New Keys

All keys except the home keys (**fdsa jkl;**) require the fingers to reach in order to strike them. Follow the *Standard Plan* given at the right to learn the proper reach for each new key.

Standard Plan for Learning New Keys

1. Find the new key on the keyboard chart given on the page where the new key is introduced.
2. Look at your own keyboard and find the new key on it.
3. Study the reach-technique picture at the left of the practice lines for the new key. (See p. R7 for illustrations.) Read the statement below the illustration.
4. Identify the finger to be used to strike the new key.
5. Curve your fingers; place them in home-key position (over **fdsa jkl;**).
6. Watch your finger as you reach it to the new key and back to home position a few times (keep it curved).
7. Refer to the set of three drill lines at the right of the reach-technique illustration. Key each line twice SS (single-spaced):
   - once slowly, to learn new reach;
   - then faster, for a quick-snap stroke. DS (double-space) between 2-line groups.

2C • Home-Key Review

Key each line twice single-spaced (SS): once slowly; again, at a faster pace; double-space (DS) between 2-line groups.

All keystrokes learned

```
1 a;sldkfj a; sl dk fj ff jj dd kk ss ll aa ;; fj a;
2 a a as as ask ask ad ad lad lad add add fall falls
3 as as ad ad all all jak jak fad fad fall fall lass
4 jj kk; jj kk; as jak; as jak; ask a lad; ask a lad
5 a jak; a fad; as a lad; ask dad; a lass; a fall ad
6 a sad fall; all fall ads; as a lass asks a sad lad
7 a fad; ask dad; ask a lass; add a lad; a sad lass;
```

Strike ENTER 4 times to quadruple-space (QS) between lesson parts.

is more widely used). Between the computer address and the filename, there may be some text preceded by a slash (*/news*). This is usually the directory in which the page is stored. Think of it as a folder in the file storage system of a computer.

To navigate the Internet and view Web sites, you need an Internet connection. You can get connected through an Internet service provider (ISP), such as America Online. You also need browser software, such as Microsoft® Internet Explorer or Netscape® Communicator. Let's go over what happens when you use a browser to visit a Web site.[2]

You connect to the Internet through your ISP and then start your browser software. Next, you enter a URL (such as http://www.bluemountain.com). The browser software connects to the computer that hosts the *bluemountain* site and requests the home page. The home page text and graphics are **cached**, or stored, on your computer. Your browser software then interprets the HTML code line by line and displays the home page text and graphics according to the HTML code. All of this can happen in less than a minute.

Let's put the information you just read to work. The following activities are for first-time Internet users. If you have experience using the Internet, your teacher may suggest ways that you can vary these basic activities. Or you may be asked to help someone in the class who is a first-timer.

MEET YOUR BROWSER

Your browser window will look much like any other software application window. At the top, the **title bar** gives the names of the browser and the Web page being viewed. At the far right of the title bar are the **Minimize**, **Maximize**, and **Close** boxes. The window includes a **menu bar** and one or more **toolbars**. There are **scroll bars** you can use to move through a page.

Your browser window includes a **Location**, **Address**, or **Netsite** box in which you key the URL for a Web site you want to visit.

Two convenient toolbar buttons that you will probably use often are the **Forward** and **Back** buttons. These buttons allow you to go backward or forward one Web page at a time. This function will work only with pages you are visiting during a single computer session. Remember also that many Web sites have hyperlinks designed to guide you through the site.

To go directly to a page you looked at some pages ago, instead of clicking Forward or Back repeatedly, you can use one of these options, depending on your browser:

- Open the Go menu and choose the page.
- Click the down arrow by the address box or by the Back or Forward button and choose the page.
- Open your browser's History feature and choose the page.

These options list pages you visited during the current computer session. Some may also list pages from past sessions, depending on your browser and its setup.

Drill 1: Browser Basics

Let's practice some of the browser basics we've just read about. We'll go to the National Park Service Web site.

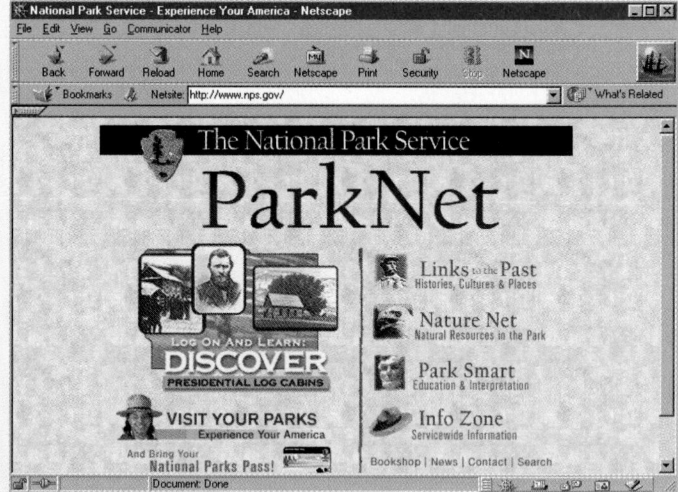

1. In the address box, key http://www.nps.gov and press **Enter**.
2. Move your mouse pointer over ***Visit Your Parks***. The pointer changes to a pointing hand icon. This indicates that *Visit Your Parks* is a hyperlink.
3. Click ***Visit Your Parks***. When the page has finished loading, note the address. You are now on a new page at the National Park Service Web site, *parks.html*.
4. You are planning to visit Lassen Volcanic National Park. Select the name of the park from the text box at the bottom of the screen and click ***Go***.
5. The Lassen Volcanic National Park page contains hyperlinks to a number of pages about the park. Use

[2] Description paraphrased from Brown, 5.

2D • New Keys: H and E

1. Use the *Standard Plan for Learning New Keys* (p. R6) for each key to be learned. Study the plan now.
2. Relate each step of the plan to the illustrations below and text at the right. Then key each line twice SS; leave a DS between 2-line groups.

h *Right index* finger

e *Left middle* finger

Do not attempt to key line numbers, the vertical lines separating word groups, or the labels (home row, h/e).

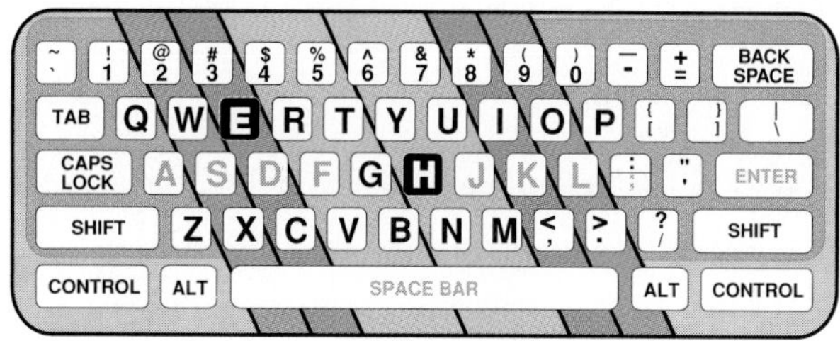

Learn h

1 j j hj hj ah ah ha ha had had has has ash ash hash

2 hj hj ha ha ah ah hah hah had had ash ash has hash

3 ah ha; had ash; has had; a hall; has a hall; ah ha

Strike ENTER twice to double-space (DS) below the set of lines.

Learn e

4 d d ed ed el el led led eel eel eke eke ed fed fed

5 ed ed el el lee lee fed fed eke eke led led ale ed

6 a lake; a leek; a jade; a desk; a jade eel; a deed

Combine h and e

7 he he he|she she she|shed shed|heed heed|held held

8 a lash; a shed; he held; she has jade; held a sash

9 has fled; he has ash; she had jade; she had a sale

Strike ENTER 4 times to quadruple-space (QS) between lesson parts.

2E • New-Key Mastery

1. Key the lines once SS with a DS between 2-line groups.
2. Key the lines again with quick, sharp strokes at a faster pace.

Spacing **C • U • E**

Space once after ; used as punctuation.

Note:

Once the screen is filled with keyed lines, the top line disappears when a new line is added at the bottom. This is called **scrolling.**

Fingers curved

Fingers upright

home row

1 ask ask|has has|lad lad|all all|jak jak|fall falls

2 a jak; a lad; a sash; had all; has a jak; all fall

DS

h/e

3 he he|she she|led led|held held|jell jell|she shed

4 he led; she had; she fell; a jade ad; a desk shelf

DS

all keys learned

5 elf elf|all all|ask ask|led led|jak jak|hall halls

6 ask dad; he has jell; she has jade; he sells leeks

DS

all keys learned

7 he led; she has; a jak ad; a jade eel; a sled fell

8 she asked a lad; he led all fall; she has a jak ad

Internet Guide with Applications

WHAT IS THE INTERNET?

The **Internet** is a network of computer networks. It is millions of computers all over the world, linked electronically to each other. The links make certain types of information stored on any one of those computers available to all the others.

To describe how much information is on the Internet, we use words like *huge* and *immense* and *stupendous* and *vast*. What kinds of information? All kinds. You (or anyone else) probably can't name a subject that is not on the Internet. Here are a few examples of things you might do there:

- Take a course
- Buy a T-shirt
- Research a school paper
- Look for a job
- Get up-to-the-minute news
- Discuss a project with an expert
- Download music

Is using the Internet like looking up topics in a humongous library? Not exactly. You see, the information is unorganized and dynamic (always changing). Using the Internet is fun because you never know what you will find.

HOW DOES IT WORK?

Although people use *Internet* and *World Wide Web (Web)* interchangeably, they are not the same thing. The Web is a network of computers on the Internet. These computers have two things in common. First, they all use the same computer language, **hypertext transfer protocol,** or **http,** to communicate with other computers. Second, all the files that they contain are Web pages, formatted using the same programming language—**hypertext markup language,** or **HTML**.

Computers on the World Wide Web host, or store, **Web sites.** A Web site is a collection of related Web pages, each of which is an individual computer file formatted in HTML.

A Web site that sells T-shirts might consist of four Web pages. The first, often called the **home** or **start page,** might welcome you to the site. The site might also include a catalog page, a page for ordering, and a page for customer service.

Web pages usually include **hyperlinks (links** for short). Clicking on a link takes you to another page on the Web site or to another Web site. Hyperlinks can appear as text that is underlined or a different color (sometimes called **hypertext**). They can also be buttons or graphics.

Every Web page has a unique address called a **URL (uniform resource locator)**:[1] The illustration shows the parts of a URL.

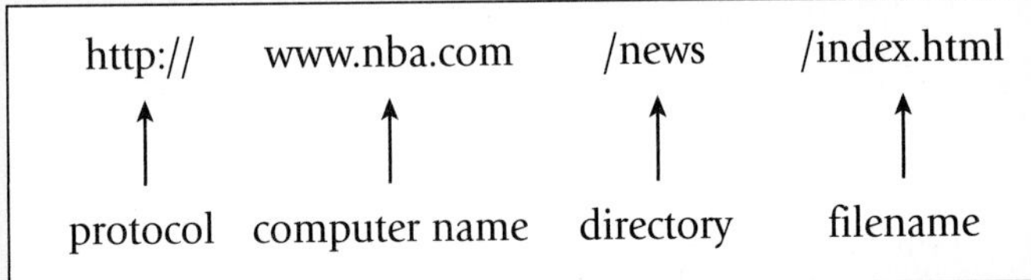

The first part is the protocol that other computers must use to communicate with the computer hosting the site. As you've learned, the protocol for Web sites is *http*. Other protocols that you may see are *Gopher, Telnet,* and *FTP*.

The second part of a URL is the name of the computer that hosts the Web site. The parts of the name are separated by periods ("dots"). The name ends with one or more codes that identify the type of organization. Here are some common codes:

.com	Commercial (for-profit) companies
.org	Nonprofit organizations
.edu	Four-year colleges and universities
.net	Network service providers
.mil	Military
.gov	Federal government
.us, .uk	Countries (United States, United Kingdom)

The last part of a URL is the filename, which ends with *.html* or *.htm* (most Web browsers recognize either, but *.html*

[1] Figure adapted from Herbert F. Brown, *Web Page Design* (Cincinnati: South-Western Educational Publishing, 2000), 5.

LESSON 3 NEW KEYS: i AND r

Objectives:

1. To learn reach technique for **i** and **r**.
2. To combine smoothly **i** and **r** with all other learned keys.

3A • 3'
Get Ready to Key

Follow the steps in the *Standard Plan for Getting Ready to Key* on p. R6.

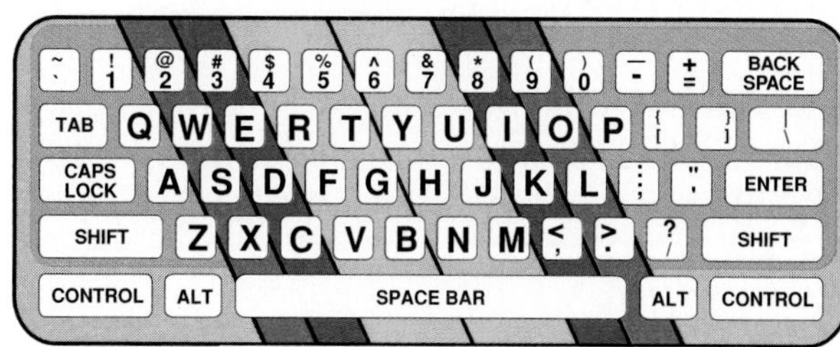

3B • 5'
Conditioning Practice

Key each line twice SS; DS between 2-line groups.

Practice **C·U·E**

- Key each line at a slow, steady pace, but strike and release each key quickly.
- Key each line again at a faster pace; move from key to key quickly.

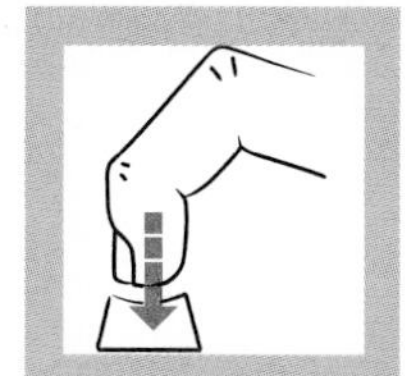

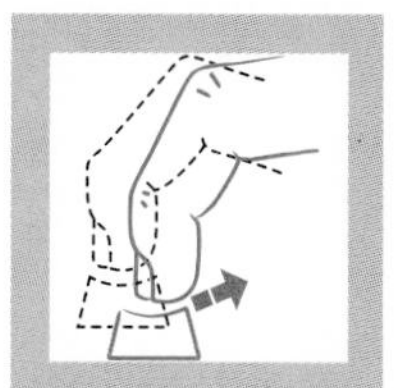

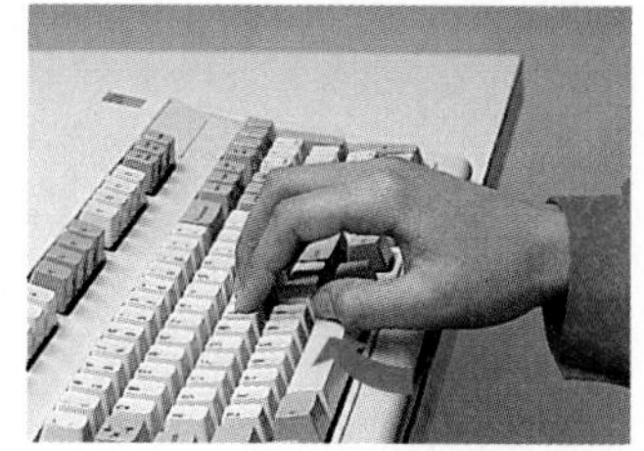

home keys 1 a;sldkfj a;sldkfj as jak ask fad all dad lads fall

Strike ENTER twice to DS.

h/e 2 hj hah has had sash hash ed led fed fled sled fell

DS

all keys learned 3 as he fled; ask a lass; she had jade; sell all jak

Strike ENTER 4 times to quadruple-space (QS) between lesson parts.

3C • 5'
Speed Building

Key each line once DS.

Spacing **C·U·E**

To DS when in SS mode, strike ENTER twice at end of line.

Speed **C·U·E**

In lines 1–3, quicken the keying pace as you key each letter combination or word when it is repeated within the line.

1 hj hj | ah ah | ha ha | had had | ash ash | has has | had hash
2 ed ed | el el | ed ed | led led | eke eke | lee lee | ale kale
3 he he | she she | led led | has has | held held | sled sleds
4 he fled; she led; she had jade; he had a jell sale
5 a jak fell; she held a leek; he has had a sad fall
6 he has ash; she sells jade; as he fell; has a lake
7 she had a fall jade sale; he leads all fall sales;
8 he held a fall kale sale; she sells leeks as a fad

After you have maximized a window, the **Restore button** will replace the Maximize button. Clicking this button restores the window to its original size and location.

Clicking the **Close button** closes a window.

To move a window, drag it by the title bar. To resize a window, move the mouse pointer to a side or corner of the window. The pointer will become a double-headed arrow (↔). Drag until the window is the size you want.

When more than one window is displayed at a time, clicking a window's title bar makes it the **active window**—the one you can work in. The other window(s) will have a gray title bar to indicate that it is **inactive**.

Drill 2: Work with Windows

1. Open file *CD-TAXES*. Practice using the scroll bars to move around in this document.
2. Minimize your word processing window. Double-click the *My Computer* desktop icon. Maximize, restore, and then minimize the My Computer window.
3. Practice switching back and forth between the word processing software and the My Computer window. Close the My Computer window.
4. Maximize your word processing window, if it is not maximized already, and open a new blank document with *CD-TAXES* still open. If the new document is maximized, click the *Restore* button.
5. Drag the new document window around the screen.
6. Practice resizing the new document window and leave it on the screen for the next drill. *CD-TAXES* should still be open, but minimized or inactive.

DIALOG BOXES

A **dialog box** displays when software needs more information to carry out a task. Selecting a menu item that is followed by an ellipsis (. . .) will open a dialog box. The illustrations at the right show how to choose common dialog box options.[3] Clicking OK excecutes the selected option; clicking Cancel closes the dialog box.

Drill 3: Use Dialog Boxes

1. Open dialog boxes in your word processing document until you have had the chance to try three different types of dialog box options.
2. Close the document without saving, close *CD-TAXES* without saving, and exit your word processing software.

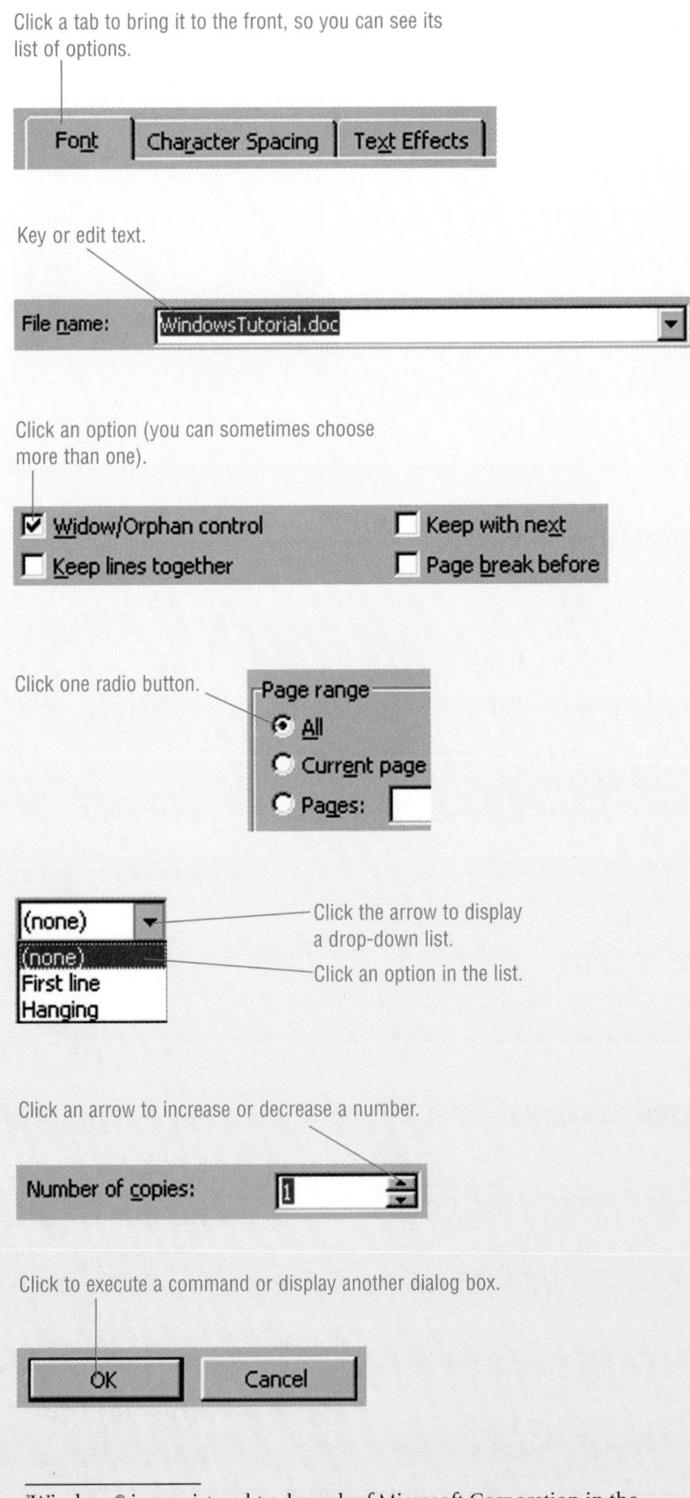

Click a tab to bring it to the front, so you can see its list of options.
Font
Character Spacing
Text Effects
Key or edit text.
File name:
WindowsTutorial.doc
Click an option (you can sometimes choose more than one).
Widow/Orphan control
Keep with next
Keep lines together
Page break before
Click one radio button.
Page range
All
Current page
Pages:
(none)
(none)
First line
Hanging
Click the arrow to display a drop-down list.
Click an option in the list.
Click an arrow to increase or decrease a number.
Number of copies:
1
Click to execute a command or display another dialog box.
OK
Cancel

[3]Windows® is a registered trademark of Microsoft Corporation in the United States and/or other countries.

3D • 18'
New Keys: I and R

Key each line twice SS (slowly, then faster); DS between 2-line groups; if time permits, key lines 7–9 again.

Technique Goals:

- curved, upright fingers
- finger-action keystrokes
- eyes on copy

i *Right middle* finger

r *Left index* finger

Follow the *Standard Plan for Learning New Keys* outlined on p. R6.

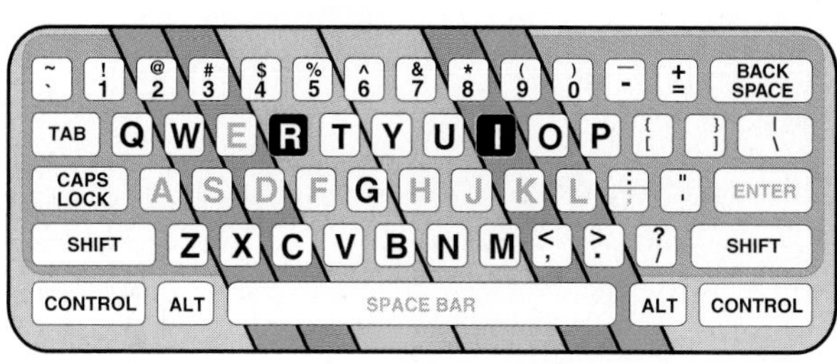

Learn i

1 k k ik ik is is if if did did aid aid kid kid hail
2 ik ik if if is is kid kid his his lie lie aid aide
3 a kid; a lie; if he; he did; his aide; if a kid is

Learn r

4 f f rf rf jar jar her her are are ark ark jar jars
5 rf rf re re fr fr jar jar red red her her far fare
6 a jar; a rake; a lark; red jar; hear her; are dark

Combine i and r

7 fir fir|rid rid|sir sir|ire ire|fire fire|air airs
8 a fir; if her; a fire; is fair; his ire; if she is
9 he is; if her; is far; red jar; his heir; her aide

Quadruple-space (QS) between lesson parts.

3E • 19'
New-Key Mastery

1. Key the lines once SS with a DS between 2-line groups.
2. Key the lines again at a faster pace.

Technique Goals:

- fingers deeply curved
- wrists low, but not resting
- hands/arms steady
- eyes on copy as you key

reach review
1 hj ed ik rf hj de ik fr hj ed ik rf jh de ki fr hj
2 he he|if if|all all|fir fir|jar jar|rid rid|as ask
DS

h/e
3 she she|elf elf|her her|hah hah|eel eel|shed shelf
4 he has; had jak; her jar; had a shed; she has fled
DS

i/r
5 fir fir|rid rid|sir sir|kid kid|ire ire|fire fired
6 a fir; is rid; is red; his ire; her kid; has a fir
DS

all keys learned
7 if if|is is|he he|did did|fir fir|jak jak|all fall
8 a jak; he did; ask her; red jar; she fell; he fled
DS

all keys learned
9 if she is; he did ask; he led her; he is her aide;
10 she has had a jak sale; she said he had a red fir;

START MENU

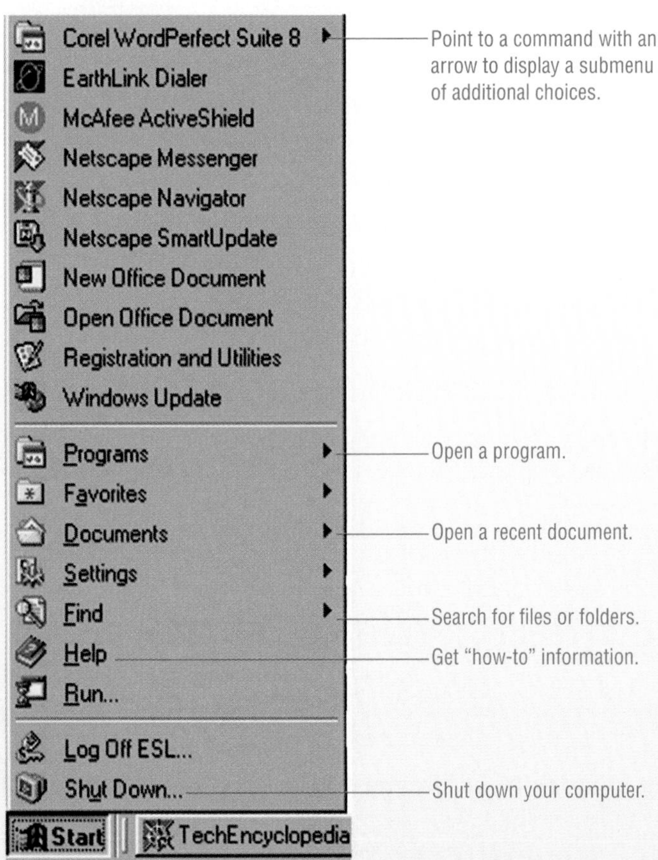

Drill 1: Open a Program from the Start Menu[2]

1. Click the *Start* button to open the Start menu. Examine the options in this menu.
2. Move your pointer to *Programs*.
3. Click the name of your word processing software to open it. Your word processing software may be inside a folder. If so, open the folder (by pointing to it) to get to the software.

BASIC FEATURES OF WINDOWS

Microsoft® Windows® displays folders, applications, and individual documents in **windows**. The basic features of all windows are the same.

The **title bar** lists the name of the window.

From the **menu bar**, you can access all the commands available in the software. Menu names are similar in

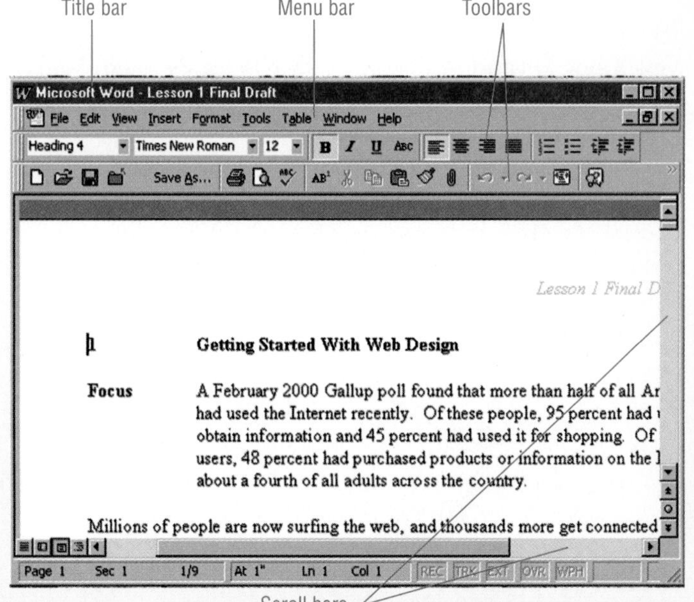

application programs that run under the *Microsoft® Windows®* operating system (as are icons and other features).

Like desktop icons, **toolbars** offer a convenient way to access frequently used commands. Application programs often have different toolbars for different tasks, like formatting text or creating tables.

If the window contains more material than you can see at once, **scroll bars** may appear at the right and/or bottom. Clicking a scroll bar arrow moves the document in small increments. Clicking a light gray area of a scroll bar moves the document in larger increments. Dragging the dark gray portion of a scroll bar moves the document exactly as much and as fast as you want.

At the right end of the title or menu bar are the Minimize, Maximize, and Close buttons. Clicking the **Minimize button** reduces a window to a button on the taskbar. This is useful when you want to **multitask** (perform more than one task at a time) and do not want to exit a program. To restore the window, click the button on the taskbar.

Clicking the **Maximize button** enlarges a window to take up almost the entire screen. Many people like to maximize application documents to have more room to work.

[2]Microsoft® and Windows® are registered trademarks of Microsoft Corporation in the United States and/or other countries.

Objectives:

1. To learn reach technique for **o** and **t**.
2. To combine smoothly **o** and **t** with all other learned keys.

4A • 8'
Conditioning Practice

Key each line twice SS (slowly, then faster); DS between 2-line groups.

In Lessons 4–8, the time for the *Conditioning Practice* is changed to 8'. During this time, you are to arrange your work area, prepare your equipment for keying, and practice the lines of the *Conditioning Practice* as directed.

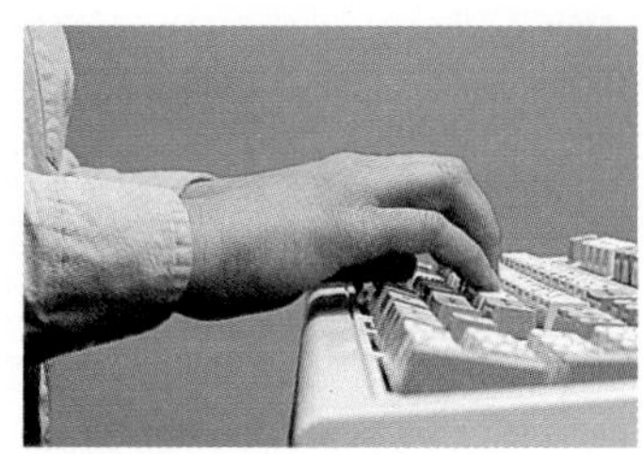

Fingers curved

Fingers upright

home row 1 a sad fall; had a hall; a jak falls; as a fall ad;

3d row 2 if her aid; all he sees; he irks her; a jade fish;

all keys learned 3 as he fell; he sells fir desks; she had half a jar

4B • 20'
New Keys: O and T

Key each line twice SS (slowly, then faster); DS between 2-line groups; if time permits, key lines 7–9 again.

o *Right ring* finger

t *Left index* finger

Follow the *Standard Plan for Learning New Keys* outlined on p. R6.

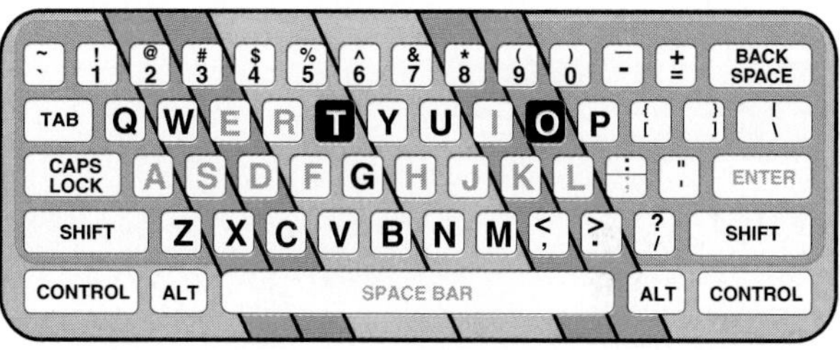

Learn o

1 l l ol ol do do of of so so lo lo old old for fore

2 ol ol of of or or for for oak oak off off sol sole

3 do so; a doe; of old; of oak; old foe; of old oak;

Learn t

4 f f tf tf it it at at tie tie the the fit fit lift

5 tf tf ft ft it it sit sit fit fit hit hit kit kite

6 if it; a fit; it fit; tie it; the fit; at the site

Combine o and t

7 to to | too too | toe toe | dot dot | lot lot | hot hot | tort

8 a lot; to jot; too hot; odd lot; a fort; for a lot

9 of the; to rot; dot it; the lot; for the; for this

Windows® Tutorial

Microsoft® Windows® is an **operating system**, a program that manages all the other programs on a computer. Like other operating systems, *Windows®* provides a **graphical user interface (GUI,** pronounced "gooey") of **icons** (picture symbols) and **menus** (lists of commands).

This tutorial will show you how to use basic *Windows®* features. A few features may look, work, or be named slightly differently on your computer, depending on your operating system version and setup.

THE DESKTOP

After you turn on your computer and it has powered up, it will display the **desktop**, your main working area. The following illustration shows a *Windows® 98* desktop.[1] Your desktop will have many of the same features; but because the desktop is easy to customize, some items will be different.

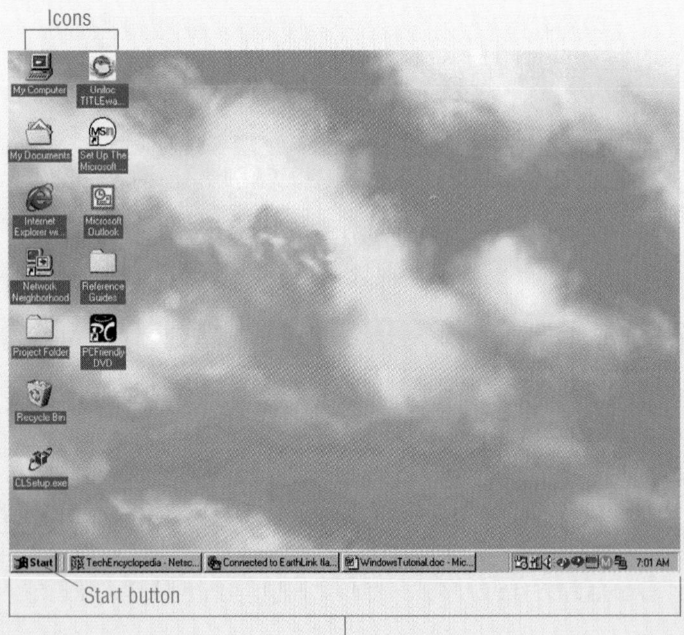

On the desktop, you will see icons and a **taskbar** (a tool for opening programs and navigating on your computer). Icons provide an easy way to access programs and documents that you use frequently. Double-click an icon to open the program, document, or **folder** (storage place for files and other folders) that it represents. (If the single-click option is selected on your computer, you will find that you can click an icon once instead of double-clicking. For more information about this option, open the Help Index—click *Help* on the Start menu—and key **single-click**.)

[1]Windows® is a registered trademark of Microsoft Corporation in the United States and/or other countries.

COMMON DESKTOP ICONS

	**My Computer** shows you the files and folders on your computer, organized by disk drive.
	**Network Neighborhood** lets you see the resources available to you if you are on a computer network.
	**Recycle Bin** contains documents that have been deleted from the hard drive. You may empty the Recycle Bin or restore files deleted in error.
	**Folders** provide a storage place for files and other folders. They are extremely useful in managing files.

The taskbar usually appears at the bottom of the screen. The standard *Windows® 98* taskbar consists of the Start button, a button for each program or document that you have open, and an icon for your computer's internal clock. Your taskbar may have additional icons.

The **Start button** opens the **Start menu**, shown on p. R38. Like a restaurant menu, a software menu offers you choices—commands you can choose. You can accomplish almost any task in *Windows®* from the Start menu.

Note: The *Windows®* operating system requires a mouse or other pointing device. For help with using a mouse, see the Computer Concepts section at the front of this text.

4C • 22'
New-Key Mastery

1. Key the lines once SS; DS between 2-line groups.
2. Key the lines again at a faster pace.

Technique Goals:

- curved, upright fingers
- wrists low, but not resting
- down-and-in spacing
- eyes on copy as you key

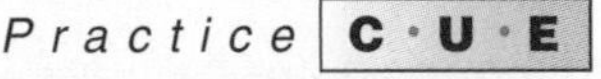
Practice **C · U · E**

In lines of repeated words (lines 3, 5, and 7), speed up the second keying of each word.

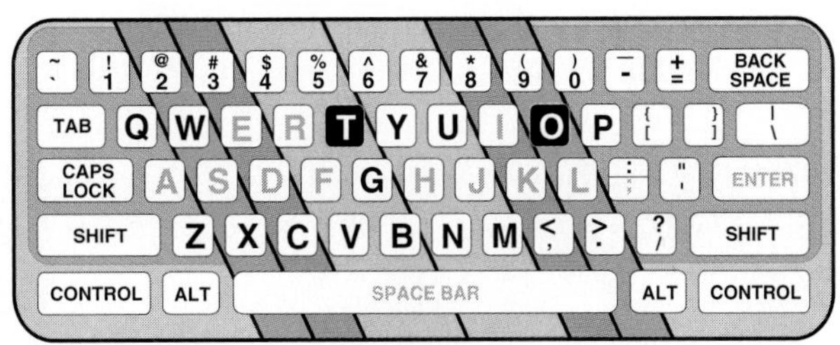

```
reach review
 1 hj ed ik rf ol tf jh de ki fr lo ft hj ed ol rf tf
 2 is led fro hit old fit let kit rod kid dot jak sit

h/e
 3 he he|she she|led led|had had|see see|has has|seek
 4 he led|ask her|she held|has fled|had jade|he leads

i/t
 5 it it|fit fit|tie tie|sit sit|kit kit|its its|fits
 6 a kit|a fit|a tie|lit it|it fits|it sits|it is fit

o/r
 7 or or|for for|ore ore|fro fro|oar oar|roe roe|rode
 8 a rod|a door|a rose|or for|her or|he rode|or a rod

space bar
 9 of he or it is to if do el odd off too for she the
10 it is|if it|do so|if he|to do|or the|she is|of all

all keys learned
11 if she is; ask a lad; to the lake; off the old jet
12 he or she; for a fit; if she left the; a jak salad
```

4D •
Enrichment

1. Key the drill once SS at an easy pace to gain control of all your reach-stroke motions. DS between 2-line groups.
2. Key the drill again to speed up your motions and build continuity.

```
reach review
 1 hj ed ik rf jhj ded kik frf a;sldkfj a;sldkfj fja;
 2 if led ski fir she ire sir jak has did jar kid rid

o/t
 3 ol ol|old old|for for|oak oak|ode ode|doe doe|does
 4 tf tf|it it|to to|kit kit|the the|fit fit|sit sits

i/r
 5 ik ik|if if|it it|fir fir|ski ski|did did|kid kids
 6 rf rf|or or|for for|her her|fir fir|rod rod|or for

h/e
 7 hj hj|he he|ah ah|ha ha|he he|she she|ash ash|hash
 8 ed ed|el el|he he|her her|elk elk|jet jet|she|shed

all keys learned
 9 of hot kit old sit for jet she oak jar ore lid lot
10 a ski; old oak; too hot; odd jar; for the; old jet

all keys learned
11 she is to ski; is for the lad; ask if she has jade
12 he sold leeks to her; she sells jade at their lake
```

FINGER GYMNASTICS

Brief daily practice of finger gymnastics will strengthen your finger muscles and increase the ease with which you key. Begin each keying period with this conditioning exercise. Choose two or more drills for this practice.

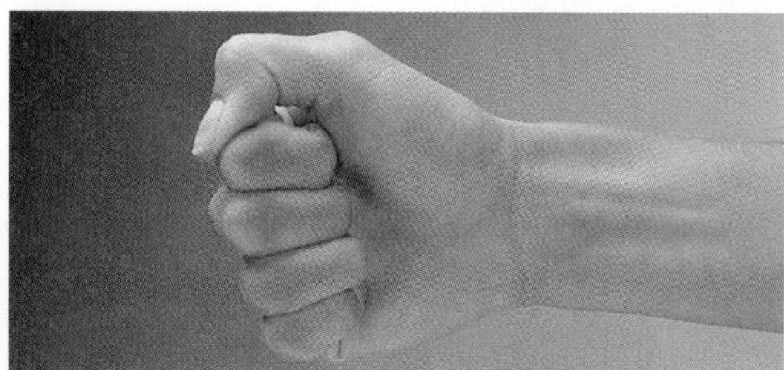

DRILL 1. Hands open, fingers wide, muscles tense. Close the fingers into a tight fist, with thumb on top. Relax the fingers as you straighten them. Repeat ten times.

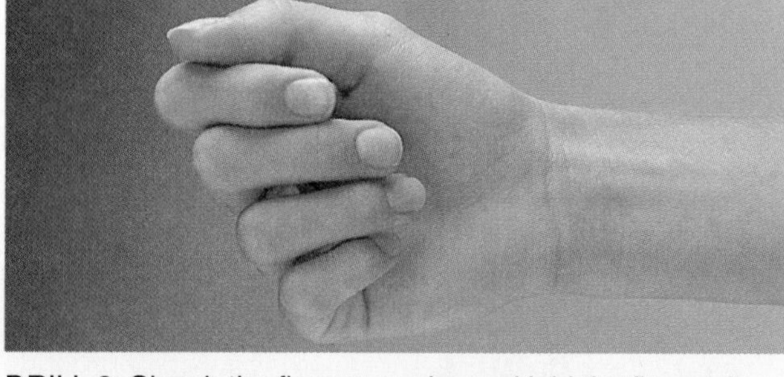

DRILL 2. Clench the fingers as shown. Hold the fingers in this position for a brief time; then extend the fingers, relaxing the muscles of fingers and hand. Repeat the movements slowly several times. Exercise both hands at the same time.

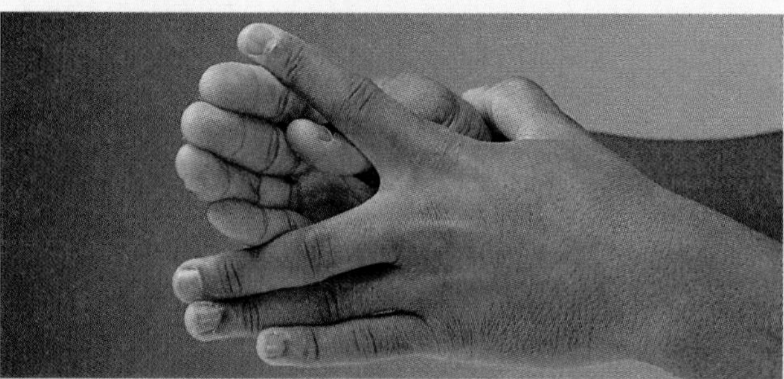

DRILL 3. Place the fingers and thumb of one hand between two fingers of the other hand, and spread the fingers as much as possible. Spread all fingers of both hands.

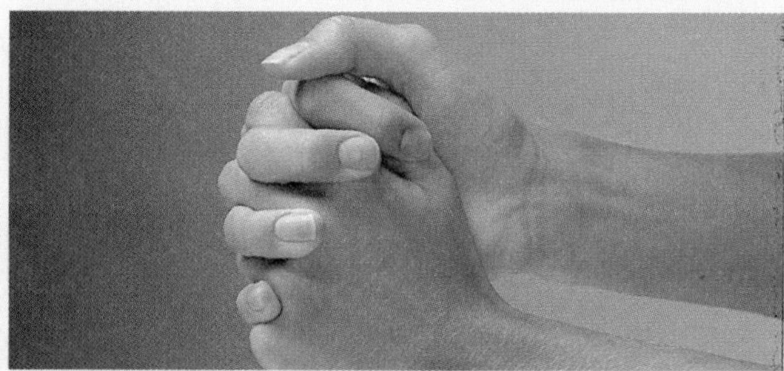

DRILL 4. Interlace the fingers of the two hands and wring the hands, rubbing the heel of each palm vigorously.

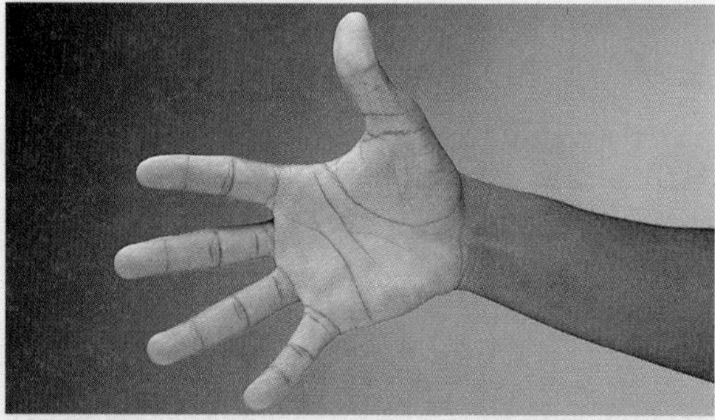

DRILL 5. Spread the fingers as much as possible, holding the position for a moment or two; then relax the fingers and lightly fold them into the palm of the hand. Repeat the movements slowly several times. Exercise both hands at the same time.

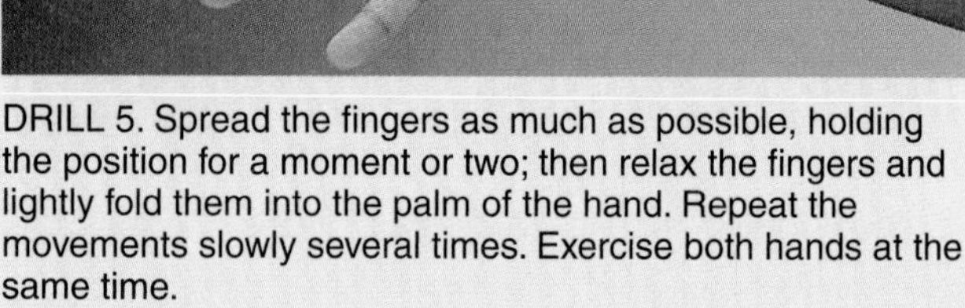

DRILL 6. Rub the hands vigorously. Let the thumb rub the palm of the hand. Rub the fingers, the back of the hand, and the wrist.

DRILL 7. Hold both hands in front of you, fingers together. Hold the last three fingers still and move the first finger as far to the side as possible. Return the first finger; then move the first and second fingers together; finally, move the little finger as far to the side as possible.

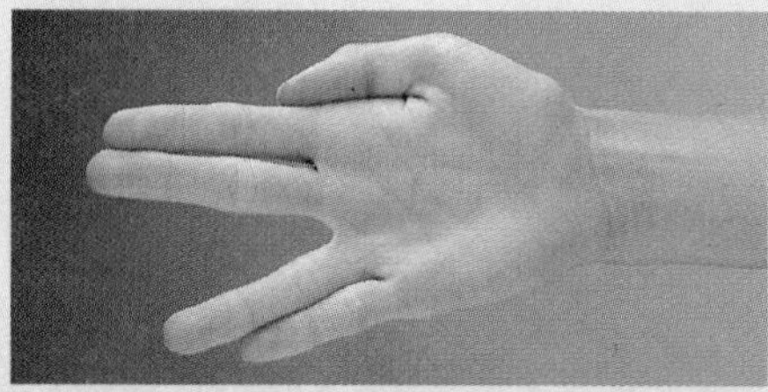

NEW KEYS: n AND g

Objectives:

1. To learn reach technique for **n** and **g**.
2. To combine smoothly **n** and **g** with all other learned keys.

5A • 8'
Conditioning Practice

Key each line twice SS (slowly, then faster); DS between 2-line groups.

```
home row  1 has a jak; ask a lad; a fall fad; had a jak salad;
     o/t  2 to do it; as a tot; do a lot; it is hot; to dot it
   e/i/r  3 is a kid; it is far; a red jar; her skis; her aide
```

5B • 20'
New Keys: N and G

Key each line twice SS (slowly, then faster); DS between 2-line groups; if time permits, key lines 7–9 again.

n *Right index* finger

g *Left index* finger

Follow the *Standard Plan for Learning New Keys* outlined on p. R6.

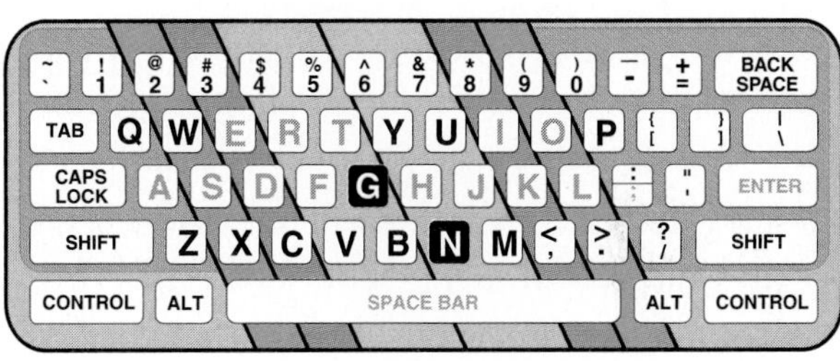

Learn n

```
1 j j nj nj an an and and end end ant ant land lands
2 nj nj an an en en in in on on end end and and hand
3 an en; an end; an ant; no end; on land; a fine end
```

Learn g

```
4 f f gf gf go go fog fog got got fig figs jogs jogs
5 gf gf go go got got dig dig jog jog logs logs golf
6 to go; he got; to jog; to jig; the fog; is to golf
```

Combine n and g

```
7 go go|no no|nag nag|ago ago|gin gin|gone gone|long
8 go on; a nag; sign in; no gain; long ago; into fog
9 a fine gig; log in soon; a good sign; lend a hand;
```

5C • 5'
Technique: Enter Key

Key each line twice SS; DS between 2-line groups.

Practice **C • U • E**

Keep up your pace to the end of line, strike the ENTER key quickly, and start the new line without pause.

```
1 she is gone;
2 she got an old dog;
3 she jogs in a dense fog;
4 she and he go to golf at nine;
5 he is a hand on a rig in the north;
```

Reach out and tap ENTER.

directly in front of the chair. The front edge should be even with the edge of the table or desk.

Place the monitor for easy viewing. Some experts maintain that the top of the screen should be at or slightly below eye level. Others recommend placing the monitor even lower. Set it a comfortable distance from your eyes—at least an arm's length away.

Position the monitor to avoid glare (an antiglare filter can help). Close blinds or pull shades as needed. Adjust the brightness and contrast controls, if necessary, for readability. Keep the screen clean with a soft, lint-free cloth and (unless your instructor tells you otherwise) a nonalcohol, nonabrasive cleaning solution or glass cleaner.

If you cannot adjust your equipment and the desk or table is too high, try adjusting your chair. If that does not work, you can sit on a cushion, a coat, or even a stack of books.

Use a straight-backed chair that will not yield when you lean back. The chair should support your lower back (try putting a rolled-up towel or sweater behind you if it does not). The back of your knees should not be pressed against the chair. Use a seat that allows you to keep your feet flat on the floor, or use a footrest. Even a box or a backpack will do.

Position the mouse next to and at the same height as the keyboard and as close to the body as possible. Research has not shown conclusively that one type of pointing device (mouse, trackball, touch pad, stylus, joystick, etc.) is better than another. Whatever you use, make sure your arms, hands, and fingers are relaxed. If you change to a new device, evaluate it carefully first and work up gradually to using it all the time.

Arrange your work material so you can see it easily and maintain good posture. Some experts recommend positioning whatever you look at most often (the monitor or paper material) directly in front of you so you do not have to turn your head to the side while keying.

EXERCISE AND TAKE BREAKS

Exercise your neck, shoulders, arms, wrists, and fingers before beginning to key each day and often during the workday. Finger exercises appear on the next page. Neck, shoulder, wrist, and other exercises appear at the Cornell University ergonomics Web site listed below.

Take a short break at least once an hour. Rest your eyes from time to time as you work by focusing on an object at least 20 feet away. Blink frequently.

USE GOOD POSTURE AND PROPER TECHNIQUES

Sit erect and as far back in the seat as possible. Your forearms should be parallel to the slant of the keyboard, your wrists and forearms low, but not touching or resting on any surface. Your arms should be near the side of your body in a relaxed position. Your shoulders should not be raised, but should be in a natural posture.

Keep your fingers curved and upright over the home keys. Strike each key lightly using the finger*tip*. Grasp the mouse loosely. Make a conscious effort to relax your hands and shoulders while keying.

For more information on mouse and keyboard use and CTS/RSI, visit the following Internet sites:

- http://kidshealth.org/kid/ (search for *ergonomics*)
- http://www.tifaq.org
- http://www.berkeley.edu (locate the Ergonomics Program and look for Computer Use Tips)
- http://www.office-ergo.com
- http://www.cornell.edu (search for *ergonomics*)

Ergonomic Keyboards

Ergonomic keyboards (see illustration at left) are designed to improve hand posture and make keying more comfortable. Generally they have a split design with left and right banks of keys and the ability to tilt or rotate the keyboard for comfort. More research is needed to determine just how effective ergonomic keyboards are in preventing RSI injuries and carpal tunnel syndrome.

5D • 17'
New-Key Mastery

1. Key the lines once SS; DS between 2-line groups.
2. Key the lines again at a faster pace.

Technique Goals:

- curved, upright fingers
- wrists low, but not resting
- quick-snap keystrokes
- down-and-in spacing
- eyes on copy as you key

reach review
1 a;sldkfj ed ol rf hj tf nj gf lo de jh ft nj fr a;
2 he jogs; an old ski; do a log for; she left a jar;

n/g
3 an an|go go|in in|dig dig|and and|got got|end ends
4 go to; is an; log on; sign it; and golf; fine figs

space bar
5 if if|an an|go go|of of|or or|he he|it it|is is|do
6 if it is|is to go|he or she|to do this|of the sign

all keys learned
7 she had an old oak desk; a jell jar is at the side
8 he has left for the lake; she goes there at eight;

all keys learned
9 she said he did it for her; he is to take the oars
10 sign the list on the desk; go right to the old jet

5E •
Enrichment

Key each line twice SS; DS between 2-line groups; QS after lines 3, 7, and 12.

lines 1–3:

- curved, upright fingers
- steady, easy pace

lines 4–7:

- space immediately after each word
- down-and-in motion of thumb

lines 8–12:

- maintain pace to end of line
- strike ENTER key quickly
- start new line immediately

lines 13–16:

- speed up second keying of each repeated word or phrase
- think words, not each letter

Reach review

1 nj nj gf gf ol ol tf tf ik ik rf rf hj hj ed ed fj
2 go fog an and got end jog ant dog ken fig fin find
3 go an on and lag jog flag land glad lend sign hand

Space Bar

4 if an it go is of do or to as in so no off too gin
5 ah ha he or if an too for and she jog got hen then
6 he is to go|if it is so|is to do it|if he is to go
7 she is to ski on the lake; he is also at the lake;

Enter key

8 he is to go;
9 she is at an inn;
10 he goes to ski at one;
11 he is also to sign the log;
12 she left the log on the old desk

Short words and phrases

13 do do|it it|an an|is is|of of|to to|if if|or or or
14 he he|go go|in in|so so|at at|no no|as as|ha ha ha
15 to do|to do|it is|it is|of it|of it|is to|is to do
16 she is to do so; he did the sign; ski at the lake;

Repetitive Stress Injury

Repetitive stress injury (RSI) is a result of repeated movement of a particular part of the body. It is also known as repetitive motion injury, musculoskeletal disorder, cumulative trauma disorder, and by a host of other names. A familiar example of RSI is "tennis elbow." RSI is the number-one occupational illness, costing employers more than $40 billion a year in health-care fees and lost wages.

Of concern to keyboard and mouse users is the form of RSI called **carpal tunnel syndrome** (CTS). CTS is an inflammatory disease that develops gradually and affects the wrists, hands, and forearms. Blood vessels, tendons, and nerves pass into the hand through the carpal tunnel (see illustration below). If any of these structures enlarge, or the walls of the tunnel narrow, the median nerve is pinched and CTS symptoms may result.

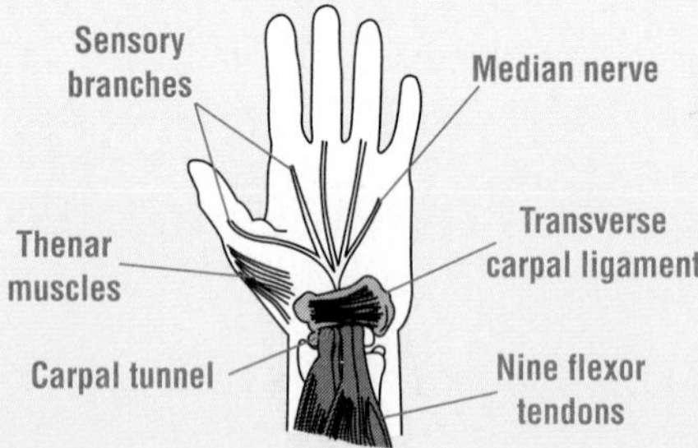

Palm view of left hand

SYMPTOMS OF RSI/CTS

CTS symptoms include numbness in the hand; tingling or burning in the hand, wrist, or elbow; severe pain in the forearm, elbow, or shoulder; and difficulty in gripping objects. Symptoms usually appear during sleeping hours, probably because many people sleep with their wrists flexed.

If not properly treated, the pressure on the median nerve, which controls the thumb, forefinger, middle finger, and half the ring finger, causes severe pain. The pain can radiate into the forearm, elbow, or shoulder. There are many kinds of treatment, ranging from simply resting to surgery. Left untreated, CTS can result in permanent damage or paralysis.

The good news is that 99 percent of people with carpal tunnel syndrome recover completely. Computer users can avoid reinjuring themselves by taking the precautions discussed later in this article.

CAUSES OF RSI/CTS

RSI/CTS often develops in workers whose physical routine is unvaried. Common occupational factors include (1) using awkward posture, (2) using poor techniques, (3) performing tasks with wrists bent (see below), (4) using improper equipment, (5) working at a rapid pace, (6) not taking rest breaks, and (7) not doing exercises that promote graceful motion and good techniques.

RSI/CTS is not limited to workers or adults. Keying school assignments, playing computer or video games, and surfing the Internet are increasing the incidence of RSI/CTS in younger people.

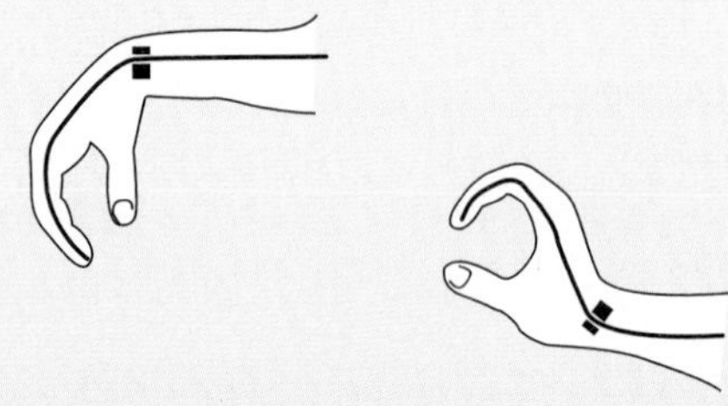

Improper wrist positions for keystroking

CTS is frequently a health concern for people who use a computer keyboard or mouse. The risk of developing CTS is less for those who use proper furniture or equipment, keyboarding techniques, posture, and/or muscle-stretching exercises than for those who do not.

REDUCING THE RISK OF RSI/CTS

By taking the following precautions, keyboard and mouse users can reduce the risk of developing RSI/CTS and can keep it from recurring. Experts stress that good computer habits like these are very important in avoiding RSI/CTS. They can also help you avoid back, neck, and shoulder pain, and eyestrain.

ARRANGE THE WORK AREA

Arrange your equipment in a way that is natural and comfortable for you. Position the keyboard at elbow height and

LESSON 6 — NEW KEYS: left shift AND period (.)

Objectives:

1. To learn reach technique for **left shift** and . (period).
2. To combine smoothly **left shift** and . (period) with all other learned keys.

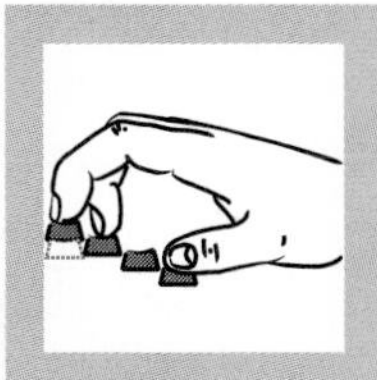

Finger-action keystrokes

Down-and-in spacing

Quick out-and-tap ENTER

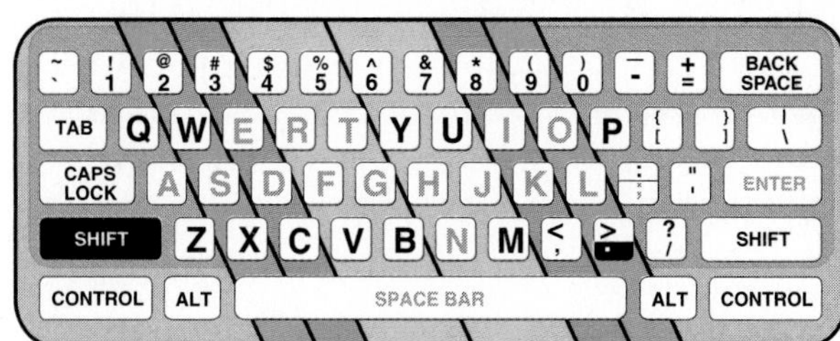

6A • 8' Conditioning Practice

Key each line twice SS (slowly, then faster); DS between 2-line groups.

reach review — 1 ed ik rf ol gf hj tf nj de ki fr lo fg jh ft jn a;

space bar — 2 or is to if an of el so it go id he do as in at on

all letters learned — 3 he is; if an; or do; to go; a jak; an oak; of all;

6B • 20' New Keys: Left Shift and .

Key each line twice SS (slowly, then faster); DS between 2-line groups; if time permits, repeat lines 7–9.

Left shift *Left little* finger

. (period) *Right ring* finger

Shifting **CUE**

Shift, strike key, and release both in a quick 1-2-3 count.

Learn left shift key

1 a a Ja Ja Ka Ka La La Hal Hal Kal Kal Jae Jae Lana

2 Kal rode; Kae did it; Hans has jade; Jan ate a fig

3 I see that Jake is to aid Kae at the Oak Lake sale

Learn . (period)

4 l l .l .l fl. fl. ed. ed. ft. ft. rd. rd. hr. hrs.

5 .l .l fl. fl. hr. hr. e.g. e.g. i.e. i.e. in. ins.

6 fl. ft. hr. ed. rd. rt. off. fed. ord. alt. asstd.

Combine left shift and . (period)

7 I do. Ian is. Ola did. Jan does. Kent is gone.

8 Hal did it. I shall do it. Kate left on a train.

9 J. L. Han skis on Oak Lake; Lt. Haig also does so.

Spacing **CUE**

Space once after . following abbreviations and initials. Do not space after . within abbreviations. Space twice after . at end of a sentence except at line endings. There, return without spacing.

15D • 10'
New Key: Tab

The TAB key is used to indent the first line of ¶s. Word processing software has preset tabs called *default* tabs. Usually, the first default tab is set 0.5" to the right of the left margin and is used to indent ¶s (see copy at right).

1. Locate the TAB key on your keyboard (usually at upper left of alphabetic keyboard).
2. Reach up to the TAB key with the left little finger; strike the key firmly and release it quickly. The insertion point will move 0.5" to the right.
3. Key each ¶ once SS. DS between ¶s. As you key, strike the TAB key firmly to indent the first line of each ¶.
4. If you complete all ¶s before time is called, rekey them to master TAB key technique.

Tab key *Left little* finger

```
Tab ⟶ The tab key is used to indent blocks of copy
such as these.
Tab ⟶ It can also be used to arrange data quickly
and neatly into columns.
Tab ⟶ Learn now to use the tab key by touch; doing
so will add to your keying skill.
Tab ⟶ Strike the tab key firmly and release it very
quickly.  Begin the line without a pause.
Tab ⟶ If you hold the tab key down, the insertion
point will move from tab to tab across the line.
```

15E • 15'
Keyboard Reinforcement

1. Key the lines once SS; DS between 3-line groups.
2. Key lines 1–9 again at a faster pace.
3. Key a 1' writing on lines 10–12.

Reach review (Keep on home keys the fingers not used for reaching.)

```
1 old led kit six jay oft zap cod big laws five ribs
2 pro quo|is just|my firm|was then|may grow|must try
3 Olga sews aqua and red silk to make six big kites.
```

Space Bar emphasis (*Think*, *say*, and *key* the words.)

```
4 en am an by ham fan buy jam pay may form span corn
5 I am|a man|an elm|by any|buy ham|can plan|try them
6 I am to form a plan to buy a firm in the old town.
```

Shift key emphasis (Reach *up* and reach *down* without moving the hands.)

```
7 Jan and I are to see Ms. Han.  May Lana come, too?
8 Bob Epps lives in Rome; Vic Copa is in Rome, also.
9 Oates and Co. has a branch office in Boise, Idaho.
```

Easy sentences (*Think*, *say*, and *key* the words at a steady pace.)

```
10 Eight of the girls may go to the social with them.
11 Corla is to work with us to fix the big dock sign.
12 Keith is to pay the six men for the work they did.
```

gwam 1' | 1 | 2 | 3 | 4 | 5 | 6 | 7 | 8 | 9 | 10 |

6C • 17'
New-Key Mastery

1. Key the lines once SS; DS between 2-line groups.
2. Key the lines again at a faster pace.

Technique Goals:

- curved, upright fingers
- finger-action keystrokes
- quiet hands/arms
- out-and-down shifting

Technique **C • U • E**

Eyes on copy except when you lose your place.

abbrev./initials

1 He said ft. for feet; rd. for road; fl. for floor.
2 Lt. Hahn let L. K. take the old gong to Lake Neil.

3d row emphasis

3 Lars is to ask at the old store for a kite for Jo.
4 Ike said he is to take the old road to Lake Heidi.

key words

5 a an or he to if do it of so is go for got old led
6 go the off aid dot end jar she fit oak and had rod

key phrases

7 if so|it is|to do|if it|do so|to go|he is|to do it
8 to the|and do|is the|got it|if the|for the|ask for

all letters learned

9 Ned asked her to send the log to an old ski lodge.
10 J. L. lost one of the sleds he took off the train.

6D • 5'
Technique: Spacebar and Enter

1. Key each line once SS; DS at end of line 7.
2. Key the drill again at a faster pace if time permits.

Spacing **C • U • E**

Quickly strike Space Bar *immediately* after last letter in the word.

Strike ENTER quickly and start each new line immediately.

1 Jan is to sing.
2 Karl is at the lake.
3 Lena is to send the disk.
4 Lars is to jog to the old inn.
5 Hanna took the girls to a ski lake.
6 Hal is to take the old list to his desk.
7 Lana is to take the jar to the store at nine.

6E •
Enrichment

1. Key each line once SS; DS between 3-line groups.
2. Rekey the drill at a faster pace if time permits.

Spacing/shifting (Use down-and-in spacing; use out-and-down shifting.)

1 K. L. Jakes is to see Lt. Hahn at Oak Lake at one.
2 Janet Harkins sent the sales sheet to Joel Hansen.
3 Karla Kent is to go to London to see Laska Jolson.

Keying easy sentences (Keep insertion point moving steadily—no stops or pauses within the line.)

4 Kae is to go to the lake to fish off an old skiff.
5 Joel is to ask his good friend to go to the shore.
6 Lara and her dad took eight girls for a long hike.
7 Kent said his dad is to sell the oak and ash logs.

LESSON 15 | NEW KEYS: tab key, apostrophe ('), hyphen (-), AND quotation mark (")

Objectives:

1. To learn reach technique for ' (apostrophe), - (hyphen), and " (quotation mark).
2. To learn reach technique for the **tab key**.

15A • 7' Conditioning Practice

Key each line twice SS; then take a 1' writing on line 3; determine *gwam.*

alphabet 1 Quig just fixed prize vases he won at my key club.

spacing 2 Marcia works for HMS, Inc.; Juanita, for XYZ Corp.

easy 3 Su did vow to rid the town of the giant male duck.

gwam 1' | 1 | 2 | 3 | 4 | 5 | 6 | 7 | 8 | 9 | 10 |

15B • 10' New Keys: ', -, and "

Key each line twice SS (slowly, then faster); DS between 2-line groups.

Note:
On your screen, apostrophes and/or quotation marks may look different from those shown in these lines. Whatever their differences in appearance, the marks serve the same purpose.

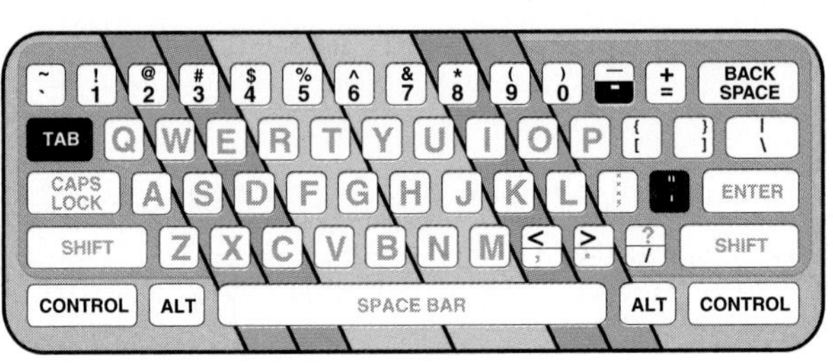

Learn ' (apostrophe)

1 ;; '; '; ;' ;' I've told you it's hers, haven't I?

2 I'm sure it's Jay's. I'll return it if he's home.

3 I've been told it isn't up to us; it's up to them.

Learn - (hyphen)

4 ; - -; -; ;- ;- -; -; -;- -;- We use a 2-ply tire.

5 We have 1-, 2-, and 3-bedroom condos for purchase.

6 He rated each as a 1-star, 2-star, or 3-star film.

Learn " (quotation mark)

7 ;; "; "; ";" ";" "I believe," she said, "you won."

8 "John Adams," he said, "was the second President."

9 "James Monroe," I said, "was the fifth President."

15C • 8' Speed Check: Sentences

1. Key a 30" writing on each line.
2. Key another 30" writing on each line. Try to increase your keying speed.

	gwam 30"
1 He bid for the rich lake land.	12
2 Suzy may fish off the dock with us.	14
3 Pay the girls for all the work they did.	16
4 Quen is due by six and may then fix the sign.	18
5 Janie is to vie with six girls for the city title.	20
6 Duane is to go to the lake to fix the auto for the man.	22

30" | 2 | 4 | 6 | 8 | 10 | 12 | 14 | 16 | 18 | 20 | 22 |

LESSON 7 NEW KEYS: u AND c

Objectives:

1. To learn reach technique for **u** and **c.**
2. To combine smoothly **u** and **c** with all other learned keys.

7A • 8'
Conditioning Practice

Key each line twice SS (slowly, then faster); DS between 2-line groups.

```
reach review 1 nj gf ol rf ik ed .l tf hj fr ki ft jn de lo fg l.
space bar    2 an do in so to go fan hen log gin tan son not sign
left shift   3 Olga has the first slot; Jena is to skate for her.
```

7B • 20'
New Keys: U and C

Key each line twice SS (slowly, then faster); DS between 2-line groups: if time permits, repeat lines 7–9.

Follow the *Standard Plan for Learning New Keys* outlined on p. R6.

u *Right index* finger

c *Left middle* finger

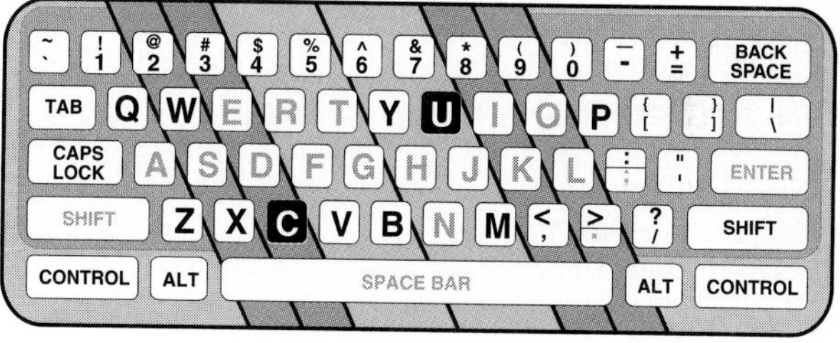

Learn u

```
1 j j uj uj us us us jug jug jut jut due due fur fur
2 uj uj jug jug sue sue lug lug use use lug lug dues
3 a jug; due us; the fur; use it; a fur rug; is just
```

Learn c

```
4 d d cd cd cod cod cog cog tic tic cot cot can cans
5 cd cd cod cod ice ice can can code code dock docks
6 a cod; a cog; the ice; she can; the dock; the code
```

Combine u and c

```
7 cud cud cut cuts cur curs cue cues duck ducks clue
8 a cud; a cur; to cut; the cue; the cure; for luck;
9 use a clue; a fur coat; take the cue; cut the cake
10 Jake told us there is ice on the road to the lake.
11 Jack asked us for a list of all the codes he used.
12 Louise has gone to cut the cake on the green cart.
```

14C • 18'
New-Key Mastery

1. Key the lines once SS; DS between 2-line groups.
2. Key the lines again at a faster pace.
3. Key a 1' writing on line 11 and then on line 12; determine *gwam* on each writing.

Technique **C • U • E**

- Reach *up* without moving hands away from your body.
- Reach *down* without moving hands toward your body.
- Use Caps Lock to make ALL CAPS.

To determine 1' *gwam*: Add 10 for each line you completed to the scale figure beneath the point at which you stopped in a partial line.

Goal: finger-action keystrokes; quiet hands and arms

caps lock/?
1 Did she join OEA? Did she also join PSI and DECA?
2 Do you know the ARMA rules? Are they used by TVA?

z/v
3 Zahn, key these words: vim, zip, via, zoom, vote.
4 Veloz gave a zany party for Van and Roz in La Paz.

q/p
5 Paul put a quick quiz on top of the quaint podium.
6 Jacqi may pick a pink pique suit of a unique silk.

key words
7 they quiz pick code next just more bone wove flags
8 name jack flax plug quit zinc wore busy vine third

key phrases
9 to fix it|is to pay|to aid us|or to cut|apt to own
10 is on the|if we did|to be fit|to my pay|due at six

easy
11 Lock may join the squad if we have six big prizes.
12 I am apt to go to the lake dock to sign the forms.

gwam 1' | 1 | 2 | 3 | 4 | 5 | 6 | 7 | 8 | 9 | 10 |

14D • 9'
Block Paragraphs

1. Key each ¶ once, using wordwrap (soft returns) if available. The lines you key will be longer than the lines shown if default side margins are used.
2. If time permits, key a 1' writing on one or two of the ¶s.

Note:

Clearing the screen from time to time between 1' writings avoids confusion when determining *gwam*. Learn how to clear the screen on your software.

	gwam 1'
Paragraph 1	
When you key lines of drills, strike the return or	10
enter key at the end of each line. That is, use a	20
hard return to space down for a new line.	29
Paragraph 2	
When you key copy in this form, though, you do not	10
need to strike return at the end of each line if a	20
machine has wordwrap or a soft return feature.	30
Paragraph 3	
But even if your machine returns at line ends for	10
you, you have to strike the return or enter key at	20
the end of a paragraph to leave a line blank.	30
Paragraph 4	
Learn now when you do not need to return at ends	10
of lines and when you must do so. Doing this now	20
will assure that your copy will be in proper form.	30

gwam 1' | 1 | 2 | 3 | 4 | 5 | 6 | 7 | 8 | 9 | 10 |

7C • 17'
New-Key Mastery

1. Key the lines once SS; DS between 2-line groups.
2. Key the lines again at a faster pace.

Technique Goals:

- Reach up without moving hands away from your body.
- Reach down without moving hands toward your body.
- Use quick-snap keystrokes.

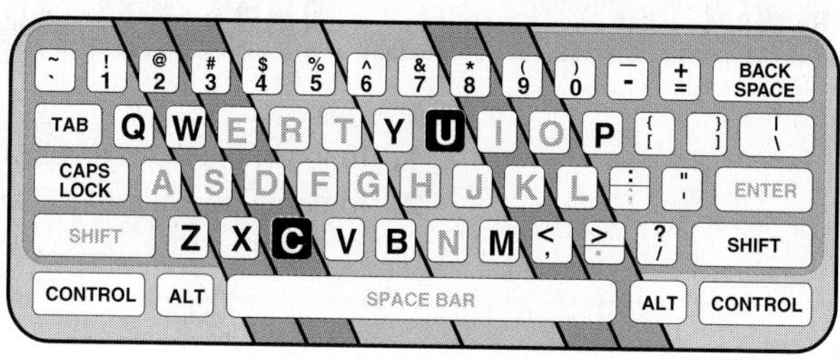

3d/1st rows
1 in cut nut ran cue can cot fun hen car urn den cog
2 Nan is cute; he is curt; turn a cog; he can use it

left shift and .
3 Kae had taken a lead. Jack then cut ahead of her.
4 I said to use Kan. for Kansas and Ore. for Oregon.

key words
5 and cue for jut end kit led old fit just golf coed
6 an due cut such fuss rich lack turn dock turf curl

key phrases
7 an urn|is due|to cut|for us|to use|cut off|such as
8 just in|code it|turn on|cure it|as such|is in luck

all keys learned
9 Nida is to get the ice; Jacki is to call for cola.
10 Ira is sure that he can go there in an hour or so.

7D • 5'
Technique: Spacebar and Left Shift

Key the lines once SS; DS between 3-line groups. Keep hand movement to a minimum.

space bar
1 Ken said he is to sign the list and take the disk.
2 It is right for her to take the lei if it is hers.
3 Jae has gone to see an old oaken desk at the sale.

left shift
4 He said to enter Oh. for Ohio and Kan. for Kansas.
5 It is said that Lt. Li has an old jet at Lake Ida.
6 L. N. is at the King Hotel; Harl is at the Leland.

7E •
Enrichment

1. Key each line once SS; DS between 2-line groups.
2. If time permits, key the lines again at a faster pace.

Practice **C • U • E**

Try to reduce hand movement and the tendency of unused fingers to fly out or follow the reaching finger.

u/c
1 uj cd uc juj dcd cud cut use cog cue urn curl luck
2 Huck can use the urn for the social at the church.

n/g
3 nj gf nj gin can jog nick sign nigh snug rung clog
4 Nan can jog to the large sign at the old lake gin.

all keys learned
5 nj gf uj cd ol tf ik rf hj ed an go or is to he l.
6 Leona has gone to ski; Jack had left here at nine.

all keys learned
7 an or is to he go cue for and jak she all use curt
8 Nick sells jade rings; Jahn got one for good luck.

LESSON 14 | NEW KEYS: caps lock AND question mark (?)

Objectives:

1. To learn reach technique for **Caps Lock** and **?** (question mark).
2. To combine smoothly **Caps Lock** and **?** (question mark) with other learned keys.

14A • 7' Conditioning Practice

Key each line twice SS; then key a 1' writing on line 3; determine *gwam.*

```
alphabet 1 Lovak won the squad prize cup for sixty big jumps.
      z/: 2 To:  Ms. Mazie Pelzer; From:  Dr. Eliza J. Piazzo.
     easy 3 He is to go with me to the dock to do work for us.
gwam 1' |  1  |  2  |  3  |  4  |  5  |  6  |  7  |  8  |  9  |  10  |
```

14B • 16' New Keys: Caps Lock and ?

Key each line twice SS (slowly, then faster); DS between 2-line groups; if time permits, key lines 7–9 again.

Caps Lock
Left little finger

? (question mark)
Left shift; then *right little* finger

Depress the Caps Lock key to key a series of capital letters. To release the Caps Lock to key lowercase letters, press the Caps Lock key again.

Learn Caps Lock

```
1 Hal read PENTAGON and ADVISE AND CONSENT by Drury.
2 Oki joined FBLA when her sister joined PBL at OSU.
3 Zoe now belongs to AMS and DPE as well as to NBEA.
```

Learn ? (question mark)

Space twice.

```
4 ; ; ?; ?; Who?  What?  When?  Where?  Why?  Is it?
5 Who is it?  Is it she?  Did he go?  Was she there?
6 Is it up to me?  When is it?  Did he key the line?
```

Combine Caps Lock and ?

```
7 Did he join a CPA firm?  I will stay on with NASA.
8 Is her dad still CEO at BSFA?  Or was he made COB?
9 Did you read HOMEWARD?  If so, try WHIRLWIND next.
10 Did Julie fly to Kansas City, MISSOURI, or KANSAS?
11 Did Dr. Sylvester pay her DPE, PBL, and NBEA dues?
12 Did you say go TWO blocks EAST or TWO blocks WEST?
```

LESSON 8 NEW KEYS: w AND right shift

Objectives:

1. To learn reach technique for **w** and **right shift**.
2. To combine smoothly **w** and **right shift** with other learned keys.

8A • 8' Conditioning Practice

Key each line twice SS (slowly, then faster); DS between 2-line groups.

reach review 1 rf gf de ju jn ki lo cd ik rf .l ed hj tf ol gf ft

u/c 2 us cod use cut sue cot jut cog nut cue con lug ice

all letters learned 3 Hugh has just taken a lead in a race for a record.

8B • 20' New Keys: W and Right Shift

Key each line twice SS (slowly, then faster); DS between 2-line groups; if time permits, repeat lines 7–9.

w *Left ring* finger

Right shift *Right little* finger

Shifting **C·U·E**

Shift, strike key, and release both in a quick 1-2-3 count.

Follow the *Standard Plan for Learning New Keys* outlined on p. R6.

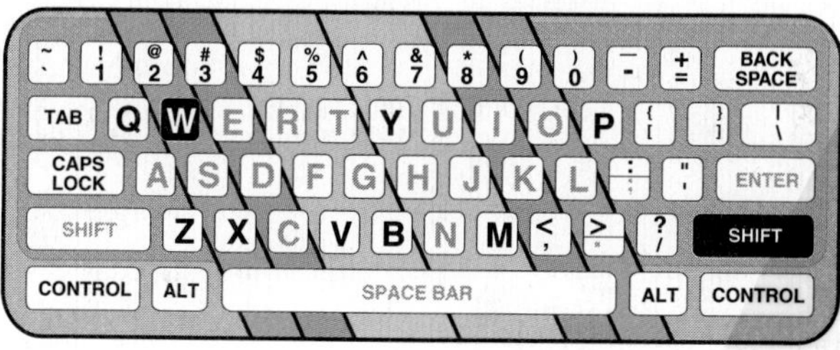

Learn w

1 s s ws ws sow sow wow wow low low how how cow cows

2 sw sw ws ws ow ow now now row row own own tow tows

3 to sow; is how; so low; to own; too low; is to row

Learn right shift key

4 A; A; Al Al; Cal Cal; Ali or Flo; Di and Sol left.

5 Ali lost to Ron; Cal lost to Elsa; Di lost to Del.

6 Tina has left for Tucson; Dori can find her there.

Combine w and right shift

7 Dodi will ask if Willa went to Town Center at two.

8 Wilf left the show for which he won a Gower Award.

9 Walt will go to Rio on a golf tour with Wolf Lowe.

10 Wilton and Donna asked to go to the store with us.

11 Walter left us at Willow Lake with Will and Frank.

12 Ted or Walt will get us tickets for the two shows.

13C • 15'
New-Key Mastery

1. Key the lines once SS; DS between 2-line groups.
2. Key the lines again at a faster pace.

Technique Goals:

- curved, upright fingers
- quiet hands and arms
- steady keystroking pace

```
      1  zoo qt. zap quo zeal quay zone quit maze quad hazy
q/z   2  Zeno amazed us all on the quiz but quit the squad.

      3  apt six rip fix pens flex open flax drop next harp
p/x   4  Lex is apt to fix apple pie for the next six days.

      5  vim mam van dim have move vamp more dive time five
v/m   6  Riva drove them to the mall in my vivid lemon van.

      7  Glen is to aid me with the work at the dog kennel.
easy  8  Dodi is to go with the men to audit the six firms.

          9  Nigel saw a quick red fox jump over the lazy cubs.
alphabet 10  Jacky can now give six big tips from the old quiz.
```

13D • 10'
Block Paragraphs

1. Key each paragraph (¶) once SS; DS between them; then key them again faster.
2. If your instructor directs, key a 1' writing on each ¶; determine your *gwam*.

Paragraph 1 gwam 1'

```
The space bar is a vital tool, for every fifth or      10
sixth stroke is a space when you key.  If you use      20
it with good form, it will aid you to build speed.     30
```

Paragraph 2

```
Just keep the thumb low over the space bar.  Move      10
the thumb down and in quickly toward your palm to      20
get the prized stroke you need to build top skill.     30
```

gwam 1' | 1 | 2 | 3 | 4 | 5 | 6 | 7 | 8 | 9 | 10 |

13E •
Enrichment

1. Key each line once at a steady, easy pace to master reaches.
2. Key each line again at a faster pace.

Technique Goals:

- Keep fingers upright.
- Keep hands/arms steady.

```
     1 xs :;|fix mix|Max:  Use TO: and FROM: as headings.
x/:  2 Read and key:  oxen, exit, axle, sixty, and sixth.

     3 qa ,k|aqa k,k|quo quo,|qt. qt.,|quite quite,|squat
q/,  4 Quen, key these:  quit, aqua, equal, quiet, quick.

     5 p; za|;p; zaza|zap zap|zip zip|size size|lazy lazy
p/z  6 Zip put hot pepper on his pizza at the zany plaza.

     7 mj vf|jmj fvf|vim vim|vow vow|menu menu move movie
m/v  8 Mavis vowed to move with a lot more vim and vigor.
```

8C • 17'
New-Key Mastery

1. Key the lines once SS; DS between 2-line groups.
2. Key the lines again at a faster pace.

Key at a steady pace; space quickly after each word.

Goal: finger action reaches; quiet hands and arms

w and right shift
1 Dr. Rowe is in Tulsa now; Dr. Cowan will see Rolf.
2 Gwinn took the gown to Golda Swit on Downs Circle.

n/g
3 to go|go on|no go|an urn|dug in|and got|and a sign
4 He is to sign for the urn to go on the high chest.

key words
5 if ow us or go he an it of own did oak the cut jug
6 do all and for cog odd ant fig rug low cue row end

key phrases
7 we did|for a jar|she is due|cut the oak|he owns it
8 all of us|to own the|she is to go|when he has gone

all keys learned
9 Jan and Chris are gone; Di and Nick get here soon.
10 Doug will work for her at the new store in Newton.

8D • 5'
Technique: Spacing with Punctuation

Key each line once DS.

Spacing **C · U · E**

Do not space after an internal period in an abbreviation; space once after each period following initials.

No space — Space once.

1 Use i.e. for that is; cs. for case; ck. for check.
2 Dr. Wong said to use wt. for weight; in. for inch.
3 R. D. Roth has used ed. for editor; Rt. for Route.
4 Wes said Ed Rowan got an Ed.D. degree last winter.

8E •
Enrichment

1. Key each pair of lines once SS.
2. Key each even-numbered line again to increase speed.

Technique Goals:

- steady hands/arms
- finger-action keystrokes
- unused fingers curved, upright over home keys
- eyes on copy as you key

u/c
1 uj cd uc cut cut cue cue use use cod cod dock dock
2 Jud is to cut the corn near the dock for his aunt.

w and right shift
3 Don and Willa|Dot or Wilda|R. W. Gowan|Dr. Wilford
4 Dr. Wold will set the wrist of Sgt. Wills at noon.

left shift and .
5 Jane or Karl|Jae and Nan|L. N. Hagel|Lt. J. O. Hao
6 Lt. Hawser said that he will see us in New London.

n/g
7 nj gf ng gun gun nag nag got got nor nor sign sign
8 Angie hung a huge sign in front of the union hall.

o/t
9 ol tf to too dot dot not not toe toe got gild gild
10 Todd took the tool chest to the dock for a worker.

i/r
11 ik rf or ore fir fir sir sir ire ire ice ice irons
12 Risa fired the fir log to heat rice for the girls.

h/e
13 hj ed he the the hen hen when when then then their
14 He was with her when she chose her new snow shoes.

LESSON 13 NEW KEYS: z AND colon (:)

Objectives:

1. To learn reach technique for **z** and : (colon).
2. To combine smoothly **z** and : (colon) with all other learned keys.

13A • 7' Conditioning Practice

Key each line twice SS; then key a 1' writing on line 3; determine *gwam.*

all letters learned	1	Jim won the globe for six quick sky dives in Napa.
spacing	2	to own | is busy | if they | to town | by them | to the city
easy	3	She is to go to the city with us to sign the form.

gwam 1' | 1 | 2 | 3 | 4 | 5 | 6 | 7 | 8 | 9 | 10 |

13B • 18' New Keys: Z and :

Key each line twice SS (slowly, then faster); DS between 2-line groups; if time permits, key lines 7–10 again.

z *Left little* finger

: *Left shift* and strike *:* key

Follow the *Standard Plan for Learning New Keys* outlined on p. R6.

Learn z

1 a a za za zap zap zap zoo zoo zip zip zag zag zany

2 za za zap zap zed zed oz. oz. zoo zoo zip zip maze

3 zap it, zip it, an adz, to zap, the zoo, eight oz.

Learn : (colon)

4 ; ; :; :; Date: Time: Name: Room: From: File:

5 :; :; To: File: Reply to: Dear Al: Shift for :

6 Two spaces follow a colon, thus: Try these steps:

Combine z and :

7 Zelda has an old micro with : where ; ought to be.

8 Zoe, use as headings: To: Zone: Date: Subject:

9 Liza, please key these words: zap, maze, and zoo.

10 Zane read: Shift to enter : and then space twice.

Language Skills **C • U • E**

- Space twice after : used as punctuation.
- Capitalize the first word of a complete sentence following a colon.

LESSON 9 NEW KEYS: b AND y

Objectives:

1. To learn reach technique for **b** and **y**.
2. To combine smoothly **b** and **y** with all other learned keys.

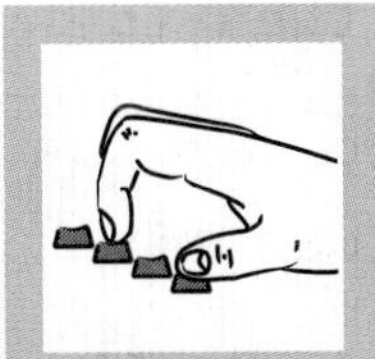

Fingers curved

Fingers upright

9A • 7' Conditioning Practice

Key each line twice SS (slowly, then faster); DS between 2-line groups.

reach review
1 uj ws ik rf ol cd nj ed hj tf .l gf sw ju de lo fr

c/n
2 an can and cut end cue hen cog torn dock then sick

all letters learned
3 A kid had a jug of fruit on his cart in New Delhi.

9B • 5' Technique: Spacebar

Key each line once.

Technique Goal:

Space with a down-and-in motion immediately after each word.

1 He will take an old urn to an art sale at the inn.
2 Ann has an old car she wants to sell at this sale.
3 Len is to work for us for a week at the lake dock.
4 Gwen is to sign for the auto we set aside for her.
5 Jan is in town for just one week to look for work.
6 Juan said he was in the auto when it hit the tree.

9C • 4' Technique: Enter

1. Key each line once SS; at the end of each line quickly press the ENTER key and immediately start new line.
2. On line 4, see how many words you can key in 30 seconds (30").

A **standard word** in keyboarding is five characters or any combination of five characters and spaces, as indicated by the number scale under line 4 at the right. The number of standard words keyed in 1' is called **gross words a minute** *(gwam)*.

1 Dot is to go at two.
2 He saw that it was a good law.
3 Rilla is to take the auto into the town.
4 Wilt has an old gold jug he can enter in the show.

gwam 1' | 1 | 2 | 3 | 4 | 5 | 6 | 7 | 8 | 9 | 10 |

To find 1-minute (1') *gwam*:

1. Note on the scale the figure beneath the last word you keyed. That is your 1' *gwam* if you key the line partially or only once.
2. If you completed the line once and started over, add 10 to the figure determined in Step 1. The result is your 1' *gwam.*

To find 30-second (30") *gwam*:

1. Find 1' *gwam* (total words keyed).
2. Multiply 1' *gwam* by 2. The resulting figure is your 30" *gwam.*

12C • 17'
New-Key Mastery

1. Key the lines once SS; DS between 2-line groups.
2. Key the lines again at a faster pace.

Technique Goals:

- Reach up without moving hands away from your body.
- Reach down without moving hands toward your body.
- Use quick-snap keystrokes.

Goal: finger-action keystrokes; quiet hands and arms

reach review
1 qa .l ws ,k ed nj rf mj tf p; xs ol cd ik vf hj bf
2 yj gf hj quo vie pay cut now buy got mix vow forms

3d/1st rows
3 six may sun coy cue mud jar win via pick turn bike
4 to go | to win | for me | a peck | a quay | by then | the vote

key words
5 pa rub sit man for own fix jam via cod oak the got
6 by quo sub lay apt mix irk pay when rope give just

key phrases
7 an ox | of all | is to go | if he is | it is due | to pay us
8 if we pay | is of age | up to you | so we own | she saw me

all letters learned
9 Jevon will fix my pool deck if the big rain quits.
10 Verna did fly quick jets to map the six big towns.

12D • 6'
Technique: Spacing with Punctuation

Key each line once DS.

Spacing **C • U • E**

Space once after , and ; used as punctuation.

Space once.

1 Aqua means water, Quen; also, it is a unique blue.
2 Quince, enter qt. for quart; also, sq. for square.
3 Ship the desk c.o.d. to Dr. Quig at La Quinta Inn.
4 Q. J. took squid and squash; Monique, roast quail.

12E •
Enrichment

1. Key each line once at a steady, easy pace to master reachstrokes.
2. Key each line again at a faster pace.

Technique Goals:

lines 1–3: fingers upright

lines 4–6: hands/arms steady

lines 7–9: two quick taps of each double letter

Adjacent keys

1 re io as lk rt jk df op ds uy ew vc mn gf hj sa ui
2 as ore ask opt buy pew say art owe try oil gas her
3 Sandy said we ought to buy gifts at her new store.

Long direct reaches

4 ce un gr mu br ny rv ym rb my ice any mug orb grow
5 nice curb must brow much fume sync many dumb curve
6 Brian must bring the ice to the curb for my uncle.

Double letters

7 all off odd too see err boo lee add call heed good
8 door meek seen huff less will soon food leek offer
9 Lee will seek help to get all food cooked by noon.

9D • 19'
New Keys: B and Y

Key each line twice SS (slowly, then faster); DS between 2-line groups; if time permits, key lines 7–9 again.

b *Left index* finger

y *Right index* finger

Follow the *Standard Plan for Learning New Keys* outlined on p. R6.

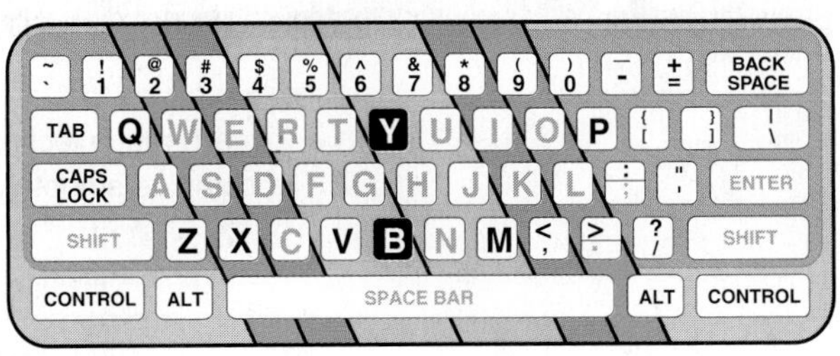

Learn b

1 f f bf bf fib fib rob rob but but big big fib fibs
2 bf bf rob rob lob lob orb orb bid bid bud bud ribs
3 a rib; to fib; rub it; an orb; or rob; but she bid

Learn y

4 j j yj yj jay jay lay lay hay hay day day say says
5 yj yj jay jay eye eye dye dye yes yes yet yet jays
6 a jay; to say; an eye; he says; dye it; has an eye

Combine b and y

7 by by buy buy boy boy bye bye byte byte buoy buoys
8 by it; to buy; by you; a byte; the buoy; by and by
9 Jaye went by bus to the store to buy the big buoy.

9E • 15'
New-Key Mastery

1. Key the lines once SS; DS between 2-line groups.
2. Key the lines again at a faster pace.

Practice 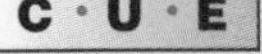 C · U · E

- Reach up without moving hands away from your body.
- Reach down without moving hands toward your body.
- Use quick-snap keystrokes.

reach review
1 fg sw ki gf bf ol ed yj ws ik rf hj cd nj tf .l uj
2 a kit low for jut led sow fob ask sun cud jet grow

3d/1st rows
3 no in bow any tub yen cut sub coy ran bin cow deck
4 Cody wants to buy this baby cub for the young boy.

key words
5 by and for the got all did but cut now say jut ask
6 work just such hand this goal boys held furl eight

key phrases
7 to do | can go | to bow | for all | did jet | ask her | to buy
8 if she | to work | and such | the goal | for this | held the

all letters learned
9 Becky has auburn hair and wide eyes of light jade.
10 Juan left Bobby at the dog show near our ice rink.

gwam 1' | 1 | 2 | 3 | 4 | 5 | 6 | 7 | 8 | 9 | 10 |

NEW KEYS: q AND comma (,)

Objectives:

1. To learn reach technique for **q** and , (comma).

2. To combine smoothly **q** and , (comma) with all other learned keys.

12A • 7' Conditioning Practice

Key each line twice SS (slowly, then faster); DS between 2-line groups; if time permits, key the lines again.

```
all letters learned  1 do fix all cut via own buy for the jam cop ask dig
p/v                  2 a map; a van; apt to; vie for; her plan; have five
all letters learned  3 Beth will pack sixty pints of guava jam for David.
```

12B • 20' New Keys: Q and ,

Key each line twice SS; DS between 2-line groups; if time permits, key lines 7–9 again.

q *Left little* finger

, (comma) *Right middle* finger

Spacing **C • U • E**

Space once after , used as punctuation.

Follow the *Standard Plan for Learning New Keys* outlined on p. R6.

Learn q

```
1 a qa qa aq aq quo quo qt. qt. quad quad quit quits
2 qa quo quo qt. qt. quay quay aqua aqua quite quite
3 a qt.; pro quo; a quad; to quit; the quay; a squad
```

Learn , (comma)

```
4 k k ,k ,k kit, kit; Rick, Ike, or I will go, also.
5 a ski, a ski; a kit, a kit; a kite, a kite; a bike
6 Ike, I see, is here; Pam, I am told, will be late.
```

Combine q and , (comma)

```
7 Enter the words quo, quote, quit, quite, and aqua.
8 I have quit the squad, Quen; Raquel has quit, too.
9 Marquis, Quent, and Quig were quite quick to quit.
10 Quin, Jacqueline, and Paque quickly took the exam.
11 Rob quickly won my squad over quip by brainy quip.
12 Quit, quiet, and quaint were on the spelling exam.
```

LESSON 10 NEW KEYS: m AND x

Objectives:

1. To learn reach technique for **m** and **x.**
2. To combine smoothly **m** and **x** with all other learned keys.

10A • 7' Conditioning Practice

Key each line twice SS (slowly, then faster); DS between 2-line groups.

reach review 1 bf ol rf yj ed nj ws ik tf hj cd uj gf by us if ow

b/y 2 by bye boy buy yes fib dye bit yet but try bet you

all letters learned 3 Robby can win the gold if he just keys a new high.

10B • 20' New Keys: M and X

Key each line twice SS (slowly, then faster); DS between 2-line groups; if time permits, key lines 7–9 again.

m *Right index* finger

x *Left ring* finger

Follow the *Standard Plan for Learning New Keys* outlined on p. R6.

Learn m

1 j j mj mj am am am me me ma ma jam jam ham ham yam

2 mj mj me me me may may yam yam dam dam men men jam

3 am to; if me; a man; a yam; a ham; he may; the hem

Learn x

4 s s xs xs ox ox ax ax six six fix fix fox fox axis

5 xs xs sx sx ox ox six six nix nix fix fix lax flax

6 a fox; an ox; fix it; by six; is lax; to fix an ax

Combine m and x

7 me ox am ax ma jam six ham mix fox men lax hem lox

8 to fix; am lax; mix it; may fix; six men; hex them

9 Mala can mix a ham salad for six; Max can fix tea.

10 Mary will bike the next day on the mountain roads.

11 Martin and Max took the six boys to the next game.

12 Marty will go with me on the next six rides today.

11C • 17'
New-Key Mastery

1. Key the lines once SS; DS between 2-line groups.
2. Key the lines again at a faster pace.

Technique Goals:

- Reach up without moving hands away from your body.
- Reach down without moving hands toward your body.
- Use quick-snap keystrokes.

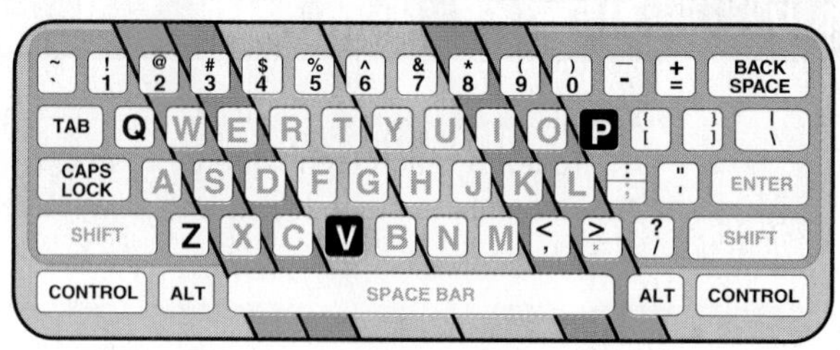

Goal: finger-action keystrokes; quiet hands and arms

reach review
1 vf p; xs mj ed yj ws nj rf ik tf ol cd hj gf uj bf
2 if lap jag own may she for but van cub sod six oak

3d/1st rows
3 by vie pen vim cup six but now man nor ton may pan
4 by six but now may cut sent me fine gems five reps

key words
5 with kept turn corn duty curl just have worn plans
6 name burn form when jury glad vote exit came eight

key phrases
7 if they|he kept|with us|of land|burn it|to name it
8 to plan|so sure|is glad|an exit|so much|to view it

all letters learned
9 Kevin does a top job on your flax farm with Craig.
10 Dixon flew blue jets eight times over a city park.

11D • 6'
Technique: Shift and Enter Keys

Key each 2-line sentence once SS as "Enter" is called every 30 seconds (30"). DS between sentences.

Goal:

To reach the end of each line just as the 30" guide ("Enter") is called.

The 30" *gwam scale* shows your gross words a minute if you reach the end of each line as the 30" guide is called.

Eyes on copy as you shift and as you strike ENTER key — gwam 30"

1 Marv is to choose a high goal 12
2 and to do his best to make it. 12

3 Vi said she had to key from a book 14
4 as one test she took for a top job. 14

5 Lexi knows it is good to keep your goal 16
6 in mind as you key each line of a drill. 16

7 Viv can do well many of the tasks she tries; 18
8 she sets top goals and makes them one by one. 18

11E •
Enrichment

1. Key each line once at a steady, easy pace to master reachstrokes.
2. Key each line again at a faster pace.

Technique Goals:

- Keep fingers upright.
- Keep hands/arms steady.

m/p
1 mj p; me up am pi jam apt ham pen map ape mop palm
2 Pam may pack plums and grapes for my trip to camp.

b/x
3 bf xs be ax by xi fix box but lax buy fox bit flax
4 Bix used the box of mix to fix bread for six boys.

y/v
5 yj vf buy vow boy vie soy vim very have your every
6 Vinny may have you buy very heavy silk and velvet.

10C • 17' New-Key Mastery

1. Key each line once SS; DS between 2-line groups.
2. Key the lines again at a faster pace.

Technique **C • U • E**

- Reach up without moving hands away from your body.
- Reach down without moving hands toward your body.
- Use quick-snap keystrokes.

Goal: finger-action keystrokes; quiet hands and arms

3d/1st rows
1 by am end fix men box hem but six now cut gem ribs
2 me ox buy den cub ran own form went oxen fine club

space bar
3 an of me do am if us or is by go ma so ah ox it ow
4 by man buy fan jam can any tan may rob ham fun guy

key words
5 if us me do an sow the cut big jam rub oak lax boy
6 curl work form born name flex just done many right

key phrases
7 or jam|if she|for me|is big|an end|or buy|is to be
8 to fix|and cut|for work|and such|big firm|the call

all keys learned
9 Jacki is now at the gym; Lex is due there by four.
10 Joni saw that she could fix my old bike for Gilda.

10D • 6' Technique: Spacing with Punctuation

Key each line once DS.

Spacing **C • U • E**

Do not space after an internal period in an abbreviation, such as Ed.D.

1 Mrs. Dixon may take her Ed.D. exam early in March.
2 Lex may send a box c.o.d. to Ms. Fox in St. Croix.
3 J. D. and Max will go by boat to St. Louis in May.
4 Owen keyed ect. for etc. and lost the match to me.

10E • Enrichment

1. Key each line twice SS (slowly, then faster); DS between 2-line groups.
2. Key each line once more at a faster pace.

Practice **C • U • E**

Keep the insertion point moving steadily across each line (no pauses).

m/x 1 Max told them that he will next fix the main axle.
b/y 2 Byron said the boy went by bus to a bayou to hunt.
w/right shift 3 Wilf and Rona work in Tucson with Rowena and Drew.
u/c 4 Lucy cut a huge cake for just the four lucky boys.
./left shift 5 Mr. and Mrs. J. L. Nance set sail for Long Island.
n/g 6 Bing may bring a young trio to sing songs at noon.
o/t 7 Lottie will tell the two little boys a good story.
i/r 8 Ria said she will first build a large fire of fir.
h/e 9 Chet was here when the eight hikers hit the trail.

LESSON 11 NEW KEYS: p AND v

Objectives:

1. To learn reach technique for **p** and **v**.
2. To combine smoothly **p** and **v** with all other learned keys.

Fingers upright

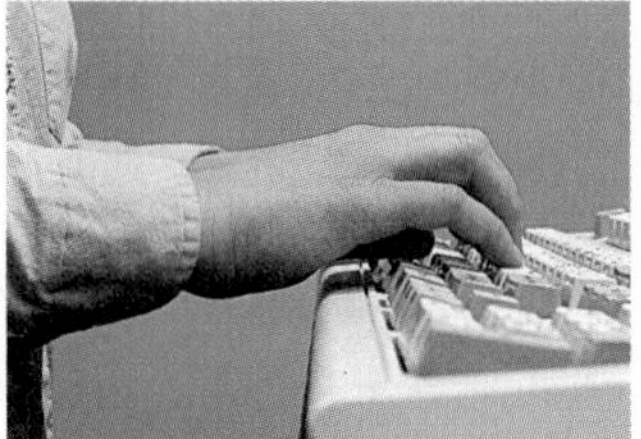
Fingers curved

Hard return

11A • 7' Conditioning Practice

Key each line twice SS (slowly, then faster); DS between 2-line groups.

one-hand words
1 in we no ax my be on ad on re hi at ho cad him bet

phrases
2 is just|of work|to sign|of lace|to flex|got a form

all letters learned
3 Jo Buck won a gold medal for her sixth show entry.

11B • 20' New Keys: P and V

Key each line twice SS; DS between 2-line groups; if time permits, key lines 7–9 again.

p *Right little* finger

v *Left index* finger

Follow the *Standard Plan for Learning New Keys* outlined on p. R6.

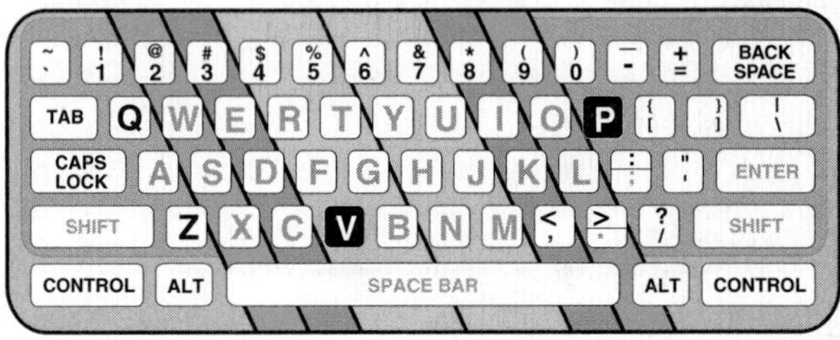

Learn p

1 ; ; p; p; pa pa up up apt apt pen pen lap lap kept
2 p; p; pa pa pa pan pan nap nap paw paw gap gap rap
3 a pen; a cap; apt to pay; pick it up; plan to keep

Learn v

4 f f vf vf via via vie vie have have five five live
5 vf vf vie vie vie van van view view dive dive jive
6 go via; vie for; has vim; a view; to live; or have

Combine p and v

7 up cup vie pen van cap vim rap have keep live plan
8 to vie; give up; pave it; very apt; vie for a cup;
9 Vic has a plan to have the van pick us up at five.

Index

0 (zero)–9 keys, 29–33

A key: control of, 2–4, 34, 45, 119, R2–R5
Abbreviations, 14, 39, R14
Active window, Windows, R39
Addresses: in business letters, 82, 88, 160, 166, 167, 168; on envelopes, 81, 86
Address lists, 126, 187, 189
Adjacent keys, 25, 89, R27
Alignment, 55, 134
Alphanumeric keys, xv
ALT key, xii, xv
Ampersand key, 42–43
Animation, xvi
Apostrophe key: control of, 17–18, R32–R33
Apposition, commas and, 156
Arrow keys, xv, 158; table navigation, 90
Asterisk key, 43–44
At Sign key, 42–43
Attachment/enclosure notation, 59, 82, 126, 128, 160, 186, 189–190
Attention line: in business letters, 160
AutoComplete feature, 158

B key: control of, 11–12, 34, 45, 119, R20–R21
Back button: browsers, R41
Backslash key, 43–44
Backspace key, xv
Balanced-hand words, 19, 22, 120, 122, 123, 152, 153, 155, 185
Bcc line (*See* blind copy)
Bibliography: unbound reports, 70
Blind copy (Bcc line), 59, 126, 129
Block paragraphs, 16, R29, R31
Bold typeface, 55, 58, 77, 81
Bookmarks: Web sites, R42
Borders, 171, 172, 179–182, 199–200, 205–206
Bound reports, 137–151, 203–204; body of, 139–141, 144–145, 148; bulleted items in, 145; endnotes in, 138, 146–147, 148–149; footnotes in, 138, 141–143, 203; formatting of, 137–151, R45; reference lists in, 138, 141, 145, 146, 204; spacing in, 137; summary in, 150; table of contents in, 138, 150–151; title page for, 137, 145, 150, 204
Bracket keys, 43–44
Browsers: parts of, R41–R42
Bulleted lists, 145, 202
Business letters, block format, 160–168, 186, 188, 196, 201, 202; addresses in, 160, 166, 167, 168; closing line, 186; dates in, 166; formatting, R44; headings in, 160; lists in, 168, 188, 191; notations in, 160, 186, 190; reference initials in, 160; subject line in, 160; two-page, 167–168; Web addresses in, 168
Buttons, Windows, R39

C key: control of, 9–10, 34, 45, 119, R16
Calculator accessory in Windows, 52
Capitalization, proofreaders' mark for, 31; rules for, 38–39; shift keys for, 9–10, R15
Caps Lock key: control of, xv, 17–18, R30–R31
Carpal tunnel syndrome (CTS), 34, R34–R36
Cc line, 59,126
Cells, table, 90–91, 169, 170, 172
Centering text, 55, 58, 69, 72, 77, 80, 92, 94
Citations: unbound reports, 70, 72–74
Clauses: dependent, 28; independent, 27, 28; nonrestrictive, 157; restrictive, 157
Close box: browsers, R41
Close button, Windows, 39, R39
Close command, xiv
Close up space: proofreaders' mark for, 31
Closing documents, xiv, R39
Closing line: business letters, block format, 186
Collective pronouns, 78
Colon key: control of, 15–16, R28–R29
Colons, 16, 184
Columns, table: 57–58, 90, 94, 169, 172–174; insert/delete, 90, 93, 169, 172; setting tabs for, 57–58, 125; shading, 170, 172, 175–176, 178–182, 199–200, 205–206; width of, 94, 172, 145–147
Combination response, 21, 26
Comma key: control of, 15–16, R26
COMMAND key, xii, xv
Commas, 156–157, 183–184
Complex sentences, 28
Complimentary close, 82
Compound predicates, 27
Compound sentences, 27
Compound subjects, 27
Computers, xi, xv
Coordinating conjunctions, 27
Copying text, 80, 124, 125, 134
Copy notation, 126, 160
Copy/Paste text, 80, 124, 125, 134
CTRL key, xii, xv, 158
Cut/Copy/Paste text, 80, 124, 125, 134

D key: control of, 2–4, 34, 45, 119, R2–R5
Date box: e-mail, 59
Dates, 49, 82, 158, 166, 183
Decimal Point key: numeric keypad, 54
Decimal tabs, 57–58, 69, 125
Declarative sentences, 132
Default settings, xiv
Default tabs, R33
Delete key, xv
Dependent clauses, 28
Desktop navigation, xi
Desktop publishing, 9
Desktop, Windows, R37
Diagnostic writing, xvi, 41
Diagonal (Slash) key: control of, 40–41
Dialog boxes, xiii, R39
Difficult-reach mastery, 25
Direct address, commas and, 156
Disk removal, 5, R5
Distribution lists, 126
Documentation, 138
Documents, in Windows, xii–xiii, R39; file/text inserted into, 136, 196; Help for, xiii, 196; naming, xiii; navigating, 158; opening, xiv, 50; printing, xiii–xiv; reading, 50; saving, xiii; tables inserted into, 90
Dollar Sign key: control of, 40–41
Dot leader tabs, 136
Double letters, 22, 36, 47, 66, R27
Drop-down lists, Windows, 39, R39

E key: control of, 5–6, 34, 45, 119, R6–R7
Ellipses (*See also* dot leader tabs), 70
E-mail, 59, 62–63, 126–127, 194, 195, 201, 203; attachments to, 59, 126, 128, 189; blind copy (Bcc) of, 59, 126; body of, 59; Cc line in, 59, 126; copies for, 126; Date box in, 59; distribution lists for, 126; formatting of, 59, 62–65, 104, 111, 126–131, R44; forwarding, 126; From box in, 59, 62, 63; headings in, 59; Internet and, 65
Enclosures: memos, 59
End key, 158
Endnotes, 135, 138, 146–149, R44
Enter key, xiii, xv, 3, 4, 20, 90, R4, R12, R13, R15, R20, R25
Envelopes, 81, 86; formatting, R44; mailing address in, 81, 86; return address in, 81, 86
Equal Sign key, 43–44
Ergonomic keyboards, R35
Escape key, xv: numeric keypad, 52
Ethics, 116, 207
Exclamation Point key, 40–41
Exclamation points, 132–133
Exclamatory sentences, 132
Exercises for keyboardists, R35, R36

F key: control of, 2–4, 34, 45, 119, R2–R5
Favorite sites: World Wide Web, R42
Finger gymnastics, 36, R36
Folders icon, Windows, R37
Folders, Windows, R37
Footnotes, 135, 138, 141–143, 197–198, 203
Formatting guides, R44–R45: bound report, 137–151, 203–204, R45; business letter, block format, 160–168, 196, 201–202, R44; e-mail, 59, 62–65, 104, 111, 126–131, 195, 201, 203, R44; endnotes, R44; envelopes, 81, 86, R44; memos, 59–61, 64–65, 105, 111, 195, 201, 202, R45; personal-business letter, 82–89, 105, 111; references, R45; table of contents, R45; tables, 91, 94–101, 108–109, 114–115, 172–182, 199–200, 205–206; title pages, R45; unbound reports, 70–77, 106–107, 112–113, R45
Forward button: browsers, R41
Forwarding, 126
From box in: e-mail, 59, 62, 63
Function keys, xii, xv

G key: control of, 7–8, 34, 45, 119, R12–R13
Games, MicroType Multimedia, xvi
Greater-than key: control of, 40–41
Gridlines, 171
Gross words per minute (gwam), 19–20, 30
Guided (paced) writing procedures, 22

H key: control of, 5–6, 34, 45, 119, R6–R7
Handwritten copy, 20, 24, 25, 31, 37, 46, 48
Hanging indents, 68, 69, 134
Hard page breaks, 57
Hard return, 3, R3
Hardware, xi
Headings, 137, 160; in e-mail, 59; in memos, 59; in tables, 94, 99–101, 108, 115, 174, 178, 179, 180, 199–200, 205–206
Help, xiii
Highlighting text, 80
Home key, 51, 53, 158
Home keys, 2–4, R2–R6
Home pages: defined, R40
Horizontal alignment: tables, 169, 172
Hyperlinks: defined, R40
Hypertext, R40
Hypertext markup language (HTML), R40
Hypertext transfer protocol (http), R40
Hyphenation, 56
Hyphen key: control of, 17–18, R32–R33

I key: control of, 5–6, 34, 45, 121, R8–R9
Icons, xi, R37
Indefinite numbers, 50
Indefinite pronouns, 102
Indents, 68, 69, 134
Independent clauses, 27, 28
Initials: capitalization of, 39
Input devices, xi
Insert: dates, 158, 168; proofreaders' mark for, 31; text into documents, 136, 196
Insertion point, xiii, 158
Insert key, xv
Insert mode, 55
Internet and World Wide Web, 65; addresses in, 88, 98; browsers, R41–R42; defined, R40
Interrogative sentences, 132
Introductory phrases or clauses, 156
Italics, 55, 58, 64, 77, 81

J key: control of, 2–4, 34, 45, 121, R2–R5
Justification of text, 55

K key: control of, 2–4, 34, 45, 121, R2–R5
Keyboard, xv, 40
Keyboard shortcuts, xii
Keying position, 2, 51, R2, R35
Keystroking technique, 3, 34, 36, 45, 47, 51, 119–123, 152–155, 185, R3, R35

L key: control of, 2–4, 34, 45, 121, R2–R5
Left alignment/justification, 55
Left indent, 68, 69, 134
Left Shift key: control of, 9–10, R14, R17
Left tabs, 57–58
Less-than key: control of, 40–41
Letter keys, 5–18, 119, 121, 122, 154
Letter response, 19, 26
Letters (*See* business letters; personal-business letters)
Line ending (*See* hard return)
Line spacing, 67–70, 134, 137, R4, R5
Lists, 168, 184, 191; bulleted, 135; numbered, 135, 188, 191
Location, Address, or Netsite box: browsers, R41
Long direct reaches, 25, 89, R27
Lowercase letters: proofreaders' mark for, 31

M key: control of, 13–14, 34, 45, 121, R22–R23
Macros, 159, 186
Mailing address, envelope, 81, 86
Margins, 67–69, 134; in bound reports, 137; in memos, 59; in personal-business letters, 82; in unbound reports, 70
Maximize box: browsers, R41
Maximize button, Windows, R38, R39
Measures, 49
Memos, 59, 126, 191, 195, 201, 202; blind copy (Bcc line), 129; formatting, 59–61, 64–65, 105, 111, 126–131, R45
Menu bars, xii, R38; browsers, R41
Menus, xii
MicroType Multimedia, xvi, 41
Minimize box: browsers, R41
Minimize button, Windows, R38, R39
Monitor placement, xv, 2
Mouse, xi, xv, R37
Movies, MicroType Multimedia, xvi
Multitasking, Windows, R38
My Computer icon, Windows, R37

N key: control of, 7–8, 47, 121, R12–R13
Navigating documents, 158
Network Neighborhood icon, R37
Nonrestrictive clauses, 157
Nouns, 27, 45
Noun/verb agreement, 27, 102–103
Numbered lists, 135, 188
Number expression: rules for, 49–50
Number keys, 29–33, 121, 122, 152, 154, 185
Number/Pound Sign key, 42–43
Numbers, 49–50; in numbered lists, 135; page numbering and, 68; subject/verb agreement using, 103
Numeric keypad, xv, 51–54; home key position for, 51, 53; MicroType Multimedia, xvi; reaching keys in, 53–54
Num Lock key, xv, 51

O **key**: control of, 7–8, 47, 121, R10–R11
Omitted characters, 46
One-hand words, 19, 154
Opening documents, xiv, 50
Opening programs, Windows, R38
Operating systems, xi
Option selection, Windows, R39
Organizational chart, 194
Orphan lines, 67
Outline format, 190

P **key**: control of, 13–14, 47, 121, R24–R25
Page breaks, 57, 67–69
Page numbering, 68–70, 137
PageUp/PageDown key, 158
Paragraphs: block, 16, R24–R25; hanging indent in, 68, 69, 134; indentation in, 68, 69, 134; left indent in, 68, 69, 134; speed building for, 22; widow/orphan lines in, 67; word wrap in, 16
Parallel adjectives: commas in, 183
Parentheses, 43
Parentheses keys, 42–43
Paste text, 80, 124, 125, 134
Percent: spelling out, 50
Percent key: control of, 40–41
Period key, R14: control of, 9–10
Periods, 132–133, R23, R27
Peripherals, xi
Personal-business letter, block style, 82–89: alignment of text, 55; formatting of, 105, 111
Personal pronouns, 78
Phrase response, 185
Plural vs. singular: subject/verb agreement, 102–103
Plus key: numeric keypad, 52
Plus Sign key: control of, 42–43
Poems, centering text, 77
Pointers, xi
Posture for keyboarding, R35
Predicates in sentence, 27, 28
Printing, xiii–xiv
Programming languages, xi
Pronouns, 27; agreement of, 78, 102–103; indefinite, 102; personal, 78
Proofreading, 31, 38
Punctuation marks, 132–133; in abbreviations, 14; colon, 184; commas, 156–157, 183–184; exclamation points, 132–133; periods, 132–133; question marks, 132–133; spacing after, 9, 14, 16, R19, R23, R27

Q **key**: control of, 15–16, 47, 121, R26
Quarter-minute checkpoints, 26
Question Mark key: control of, 17–18, R30–R31
Question marks, 132–133
Questions: colon to introduce, 184
Quotation marks, 46, 48; commas and, 156
Quoted material: bound reports, 137, 145; bulleted, 202; colon to introduce, 184; commas used in, 156

R **key**: control of, 5–6, 47, 122, R8–R9
Radio buttons, Windows, R39
Reaches with outside fingers, 25
Reading documents, 50
Recycle Bin, R37
Redo feature, 56
Reference initials, 82, 160
Reference lists, 69; in bound reports, 138, 141, 145, 146, 204; formatting, R45; in unbound reports, 70, 75, 107, 113, 197–198
Repetitive stress injury (RSI), R34–R36
Reply to: bound reports, 126
Reports (*See* bound reports; MicroType Multimedia; unbound reports)
Response patterns, 19–20, 26, 185; combination response, 21, 26; letter response, 19, 26; phrase response, 185; word response, 19, 26, 36, 47, 89, 185
Restore button, Windows, R38–R39
Restrictive clauses, comma use, 157
Return address, 81–82, 86
Return key, xiii
Rhythm in keying, 34, 36, 45, 47, 119, 121
Right alignment/justification, 55
Right Shift key: control of, 11–12, R18–R19
Right tabs, 57–58
Rough draft, 24, 31
Rows: height of, 92–94, 172; insert/delete, 90, 93, 169, 172; shading of, 170, 172, 175–176, 178–182, 199–200, 205–206; table, 90, 94, 169, 172–174

S **key**: control of, 2–4, 47, 122, R2–R5
Salutation, 82
Save As, xiii
Saving documents, xiii
Script copy, 20, 24, 25, 31, 37, 46, 48
Scroll bar, xii, R38; in browsers, R41
Scrolling text, R7
Search engines, 75, 127, 168, 186, R42–R43
Second-page heading, 160
Selecting text, 80
Semicolon key: control of, 2–4
Semicolons, R2–R5
Sentences: capitalization in, 38; complex, 28; compound, 27; declarative, 132; exclamatory, 132; interrogative, 132; simple, 27; speed building for, 21
Series comma, 156, 183
Shading: columns/rows in tables, 170, 172, 175–176, 178–182, 199–200, 205–206
Shifting for capitalization, 9–10, R15
Shift keys, xv, 22, 89, R14, R18–R19, R25, R33; control of, 9–12
Shortcuts, xii
Side-by-side keys, 25
Side headings: bound reports, 137
Signature line, 82
Simple sentences, 27
Skill building, 19–20, 25
Slash key (*See* Diagonal key)
Soft page breaks, 57
Soft returns, 16
Software, xi; closing, xiv; starting, xii
Sorting: tables, 92, 93, 172
Spacebar key, xv, 20, 22, 36, 47, 89, R3–R4, R13, R15, R17, R20, R33; control of, 3–4
Spacing (*See also* line spacing), 134, R3; abbreviations, R14; around ampersands, 42; in bound reports, 137; commas and, R27; in desktop publishing, 9; number signs and, 42; between paragraphs, 16; between parentheses, 43; periods and, R19, R23, R27; proofreaders' mark for, 31; after punctuation, 9, 14, 16, R23, R27; in unbound reports, 70
Speech recognition technology (SRT), 118
Speed building, 20, 22, 23
Speller/Spell check feature, 56
Standard words, R20
Start button/Start menu, Windows, R37–R38
Straight copy, 24; speed building for, 23
Street names/numbers, capitalization of, 39
Subheadings: bound reports, 137
Subject box: e-mail, 59
Subject line, 160
Subject of sentence, 27, 28
Subject/predicate agreement, 102–103
Summary, 150
Superscript, 135
Symbol keys, 40–44

T **key**: control of, 7–8, 47, 122, R10–R11
Tab key, xv, 35, 57, 90, 119, 121, 122, 152, 154, R32–R33; control of, 17–18
Table of contents, 138, 150–151, R45
Tables, 90–93, 169–182, 189, 190, 199–200, 205–206; alignment in, 92, 94, 169, 172; centering page for, 92, 94; columns in, 90–91, 93–94, 169, 172–174; data in, 94; formatting 91, 94–101, 108–109, 114–115, 169–171, 172–182; four-column, with headings, 100–101; headings in, 94, 96–101, 108, 115, 174, 178–180, 199–200, 205–206; macros used in, 159; rows in, 90, 92–94, 169, 172, 173, 174; shading in, 170, 172, 175–182, 199–200, 205–206; three-column, with headings, 99–100, 108–109, 174, 178, 180; titles in, 94, 174; two-column, with headings, 96–98, 108, 115, 174, 179, 199–200, 205–206
Tabs, 57–58, 119, 121, 122, 152, 154; decimal, 57–58, 69, 125; default, R33; dot leader, 136; left, 57–58; right, 57–58; setting, 57–58, 69, 119, 121, 122, 125, 152, 154; Windows, R39
Taskbar, Windows, R37
Textual citations, 70, 72–74, 138
Three-dimensional animation, xvi
Time, 49, 184
Title bars, xii, R38; in browsers, R41
Title page: in bound reports, 137, 145, 150, 204; formatting, R45; in unbound reports, 197–198
Titles: capitalization of, 39; italics in, 64; in tables, 94, 174; in unbound reports, 72; underline in, 64
To box: e-mail, 59, 62, 63
Toolbars, xii; browsers, R41
Trading Partners, global, 117
Transpose: proofreaders' mark for, 31
Turning off the computer, xiv, 4
Typeover mode, 55

U **key**: control of, 9–10, 47, 122, R16
Unbound reports, 70–77, 106–107, 112–113, 186, 192–193; footnotes in, 197–198; formatting, R45; reference list in, 70, 75, 107, 113, 197–198; title page for, 197–198
Underline, 55, 58, 64
Underline key, 43–44
Undo feature, 56
URLs, R40–R41

V **key**: control of, 13–14, 47, 122, R24–R25
Vertical alignment, 92, 94, 169, 172
View feature, 57

W **key**: control of, 11–12, 47, 122, R18–R19
Web addresses, 168, 186
Web pages: URLs, R40–R41
Web sites (*See also* Internet and World Wide Web), 88, 98, 168; defined, R40
Weights, numbers in, 49
Widow/orphan lines, 67–69
Width, columns, 91, 93, 94, 169, 172
Windows, xii; size and placement of, R39; in Windows, R38
Windows software, R37–R39; starting, xii
Word processing, 55–58, 67–69, 80–81, 124, 134–135, 158; copying text, 80, 124, 125, 134; envelopes, 81; macros, 159, 186; tables, 90–93, 169–171; tab setting, 69
Word response, 19, 26, 36, 47, 89, 185
Word wrap, 16
Work area arrangement, 2
Works cited page, 70
World Wide Web (*See also* Internet and World Wide Web): defined, R40–R41; favorite sites, R42; home pages, R40; hyperlinks, R40; hypertext, R40; search engines, R42–R43; Web sites, R40

X **key**: control of, 13–14, 47, 122, R22–R23
X-rays and computers, xi

Y **key**: control of, 11–12, 47, 122, R20–R21

Z **key**: control of, 15–16, 47, 122, R28–R29
Zoom feature, 57

Concentration drills
a, 2–4, 34, 45, 119, R2–R5; **a/l**, 29; **a/z**, 66; **b**, 11–12, 34, 45, 119, R20–R21; **b/7**, 66; **b/x**, R25; **b/y**, 13, R22, R23; **c**, 9–10, 34, 45, 119, R16; **c/n**, R20; **c/x**, 66; **d**, 2–4, 34, 45, 119, R2–R5; **d/3**, 32; **d/w**, 66; **e**, 5–6, 34, 45, 119, R6–R7; **e/v**, 66; **ed/de**, 23; **f**, 2–4, 34, 45, 119, R2–R5; **f/4**, 30; **f/5**, 31; **f/u**, 66; **g**, 7–8, 34, 45, 119, R12–R13; **g/t**, 66; **h**, 5–6, 34, 45, 119, R6–R7; **h/e**, 5–7, 9, R7, R8, R9, R11, R19, R23; **h/s**, 66; **i**, 5–6, 34, 45, 121, R8–R9; **i/r**, 5–6, 9, 66, R9, R11, R19, R23; **i/t**, 7, R11; **ik/ki**, 23; **j**, 2–4, 34, 45, 121, R2–R5; **j/6**, 32; **j/7**, 31; **j/q**, 66; **ju/ft**, 23; **k**, 2–4, 34, 45, 121, R2–R5; **k/8**, 29; **k/p**, 66; **l**, 2–4, 34, 45, 121, R2–R5; **l/o**, 66; **m**, 13–14, 34, 45, 121, R22–R23; **m/n**, 66; **m/p**, R25; **m/x**, R23; **n**, 7–8, 47, 121, R12–R13; **n/g**, 8, 9, 11, R13, R17, R19, R23; **o**, 7–8, 47, 121, R10–R11; **o/r**, 7, R11; **o/t**, 9, R11, R19, R23; **ol/lo**, 23; **p**, 13–14, 47, 121, R24–R25; **p/v**, 15, R26; **p/x**, 16; **q**, 15–16, 47, 121, R26; **q/p**, 31, R31; **q/z**, 16; **r**, 5–6, 47, 122, R8–R9; **s**, 2–4, 47, 122, R2–R5; **s/2**, 32; **t**, 7–8, 47, 122, R10–R11; **u**, 9–10, 47, 122, R16; **u/c**, 11, R17, R18, R19, R23; **v**, 13–14, 47, 122, R24–R25; **v/m**, 16; **w**, 11–12, 47, 122, R18–R19; **ws/sw**, 23; **x**, 13–14, 47, 122, R22–R23; **y**, 11–12, 47, 122, R20–R21; **y/v**, R25; **z**, 15–16, 47, 122, R28–R29; **z/v**, R31; **za/az**, 23; **z/colon**, 17, R30; **Apostrophe (')**, 17–18, R32–R33; **Caps Lock**, 17–18, R30–R31; **Colon (:)**, 15–16, R28–R29; **Comma (,)**, 15–16, R26; **Enter key**, R15, R20; **Home keys**, 2–4; **Hyphen (-)**, 17–18, R32–R33; **Left Shift**, 9–10, R14, R17; **Period (.)**, 9–10, R14; **Question Mark (?)**, 17–18, 23, R30–R31; **Quotation Mark (")**, 17–18, R32–R33; **Right Shift**, 11–12; **Semicolon (;)**, 2–4, R2–R5; **Shift keys**, 9–12, R14; **Spacebar**, 7–8, R15, R17, R20; **Tab**, 17–18, 35, R32–R33

Models illustrated in text
B Bound reports, 137, 142; business letter, block style, 160
E E-mail, 62, 126; endnotes page, 137; envelopes, 86
F Footnotes, 142
M Memo, 59, 60, 126
O Organizational chart, 194
P Page numbering, 68; personal-business letter, block style, 82, 83
R Reference list (citations), 74
T Table of contents, 138; tables, 94, 95, 172; textual citations, 54; title page, 137
U Unbound reports, 70, 71, 73–74
W Widow/orphan lines, 67